Contents

ACKNOWLEDGMENTS   vi

1. INTRODUCTION   1

The Concept of Mystical Power, 4
Initial Comparisons between Traditional and World Religions, 5
Our Orientation in This Book, 7

2. MYSTICAL POWER AND ITS SOURCES   10

Mana, 10
Mystical Power in the Person, and How It Gets There, 14
Relation between Personal Mystical Power and the Economy, 21
Mystical Power Outside the Person, 24
Summary, 27

3. ANIMALS AND PLANTS IN RELIGION   28

Totemism, 28
Understanding Animals and Interacting with Them, 30
Hunting and Herding Societies, 33
Hunters, 34
Herders, 39
Plants, 43
Summary, 45

4. MYSTICAL BEINGS   47

Major God, 48
Spirits of the Dead, 51
Other Gods and Spirits, 55
Culture Heroes, 60

Self as Mystical Being, 61
Character of the Supernaturals, 61
Summary, 64

5. COMMUNICATION WITH MYSTICAL BEINGS   66

Communion versus Reciprocation, 68
Modes Stressing Communication *to* Mystical Beings, 70
Modes Stressing Communication *from* Mystical Beings, 81
Summary, 95

6. WIZARDRY   96

Sub-Saharan Africa, 97
North America, 103
South America, 105
Oceania, 106
The Setting and Meaning of Wizardry, 108
Wizardry and the Individual, 109
Wizardry and Society, 113
Psychological and Societal Costs of Wizardry, 119
Summary, 119

7. ILLNESS AND HEALING   120

Reactions to Illness, 121
Similarities and Differences, 131
Summary, 140

8. RITES OF PASSAGE, AND RELATION
    BETWEEN THE SEXES   141

Rituals of Pregnancy and Birth, 142
Rituals of Advancement toward Adulthood, 148
Why Initiation Rites?, 152
Males as Agents of Social Continuity, 153
Male Envy of Women, 155
Summary, 163

9. DEATH AND THE AFTERLIFE   165

Survival of the Soul, 168
Mortuary Rites, and Becoming an Ancestor, 179
Reincarnation, 185
Summary, 186

Religion and Magic
in the Life
of Traditional Peoples

Alice B. Child

Irvin L. Child
Yale University

Prentice Hall, Upper Saddle River, New Jersey 07458

Library of Congress Cataloging-in-Publication Data

Child, Alice B.
  Religion and magic in the life of traditional peoples / Alice B.
Child, Irvin L. Child.
    p.   cm.
  Includes bibliographical references and index.
  ISBN 0-13-012451-6
  1. Religion, Primitive. 2. Magic--Religious aspects. I. Child,
Irvin Long. II. Title.
  GN470.C45 1992
  291'.042--dc20   92-34183

To the memory of

Clyde Kluckhohn, and to the many ethnographers
of the past and the present whose devoted work
has made this book possible

Acquisitions editor: Nancy Roberts
Production editor: Elaine Lynch
Copy editor: Mary Louise Byrd
Editorial assistant: Pat Naturale
Cover designer: Ben Santora
Pre-press buyer: Kelly Behr
Manufacturing buyer: Mary Ann Gloriande

© 1993 by Prentice Hall, Inc.
Upper Saddle River, NJ 07458

Printed in the United States of America

10 9 8

ISBN 0-13-012451-6

Prentice-Hall International (UK) Limited, *London*
Prentice-Hall of Australia Pty. Limited, *Sydney*
Prentice-Hall of Canada, Inc., *Toronto*
Prentice-Hall Hispanoamericana, S. A., *Mexico*
Prentice-Hall of India Private Limited, *New Delhi*
Prentice-Hall of Japan, Inc., *Tokyo*
Prentice-Hall Asia Pte. Ltd., *Singapore*
Editora Prentice-Hall do Brasil, Ltda., *Rio de Janeiro*

10. **FESTIVALS**   187

Festival in North America, 187
Festivals in Oceania, 191
Festival in Africa, 197
Summary, 200

11. **RELIGION IN SOCIETIES UNDERGOING
   RAPID CHANGE**   201

Cargo Cults, 201
Prophet Dance and Ghost Dance, 203
A Comparison, 205
Other Syncretism in the Americas, 207
Religious Change in Africa, 212
Indonesia and Asia, 219
Summary, 219

12. **WHAT TRADITIONAL RELIGIONS DO FOR PEOPLE**   221

Gains and Losses, 221
Norms of Sexuality, 224
Norms of Aggression Control, 226
Self-Assertion versus Dependence
  (Norms of Humility and Competence), 228
Norms of Confidence, 230
Cognition: Continuity versus Change, 233
Summary, 236

REFERENCES   237

INDEX OF NAMES   260
INDEX OF TOPICS   264

Acknowledgments

For their kind permission to quote, we are greatly indebted to

Professor Jack Goody, of St. John's College, Cambridge, for extensive passages from his book, *Death, Property and the Ancestors.*

Professor Lester R. Hiatt and Angus & Robertson Publishers, for passages from *Anthropology in Oceania,* the festschrift edited by Hiatt and the late Professor Chandra Jayawardena in honor of Professor Ian Hogbin.

The Oxford University Press, for passages in Professor Godfrey Lienhardt's book, *Divinity and Experience,* published by them in 1961.

The International African Institute, for passages from *African Systems of Thought*, edited by Meyer Fortes and Germaine Dieterlen.

The Royal Anthropological Institute, for passages in Professor Robin Horton's article, "The High God: A Comment on Father O'Connell's Paper," published in volume 62 of *Man.*

We are also greatly indebted to the authors and copyright owners of many additional passages, some quoted and some only cited, that under customary rules of fair play under copyright laws, are brief enough not to require express permission. All quotations and most citations are accompanied by name of author and date of publication, so the reader can identify the source in the list of references that appears after Chapter 12 of this book.

Chapter 1

Introduction

Gods, ghosts, and totems were thought to be corporeal and to live on the earth with men rather than in a distant Valhalla. Religion stressed material rather than spiritual values. It was concerned with physical benefits in this life rather than spiritual rewards in the next.... Through myth, it explained and validated the cosmic order. Gods invented and gave men crops, artefacts, valuables, and domesticated animals. Religion provided the ritual techniques believed to harness the power of gods and spirits in agriculture, manufacture, trade, and animal husbandry. (Lawrence, 1971, 140)

The Australian anthropologist Peter Lawrence offers here an example of the role of religion in the life of a traditional people, before their contact with the Western world. Lawrence was writing of a particular group he had studied in New Guinea, but his general characterization would apply to the religions of many other traditional societies. It differs from the role most conspicuous in the religions of Western nations, where beliefs about the supernatural and modes of communicating with the supernatural are at least superficially more conspicuous. Yet everything Lawrence says about the religion of an aboriginal group has its parallels in aspects of a Westerner's religious life. By searching for what religion means in the life of traditional peoples, we may be better able to discern the rich and varied meanings of religion in our own society.

By *traditional societies*, we mean essentially those whose ways—especially the religious aspects—have developed in the absence of writing and have been perpetuated by oral and behavioral traditions alone. The religion of a traditional society may survive the introduction of writing and of one or more world religions sufficiently intact to provide useful material for our study. But to the extent possible (except in Chapter 11), we are concerned here with the traditional aspects as they probably existed before such intrusions.

In some traditional societies, European visitors of the nineteenth century and before could think religion completely absent. Defining religion solely after the pattern of their own practices and beliefs, some could not see the basic similarity. But to scholars with a scientific mode of thought, like James Frazer (1922), even their limited knowledge about religions of traditional societies called urgently for comparison with the world religions and with the early history of these (while they were still local rather than widespread). Dominated like so many of his contemporaries by the concept of evolution, Frazer emphasized and exaggerated a steady sequence of change from modes of thought characterizing more primitive religions to modes of thought characterizing science in its gradual replacement of much of the Christian tradition. Humanity, in his view, began with reliance on magic (which he distinguished from religion), progressed to reliance on supernatural beings, and finally moved gradually on to reliance on the rational processes of human intellect.

From the perspective of modern anthropology, Frazer had little ethnographic knowledge to draw upon, and he looked forward to a time when a rich variety of information might be available. That time has come. Even as the number of isolated traditional societies has sorely diminished, the adequacy of ethnographic work has increased, and especially the adequacy of information about religion. Many scholars in recent decades have spent long periods in study of a traditional society, learning the local language and working through it in attempting to understand the actions, thoughts, and feelings that characterize the religious aspects of life and their role in the general life of the society. We draw on the vast body of anthropological data on religion, both the older and the more recent. We seek to review the similarities, and at the same time the range of variation, in religion, as they can be seen in traditional societies and to consider their role in the life of the individual and society.

Our effort differs from accounts that are based primarily on mythology. Such accounts proceed, basically, from trying to make sense of the diverse myths that constitute the principal evidence we have about the religions of ancient peoples. How these religions operated long ago in daily social life must be guessed or else neglected. Our inquiry is based, instead, on ethnographic study of societies still functioning to some extent when studied, and thus religious aspects of their life could be directly observed or else reported from the memory of elders.

To *religion,* we give the broadest possible meaning. In many societies no aspects of life are segregated with any such label as "religion." We have tried to be inclusive. Various anthropologists have formulated definitions of religion. We find each of the following samples, for instance, useful as a general guide, but we would not for our purposes exclude any aspect of thought or action because some of these definitions would exclude it.

1. Religion can be looked upon as an extension of the field of people's social relationships beyond the confines of purely human society. (Horton, 1960, 211)

2. I shall define "religion" as "an institution consisting of culturally patterned interaction with culturally postulated superhuman beings." (Spiro, 1966, 96)

3. . . . . A *religion is (1) a system of symbols which acts to (2) establish powerful, pervasive, and long-lasting moods and motivations in men by (3) formulating conceptions of a general order of existence and (4) clothing these conceptions with such an aura of factuality that (5) the moods and motivations seem uniquely realistic.* (Italics in original.) (Geertz, 1973, 90)

These definitions vary greatly. The first two are behavioral definitions; religious actions are those in which a person acts toward nonhuman entities (real or imagined) as though they were human. The third refers to cognitive events within people; in distinguishing religion from other systems of symbols by its effects on moods and on sense of what is real, moreover, Geertz introduces in his definition ideas about what religion does for people. Yet, as guides to delimiting a subject matter, they might be more or less equivalent. The behavior referred to by Horton and Spiro would, if we looked at what is going on inside people, most likely make the same incidents relevant to a study of religion as would a search beginning with Geertz's definition.

The major implication of our defining our subject matter more broadly than these writers do is that we would not exclude magic. Magic is often distinguished from religion, following Frazer and his contemporaries, as not involving relations with a superhuman entity. Magical explanations attribute events to mechanical, though mistaken, cause-effect relations, such as misfortune being brought about by a black cat's walking across one's path. Magical practice involves the application of the knowledge and skills the magician has acquired about these relations, such as how to stick needles into a doll symbolizing one's intended victim. Because supernatural beings are not necessarily involved, the definitions of religion by Horton and by Spiro would exclude magic. Geertz's definition might exclude magic except when it happens to be integrated into a system of symbols that constitutes the religion of a particular society.

We are not alone in including magic within the category of religion. Two American anthropologists, for example, offer a definition that clearly includes magic (though they later proceed to narrow their definition): "Every society that we know develops certain patterns of behaving, designed to guard, by one means or another, against the unexpected, and better to control man's relationships to the universe in which he lives. It is this area of culture that we shall call religion" (Beals & Hoijer, 1965, 528). Inclusion of magic within the definition of religion is implicit also in a general introduction to anthropology by another pair of American anthropologists, Carol Ember and Melvin Ember, as they say, "We will define *religion* as any set of attitudes, beliefs, and practices pertaining to *supernatural power*, whether it be forces, gods, spirits, ghosts, demons, or any other imagined power" (1973, 417). More explicit is the British anthropologist Raymond Firth (1951, 223) as he says, approvingly, "Many modern anthropologists include magic under the general head of religious behavior."

In the title of this book we refer to "religion and magic." We have not done so to emphasize a distinction. Rather, it is simply to indicate, to readers accustomed to making the distinction, that magic is indeed part of our subject matter.

THE CONCEPT OF MYSTICAL POWER

We agree essentially with Ember and Ember's definition of religion, but their term *supernatural power* seems excessively tied to modern Western conceptions of nature and the limits of nature (see Saler, 1977). A term we prefer, because it seems less likely to involve attribution to other cultures of ideas developed or refined under the influence of Western natural science, is *mystical power*. The general unpredictability of such power, and the recognition that it differs from everyday realistic power, are perhaps as well expressed cross-culturally by the term *mystical* as by any other, and this usage is prevalent among British anthropologists. In using this, or any other term, we need to keep in mind that its distinction from ordinary realistic power is difficult, perhaps impossible, to apply in any uniform way for every culture. In some societies people are just not greatly concerned with any such distinction, as Hallowell (1938) pointed out for the Saulteaux, an Ojibwa-speaking people of northern North America.

The distinction between realistic and mystical power comes to us most clearly from our own cultural tradition, but it does transcend that origin and certainly could have arisen solely from a study of cultures very different from ours. We venture the guess, though we can hardly prove it, that some such distinction, however blurred and shifted, is present in every culture. The basis for its development must everywhere be present; for what we call mystical power there seems nowhere to be seriously claimed the dependability, the regularity, of success that obviously marks the realistic power of the skilled practitioner of cooking, canoe making, or an infinity of other realistic skills. Yet some share of credit for what might seem to us the simple outcome of practical skills is often claimed for mystical power. Kenneth Read says of the New Guinea group he studied:

> In Gahuku belief, strength and power, every human achievement testified to the operation of supernatural forces. Men were not thereby the passive recipients of supernatural benefits. Time and effort, the application of human skill and knowledge were necessary to every enterprise, but alone they did not guarantee success. (1965, 78)

Even when it is argued that the two kinds of power are intermeshed, are inextricably fused in actual practice, a basic distinction is asserted or implied. Consider, for instance, I. M. Lewis's account of the relation between a religious power and a warlike power among the Somali (of the horn of Africa) who think of these two powers as ideally distinct. The distinction often breaks down in actuality; yet, as Lewis says:

> Power in general is not readily defined in a single cultural idiom, or divided into separate secular and spiritual spheres any more than those whose social roles are primarily defined in either of these two spheres can entirely limit their interests to that realm alone. And in Somaliland the vital social interests which warriors and men of religion share, and particularly those which make . . . [religious specialists] dependent on warriors for their ultimate safety, prevent any rigid and permanent division between the two spheres. (1965, 219)

Even where mystical power is thought to derive partly from realistic power and yields in turn an increment in realistic power, a distinction seems implied, as when Harner reports of an Amazonian society that

> the personal security which the Jívaro believe comes from killing has some social reality. A man who has killed repeatedly, called a . . . "powerful one," is rarely attacked, because his enemies feel that the protection provided him by . . . [increments in mystical power gained from the souls of his victims] would make any assassination attempt against him fruitless.(1973, 142)

We would define religion, then, as all behavior, thoughts, and feelings that imply mystical power, whether that power is believed to reside in people, animals, inanimate things or events, or in beings that so far as observation can tell us are imaginary.

INITIAL COMPARISON BETWEEN TRADITIONAL AND WORLD RELIGIONS

The passage from Lawrence with which this chapter begins brings out very clearly some of the features appropriate for comparing traditional religions with world religions (such as Christianity, Islam, and Judaism). The focus of religious interest in Lawrence's New Guinea group was generally on this world rather than on an afterlife; ideas about salvation were lacking. Rituals were of paramount importance in attempting to gain the support of supernatural beings, who were seen as the source of good fortune and of misfortune, of health and of illness. Knowledge about the world, both the present and the past, was largely knowledge about supernaturals. With the power behind events residing primarily in supernaturals, people would, of course, turn to supernaturals for help and depend on tradition for guidance in this quest. And so, of course, do many participants in the world religions of modern nations when they appeal to divinity in whatever way they have been trained to use. For most of these features, there is perhaps no uniform difference between traditional and world religions.

The religions of traditional peoples are somewhat distinctive in ways that Lawrence does not mention in this passage. He takes for granted that his readers know that religious traditions were passed on orally from generation to generation. There can be no holy scriptures in an illiterate society; verbatim texts may be systematically memorized, but these are more often rituals or myths than statements of doctrine.

Another common feature is tolerance of other peoples' religions. It is as though traditional peoples readily appreciate that their religion pertains to their way of life. Alien peoples with a different way of life can hardly be expected to share it and must be expected to have their own religion appropriate to their own ways. The world religions, on the other hand, tend to emphasize claims to universal validity. Although a single world religion does vary greatly in the way it fits into the lives of different individuals or groups, this variation is overshadowed by the universalities of dogma or practice.

Another feature, which might be guessed by a reader of Lawrence's passage but is not explicit there, is that morality often plays a lesser role in the religions of traditional peoples than it does in the religions of complex societies such as ours. Morality may be at least as much a concern as in modern nations, but it seems often to be less connected with religion than we are inclined to consider it; and, of course, the ideas of morality, whether or not connected with religion, may vary in specific form. Perhaps a good way of expressing a frequent departure of traditional peoples from what Westerners are used to is to say that violation of moral rules is not commonly thought of as sin; the concept of sin, central to the moral teachings of Western religions, seems alien to the ways many traditional peoples think about wrongdoing. Where misfortune, bad luck, and misbehavior may be explained as punishment of mystical origin, feelings corresponding to a sense of sin are often not easy to find.

The term *worship* is also less appropriate for many traditional religions than for some of the world religions. Some mystical beings are considered to be remote and aloof; when they are thought to be close to people, it is often as sources of danger rather than of benefit.

A prime aim in the religious life of traditional peoples seems to be to establish the view that there is order in the universe, including an expectation that at least certain happenings will be repeated year after year. Prescribed behavior is aimed at maintaining this order and harmony in interpersonal relations as well as between people and all the other entities in this world. Richard Gould sums up this aspect of the religion of Australian aborigines:

> Gradually I experienced the central truth of Aboriginal religion: that it is not a thing by itself but an inseparable part of a whole that encompasses every aspect of daily life, every individual, and every time—past, present, and future. It is nothing less than the theme of existence, and as such constitutes one of the most sophisticated and unique religious and philosophical systems known to man. . . . For me the striking thing was the absolute relevance of

> every part of it to the problems and situations of daily life. In a sense, everything within the Aborigines' environment is holy, not in some vague, pantheistic sense but in terms of concrete ties which the rituals use and revitalize. (1969, 104)

In our society, popular comparison of religions centers on *isms*. Everyone tends to be considered a member of an institution thought of superfically as unitary: Catholicism, Protestantism, Judaism, Islam, Buddhism, and the like. Sorting people out by religious affiliation is perhaps inevitable when one's personal identity and place in relation to others are partly defined by a religion; to serve this purpose, each religion must have a label. But in a traditional society, before the intrusion of world religions, religion serves no such purpose. It does not separate some individuals from others; it simply is a part of the life of all the individuals in the community.

OUR ORIENTATION IN THIS BOOK

By avoiding ism labels, we will be able to give a more realistic picture of religion in traditional societies. But there is another advantage: By presenting the religions of traditional societies as they exist there, we may make more apparent the similarities they bear to religion as it exists in modern nations. The broad categorical labels that distinguish the major world religions may exaggerate the differences and distract our attention from what all those religions have in common. At a period when the decline of religion is often felt to be a major part of the deterioration of modern societies, improved understanding of the social values of religion elsewhere may be a help in constructive change of our own society.

A thorough understanding of the religion of any particular traditional society can be gained only as part of a thorough understanding of its total culture. The reader who wishes to gain such an understanding may approach it by way of some of the ethnographies we have drawn on. But our aim here is to look at individual cultures from a comparative point of view. We hope that our understanding of particular religions is based on at least a modest grasp of the culture in which they are embedded, but we have tried to communicate principally ways in which they illustrate points whose validity extends at least to similar traditional societies.

The features we have mentioned as more common in the religions of traditional societies are not absent in the world religions as they are found in modern nations. We hope that seeing them in the unfamiliar setting of traditional societies will help in seeing them where they occur among us.

We hope, too, to exhibit a basic similarity between traditional religions and world religions. In our treatment of the former, which provide the subject matter of this book, we will maintain that the variations found from one society to another are related to the differing situations and histories from which they emerge, and that traditional religions serve

similar basic functions in diverse societies, that they play a similar role in
the life of people. From this comes the suggestion that world religions may
likewise serve the same human needs. Our ready classification of people
in our community as participants in one or another ism encourages us to
think of each of the world religions as a uniform entity. But the fact is that
each of those religions, and especially its role in the life of its adherents,
vary among nations and even within a single nation or community, and
some of these variations may result from different social conditions, past
and present, to which the religion has adjusted.

Like some of the earliest writers on this subject, we are oriented
toward what might be learned about human nature, about universalities
in the way people think and act. But two circumstances give us a better
position than the earliest writers had:

1. Information about religions of traditional peoples has vastly improved. The fieldworkers who supply it have gained from the increase in
general methodological skill of anthropologists, and in recent decades an
ever larger proportion of them have devoted major attention to religion. As
a result, religion is increasingly known as an aspect of the total life of a
group, not as a separate category. This direct kind of knowledge of how
religion enters into everyday life provides a much better basis for our study
than the conjectures to which earlier writers were of necessity so largely
confined. At the same time, we also draw heavily on the factual reports of
earlier fieldworkers, because they had the advantage of gathering data at
closer to aboriginal times. As we want to survey the whole range of
variation in religion developed by human beings before the spread of a few
dominant world religions, the earlier work is especially pertinent.

2. Advances in psychology prepare us better to see similarities between
our own thought processes and those of traditional peoples. Clinical study of
people with problems and the experimental study of judgment and belief
conspire to disprove the naive nineteenth-century assumption that Westerners are rational and traditional peoples are irrational or prerational.

We seek to present a general review of the religions of traditional
societies, of their character and the variations among them. Such a review
is relevant to many intellectual interests. Our special bias is one that many
readers will share, whatever be the special interests they also bring to the
inquiry. Our bias is toward asking what various religious features contribute to the life of people. This may seem a psychologist's bias, and this is
not surprising, as one of us is a psychologist. But it does not require a
psychological background, as is well illustrated by the similar position
taken by anthropologists Raymond Firth and S. F. Nadel. Firth (1951), in
considering religion humanistically, asked what human needs are met by
beliefs that do not correspond to objective reality. He proceeded from his
study of a remote island in the Pacific, and Nadel from his study of a society
in Nigeria, but both were led to the same view of religion as diversely useful
to people. Nadel introduced the general conclusions to which his study of
Nupe religion had led him with this statement:

Let me here speak of "competences" of religion; for what I mean is, crudely speaking, the things religions "do" for individuals or societies; the effects they have upon their lives and actions or, if you like, the "needs" they are capable of satisfying. There is no need to refine our terminology further. (1954, 259)

With Nadel's resolve to use the language of everyday discourse, we are in complete agreement. For technical purposes of anthropology, sociology, or psychology, many writers on religion have used diverse refinements of language. We have tried to write in a way that would make our discourse immediately clear not only to specialists in any of these social sciences but also to people whose interest in world religions, in political problems, or in their own lives is what leads them to be curious about the religions of traditional peoples.

The broad purposes we seek to achieve in this book are two:

1. To portray what the religions of traditional peoples the world over have in common, and what variations stand out as of general importance. To describe the uniformities and the variations, we will rely not only on general statements but also on examples we can cite from the writings of the many fieldworkers who have reported on the religions of traditional peoples. Except in Chapter 11, we will be concentrating on religion as it developed before the advent of direct influence from the world religions. Because that influence has often been profound, our account of particular societies may be about their religion in an earlier generation. We do not aim to survey religion as it would be found at present, but religion as it developed in many different societies under more or less aboriginal conditions.

2. To indicate as best we can the way that the features of religion enter the lives of traditional peoples, to consider throughout the question: What does religion do for people? We have two principal sources to draw on in attempting an answer to this question. One is the interpretation of particular instances; many an ethnographer has reported his or her understanding of what role religion plays in the life of the people studied. The other source lies in systematic cross-cultural comparisons. Where some feature of religion varies from one society to another, it is possible to study what other features of culture vary with it. When two features of culture are found to vary together, plausible conjectures may be made about the functional relation between them. An especially important influence on many features of religion is the general mode of life and basic economy. Where knowledge justifies it, we have much to say about how religion contributes to effective pursuit of hunting and gathering, horticulture, animal husbandry, and agriculture. But religious features contribute also to other aspects of life—to maintaining traditional definitions of the roles of men and women, for example—and these, too, will be considered where knowledge permits.

Chapter 2

Mystical Power and Its Sources

What religions have in common is a concept of mystical power—power different from the material power of physical forces and from the personal forces of social interaction. However, conceptions of where the power resides, and how it gets there, vary widely. Mystical power is often explicitly attributed to living persons in this world or to gods or spirits in some other reality. Mystical power, with or without a specific locus, is often appealed to in explaining events, and it is at least implied in many feelings and actions. In attempting to understand the religions of traditional peoples, many early writers gave first place to a version of mystical power for which they used the term *mana*. This term continues to be much used, and it is important to see what is valid and what is doubtful in the way it is used.

MANA

When missionaries first visited traditional societies in the Pacific, a prominent feature they found in the aboriginal religions was a concept of mystical power to which the natives over a wide area gave the name *mana* (or slight variants). Most influential in introducing the concept of mana to the West was the English missionary R. H. Codrington. After traveling and working among peoples of the Solomon Islands, the Banks Islands, and other parts of Melanesia, Codrington published in 1881 an article on their religion and in 1891 a more general book on their culture. He summarized the Melanesian concept as follows:

> This Mana is not fixed in anything, and can be conveyed in almost anything; but spirits, whether disembodied souls or supernatural beings, have it and can impart it: and it essentially belongs to personal beings to originate it, though it may act through the medium of water, or a stone, or a bone. (1891, 119)

Codrington's study of Melanesian religions, with its focus on mana, attracted great interest among scholars and led to many speculations and theories about the concept. The speculations went far beyond the facts and beyond the regions from which the facts had been learned, so that mana came to be represented at times as though it were a substance diffused through the world, belief in which was fundamental to all "primitive" religions and distinguished them from the world religions. Codrington had confined his report to Melanesia (islands of related cultures, generally in the western Pacific), although he was aware that the concept had been reported also for Polynesian peoples (who lived, for the most part, in the more easterly regions of the Pacific), and indeed he suggested that it might have spread to Melanesia from Polynesia. Many European writers took off from Codrington's writings, and other early reports, to speculate, often very loosely, about primitive religion. Though Codrington had reported mana to be always tied in some way to persons, real or supernatural, these writers often changed the concept into that of an impersonal mystical power spread throughout the universe.

Raymond Firth (1967a, 177-178), an anthropologist of a later generation who specialized in Oceania, reported that the mana concepts found in Polynesia differed considerably in general form from the widespread accounts that had been inspired by what Codrington described for Melanesia. In his review of these accounts, Firth reported considerable confusion in the great variety of meanings ascribed to mana, meanings often seemingly derived from the theoretical preconceptions of the various authors rather than from actual data about Polynesian beliefs. Even in a single treatise, Firth said, mana may be represented as a force, a being, an action, a quality, and a state (1967a, 175).

What Firth found lacking in these early speculations about mana was empirical data, examples of how mana is represented in native actions and statements, obtained through the fieldworker's observations and interviews. Firth attempted to fill this gap for two Polynesian societies, on the basis of his own fieldwork among the Maori and the Tikopia. He offered an especially full and dependable account of the concept as it appears in the society where he did his most extensive and intensive work, the Tikopia. He reported, for instance, that a Tikopian chief

> is considered to be able through his relations with his ancestors and gods to control natural fertility, health, and economic conditions, in the interests of his dependants. Material evidence of his powers is given in native belief by the condition of the weather, of crops, of fish, and of sick persons whom he attempts to cure. Success or failure in these spheres are symptoms of his *mana*. (1967a, 179)

In Tikopia, mana is ascribed especially to chiefs but also to mediums (persons who specialize in contact with spirits). When the source of a person's mana is stated or implied, Firth found in Tikopia, it is always ascribed to spirits; it never appears as an impersonal force inherent in physical objects or in the world generally, and is never held to flow into a person from such an impersonal outside source. Although there are no comparably detailed studies of mana in other Polynesian societies, Firth indicated that this finding for Tikopia may well apply to the rest of Polynesia. There is no satisfactory evidence against it, and early statements to the contrary were probably based on misinformation. But mana in the sense of a mystical force characterizing individual human beings and the spirits who have given it to them is indeed important in Tikopia and in other Polynesian societies.

The concept of mana is applied to a much greater variety of people in Melanesia than in Polynesia, and the reason seems to lie in the lesser stratification of Melanesian society. Chiefs have a very important role in Polynesia, and thus they are the ones who principally demonstrate mana. In most Melanesian societies, the closest anyone comes to the status of chief is that of "big man" (an adult male respected for his character and achievements), and this role is less clearly defined than that of Polynesian chief. The big men demonstrate mana, but so do religious practitioners not known as big men, who have magical skills such as formulas to enhance success in growing yams or taro (Serpenti, 1965, 218-219). Individuals in Melanesia who gain prestige through demonstrating mana must, unlike Polynesian chiefs, continue to demonstrate their power by producing results. In both these Oceanic areas, then, mystical power is associated with realistic power in everyday social relations, but more rigidly in the more stratified societies.

In Tikopia—and this seems likely to hold true for Polynesia generally—the possessor of mana is able in some way to pass it on in the family line, just as he can his political power. When a Tikopian chief dies, one of his sons is elected chief, and the spirit of his deceased father is asked and expected to give mana to the successor. Apparently all Tikopian chiefs are considered to demonstrate mana, though to varying degrees, and any individual chief may have more at some times than at others. If things go wrong, a chief may be said to have developed a sort of negative mana, temporarily or permanently.

In Melanesia, on the other hand, there seems to be no corresponding expectation that a child of anyone who has possessed mana will come to have it too. (Gardening experts seem to constitute an exception here. Among the Trobriand Islanders, at least, Malinowski [1916, 193] reported that garden magic can be carried out only by a man whose maternal ancestors have "always been the lords of that village and of that soil." Perhaps it is significant that the Trobrianders are a Melanesian people who do have chiefs and that the garden magician of a village is next to the chief in importance. Here, too, then, possession of mystical power is a direct reflection of position in the social order.)

Firth's analysis of what mana means in Tikopia has been paralleled by studies in Melanesia, and none of them report belief in a diffuse, impersonal power such as early European writers had inferred. For both Polynesia and Melanesia, Hogbin (1936) found the concept of mystical power much more variable than had been supposed. On the basis of his own wide-ranging fieldwork, he provided details about religion in two Melanesian societies (on the islands of Guadalcanal and Malaita) in which mana is important and in one Melanesian and one Polynesian society (Wogeo and Ontong-Java, respectively) where the concept is absent. In no case did he find belief in impersonal mystical power. In Wogeo and Ontong-Java, power is indeed ascribed to spirits, but no special term such as mana is used in speaking about it, and people do not seek to have spirits transfer mystical power to them; instead, people use their own mystical power to try and compel spirits to act in their favor. Hogbin argues, then, that belief in anything like diffuse mystical power is no universal characteristic of the religions of traditional peoples. An analysis of the power concept among Melanesians of southeast Ambrym in the New Hebrides (now the independent nation of Vanuatu) by Tonkinson (1981, 260) finds mystical power important both in the traditional religion and in the local interpretation of Christianity, but it is always clearly localized in persons or spirits.

The writers who popularized the concept of mana as a diffuse, impersonal power had little or no knowledge of the languages of Oceania and apparently little appreciation of the difficulty—sometimes the impossibility—of adequate translation of abstract ideas from one language into another. The greater linguistic sophistication of modern anthropologists has brought new reasons to reject the notion that a concept of impersonal power was basic to Oceanic religions. Roger Keesing (1984) has analyzed ethnographic evidence in the light of the ways mana and related terms are used in various Oceanic languages and finds no evidence that the idea of a diffuse, impersonal power was ever basic to the religion of Melanesians or Polynesians. It seems to have arisen sporadically where social conditions favored the elaboration of theological speculation. But, for the most part, the notion of mana as a substance appears to have been a misunderstanding to which Westerners were led by their own religious and philosophical traditions. Fieldwork in Vanuatu by MacClancy (1986), done with careful attention to words and their usage, confirms, for one of the regions for which Codrington had originally reported, the absence of any idea of mana as a substance filling the void. But mana as a word for a mystical power believed to be present in certain people, animals, things, or places is indeed important in most societies of Melanesia and Polynesia.

The concept of mana is a useful introduction to the general topic of mystical power. Early writers exaggerated the extent to which mana was seen by Polynesians and Melanesians as existing in the outside world rather than in people because their own religious preconceptions placed mystical power almost exclusively in supernatural figures. In Christian Europe, only in the folk religions was mystical power granted also to living human beings—sorcerers, mediums, and the like.

Going beyond the concept of mana, we will proceed now to consider two aspects of mystical power already alluded to in connection with mana: mystical power as it is conceived to reside in individual living persons, and, more briefly for the present, mystical power as it is conceived to reside elsewhere. Because mystical power in world religions is rarely placed in living persons, that location is what most needs introduction, to prepare the reader for the great variety of ways in which religion has personal relevance to daily life in traditional societies.

MYSTICAL POWER IN THE PERSON, AND HOW IT GETS THERE

Mystical power in the person is perhaps most widely known to the modern public as it appears in many Native American societies, as part of the vision-quest complex.*

In such societies the power generally comes to a boy or girl from a spirit helper or guardian, in a one-to-one relationship between the individual and guardian spirit. The gift of power is often made during dreaming or in waking visions, after some days and nights of searching, and it may be thought of as knowledge conveyed. Among some of the most northerly tribes of North America, according to Ridington (1990, 12), "knowledge and power are one." Once having granted the power, the helper is not always immediately involved each time the power is exercised. As Flannery (1952) points out, this differs from the mystical power a spirit is thought to provide to a spirit medium, permitting communication with the dead; the medium is conceived to depend upon spirit cooperation anew on each occasion, just as are mediums in the spiritualist tradition in our culture.

The idea that mystical power may be gained through a vision quest is not limited to Native Americans; similarities in the way it appears in diverse places can be illustrated by an example from North America and one from Melanesia, though in the latter a supernatural stone takes the place of a spirit. Spier, writing about the Klamath of the western United States, says,

> The formula prescribes fasting for a number of nights on the mountains, continually running about and piling up rocks, combined with diving into lonely pools, or following the latter plan alone by diving beneath whirlpools in the river or lakes which spirits are known to haunt. The supplicant loses consciousness and wakes to find himself on the shore bleeding profusely from the mouth and nose. He does not ordinarily have a vision, but success is manifested in a song heard in a dream on a night soon following. (1930, 239)

Here is Lane's account for the Ragans, a Melanesian people of Vanuatu:

*Following present-day usage in the United States, we occasionally use the term *Native American* for aboriginal societies of the area now the United States; but because similar societies existed to the south and to the north of present borders, we extend the term to cover them too.]

One way of obtaining power from stones was by diving into lakes and pools. A person planning such a quest would prepare by fasting, purification, and by abstaining from sexual activity. He would then go to the pool, either alone or in the company of a tutor. At the pool, he would anoint himself or be anointed with coconut juice. He would then dive as deep as he could and remain under water for as long as he could. The aim was not to search for a stone in a direct way. Rather, the seeker tried to achieve a quiescent state, drifting near the bottom. The hope and expectation was that a mysterious stone would miraculously appear in the hands of the seeker. (1977, 367)

The pattern of the vision quest is highly variable, even within a single culture. Both the source from which a person acquires power and the way he or she acquires it vary widely. Often the source is not clearly specified. In the passage on the Klamath, for example, Spier goes on to say: "The spirit is not the suppliant's guardian and later quests are not necessarily for renewed experiences with it. Power may also come involuntarily, when a dreamer hears a spirit song. There is no obligation to accept, but resistance brings illness" (1930, 239-240).

In some Native American societies, on the other hand, the source of power gained in the quest seems to have been quite clear for most persons. The Saulteaux, for instance, considered the supernatural "masters" or "bosses" of various animal species to be the main source of mystical power, communicated in dreams; the boy or girl seeking power apparently dreamed of one or more particular masters, though a custom of concealing the vision dreams from others prevented the ethnographer from gathering detailed information (Hallowell, 1934). Among the Beavers (also known as Dunne-za) of British Columbia each person's power is derived from a specific person-animal figure of mythology, such as Spider-Person or Frog-Person (Ridington, 1976).

In South America, among the Jívaro (Harner, 1973) and Yanomamo (Chagnon, 1968), for example, psychedelic drugs play an important role in obtaining mystical power. In North America and in Melanesia purchase or inheritance is a more likely alternative to the vision quest. Another, though rare, way to acquire power is from ghosts of the recently deceased. Inborn power might come, too, by reincarnation. Among the Chipewyan (a northern Athapaskan group in Canada), the maximum of mystical power is found only in a person who is a reincarnation of Lived-with-the-Wolves, an immortal being who from time to time incarnates, perhaps in response to the wish of a pregnant woman expressed by her eating wolf-flesh. Among the Chipewyans, at least, even power conferred in this way can be lost, as shown in the life history of a recent incarnation (Sharp, 1986).

Where power is purchased or is acquired by taking a psychedelic drug, there may be a period of training and instruction about the dangers inherent in the possession of power and about how to use it safely. In some societies, indeed, formal instruction appears to be the principal route to power, and the instruction may be a blend of the realistic and mystical. In Melanesia, as we have indicated, a horticultural expert among the Kimam of western New Guinea has, besides technical knowledge and skill, special medicine to make yams grow well (Serpenti, 1965, 218-220). He may on request undertake to train another individual to use this medicine. However, the medicines are considered so dangerous that many men choose not to undergo the training, either for fear of the danger itself or because they are reluctant to submit to the food taboos and sex restriction that would be needed to protect them from it (Serpenti, 1965, 219, 222).

Achievement of mystical power is sometimes an objective of ceremonials. This is true of girls' puberty ceremonies among the Cibecue Apache. The power of the mythological figure Changing Woman enters the girl's body for a period of four days, during which "the girl acquires all the desirable qualities of Changing Woman herself, and is thereby prepared for a useful and rewarding life as an adult" (Basso, 1970, 64). In particular, the power of Changing Woman brings longevity and usefulness. During the four days the power is in her, the girl is, like a medicine man, able to heal and to bring rain. Male initiation rites are also often seen as a source of personal power. Among the Abelam of the Sepik district in Papua New Guinea, for instance, initiation into a major cult contributes to gardening success; it gives the youth "a supernatural power that is transmitted through his hands to the yams which he handles" (Kaberry, 1941, 355).

Ceremonies may be seen, too, as strengthening mystical power that a person already has. The medicine men of the Pawnee (a horticultural people in the Platte Valley, in Nebraska) originally obtained power from a guardian spirit or from instruction by a medicine man. Each year, however, they held a ceremony that served to renew their power as well as to demonstrate it to the laity (Linton, 1923).

In many Native American tribes mystical power might be obtained from "medicine bundles" or "holy" or "sacred" bundles, as they were variously called by English-speaking whites. A bundle often included sacred stones, plant and animal parts, sacred dolls, and the like, typically wrapped up as a package. A bundle could, in some cases, be inherited or sold, the mystical power going with its legitimate ownership but also by contact (for the owner often carried the bundle on his body when engaged in combat, healing, etc.). These sacred bundles and their use have been described for many Native American peoples, for example, the Crow (Lowie, 1935) and the Pawnee (Weltfish, 1965). Descriptions, however, do not make clear how consistently the rationale involved a gain of internal mystical power, as opposed to purely external power in the bundle itself. Sometimes bundles were the property of groups rather than individuals (Linton, 1922b), and here it may be less likely that the power was thought to be internalized by the owner. In an African instance of individually owned bundles or medicines (Boston, 1971), there is no suggestion that the power is internalized. Nor is there in a detailed account of bundles among the Plains Cree of Canada (Mandelbaum, 1940, 258-261). Instructions for the assembly and use of a bundle are given in a dream by a spirit helper; the owner can subsequently transfer the bundle with its power intact to someone else. Among the Beaver, on the other hand, it seems clear that mystical power gained in the vision quest resides partly in the medicine bundle and partly in the person, where it may vary in strength from time to time, swelling to dangerous strength if the proper taboos are not observed (Ridington, 1976).

Sometimes mystical power seems to be considered a direct gift from divinity. In Polynesia, as we have mentioned, it is primarily the chiefs who have mystical power. For the Maori (the Polynesians of New Zealand), both Best (1924) and Buck (1939) indicate that although knowledge and skill are part of the authority of a chief or other expert, something more is involved that makes the chief or expert subject to a multitude of taboos related to the "sacred"; that extra something comes from the gods. This Polynesian focus on the mystical power of the chief, and the significance of his mana for the welfare of the community, are paralleled in some African societies in conceptions of "divine king" or "divine breath of kings," as among the Nyakyusa and Shilluk. In Polynesia, however, the origins of the power are fused with something like inheritance (resembling at times our conception of biological heredity, at other times our conception of the passing on of property). In ceremonies at the time of accession of a king, he becomes the incarnation of earlier kings, who have by now become gods.

Taboos associated with the sanctity of Polynesian chiefs seem to imply personal mystical power, and the same may be said of high status generally in these stratified societies. A chief had to be approached with deference, always leaving him elevated above the humble person. In Tonga an inferior was forbidden to touch any superior. Because the head and back were the most sacred parts of a chief's body, an inferior could not pass behind a chief, particularly during a ceremony. Similar taboos were imposed in other regions of the world, such as North America, to show respect for a shaman, especially when actively engaged in a ritual. Tongans also considered it dangerous for ordinary people to eat food left by a chief, as illness might be expected to result (Collocott, 1921). All these taboos seem to imply a mystical power in the high-status person that might threaten the welfare of any violator of the taboo.

Some other taboos also suggest mystical power residing in a person, though often only temporarily. A woman giving birth, a person undergoing initiation, a warrior who had just killed an enemy—may each be thought of as in a sacred state. The implication is that, sometimes, this person is vulnerable to injury from mystical sources or ordinary physical dangers. But also, at times, this person in a temporary sacred state seems to be a source of unintentional danger to others if they do not observe the taboos on interaction with him or her that are appropriate to the sacred state, taboos that protect others from the mystical power occasioned by the sacred state.

Another route to more lasting mystical power, found both in South America and on the far side of the Pacific, is through killing other human beings. In headhunting societies, a head taken is not merely a trophy of prowess, a source of pride and glory; it also brings an increment of mystical power. For the Jívaro, the warrior who killed an enemy and took his head home thereby stole one of the several types of soul each person may have. (The Jívaro had complex beliefs about multiple souls.) The Jívaro boy at first goes out on what might be viewed as something in the nature of a vision quest. As Harner reports:

> His dream visitor is in the form of an old Jívaro man who says to him, "I am your ancestor. Just as I have lived a long time, so will you. Just as I have killed many times, so will you." Without another word the old man disappears and immediately the . . . [vision-producing] soul of this unknown ancestor enters the body of the dreamer, where it is lodged in his chest. (1973, 138-139)

After such an initial experience, a Jívaro male would go on to seek more souls to protect him or his relatives. Headhunting was the most important way of adding a soul and gaining power; though the soul did not remain permanently, some of the power gained from it could still be kept. Jívaro men had to renew their power by stealing more souls, with the help of headhunting or psychedelics, in order to protect themselves from death at the hands of other headhunters. Here, too, there was an element of inheritance, so that the first vision-producing soul a boy acquired had to be from an ancestor; thus, an ancestor who had been successful in life was now, even if long since dead, able to pass on power to his descendants.

The Mundurucú (Murphy, 1958, 55) are another South American group that view headhunting as a source of mystical power. They explicitly saw the successful headhunter's power as a gain to his group as well as to himself; his proximity ensured the success of his fellows in the food quest.

Early accounts of headhunting in various other parts of the world—among the Ifugao and Iban of Indonesia and some people of southern New Guinea, for instance—associate the practice with fertility, and that association seems also to imply a notion of personal mystical power. Some writers have suggested that power flows from the captured and severed head, or resides there. But Needham (1976) shows that for a Borneo people, and perhaps others, this, like some notions of mana, is an unwarranted extension by Western writers of their tendency to ascribe mechanisms. In some headhunting societies, the taking of a head is seen as producing a gain of personal power without any beliefs about how it happens.

Killing as a route to mystical power is not confined to headhunters. The same implication is to be found in a notion about sorcerers in both Africa and North America, that to gain their power they must have killed a near relative. Transfer of mystical power from a deceased person does not necessarily depend on killing alone or on inheritance. It may also occur through ritual cannibalism, the ceremonial eating of some part of the corpse. Linton (1922a, 16) reports for the Skidi group of the Pawnee that at the annual Morning Star ceremony members of the Bear Medicine Society ate the liver of the human sacrificial victim in order "to acquire magical powers." The eating of the victim's heart is reported for the pre-Columbian Aztecs of Mexico. In both these cases the deceased was a captive from outside, and in many such cases it has been assumed that a transfer of mystical power provided part of the motive for cannibalism (Sagan, 1974, 8-9). Ritual cannibalism in some societies is a part of the mortuary ceremonies for their own members. Widely believed at one time to be such a case was the cannibalism of the South Fore in New Guinea. Kuru, a fatal nervous system disease attributed by the Fore to sorcery, was found to be a virus disease transmitted by the eating of portions of the body of deceased kin. But it was eventually learned that this endocannibalism lacked ritual significance (Lindenbaum, 1979, 22). In another New Guinea society, however, the Bimin-Kuskusmin, a deceased person's ritual and reproductive power were thought to be transferred to kin by their eating of ritually significant parts of the body (Poole, 1983, 15-17).

In some of the African societies where personal mystical power is widespread in at least the male population, the source is vaguer. Among the Kung San, men employ an "invisible potency" in their rituals of curing, marked by dancing and going into trance (Katz, 1982). The ultimate source appears to be a supernatural being of the type anthropologists call a *culture hero* (mythical author of some feature of the culture). In two pastoral societies of North Africa, the Riffians and the Tuareg, the personal mystical power referred to there as *baraka* appears to emanate from God, and this is perhaps an Islamicized version of a pre-Islamic conception of mystical power. Coon, writing of the Riffians, reports that baraka

> is usually confined to supposed descendants of the Prophet, and is dependent upon their possession of a magical emanation supposedly transmitted to them by him. A man possessing it is equipped with supernatural powers; he is able to predict the future, to perform miracles, and to heal or destroy by touch, or, through extension, by employing some object which has been in contact with his body, such as a part of his clothing, a piece of bread, or an egg which he has kissed. (1931, 157)

A wedding confers the same mystical power on the bride and bridegroom, so that persons who take part in the wedding, and even other people, expect to derive certain benefits. The bride throws barley, and people catch of it what they can and mix it with their own barley in order to derive benefits from mere contact with the "holy" barley.

Among the Nuer and the Dinka, pastoralists of East Africa, personal power is related to something more general—"Spirit," as Evans-Pritchard (1956) says of the Nuer, "Divinity," as Lienhardt (1961) says of the Dinka. Dinka seers, diviners, and prophets all have "Divinity," a concept used to explain a person's internal power, his skills and abilities, just as it is used to explain the mystical qualities of supernatural beings. These two authors speak of "refractions" of Spirit or Divinity, and these refractions seem to include the individual mystical powers of the Nuer and Dinka.

Does mystical power also reside at least momentarily in a person who utters words that produce a mystical effect? In many societies, spells and incantations must be learned and recited correctly in order to be believed effective; knowledge of them, and the right to utter them, may be a valuable personal possession, learned from someone privileged to teach them, and often paid for. Reliance on the mystical power of words appears especially often among horticulturalists and agriculturalists. Malinowski, in his *Coral Gardens and Their Magic* (1935), reported in detail the chants that must be used by specialists among the Trobriand Islanders to ensure successful crops. Serpenti, in *Cultivators in the Swamps* (1965), gives a similar picture for another Melanesian horticultural society, the Kimam.

Peoples with a nomadic or migratory type of life, on the other hand, particularly those living in small bands rather than communities, do not have the strong oral traditions of more stable groups with dense populations and close face-to-face interactions; foragers and some pastoralists share a tendency toward isolation and movement, whereas agriculturalists and horticulturalists tend to live a sedentary life in larger groups. The sacred knowledge and traditions of the more stable groups make for the persistence of rich religious traditions of verbal expression, particularly where there are religious cults. An agriculturalist example from southern Africa that explicitly indicates the importance of the power of words appears in Krige's (1968) description of the Zulu girls' initiation rites. The Zulu girls sing on this occasion songs of sexual character that the Zulu would under other circumstances consider obscene. These songs are tolerated when girls are reaching menarche because they are thought to promote the sexual maturing of young females, preparing them for marriage and childbearing.

In complex traditional societies, there may be great variation among individuals in their access to mystical power. Such variation is conspicuous in many horticultural and intensive agricultural groups in Africa, Oceania, and Asia, as well as in North and South America. Often, supernatural power can be inherited by the select few who are also inheriting a status that carries great realistic power. Firth, for example, tells how a deceased Tikopian chief was believed to be crawling to the god asking for mystical power to give to his successor, his son (1967a, 181). Reincarnation of the spirits of dead ancestors also appears as a source of mystical power that differentiates individuals from one another, and this too appears to be frequent in the more complex societies. Among the Tongans, even the possession of a soul is reserved to those of high status (Collocott, 1921, 424).

The economy of foragers is such that all persons need to be self-reliant, so a need for individual power is more uniformly present. This is even true of the temporary mystical power that may be gained while engaging in special activities or during a period of life when they are practiced. A comparison between the Balinese and the Kung San seems instructive on this point. Among the Balinese, an agricultural society of Indonesia, some adults choose to engage in the special trances that permit them to do dangerous sword dances with apparent impunity (in part, protected by participants not in trance); so also certain young girls go into trance and do dances they are felt to be incapable of performing in a normal state. In most instances, only a fraction of the population seems to take part. Among the Kung, on the other hand—African foragers—temporary participation in dances in a state of trance seems to characterize all young men, even though only a few go on to develop in this way skills on which healing may depend (Katz, 1973). In the North American vision quest, lasting mystical power was among some peoples, mostly foragers, expected to be gained by everyone, though the strength of the power might vary greatly.

Again, the outcome of possessing mystical power could vary greatly. Appeal to it in coping with sickness and preventing misfortune is considered in Chapter 7, on illness and healing. Some of the same persons who functioned principally as healers, however, might turn their powers to evil use in sorcery or witchcraft, and others might attempt to use mystical power only for those evil purposes, which are considered in Chapter 6, on wizardry.

Temporary changes in use of mystical power were expected and feared in some societies. Among the Beaver and some other Native American groups, an excess of power might be involved in a person's gaining the reputation of compulsive cannibalism, in an evil role provided for in their cultures. Fears of this distortion are most often mentioned in accounts of northern societies where starvation was enough of a threat so that cannibalism could be at times a real temptation. Ridington (1976, 119) tells of seeing a young girl handing her father his medicine bundle, as though to drain off into it some of the excessively strong frog power that seemed to be leading him toward cannibalism.

RELATION BETWEEN PERSONAL MYSTICAL POWER AND THE ECONOMY

Through most of the varied forms of personal mystical power, there seems to be a fairly regular background fact. It is that personal mystical power is most conspicuous in societies with a hunting and gathering economy. Various kinds of cross-cultural research have shown that such economies are associated with an emphasis on self-reliance (Barry, Child, & Bacon, 1959). The widespread distribution of the vision quest in Native American groups is consistent, then, with the predominance in North America of hunting-gathering economies that require individual skill and achievement. In other parts of the world, personal mystical power is especially important where similar economies place the same premium on self-reliance. In our African example, where emphasis on personal mystical power is generally much less conspicuous than in North America, the clearest case of strong emphasis appears in a hunting-gathering society, the Kung San. Among other African societies, personal mystical power is more developed in the pastoral than in the agricultural societies. We would relate this to the pastoralists' need, pointed out by Goldschmidt (1971), for self-reliance, occasioned by the greater uncertainties of their economy in comparison with that of agriculturalists.

Among the Native American tribes that inhabited the Great Plains and adjacent areas when the Europeans came, the role, at later times, of mystical power gained in visions varied with the economy and the social system developed to support the economy (Albers & Parker, 1971). Europeans introduced horses to the New World, and horses had been acquired by Plains tribes long before Europeans came in numbers to their region. Horses made possible a new and efficient way of living, by group hunting of the buffalo—a kind of hunting that stressed cooperation more than outstanding individual skills. Reliance on individual visions was diminished in these societies, in the enterprise of food getting, in favor of group rituals, whose validity was traced to visions, perhaps mythical, in the past. The mystical power was thus a property of the group rather than of the individual. In societies that continued a simpler foraging and horticultural existence, visions continued to be a source of individual mystical power, sought for by each boy as a basis for success in adult life. (Even in some of the buffalo-hunting tribes, individual visions continued as an important source of mystical power supportive of self-confidence and reputation in warfare.)

Albers and Parker adduce evidence that even within a single society of this region the role of mystical power in the individual's life was also subject to change in adaptation to the position the individual was finding for himself. Among the Crow, Robert Lowie's impression (1935, 254) was that a person's description of his power-granting vision—the way he described it to himself, presumably, as well as to others—was characteristically "remodeled by his individual fancy and the needs of the moment." Verne Ray was even more explicit in his conclusions about the Sanpoil, where a person was expected to experience mystical visions before puberty but not to reveal them, or even remember them clearly, until adulthood.

> The results of a quest . . . were not disclosed. Soon after the vision the whole experience was completely "forgotten." Informants insisted strongly on this point. The visionary, they claimed, was powerless to recall any details of the incident until he was again visited by his spirit. This did not occur until many years later, usually when the person reached twenty-five or thirty years of age. . . . By the time the spirit returned the individual had more or less definitely found his place in the community. His talents were known to himself and to others, and his character likewise. The type of activity which was to predominate in his life was usually fixed. . . . When recalled after this period of enforced forgetting the details of the experiences would naturally, without conscious falsification, be reconstructed to fit the situation in which the individual found himself established. (1933, 186)

These accounts of how the visionary mystical power fitted into the individual's life are remarkably similar to Alfred Adler's account, based on his clinical experience in Vienna, of a person's early memories. A person remembers his earliest experiences, Adler said (in passages brought together in Ansbacher & Ansbacher, 1956, 350-365), in a manner consistent with the way he now lives and hopes to live in the future. The memories are gradually modified—by selection of memories and by modification of those that are recalled—as the person's whole conception of himself and his interaction with others changes. They form a part of the guiding fiction, only partly conscious, that helps motivate and provide a cognitive framework for life activities. Here in everyone's lifetime is to be seen a psychological mechanism that would facilitate the adaptation of the vision quest to the adult role, so that in societies with a vision quest a person's sense of his own mystical power would be appropriate for his role in the life of the community.

Another pertinent aspect of the variation among economies is degree of egalitarianism. The idea that a person's power comes from a direct relationship with a guardian spirit allows for the possibility that any member of a society might establish such a relationship and receive a gain of mystical power. It is understandable, then, that such a belief is more likely to be found in relatively egalitarian societies. Foragers are especially likely to be egalitarian, with little variation in status among members. The widespread distribution of the vision quest and guardian spirit among Native American societies is consistent with their living by foraging. But Melanesian societies, which add horticulture and pig raising to foraging, are also rather egalitarian, and this is consistent with the presence among them, too, of a kind of quest for mystical power; in some instances, this quest takes forms almost identical with those found in North America.

A relation to basic economy seems also to hold true for the proportion of individuals in a society who seek or gain mystical power. All societies seem at least to have healers who are credited with mystical power. But how widespread is personal mystical power in the rest of the population? In North America its breadth is associated with variations in the economy and the pattern of social interaction. Among the Paiutes of the Great Basin area, in the state of Oregon, for example, a gathering and hunting society with considerable individualism, mystical power is sought by many (Whiting, 1950). Among the Zuni of New Mexico, on the other hand, who are primarily agricultural and very group-oriented, mystical power is little sought and does not even come to many persons involuntarily through their dreaming. The correlation with economy suggested by these extreme cases seems to be typical.

At the extreme, everyone in a society may have mystical power. This is well illustrated by Pygmy groups in southern Africa, foragers whose physical environment ties their welfare closely to the amount and timing of rainfall. Among the Kung San, each child is born with mystical power that may tend toward production either of favorable or of unfavorable weather conditions, and its character may be diagnosed around the time of birth.

> It is discovered what kind of . . . [mystical power] a child has by observing the weather at the time of its birth or soon after. If it rains the people believe the ...[power]...of the child has brought the rain and are sure the . . . [power] is good. If water should freeze when the child was born or soon after, the child's . . . [power] would be known to be bad. (Marshall, 1957, 236)

When the weather surrounding a child's birth is extreme—very rainy or bitterly cold— this strengthens the confidence felt in the diagnosis. The Khoikhoi (Hottentots) (though they combine foraging with some animal husbandry) share this belief in universal mystical power. With them, the child's power can also be diagnosed from the weather conditions surrounding the birth. People who are endowed with good power seem able to help protect their group from bad weather and from other bad effects that may be brought about by "an unknown and overwhelmingly great power" (Hoernlé, 1918, 68).

As the role of hunting and gathering in subsistence decreases, mystical power increasingly has a purely protective function. This is highlighted by the contrast between societies of North America that depend exclusively on hunting and gathering and some of the South American societies for whom hunting and gathering is less important. In the former, mystical power provides much that is positive—success in the food quest, success in war, success in love and family life, prestige. In the latter, mystical power is more often protective, increasing a person's safety in confronting an enemy but not necessarily forwarding his positive subsistence aims. For some very warlike South American tribes, in which personal mystical power is greatly elaborated—the Jívaro (Harner, 1973), the Yanomamo (Chagnon, 1968), and the Mundurucú (Murphy, 1958)—its protective function is very obvious, as evidenced in the details of the ethnographic reports.

MYSTICAL POWER OUTSIDE THE PERSON

Mystical power outside the person seems to be found in every society, though its relative importance and precise form vary greatly. Franz Boas, an early leader of anthropology in the United States, wrote that fundamental to the religions of Native Americans is a concept of mystical power that

> must be understood as the wonderful qualities which are believed to exist in objects, animals, men, spirits or deities, and which is superior to the natural qualities of man. . . . It is what is called manito by the Algonquian tribes; wakanda by the Siouan tribes; orenda by the Iroquois; sulia by the Salish; naualak by the Kwakiutl; and tamanoas by the Chinook. (1910, 366)

Any of these terms from Native American languages would have deserved the expansion that was instead given to the Oceanic term mana. The diversity of Native American languages has spared us from having any one of them over-generalized. For all of these terms, as well as for mana, which by historical accident received greater attention, we can substitute the English term *mystical power*. This fact seemed to be realized by Boas and some of his students. Ruth Benedict, who became a distinguished anthropologist in her own right, was one of the most eloquent. In her chapter on religion in Boas's *General Anthropology*, she considered what the native terms for mystical power meant in various American tribes, and concluded,

> The fundamental concept that is represented by these native terms is the existence of wonderful power, a voltage with which the universe is believed to be charged. This voltage is present in the whole world in so far as it is considered supernatural, whether it is regarded as animate or inanimate. . . . Always, moreover, the manipulation of this wonderful power, and the beliefs that grow out of it, are religion. (1938, 630)

A good example of the ethnographic accounts that justified the statements by Boas and Benedict is provided by the early American anthropologist Alice Fletcher and her Omaha Indian collaborator Francis LaFlesche. The passage also illustrates that traditional religions may be very much concerned with morality. They begin by correcting the common impression that Wakonda refers simply to "the great spirit," and then go on to say:

> Wakonda stands for the mysterious life power permeating all natural forms and forces and all phases of man's conscious life. The idea of Wakonda is therefore fundamental to the Omaha in his relations to nature, including man and all other living forms. . . . Visible nature seems to have mirrored to the Omaha mind the ever-present activities of the invisible and mysterious Wakonda and to have been an instructor both in religion and in ethics. The rites pertaining to the individual reveal clearly the teaching of the integrity of the universe, of which man is a part; the various. . . rites emphasize man's dependence on a power greater than himself and the idea that supernatural punishments will follow disobedience to constituted authority. Natural phenomena served to enforce ethics. (1911, 597-598)

Another explicit placement of power in natural objects is seen in the North African concept of baraka, mentioned earlier. To the Berbers, animals, trees and other plants, even the ground where grass, corn, and fruit were grown, were considered holy and participating in this mystical power.

As we will refer in most of our chapters to mystical power outside the person, we will only introduce it briefly here. In considering it, we run the risk of becoming involved in theological speculations such as are generally a major concern of only a small minority, the philosophically minded members of any community (see Radin, 1927), and that often reach us only through a haze created by barriers of language, religion, and colonialism.

A prime example of issues difficult to resolve is whether some of the mystical power outside human beings is sometimes conceived of as thoroughly impersonal or is thought always to be associated with person-like beings. Australian aborigines, for example, feared the mystical power associated with specific places. In some instances, the power originated in a person who had died or was buried in that spot; in other instances, the power remained from events in distant mythical times, and it is not clear whether it was then still thought of as personal in character (Biernoff, 1978).

Paul Radin (1914, 350) argued that Native Americans do not believe in an impersonal force, that they always hold mystical power to reside in definite spirits. The assumption that they believe in an impersonal force was, he held, a mistaken interpretation by earlier investigators. Hallowell's intensive study, in the 1930s, of religious concepts of the Ojibwa led him to the same conclusion about that particular group, and he seemed to agree with Radin's view about other Native American groups. Analysis by Firth and others of the mana concept in Oceania, which we have summarized earlier, suggests a similar conclusion for Polynesia and Micronesia. Ruth Benedict (1938), on the other hand, summarizing knowledge in the 1930s about traditional religions, writes of impersonal mystical power as though it were of great and widespread importance.

Resolution of such controversies may be impossible. Anthropologists who were able to do fieldwork with societies still close to their aboriginal condition have not been able to agree. Perhaps further fieldwork on a large scale, with the improved facilities and techniques of today, might lead to resolution, except that few societies close to their aboriginal state are now available for study. These difficult issues are of great interest even if they cannot be definitively resolved. But we prefer to emphasize in this book what can be more simply evidenced and reported, and more confidently known from existing reports of fieldwork: what people *do* in relation to external mystical power.

At the outset we might ask, do they necessarily do anything? In some cases, they seem not to. Among the Berbers of North Africa, it is not clear just how or whether their ascription of mystical power to plants and fields was expressed in action. Among the Native Americans of North America, the emphasis was on individuals utilizing the mystical powers they themselves possessed. This contrasts greatly with the concern with divine power in Judaism, Christianity, and Islam. Yet the individual's power was thought by these Native Americans to originate as a gift from mystical beings. Their hunting was regulated, too, by reference to the power of mystical "owners" or "masters" of the game. They also prayed to the sun—indispensable source of great external power—and accompanied their prayers with tobacco smoke, pollen, and other small offerings. Some action in relation to external power seems to be everywhere present to some degree. Belief in mystical power outside the person seems to increase with increasing complexity of the society. Appeal to external power becomes more conspicuous, and appears in several different forms.

In Chapter 3 we consider how plants and animals enter into traditional religions, sometimes as loci of power and sometimes in other ways. Then, in later chapters, we turn to the variety of other forms in which external power appears, to the variety of what in our culture might be called supernatural figures possessing mystical power, and to the ways in which people seek to establish and maintain communication with those supernatural figures. We follow that with a chapter on magic and aspects of sorcery and witchcraft that have not been considered earlier; here are practices that, in not depending on realistic techniques of manipulating the world, are attempts to exert mystical power.

SUMMARY

Mystical power as the core of religious thought was stressed in early accounts of mana in cultures of the Pacific. Those accounts were oversimplified, but were useful in directing attention to concepts of mystical power, which in their various forms can indeed serve to define what is common to religions.

Mystical power in the person is generally of greater importance in traditional religions than in world religions. It is sought in the spiritual quest of North American tribes. Mystical power is believed in different societies to be gained in a great variety of ways: by inheritance or purchase, by psychedelic drugs, by use of medicine bundles, by special temporary or permanent social status, by killing (as in headhunting), by use of powerful words. Personal mystical power is especially stressed in the religion of foragers, where it may contribute to the reliance on individual skills in the food quest, and by pastoralists rather than agriculturalists.

Mystical power outside the person, in supernatural figures, characterizes religious thought everywhere and is elaborated in Chapter 4.

Chapter 3

Animals and Plants in Religion

In the nineteenth century, scholars in Europe and America were beginning to acquire detailed knowledge about peoples outside the various great civilizations of the world. They sought to make sense out of this knowledge by contrasting it with their own culture and history. Today we are likely to call those newfound peoples "traditional" or "preliterate," as a way of indicating that before contact with literate societies they had to depend on behavioral and oral tradition alone rather than on writing in transmitting their culture from one generation to another. Seeking a simple view, or perhaps unthinkingly adopting one, Western writers labeled these peoples "primitive" or "savage." These terms suggest additional ways in which such peoples supposedly differ from "advanced" or "civilized" societies, and many of the supposed differences may not be very genuine. In religion, an apparent distinction from the most familiar complex societies could be created by calling all the traditional peoples "pagan" or "heathen." All these words were misleading in suggesting much more uniformity among traditional peoples and more consistent difference from "advanced" peoples than in fact prevailed.

TOTEMISM

When nineteenth-century writers looked at the role of animals and plants in the religious life of traditional peoples, they too hastily developed again a simple concept, that of totemism. Their assumption that totemism was characteristic of traditional peoples has given way in the face of the vastly more detailed knowledge of many traditional societies, gained by ethnographers in the intervening century. But the aspects of religion that gave rise to the concept of totemism are indeed important for many societies, and they provide a good starting point for considering the religious significance of animals and plants.

The nineteenth-century writers held that traditional peoples' ties with the animal and plant worlds were of a mystical nature and centered on the relation of human groups to *totems*. Each major group in a society was distinctively associated with a particular kind of plant or animal (sometimes, a material object), and this was its totem. Usually, it was held, members of the group claimed descent from their totem. A god or spirit might incarnate itself in the form of a totem. Members of the group observed various taboos related to their totem, avoiding killing, eating, or showing disrespect to it.

All these features are indeed found in the religions of various traditional societies. But they are not present everywhere, and they are not always found together. Later fieldwork, primarily by anthropologists, has filled out and corrected the picture. The supernatural or mystical forces that traditional peoples associate with animals, plants, and even inanimate objects in nature involve much more than merely special ties between a clan, sib, or cult group and its totem. Especially in North and South America there is often the added element of tracing a group's origin to descent from the animal whose name it bears, though this sort of belief is perhaps not generally taken very literally. Some complex hunting and fishing groups, such as those of the Northwest Coast of North America, go to great lengths in their folktales, mythology, rituals, and artistic expression to portray and present humanlike personalities in accounts of the various animals (including such fictitious animals as thunderbirds) with which they people their real and imaginary environments, and this seems to facilitate a belief in animal origins of humanity. Symbolically for these groups, people seem to be portrayed as getting their start long ago as humans cloaked in animal forms (Goldman, 1975). Traditional peoples in northeast Asia and Japan held the belief that they were descended from trees: the Orok from a birch, the Gilyak from a larch, the Ainu from a fir.

Sometimes descent from other species is present even though other features of totemism are not conspicuous. Laura Thompson (1949, 256), for instance, in describing the beliefs of the Lau Fijians about their origins, reports no tradition of their ancestors having arrived, as we know they must have, by boat; instead, she reports that various groups are said to be descended from various species of trees and animals. Yet she cites for the Lau Fijians no general totemic tendency. Similarly, the Barasana of South America trace their ultimate ancestry to anacondas (giant water snakes), yet seem to show no other evidence of totemism (C. Hugh-Jones, 1979; S. Hugh-Jones, 1979). In some of the societies already mentioned, likewise, other features of totemism may be inconspicuous or absent.

Raymond Firth (1967a) judges much of the early writing on totemism to betray wide confusion; most of the statements made about totemism do not fit with the ethnographic data. Firth shows, for example, that the relation social groups have with animals or plants is quite different in the two areas in Oceania, Melanesia and Polynesia, from which the first, superficial reports had suggested the concept of totemism. The relation varied with other aspects of the religious system. In Tikopia, the Polyne-sian society Firth had studied at length, each of the four clans has a special relationship with one of the four basic food products—yam, taro, bread-fruit, and coconut. These are not totems, however, and unlike most totems, these plants are basic to the diet of the Tikopia and are eaten regularly by everyone. The chief of each clan is responsible for protecting and promoting the growth of its special food-producing plant and seeing that the proper use is made of the crop it yields. In order to punish misuse of his food product, the chief responsible for the coconut may send his totem animal, the bat, to pilfer the coconuts belonging to those who are careless or wasteful. He may also, in turn, appeal to the eel god, another totem of his clan, to prevent the bat from feeding too much on the coconuts and to turn the bat to eating the wild fruits of the forest instead (Firth, 1967a, 242). The totem, in this case, is the vehicle of a god and is associated with the chief in his role of protector of valuable plant products.

The Tikopian taboo on harvesting coconuts at inappropriate times may be effective just by being known. Its observance is doubtless helped, however, by the belief that if the taboo is violated, the chief can get the animals in whom a god is incarnate, like the special bat and eel, to prevent further loss. Such animals are considered sacred; their incarnation is apparent in special behavior that distinguishes them from others of their species. Concludes Firth:

> In Polynesia. . .the members of the social group are affiliated with the individuals of the totem species, not by the immediate linkage which obtains in Melanesia, but through a spiritual being as intermediary. The system of totemism is dependent on the belief in the gods, not separate from it. (1967a, 265)

Among other effects of belief in the gods, then, is in this instance support of totemism's role in conservation and ensuring equitable use of food products.

UNDERSTANDING ANIMALS
AND INTERACTING WITH THEM

A fundamental fact about traditional societies is that living animals are generally much more important to them, more continuously vital to the life of a society than they are among us. The way people understand and interact with animals is, therefore, a major factor in developing the role of animals in religious thought and practice.

A feature underlying many of the specific beliefs and practices is the assumption that every animal is a center of conscious experience. Any thoughtful person, we would guess, spontaneously considers every human being to be like himself or herself in this respect; expressing doubt about the presence of awareness in every human being is presumably an extremely sophisticated development of rarefied intellect. Extending the presumption of awareness to animals, at least to mammals and perhaps more generally, may be supposed to be likewise a spontaneous development everywhere.

In the history of our own culture, when science had become sharply differentiated from religion and came, in the nineteenth century, to be applied specifically to the psychological study of animals, there developed a tendency to reject—at least for the purposes of science—this hypothesis of conscious experience in other animal species. In the behavioristic movement we saw an extension of this rejection even to human beings. This rejection had for some scientific problems a temporary heuristic value, in that it increased the emphasis on objectivity of evidence that is valuable for scientific progress. From a long-range point of view, however, it seems to be a retrogression, temporarily rendering scientific understanding in this one respect inferior to the understanding of animals shared by simpler societies and by nonscientists in our society. Along with much else in the behavioristic position, this rejection of consciousness is crumbling. One sign is the argument by the behavioral biologist Donald Griffin in his books *The Question of Animal Awareness* (1976) and *Animal Thinking* (1984) that the hypothesis of more or less uniform animal consciousness might now be more useful to science.

If science has moved backward here, it may be for the sake of an ultimate forward movement. The beginnings of real progress are to be seen in the research initiated a few years ago by Gordon Gallup, Jr. (1977), on the specific issue of self-awareness in other animals, research that could hardly have been done without the orientation toward objective method that behaviorism had sponsored. Gallup started with the observation that a chimpanzee, when faced for the first time with a mirror, soon comes to respond as to an image of itself. (Seeing in the mirror image a spot of red paint that has been placed on its head during sleep, the chimpanzee will reach directly for that spot on its head.) This very human development is presumably shared by the other higher primates, but has been found to be absent in monkeys and other animals even after prolonged exposure to mirrors. The inference seems to be that one central component of our own conscious awareness, a sense of identity, a sort of consciousness of being conscious, is not shared by all animals—indeed, is shared by none of the animal species that many societies have regular contact with. So modern science leads us, after a lengthy detour, to an improvement over the initially reasonable inference that seems to underlie some of the animal beliefs of traditional societies.

On the basic assumption that animals are like people can be built, of course, many specific beliefs. In the absence of high standards of evidence, many of those beliefs will turn out to fall clearly into the category of religious rather than scientific thought. We can suppose that the person of inquiring mind among traditional peoples faces the same difficulty that animal psychologists face, that the evidence available for deciding what to believe about the inner life of animals is very much poorer, because animals cannot talk about it, than the evidence available for deciding about the inner life of human beings. If we can agree that a great variety of specific beliefs about animals will be invented through the imaginative activity of people anywhere, we can see why those beliefs could not be as carefully tested as those about people, and why many beliefs that were quite unrealistic (were, in our modern sense, religious rather than scientific) might, therefore, have become established in a particular culture.

A prime example of such a belief found in many societies is the ascription of souls to animals. In all or most societies human beings are believed to have souls, but so, very widely, are many animals. Attribution of a soul to people must find support in many facts of self-observation, buttressed by interaction with others, as we consider in more detail in Chapter 9. Attribution of a soul to animals seems to be less directly based on observation and to be an instance of extending to animals an inference that is first of all about human beings.

In the extreme north of Siberia, hunters and herders alike consider their dogs to have souls (and, indeed, consider them to be mediators with or messengers from the dead, as well as guardians and protectors against evil spirits). In general, it seems to be the animals of greatest economic or religious significance that are most likely to have a soul—bear rather than rat, cattle or caribou rather than chicken. Even the details of the ascription of soul are similar for people and for animals. Among the Buryat of Siberia, people are held to have several souls, of which one resides in the bones. Animals have this kind of soul, too. Hence, "at a sacrifice, a deep concern is to protect the bones of the sacrificial animal. For if the bones of the offering are broken, the soul would be injured and the sacrifice would be rejected by the deity to whom it was offered" (Krader, 1954, 327).

In societies where people are believed to undergo successive reincarnations, the ascription of a soul to animals is sometimes expressed in a belief in reincarnation for animals, either independently of human reincarnation or as part of the human cycle. This idea is particularly widespread among foragers of the Americas, but is not limited to them. It is also found in parts of Africa, Europe, and Asia.

Some tropical forest tribes of South America, whose economy was a mixture of horticulture and hunting, tabooed the killing or eating of certain animals, especially deer, because the souls of ancestors were believed to be incarnated in them. In these societies, belief about the particular species in which ancestors were reincarnated showed some association with their status. Shamans tended to become jaguars, and shamans were also said to be able, while alive, to transform themselves into jaguars or other animals of high prestige; among the Barasana of the Colombian jungle, transformation into jaguars is ascribed especially to the most powerful shamans (S. Hugh-Jones, 1979, 124).

Such conjectural extensions from humanity to other animals may be the basis for many additional beliefs and for the practices associated with those beliefs. Some of the beliefs and practices we will review seem, on the other hand, likely to grow more out of practical than cognitive interests, out of the need for effective interaction with animals and with the food supplies they yield. Two very different kinds of influence on the ways that animals enter into the religions of traditional societies can, then, be seen very clearly. One is the influence of observed fact on people seeking to understand the world they experience. That aspect of religious experience and belief is like science and is not necessarily at all points or for all purposes inferior to highly developed science. The other is the influence of social utility; beliefs and practices, once they have appeared, seem more likely to be retained if they are useful in promoting health, happiness, and personal and social survival.

HUNTING AND HERDING SOCIETIES

Animals have greatest religious significance in those societies where food is obtained principally from animals. Hunting societies are dependent on success in killing game (including fish or sea mammals). Herding societies are dependent on the growth and health of domestic animals from which they obtain milk (with its product, cheese) or meat or both.

Before we turn to the distinctive ways in which animals are incorporated into the religions of hunters and herders, we should acknowledge that both kinds of societies may make religious use of animals in ways that are found frequently in societies of all kinds. For one thing, in any kind of society body parts of animals (hair, skin, bones, feathers, etc.) enter into religious rites or serve as amulets and charms having magical or spiritual value. Such uses occur regardless of type of economy (as might indeed be guessed by any observer of automobile charms in the United States). The elaborate rituals with prayer sticks of the Pueblo peoples and the Navaho of the southwestern United States, for instance, depend on feathers, although hunting was in neither case the main source of food. The medicine bundles of the hunting tribes of the North American Plains made use of bones, feathers, and skin from many species. It is especially in medical practices of traditional peoples that animal parts—joined, of course, with other objects from the physical environment—are put to use. These varied uses are often related to mystical power attributed to the animal species whose parts are incorporated in the ritual practices or in the medicine bundles.

Communication between animals and people, going far beyond what we would consider realistically possible, is a very general part of religious belief in traditional societies of widely varying economies. Some of the communication from or through animals to people is thought of as quite involuntary on the part of the animals. It is implied in the widespread practice of divination through the use of shoulder blades, livers, entrails, and circumstances surrounding the death of animals—especially the sacrifice of domestic animals. Also common among traditional peoples is the idea that animals are associated with omens and auguries. Usually these involve the special appearance and behavior of animals, birds, and even insects. Owls are usually foretellers of death. The path that a snake follows may determine whether a person should take a journey that day or postpone it, the snake's path being predictive of a favorable or an unfavorable outcome. In some cases animals are even thought to indicate in a mystical way the direction that needs to be taken in order to be successful in the hunt. This religious use of animals, along with other devices for foretelling the future, serves to reduce uncertainty and to increase the probability of novel choices, a value that was pointed out by sociologist O. K. Moore (1957).

HUNTERS

Four kinds of religious involvement with animals are especially characteristic of hunting societies, functioning to ensure a future supply of game, success in the hunt, equitable distribution of the catch, and gain in mystical power.

Ensuring Future Supply of Game

Some of the religious differences pertaining to animals that distinguish hunters from herders seem to emerge from the greater degree of realistic control that can normally be exercised by herders than by hunters. This is a difference that has been clearly brought out by Paine (1971) in his comparison between hunters and herders of the Far North. Herders are in constant contact with their animals, can control their movements, and can feel confident of the yearly increase as the normal reproductive cycle moves around. Hunters, on the other hand, see little of their prey except while hunting, may see them not at all at certain seasons, and feel uncertain whether they will ever return; nor do they generally witness the various stages of the reproductive cycle. Consequently, as Paine points out, hunters must feel they depend on supernatural mediation for contact with their prey species.

Thus hunters may be expected to work more strenuously than herders toward influencing supernatural processes in the direction of increasing or at least maintaining the supply of the animals on which they depend. A conspicuous instance of this appears in societies where animals as well as people are believed to appear only through reincarnation. Northwest Coast tribes in North America, to ensure reincarnation of the salmon, would throw back into the river the bones of the salmon they had eaten or preserved. Many societies, for the same reason, took good care of the bones of larger animals of the hunt—never, for example, throwing them to the dogs. The Ainu and other Siberian groups placed the skulls of bears and other animals in trees or on poles. The Ainu made a sort of "sacred hedge" of the skulls of sacrificed bears. The Gilyak aimed to promote reincarnation in throwing the decorated heads of seals into the ocean and carefully burying the bones of bears. Even the Lapps of northern Europe, though they herded as well as hunted, carefully buried the bones of bears.

A variety of other rituals were directed by hunters at maintaining or increasing their prey. Some rituals were built especially around animal fertility. Mainland Australian hunters had increase rites to ensure the fertility of various animals. The Mundurucú, tropical forest hunters of South America, also had increase rites. But more characteristic of hunters are rituals that seem to have as their direct aim demonstration of respect for the prey species.

Ensuring Success in the Hunt

Success in hunting was in many societies believed to depend on the cooperation of the game animals or of their supernatural masters. This was conspicuous in the foraging societies that formed the bulk of the aboriginal peoples of North and South America. For example, as Hallowell says,

> to these Northern Ojibwa, hunting in the aboriginal period of their culture was not a secular occupation as it is among white men. Success depended as much on a man's satisfactory relations with the superhuman"masters" of the different species of game and fur-bearing animals, as on his technical skill as a hunter and trapper. (1955, 120)

One function of the superhuman entities Hallowell is speaking of is the punishment of improper behavior and the reward of proper behavior toward prey animals so as to ensure success. But these entities were often seen as gaining in turn from human attention. Clear evidence of such reciprocity appears in Murphy's comments about the propitiation of the "spirit owners" or "spirit mothers" of game animals in a tropical forest society of South America: "The Mundurucú depended on the animals for subsistence and the animals, through their spirit mothers, depended on the Mundurucú for the performance of rituals essential to their well-being and increase" (1958, 133).

The concept of "owners" or "masters," though especially characteristic of foraging societies of the Americas, is found sporadically among peoples around the world who do some hunting, fishing, or gathering and even those whose economy is principally of some other sort. The African Bambara, for example, have a "Mother of Fish" who is both creator and guardian of all species of fish. The Bemba, another African group for whom the hunt is a highly valued pursuit, though of little economic importance, have a hunting god who appears to function as guardian for all game. The Afkhaz of the Caucasus have a god of game, and the Lepcha of the Himalayas have a huge bull as a hunter god.

The way this idea of a guardian, boss, or master of a species or group of animal species is conceived may vary. The master of a species, viewed as endowed with mystical power, may be an actual animal. That is, the guardian of a species may be an especially big member of the species, or one that is distinctive in color, or one living in a particular locality. Unusual behavior is another criterion that may identify an individual animal as the master of its species. Hunters should avoid killing the special animal because misfortune might follow, even the death of the hunter. Some societies believe that the master animal cannot be killed. The gigantic bull that is the hunter god of the Lepcha, for instance, is considered to be proof against wounds.

Through all these variations persists the notion of control by some entity with powers we would call supernatural or mystical, and often the entity is purely supernatural—either a special deity who has no other attributes or a deity who has this attribute among others. The sea goddess of the Inuit or Eskimo is thought of in somewhat different ways in different localities, but in general is considered to be in charge of all sea animals, willing to release them only if people obey her dictates. For the Mbuti, African Pygmies, on the other hand, each species is represented by an individual deity with a definite locality and a specific honorific name. The Great God, however, is among the Mbuti the real owner and master of all things; the master of each species is a delegate or representative.

Masters of animals are thought of as surrounding the hunt with taboos. In many societies men must abstain from sex before going on the hunt. The ethnographic reports present frequent statements about the importance of showing respect for animals and even fish, and sexual abstinence is one such way. There are also strictures on the manner of killing and treating the dead animal. Anne Gayton, reporting on the California Yokuts, put it this way:

> The reverence for Eagle, Falcon, Cougar, Bear, Coyote (and lesser creatures in lesser ways) was actualized in ceremonies performed over their carcasses by persons of those lineages they symbolized, and witnessed by the usual audience of interested and, in part, participating villagers. The hunters of deer had to observe care in handling their kill. The underlying motive of these acts was that animals who were not "treated right" on this earth, at death reported to their prehistoric counterparts in their eastern home, and the offended creatures would no longer give their support (as either a subsistence or a power source) to the transgressor. (1946, 263)

The Copper Eskimo or Inuit of northern Canada provide a good example of the way hunting peoples use taboos to keep on correct terms with both the animal and plant worlds. The Copper Inuit show respect by enforcing sharp separation between food sources from land and from sea.

> Almost every detail of hunting and utilizing the catch is regulated in some respect by taboo. The outstanding feature of the system is the rule that land animals and sea animals must be kept separate. Seals, walruses, and whales must not be defiled by caribou and other creatures of the land. From this basic differentiation the system ramifies to many less obvious restrictions. For example, certain groups prohibit the working-up of soapstone, a product of the land, during the time they are living on the ice; and in some sections it is forbidden to work on wood back from the coast while the hunters are

catching seal in the sea. All such taboos are based on the theory that to associate the products of these two realms will offend either the souls of the animals or the spirit who controls them. (Weyer, 1932, 367)

Like the Inuit, the Samoyeds of northern Siberia must never eat fish and bear at the same meal because this mixture would cause all the fish to disappear from the rivers. In the ethnographic accounts, when the local rationale for these practices is recorded, it is often expressed as the necessity for displaying respect toward the prey animals.

The dependence of foragers on prey animals may be expressed in feelings that appear to be based on dependence of people on each other. Robin Ridington, in an intensive study of the Beaver, or Dunne-za, of British Columbia over several decades, was repeatedly impressed by their sense that success in the hunt depends on the prey's willingness to give itself for people's nourishment, and that a benevolent relationship is essential. The Dunne-za view the prey species as expecting to be treated benevolently and as requiring that the people to whom they are giving themselves be a harmonious group: "The animals will not give themselves to people unless people are equally willing to accept that human life depends on people giving to one another" (Ridington, 1988, 78).

In ethnographies of African foragers appear several instances where supernatural sanctions were thought to follow lack of respect for animals. In *The Harmless People*, Thomas (1959) gives an example where revenge for improper treatment comes from other animals of the same species. Because one individual of a Kung group had scorched some bees instead of simply smoking them out of their hive, the group felt it was understandable that bees from the next hive they found, some distance away, attacked them in advance. In the first attempt they had failed to go about the task in the proper way, and they suffered the consequences. In the case of the Mbuti Pygmies, Turnbull indicates that boys may on occasion make fun of dead animals or even toy with or torture birds or small animals, but that this is not characteristic behavior of hunters, even the youngest. Turnbull describes the emotional tone of the Mbuti hunt: "There is no expression of joy in the capturing and killing of an animal, though the excitement still runs strongly. The moment of killing is best described as a moment of intense compassion and reverence" (1965, 161).

Ensuring Equitable Distribution of the Catch

Definite patterns of dividing game are widespread, and they are often ritualized. The seal-hunting Netsilik Inuit of northern Canada had a ritual sharing of the liver of each seal caught at the breathing holes out on the ice. A similar practice is cited for the Kung San, whose hunters share the liver and possibly other perishable parts before returning to camp with the rest of the meat, whose distribution is then also regulated. In the case of the Kung, the arrow judged to have killed the animal is the one whose owner or maker will be the distributor of the meat. Because the owner or maker is not always the person who shot the arrow, this rule tends to increase the communality of the hunting enterprise: Those Kung who are not highly skilled in the hunt may instead be good craftsmen in making arrows and coating them with poison. Among the Bororo of tropical South America a man passed on his entire catch to others, eating only meat given to him by other hunters.

Thus a hunter's catch is not exclusively his own property; it comes to him with obligations attached. Although ethnographic reports often do not explicitly cite the sanctions involved, a fear of misfortune on violation of sharing rules seems clear, and misfortunes are very generally given a mystical interpretation. The rules about sharing, moreover, seem related to the feeling that the prey animals come to the hunter from somewhere outside the human realm, and that suitable relations with that external realm must be maintained in order to ensure continued success.

Ensuring Gain in Mystical Power

In Chapter 2 we considered the concept of a guardian spirit from whom an individual obtains supernatural power. What is relevant here is that the guardian spirit may be an animal. This sort of belief, perhaps not phrased in a way that would be translated as "guardian spirit," has been reported from Melanesia. For the Pentecost Islanders, "power derived from pigs and snakes assures success in the graded society and in making and preserving peace. Eels bestow power for success in pig-breeding and in raising tusked boars" (Lane, 1965, 258). In North America animals often appear in this role of source or donor of mystical power. The bear, for example, is often associated with giving power for healing the sick and the buffalo with giving protection to warriors.

Animals are also involved in some of the supernatural practices to which the possession of mystical power leads. Communication with animal spirits is in some peoples an important activity that becomes possible once one has gained power from whatever source. An example we will look at more fully in Chapter 5 is provided by the Ojibwa and other groups of north central and central Canada, where the shaman or conjurer is believed able to talk with animal spirits while secluded in a small hut with an audience outside. Not only do the voices of animal spirits issue from the hut, but the audience could put questions to the animal spirits for help in finding lost items, learning the fate or whereabouts of people at a distance, or obtaining a prediction of events about to happen.

The tendency of hunting peoples to depend on animal rather than human sources of mystical power may well originate in the greater individualism or independence of hunting peoples, which has been shown to characterize also their child-rearing practices (Barry, Child, & Bacon, 1959). Animals may be equally important to herders, but the orientation of hunters toward individual skill may lead them to seek individual powers from that part of the environment of greatest importance, whereas herders, whose livelihood depends somewhat more on cooperation and responsibility, express toward their animals an interest in friendly cooperation as they dominate or control their behavior. Hunters, moreover, being already dependent on supernatural powers of animals for success in the hunt, need only change their orientation slightly to seek other supernatural help from animals.

HERDERS

Identification with Domestic Animals

Living in intimate contact, and taking constant care of, animals they think of as conscious creatures with a soul, herders are prone to identify with them. Cattle are thus humanized and given a familial and personal status, expressed in the way cattle enter into mystical aspects of the worldview. The Dinka, for instance, pastoralists of East Africa,

> often announce to a beast that is to be sacrificed the important and necessary purpose for which it is victimized. Further, in compensating the beast for its death by naming the next child after it, they are preserving its memory in a way which is very characteristic of their thought about perpetuating the names of their families' dead in naming the living. They complain that in the government herds of cattle which have been taken as fines, it is wrong that the cattle of different families should be all mixed together, for cattle "have their own names"—their own affiliations and groupings in relation to human groupings—and are not merely so many individual "head of cattle" as they are officially regarded. (Lienhardt, 1961, 22)

Many cultures of African herders have in common the theme of identification of people with cattle. Among the Chaga, for instance, the ethnographer notes that a cow with a calf is treated with the same respect as a woman with a newborn infant. The Chaga forbid marrying off a daughter while her mother is still able to give birth. For their cattle they have a less drastic rule, which is obviously based on identifying the cattle with people: After a calf is weaned from its mother, the two are separated so there can be no conflict over procreation. The Ila-speaking peoples of Zambia have a cosmetic practice of knocking out their front teeth, and they say that the practice originated in a desire to resemble cattle (Smith & Dale, 1920, 127-128); the same practice and reason are present among the Dinka and perhaps the Nuer (Evans-Pritchard, 1953, 187).

Particularly rich material on this theme is available in the ethnographies by Lienhardt on the Dinka and by Evans-Pritchard on the neighboring Nuer (both societies live near the convergence of Sudan, Uganda, and Kenya). Both ethnographers stress the identification of a typical young man with his own special ox. A young man is addressed by another person by the name of the ox he owns. A young man gives his ox great care, shows aesthetic appreciation of its physical beauty, and feels great sorrow if he loses the ox through sacrifice or other death. Dances of young men emphasize an imitation of the beautiful shape of cattle horns.

Some of the milking rituals of the Thonga, Ovimbundu, and Chaga—all Bantu-speaking tribes—seem to be based on identification of human beings with their cattle. People who have loaned out some of their cattle may not drink the milk of these cows until, on their return to their herd, a ritual is performed. This ritual seems to have as its purpose, a reestablishment of the identification between the cattle that have been loaned out and the group of people to whom they belong and have now returned. Identification is also suggested in a ritual through which a bride becomes a member of her husband's sib. This occurs on a special occasion when the bride partakes for the first time of the milk from her husband's cows.

Among the Garia and other groups of eastern New Guinea, a comparable idea about the pigs one has raised is extended to close relatives as well as the person principally responsible for care of the animals.

> Garia explain the taboo thus: "A pig's flesh is like a man's flesh"—or, in greater detail, "Our wives suckle our children and, if it is essential, our piglets. Later we and our wives cook food for our children and our pigs. Our pigs and those of our close kinsmen, therefore, are like our own flesh and blood. We cannot eat them." (Lawrence, 1971, 151)

Identification with animals is seen here to depend on the close relation people have with their domestic animals, even if these are not their main source of food, for the Garia are primarily horticulturalists.

In South America, too, people are identified with animals. In one case we have noted, the evidence pertains to the special circumstance of sacrifice at funeral ceremonies. The Goajiro believe that when an animal is sacrificed as a part of the death rites, close relatives of the deceased must not eat the meat of the victim because "it would be like eating the flesh of the relative himself" (Pineda Giraldo, 1961, 43). Though this is related, of course, to the prohibition of cannibalism, its extension in this way is dependent on an identification of the sacrificed animal with the person for whose good the sacrifice took place.

Identification with animals seems also to underlie the widespread belief about an individual's fate being tied to that of some animal, known as the person's "destiny animal." Whatever happens to the animal whose destiny is intertwined with that of a human being must have its effect on that person. Should the animal die, the man or woman or child will also die. In the Western Hemisphere this idea is found, for instance, both among the Yanoama hunters of South America and among the sedentary agricultural Quiché of Central America. In Europe the Lapps are reported to believe in destiny animals. The Somali herders of the horn of Africa see the fate of humans as tied up with their camels.

Similar beliefs in a form more beneficent for people are also found. The Ashanti of West Africa believe that a sickness threatening a person can be assumed by an animal, thus restoring the person to good health. The Goajiro, herders of South America, also have the idea that an animal's death spares a member of the family. The reindeer-herding Chukchee of Siberia feel that protection from the bad influence of strangers, such as infectious illnesses they bring, can be gained by rubbing the influence off onto their own dogs.

In ethnographies of foraging societies we have not (outside the customs labeled as totemism) encountered evidence of similar close ties with the wild animals important to them, except in a single instance, the eland or "sacred" animal of the northern Kung. One article on their hunting rituals (Lewis-Williams & Biesele, 1978) describes the rites surrounding a young man's killing of his first eland. It is a rite of passage that includes the establishment of a special relationship between the boy and the specific eland he has killed. But this is, as we have said, an exception. Identification of a person with a ritually significant animal is found principally in herding societies.

Sacrifice of Domestic Animals

Whereas rules relating to the treatment of prey animals are the characteristic emphasis of hunters, sacrifice of domestic animals to please the supernatural is that of herders.

Sacrifice of some sort is perhaps universal. It is certainly not absent in hunting peoples, who may often throw some food into the fire, send tobacco smoke toward sun or sky, or even set aside part of the prey animals as offerings for the masters they consider responsible for their success in the hunt. Scholars sometimes refer to these smaller sacrifices as offerings or bloodless sacrifices. Such offerings seem at once an acknowledgment of indebtedness, an expression of gratitude, and a petition for future help. The net effect is to bring the supernatural firmly into the real social world of everyday life. In herding societies, domestic animals are a parallel to the food or tobacco offered by hunters. That is, they are a part of the human world; men and women have fed, bred, and cared for them. In a single society, of course, both bloodless sacrifices (offerings) and bloody sacrifices may be found.

In pastoral societies, however, bloody sacrifices are more typical, and an emphasis appears on the killing of the animal as an intrinsic part of the offering to the supernatural. Though the meat of the sacrificed animal is almost always eaten, the need for food is not generally thought an adequate reason in itself for killing an animal of the species the society uses for sacrifice. The religious significance of animals of the kind to be sacrificed may dominate the whole view of them, as Evans-Pritchard (1953) argues is true for the Nuer view of oxen.

The occasions appropriate for sacrifice, though they may be numerous, are each culturally defined. The sacrifice is a social occasion, with its social significance sometimes enlarged by invitation to deceased ancestors to share in the feast. The animal to be sacrificed may, in various symbolic ways, be made a part of the social occasion. The passage we have quoted earlier about the Dinka illustrates this, as does the following statement:

> A beast which has been killed for no good reason and without ceremony (and the desire for meat, as distinct from the necessity of preserving life in famine, is not a good reason) may haunt . . . its killers, as may a human person unjustly slain, and I have been told that "ghosts" of such cattle might return to reproach their owners. (Lienhardt, 1961, 21-22)

Bloody sacrifices are rarer in the Western Hemisphere, where domestication of animals was a later development, than in the Eastern Hemisphere, where most domestication of animals originated. Some tribes of the North American Plains had a practice of killing a man's horse to accompany his soul to the realm of the dead, but the rationale does not seem to justify classifying this practice as sacrifice (and the horse, of course, had been introduced by Europeans). In Peru the Inca, who had a domestic animal before the arrival of Europeans, sacrificed white llamas. In the American Southwest the Navaho, who became herders only after the arrival of Europeans, neither made the killing of their sheep and goats a sacrificial act nor established these animals as the subject for any other religious rites or beliefs. The contrast between Inca and Navaho suggests that many generations may be necessary before a shift in economy is followed by a shift to more appropriate religious customs. The Goajiro, located in Venezuela, are an intermediate case. At funerals, they sacrifice animals that the deceased had owned. They are herders of cattle, sheep, and goats, all introduced from Europe. It may be significant that the Goajiro appear to be more thoroughly dependent on herding than are the Navaho.

Among the Plains tribes, the sacred animal around which much ritual centered was not the horse they had acquired through European contact but the buffalo they had hunted less efficiently before they acquired the horse; and, as is almost universally true of prey animals, bloody sacrifice was not involved in these rituals.

Bloody sacrifice is almost entirely confined to domesticated animals. (A possible exception is wild reindeer in some societies that also have herds of domestic reindeer. The sacrifice of bears, discussed in Chapter 5, does not seem to be an exception, as the animals sacrificed in this case were captured as infants and reared in captivity.) The species whose sacrifice is most widespread is the dog, the one domestic animal that most peoples around the world seem to have had before any direct contact with complex civilizations. Sacrifice of dogs occurs in all the major regions of the world—in societies of the North American Plains, the northeastern United States, the Northwest Coast, and Central America, to cite only regions with no herding where other animal sacrifice was not present. Yet sacrifice of dogs seems not to be frequent and regular, and the rituals are rarely elaborated as are those of cattle sacrifice.

Jochelson (1905-1908) speculates as to whether the Koryak of Siberia had "made offerings of dogs prior to the time when a part of them began to keep reindeer-herds," and seems to conclude that they probably did. He points out that the reindeer-herding Koryak sacrificed reindeer, not dogs, to the "one on High" (a master). It was the Maritime Koryak, who rarely had reindeer, who sacrificed dogs. The same contrast in sacrificial animals is found in another Siberian culture, the Chukchee, where again some are herders and some are hunters of the sea. A domestic animal that is a major source of food is very likely to be subject to elaborate rituals of sacrifice; the dog, which is at most a trivial source of food, is not likely to be. Is this because sacrifice arises out of a whole pattern of life that is found only where there is a domestic animal around which the food quest centers?

In Siberia and northern Europe there are societies that depend on both hunting and herding. They share with the hunters of northern Canada and Alaska their respect for prey animals, and they share with the herders their sacrificial practices. They are, thus, a sort of intermediate group, and tend to confirm the dependence of each religious aspect on the corresponding aspect of economy.

Ensuring Equitable Distribution of Meat

Religious rules take different form in serving the same function in different economies. A clear instance is provided by food sharing. Hunters share their meat from large animals, as we have seen, and various taboos and other rules support this practice. Owners of herds, on the other hand, are pressured (by religious considerations among others) into killing some of their animals as sacrifices, and the meat of the sacrificed animals is not consumed just by the owner and his immediate family but is shared more widely in the community. Many societies have elaborate rules, supernaturally sanctioned, about how the meat is to be divided up.

PLANTS IN RELIGION

Certain plants have a special relation to religion because a person swallowing them or their products has experiences that may have a profound effect on religious belief and may themselves be felt as religious revelation. These are the many plants that are psychotropic, psychedelic, or hallucinogenic. Their very important contribution to religion in traditional societies is considered in Chapter 5. Here we are concerned only with the other religious roles of plants.

Plants do have some resemblance to human beings, but less resemblance than animals do. So it is not surprising that some of the assumptions people make about mental properties of animals are also made, if more rarely, about plants.

To show respect is the most common form of prescribed behavior observed by traditional peoples toward members of the plant, as well as the animal, world and it seems to imply a humanizing attitude. Taboos may be imposed on the use of plant as well as animal products to ensure that they continue to be available, and compliance with the taboo seems often to be accompanied by a feeling of respect. An instance of respect, and rituals expressing that attitude, are reported by the theologian Harvey Cox (1977, 42) in his account of a visit to the Huichol of Mexico. Accompanying a group on their annual peyote hunt, he was taught not only how to sever a peyote button neatly from the plant on which it was growing but also how, then, to intone a prayer of apology for removing the button.

The behavior of people toward plants, under the influence of traditional beliefs, fairly often seems to imply the ascription of a soul, and sometimes the belief is explicit. When cutting down a tree, the Gilyak of Siberia were anxious because they would be destroying the soul-creating substance that is supposed to return soul and life to the tree; the attitude here seems to be the same as underlies the Gilyak's cautious treatment of the skulls of bears. This practice constitutes just one of the ways in which respect is shown to animals and plants; their reincarnation is often assumed to be favored by respectful treatment.

Ascription of a soul to plants seems most likely for plants of great economic significance. Both the Balinese of Indonesia and the Ifugao (in the Philippines) ascribe souls to rice plants, their principal source of food. Economic value must join with experiential significance in motivating the extension to a plant of the ascription of a soul, in the case of the Huichol belief that the plant that yields peyote has a soul visible to shamans and to be taken account of by everyone else (Myerhoff, 1974, 154). This sort of belief is no isolated idea; the ascription of a soul to rice plants by the Balinese and the Ifugao is in both groups part of a very complex structure of religious belief and practice. The plants themselves may enter religious practices in a complex way. For Balinese ceremonies, for instance, elaborate figures of a rice spirit are made from rice plants.

Perhaps more common than the idea that animals and plants actually have a soul is the idea that spirits or gods are associated with them. Some tribes in Oceania have human crop guardians, who declare taboos on various crops to prevent their being harvested at inappropriate times. Some other Melanesian groups did have supernatural guardians or masters of plants, though these are rarer worldwide than for animals. The Orokaiva are reported to have "food spirits" and the "spirit of the taro" (Thompson, 1949, 260). These supernaturals were thought, like the bat of the Tikopia, to destroy the gardens of those who did not work their gardens well.

In societies of greater complexity, the supernatural beings or spirits involved in relations with plants and animals may be tribal ancestors rather than masters or guardians. Ivanoff writes of the beliefs of headhunting Dyaks he visited in Borneo:

> In order that the tribe shall be blessed with abundance and fecundity it must clearly have some powerful protector. Only a benevolent spirit can assume this role, of course. Now the sacred tree *mahang* harbours such a benevolent spirit, none other than the spirit of Oton Tawim, the woman of Dyak legend.

Apart from this sacred *mahang* tree only a freshly severed head is a suitable dwelling place for a benevolent spirit. As the new head is now available the transfer of the good spirit to its shelter has to be arranged. This is not easy. These benevolent spirits are the souls of certain tribal ancestors, and if just anyone went to seek them in the *mahang* tree they might well flee underground by way of the roots of the tree; so, in fact, only the members of certain families, the descendants of the spirits in question, can retain them above ground by maintaining close contact with the sacred tree. (1958, 66)

This mahang tree is later relocated to near the tribal communal house after the proper male descendant has climbed into the crown of the tree to have a conversation with the spirit. The tree is positioned so that it faces the inside of the communal hall where a freshly severed head has been placed. "An old woman now comes forward. She performs a sensual dance, miming the act of congress with the tree, and gradually approaching closer and closer to the spot where the freshly severed head has been placed" (Ivanoff, 1958, 67).

Even identification with domestic plants is possible. Among the Kwoma, who live on the Sepik River, in New Guinea, men believe that they should not eat the yams they themselves have planted. A man will get someone else to plant the yams that he will eat. In eating the yams one grows, one would be eating something associated with one's own body (Whiting, 1941).

Ethnographers, in attempting to interpret fully the symbolism of ritual and belief in particular societies, have portrayed ideas about plants as well as animals as intricately woven into a complex fabric. A relatively simple instance is provided by Barbara Myerhoff's study of the sacred journey of the Huichol Indians of Mexico. Their deer-maize-peyote complex involves connections among animals and both wild and cultivated plants:

> The maize cannot grow without the deer blood; the deer cannot be sacrificed to the Sun until after the peyote hunt; Parching the Maize, the ceremony which brings the rains needed to make the maize grow, cannot be held without peyote from Wirikuta; the peyote may not be hunted until the maize has been cleansed and sanctified and the children told the stories of the First Peyote Hunt. Every ceremony is dependent on the presence of the three symbolic items, and their sequential procurement makes the entire religious calendar a closed circle. (1974, 221)

SUMMARY

Animals and plants entered nineteenth-century accounts of traditional religions in exaggerated emphasis on totemism as a uniform feature. Varying from one society to another, and often not present at all, use of animals and plants (and sometimes things) as symbols of groups, symbols associated with beliefs and practices implying mystical power, is indeed important. Along with these totemic uses go other religious roles of animals and plants, where they are associated in quite different ways with ideas of mystical power.

The religious role of animals has its base in the spontaneous ascription to animals of consciousness and hence of souls. Various conceptions that result may be strengthened by their utility in a people's mode of life. Hunting societies seek to ensure future supply of game by encouraging reincarnation to replace what they have killed and by showing proper respect for the prey species and the supernaturals who control them. They follow rules to ensure equitable distribution of the catch, and they readily appeal to animals as mystical helpers. Herders tend to humanize relations with their domestic animals. Also, they sacrifice domestic animals as an offering to supernatural figures; this is sometimes seen as a way of sending a message that the victim will transmit to the god or ancestral spirit.

Plants appear in traditional religions in some of the same ways as do animals, but less regularly. Of special importance for religion is the ingestion of psychotropic plant material, discussed in Chapter 5.

Chapter 4

Mystical Beings

We will generally speak of *mystical beings*, as the equivalent of the more common term, *supernatural beings*. This latter term is a Western one, based on Western culture's fairly clear distinction between natural and supernatural. As we implied in discussing power, in many other cultures the distinction is not clear. But something like our distinction between mystical power and normal power seems to be present everywhere, though sometimes it is of little importance. The Western conception of supernatural beings can be extended to other societies by way of the idea of mystical power. Supernatural beings are, first of all, beings that possess mystical power. As a total definition, this would include—as follows from Chapters 2 and 3—the many people and animals believed to have mystical powers, yet ordinarily they would be excluded from the Western category of supernatural beings. It would be more harmonious with general Western usage to restrict the term to loci of mystical power that normally have no material existence. But this would do violence to the view in some cultures that certain mountains, plants, or animals have mystical properties that make them more akin in the life of the people to purely mystical entities than to other more purely physical mountains, plants, or animals. So we will exclude from our main concept of supernatural beings only actual human beings, and we will consider them briefly at the end of our discussion. We prefer, however, to speak generally of mystical beings, providing thus a recurrent reminder that Western culture's distinction between natural and supernatural should not constantly intrude on what is said. When we discuss the work of researchers who have used the term *supernatural*, we often retain their terminology.

We will organize our account of mystical beings into four principal categories: major god, spirits of the dead, other gods and spirits, and culture heroes. All four groups are found in each kind of basic economy, and indeed most individual societies have some representative of each principal category of mystical being. Different economies do, however, lead to different emphases. For this reason, to some extent our presentation of each kind of mystical being is organized around type of economy.

MAJOR GOD

Discussion by anthropologists of single gods of special importance often centers on the conception of *high god*, to which the sociologist Guy Swanson (1960) tried to give a more precise meaning than it had previously enjoyed. Religious beliefs in a culture might identify a particular god as the creator of the world. They might identify a particular god as the present ruler or controller of everything that happens (perhaps with no clear theory about creation). A god distinguished in either or both of these ways, Swanson pointed out (1960, 56), is seen as "ultimately responsible for all events, whether as history's creator, its director, or both," and to such a god Swanson applied the label *high god*. As this term has come to be used, it is often associated with Swanson's particular theories about how people come to believe in such a god, and it has also retained some of the less precise usage that had previously characterized it. Preferring to stay closer to observed fact about religion, we will use, instead, the term *major god*, with essentially the same intended meaning.

Those foraging societies whose members live in small groups, without sharp distinctions of status or of family line, generally believe in a major god to whom they trace the creation of their world. Though the god may be thought of as remote from current human affairs, it is still likely to be the supernatural figure to which people give the most attention. The anthropologist Carleton Coon, who was particularly interested in the hunting peoples, reviewed the religion of all for whom relevant information was available and concluded: "Believers in a single creator include the Bushmen, Pygmies, Great Andamanese, Semang, Philippine Negritos, some of the Southeast Australian aborigines, probably the Tasmanians, the Yaghans, Onas, Central and Eastern Eskimo, the northern Algonkians and most of the northern Athabascans" (1971, 286). These foragers he names, mostly with simple social organization, are scattered through all the continents but Europe. Their mode of life seems to be one of the "various situations, in many different degrees of cultural complexity" that have, according to Ruth Benedict (1938, 661-662), brought about "the idea of one highest and supreme god." For the Americas alone, Hultkrantz (1967, 15-26) has reviewed the evidence for aboriginal belief in a major god and concludes that the belief was present in a large number of societies, though with emphasis less on creation than on current control of events. Many of the examples he gives are of simple foraging societies.

Almost as widespread are foraging societies that are more complex in either (or both) of two ways. Their local community may contain people of varying descent groups or of widely varying wealth or social status; both kinds of complexity, for example, characterize the Kwakiutl and some of the other tribes of the Northwest Coast of North America. Either of these conditions works against homogeneity of the community, and makes for recognizing what distinguishes each person from others. As Coon (1971, 186) summarizes, people in such societies "care less about an overall creator than about the fabulous deeds of their particular ancestors," and may show no evidence of having a conception of a single creator god. In their stories about creation they may resemble the Shoshone of the American West, who assign some creation role to Coyote, but some also to Wolf and other mythical figures (Lowie, 1909, 233).

Other specific conditions of economy and social structure may affect belief in a major god. Nomadic herders, whose surroundings differ so radically from season to season, may well find that belief in a major god directly interested in their affairs helps give continuity and cohesion to their life. But the feature for which there is the best evidence for a role in belief in a major god is social complexity. The evidence is most clearly organized and assembled in Swanson's *Birth of the Gods*.

Swanson defined high god as either a single creator or a single god actively directing the present world. He looked for evidence of belief in a high god in each of 50 societies worldwide, chosen systematically to represent diversity among traditional societies. For 11 societies the evidence was not sufficient to permit classification. The rest were divided almost evenly; 20 were judged to lack a belief and 19 to have a belief in a high god. (These 19 were again divided about equally between those who conceived their high god to be remote from human affairs and those who conceived the god to be active in human affairs.)

In planning his research, Swanson was influenced by the French sociologist Emile Durkheim (1965, orig. 1912), who had held that the pantheon of a society mirrors the social structure of the society. A case that clearly illustrates this possible role of a major god is that of the Incas during the century before their conquest by Europeans. A religious reform was introduced by Emperor Pachakuti, who had extended the Inca Empire by conquest of other tribes and reorganized its administration. The reform either strengthened the religious position of, or even introduced, a supreme being who was "the maker and ruler of the universe, and lesser divinities, including the Sun, were his agents and assistants" (Rowe, 1960, 408). The worship of this great god was, Rowe argues from historical evidence, "a necessary part of the effort made by the great organizer to provide new and coherent central institutions which might integrate the diverse peoples over whom Pachakuti had recently extended Inca rule."

Swanson took the presence of a high god to indicate that a society's pantheon was complex, and looked for a relation to the complexity of the social structure. He defined degree of complexity as the number of different types of "sovereign groups" found in a society. Groups were considered sovereign if they "exercise original and independent jurisdiction over some sphere of social life." In a simple society, there might be no sovereign group except for the nuclear family. In a very complex yet traditional society, family, village, kin groups, kingdom, and other organizations, each sovereign in relation to some aspect of social life, might coexist in a hierarchical arrangement.

Swanson found a marked tendency for belief in a major god to appear in societies of high complexity, rather than in societies of lower complexity, within his sample. Because of the small size of his sample, he missed the fact that many simple foraging societies also share this belief, more frequently than do societies of intermediate complexity. Although we cannot accept Swanson's apparent implication that a major god bringing unity to the worldview could be invented only in a society with a hierarchy of social groups culminating in a single head with overall responsibility or power, his theory in less extreme form indicates one important support for belief in a major god. The presence of a major god in the simplest societies as well would indicate, however, that the idea of a major god may have diverse origins or supports.

What some of these other supports are has been suggested by Robin Horton, the British anthropologist, on the basis of his broad knowledge of African religions. Belief in a major god is found in almost all African societies, but the nature and importance of this belief varies radically. At one extreme, a creator god is thought to keep aloof from humanity and is given no worship or other attention; there may not even be any well developed idea of the characteristics of the creator. At an opposite extreme, the major god may be considered an active controller of the present world, an intervenor in daily life, the object of individual and group worship, and subject of theological inquiry.

Horton suggests two variable conditions that help account for this variation. One is the degree to which people are brought into contact with the world outside their local community. Horton argues that the lesser gods provide people with a way of interpreting events and relationships within their fairly immediate territory, whereas a high god provides a way of interpreting their more immediate world in relation to the outside and to the world as a whole. The greater a people's actual contact with the outside world,

> the greater its need to take practical account of that level of theory which relates the microcosm to the wider world—*i.e.* the level of ideas about the high god. Again, the greater the active contact with the wider world, the greater the area of experience within the microcosm which comes to be seen, not as peculiar to it, but as part of a general human predicament. Hence the larger the number of occasions within the microcosm when people's practical concerns force them to take active account, not of the lesser gods who are concerned with its peculiarities, but of the high god who is concerned with its universal features. (1962, 139)

A second variable condition that Horton relates to the importance of the major god is the degree to which an individual's status is ascribed or achieved—that is, is determined by the circumstances of his birth (and how the cultural rules are applied to them) or is determined by his own later personality and actions.

Where the individual's status is largely determined by ascription, his peculiar lot will appear to be something largely dictated by his community. Hence
the ideas appropriate to the explanation of his lot will be drawn from the
realm of those lesser gods who are concerned with the community and its
peculiar features. On the other hand, where achievement plays a greater
part, individual and community are likely to appear as partially independent
variables. Here, then, explanations of individual vicissitudes may well refer,
not to the parochial lesser gods, but to the high god who is concerned with
the wider order of things. In the latter situation, one would expect individual
worship of the high god to be far more developed than where ascription
determines status.

Horton cites African examples that suggest the relevance of these two
variables. The Tallensi live in self-contained groups whose customs largely
determine the status of each individual, and their major god is remote. The
Ashanti and Benin live in a highly organized state system, with less
emphasis on ascribed status, and they actively worship their major god.
Horton also suggests that the openness of many African groups to Islam
and Christianity is related to the fact that in Africa "missionary enterprise
has tended to coincide with a great opening-up of previously self-contained
communities, and with an increase in the importance of achieved rather
than ascribed status."

SPIRITS OF THE DEAD

Belief in the reality of spirits of the dead is almost universal. Among 65
societies surveyed by Rosenblatt et al. (1976), evidence for the belief was
found in 64; its absence in the one remaining was probably due to paucity
of information. Societies vary greatly, however, in the importance of this
belief and in which spirits of the dead are stressed. In the more complex
foraging societies, where a major god is absent or relatively unimportant,
the spirits of the dead are the supernaturals likely to receive most attention, and prime attention is often given to spirits of the recently deceased.
The Vedda of Sri Lanka, for example, perform a mortuary ceremony
thought to encourage the spirit of the person just deceased to bring luck in
hunting and honey gathering (Seligmann & Seligmann, 1911, 152-153). In
many societies, spirits are thought to be especially dangerous during the
first few days after death, as they confront being deprived of the life they
have known and may seek to bring companions to share their new and
perhaps ill-defined afterlife.

Spirits of mythical distant ancestors are the principal objects of
attention among many Australian aborigines. As with more immediate
ancestors elsewhere, the tie to these mythical ancestors helps define the
personal identity and the social relationships of each individual. In some
Australian groups, the mythical ancestors have a special importance as

reincarnators, the spirits that provide the spiritual part of new human life (Strehlow, 1964, 730). In several societies of the North American Northwest Coast, it is the more immediate ancestors or relatives whose spirits are thought to be reincarnated in new members of the family. Ancestral spirits have a similar role in some African societies.

Ritual relation to ancestral spirits is often very different in quality from what Westerners might mean by "worship," and the common use of that term in referring generally to all societies where attention is given to ancestral spirits is quite misleading. Very often the ancestors are principally an object of fear, in expectation that they may quite arbitrarily harm their living descendants. On the other hand, they may instead be objects of friendly attention. Among the Zuni, attitude toward ancestral spirits is said to be dominated by a wish to be helpful and respectful. The oldest man at a family meal throws a bit of bread and meat into the fire as he says, "Grandfatherly people, eat!" and this is said to express Zuni ideals about their relation to the world as a whole (Tedlock, 1975, 256-257).

Ancestral spirits are most uniformly conspicuous in the religions of sub-Saharan Africa; in several societies there, ancestral spirits enter into the religion in a way that especially merits the term "ancestor worship." The Tallensi, studied by Meyer Fortes, are one of these societies, and Fortes has provided a clear summary and interpretation of the form ancestor worship takes there and of how it differs from the still conspicuous role of ancestral spirits in the religions of some other African societies (Fortes, 1965b).

Among the Tallensi ancestor worship is a projection into the supernatural world of the authority structure of the family (or, more exactly, the lineage)—an extension, as worship after death, of the respect and obedience due to a living father—and it is a continuing source of strength for maintaining that authority structure in this world, where each child sees his or her father treating his own deceased father in the way he expects to be treated now by his children. In the patrilineal societies that share this pattern, the present head of the family is, in effect, the high priest, the only one who communicates, by sacrifice, prayer, and other accompanying ritual, with ancestral figures. He communicates directly with the ancestor who while alive had authority over him, that is, the previous priest (normally his father), and through that figure with earlier priests of their lineage. The present head of the lineage has not only the sole privilege but also the heavy responsibility of properly worshiping the ancestors, representing the interests of all the living members and of the deceased authority figures. In this system, in contrast with the many societies where the ancestral spirits are important but not worshiped,

> the persecuting ancestor is not a supernatural being capriciously punishing wrong-doing or rewarding virtue. He is rather to be thought of as an ultimate judge and mentor whose vigilance is directed towards restoring order and discipline in compliance with the norms of right and duty, amity and piety, whenever transgressions threaten or occur. When misfortune occurs and is

interpreted as a punitive, or to be more exact, corrective intervention by the ancestors, they are believed to have acted rightfully, not wantonly. Moreover, they are subject to the moral constraint that emanates from faithful worship. Though one cannot be certain that one's offerings and tendance will gain their benevolence, one can rest assured that they will bind the ancestors to act justly. (Fortes, 1965b, 136)

The Tallensi attribute all deaths to the ancestors, but without blaming them; even the death of the head of the family is necessarily just. Succession to the headship is a doubly saddened occasion; to the usual regrets at the death of the family head is added the fact that the death was just punishment for some failure for which the deceased bore responsibility. This enters clearly into the series of ceremonies in which the successor must take part, ceremonies by which the deceased enters the new status of ancestor and his son replaces him in the status he had while alive:

These are, firstly, the rites by which the deceased is established among his ancestors and is thus transformed from a living person into an ancestor; and secondly and consequentially, those by which the son is invested with his father's status or is made eligible for this. Significantly, it is the eldest son who should make the rounds of all the ancestor shrines that were in his father's custody and, with the customary libation, apprise them of his death. Then, he must attend the divination session at which the ancestral agent of his father's death is determined; for he must concur in the verdict since the sacrifices to appease the ancestors and to reconcile them with the living are his responsibility. Finally, he . . . is the main actor in rites which free him to do those things which were forbidden to him in his father's lifetime. (Fortes, 1961, 175)

Much the same pattern of ancestor worship is found in some other African societies with similar social structure, notably the Lugbara (Middleton, 1960). Along with it go expectations of benefits and harms from ancestral spirits on the mother's side; though there is great variation in detail here from one patrilineal society to another, there is agreement in not offering to maternal ancestors the formal worship that is provided for patrilineal ancestors. (Anthropologists have exaggerated the *worship* of ancestors in Africa, Kopytoff [1971] argues. The power of the oldest of a lineage, and the respect accorded him, may in some societies simply continue after his death, rather than being increased by virtue of his having become an ancestral spirit.)

There is variation, likewise, among matrilineal societies in Africa; McKnight (1967), in reviewing the best studied cases, argues convincingly that both the organized worship and the other forms of relationship with ancestral spirits can be understood in each society as an outcome of the customary relationships there among living family members. The same point is made by Gough (1958) in a study of an Asian case, cults of the dead among the Nayars, a matrilineal group in India.

An African instance where ancestral spirits are central to the religion, yet ancestor worship is absent, is provided by the Lovedu, a matrilineal society described by Krige and Krige in *The Realm of a Rain-Queen* (1943, 231). The Lovedu believe in a remote creator god; he is not thought of as entering into current human activities. The ancestral spirits acting on their own are the source of help and protection. Illness or other misfortune can come only if the ancestral spirits fail to provide the help and protection expected from them. Even the attempts of wizards to bring illness can be effective only if the victim's ancestors permit. Sacrifice and prayer help in maintaining ancestral benevolence; in some families, including the royal family, ancestral spirits are felt on ceremonial occasions to take part joyously in drinking, dancing, and singing. Yet there is no general pattern of organized worship. The ancestors, it is said, "desire mainly to be remembered" (p. 233), and are likely to be addressed by prayer and sacrifice only when some misfortune is interpreted as an ancestral complaint of not being remembered. Ceremonies of the royal family are crucial to the welfare of everyone, because the queen's ancestors are responsible for rainfall. Otherwise, "Each family has its own ancestors, and religious observances are thus peculiarly a family concern."

In some African societies, ancestral spirits are even less important. The Lozi (of Zambia), for instance, believe in their reality but rarely attribute occurrences to their influence. Turner (1952, 50) thought the unimportance of ancestors in Lozi religion was probably due to the lack of lasting attachments to places with which ancestors could be associated, in view of the migratory character of Lozi life. The same point emerges in our account elsewhere of Asian nomads. Ancestral spirits are more easily and frequently thought of and attended to if they are associated with a well-marked grave, or a long-lasting shrine in permanent home territory.

Societies that depend primarily on herding (referred to alternatively as herders or pastoralists) are often nomadic, moving from one region to another as their animals exhaust the available food or must be moved in anticipation of seasonal changes. This is doubtless a reason that spirits of the dead figure less in their religions. Having to dispose of their dead in places to which they may not soon return, they lack the reminder offered by a grave and by the scenes of their living interactions with the now deceased.

Societies depending primarily on intensive agriculture, with plowing or irrigation or both, are more sedentary than most foragers and herders; often they are also more sedentary than horticulturalists, who may have to move their gardens every few years. From their sedentary way of life may come their more frequent sense of interaction with spirits of the dead. More than in other societies, everyone has ancestors whose remains are nearby; their burial places serve as reminders of their earlier roles as living parents or grandparents and make more likely a sense of their continuing presence.

Swanson (1960) found belief in active ancestral spirits to be related to another cultural feature—a social system in which kinship is the basis of membership in groups (larger than the nuclear family) that make and enforce decisions ("sovereign groups", as Swanson called them). Such groups, Swanson argued in effect, give kinship a definition that reaches into the past and facilitates extending to the deceased the deference and dependence due to living elders.

More complicated consistencies in the interaction between family and the religious role of ancestral spirits have also been suggested. If the relation with spirits of the dead is based in part on relations among the living, then the former might be expected to vary from one society to another in accordance with differences in general relations among the living. Tatje and Hsu (1969) have suggested that kinship relations are one important source of this variation. In many societies, Hsu (1965) has argued, the relation within one particular kind of kinship pair is dominant—that is, it has a prime importance for the whole social system—and its characteristics tend to spread to other relationships as well. Father-son relationship has this position of dominance in many societies.

Father-son relationships anywhere tend to share certain character-istic features, such as persistence, authority, and asexuality. These fea-tures, then, according to Tatje and Hsu, tend to color many other social relationships. In societies where the father-son relationship is stressed, these features support a tendency for men to look toward the dead as toward their father, to be especially concerned about deceased male elders and to expect benevolent help from them (perhaps accompanied by pun-ishment for serious infractions). The ancestor worship found in the Tallensi and the Lugbara fits this pattern.

Where, on the other hand, relation between husband and wife is the dominant influence on social relations, kinship behavior offers no special support for concern with ancestors, and interest in spirits of the dead may be absent or diffuse, not focused on ancestors. Tatje and Hsu argue that domi-nance of other particular pairs of kin will have their own characteristic influence on attitudes toward ancestral spirits. Discussion of this question by several ethnographers in a book edited by Hsu (1971) suggests that such influences are variable and complicated, but that attitudes toward ancestral spirits do tend to be consistent with patterns of relationships among the living.

With increasing complexity of societies, a major god does not always replace ancestral spirits as the mystical being of greatest importance. For the Tallensi of Ghana, despite the complexity of their agriculturally based existence, ancestral spirits seem to remain the most important mystical beings. Fortes says that ancestor worship so dominates their thought that "the other occult agencies postulated by them, the mystically powerful Earth or the magically efficacious medicines, for instance, are all conceived of as being under the ultimate control of the ancestors" (1987, 12).

OTHER GODS AND SPIRITS

Probably no traditional society recognizes only a single mystical being other than ancestral spirits. Even the monotheistic religions of complex societies of West or East generally admit of additional supernaturals, in popular practice even when not in official dogma. The number of mystical beings is extremely variable, and sometimes reaches astonishing heights; we are not including here the spirits of deceased members of the society, which might always be innumerable, but only other mystical beings. E. G. Parrinder (1950) reported that Yoruba tradition claims more than 400 deities as objects of worship.

The extreme in number of mystical beings is perhaps found in the religion of the Ifugao, Indonesian agriculturalists of the Philippines, and they serve well to illustrate also the diverse kinds of mystical beings in which people believe. After many years of observation and study, Barton (1946, 14) listed 1,240 gods and estimated that the total probably exceeds 1,500, grouped by the Ifugao into more than 40 categories. Various criteria define the categories. One large group, whose label Barton translates as "Paybackables," are gods with whom the Ifugao believe their forebears long ago had trading relations through which they obtained their domestic animals, technological equipment, and rites; to gods of this category are due the principal offerings in general festivals. The Ifugao group other gods on the basis of the human activities they sponsor (such as persuasion, hostility, divination, maintenance of property, and prestige), the diseases they cause or control, the natural phenomena they produce, and so on. Within each category, the gods are often very specifically defined. They include, Barton reports, neither creator gods nor a supreme god. Of the multiplicity of gods, Barton says they

> share in the attributes usually attributed by men to their supernatural beings: immortality, ability to change form at will, to become invisible, to transfer themselves quickly through space, and so on. . . . Broadly speaking every deity participates in three sorts of powers: (1) common or general, shared by all, such as the powers mentioned above, plus another shared by all or nearly all Ifugao deities, the power of afflicting men with disease, misfortune, and ill-luck; (2) special powers possessed by the class to which the deity belongs; and (3) *individual* powers within the frame of the powers of the class. To illustrate: Anobok, as a deity, can make men sick or visit misfortune in general on them; as one of the group of social-relations deities of the class of "Convincers," he participates with the others of that class in the ability to control men's minds and to suggest courses of conduct; his individual forte is to make debtors who have publicly refused to pay debts or demands and who cannot, therefore, pay openly and publicly without losing face weaken and pay secretly. (1946, 17-18)

Societies with fewer basic categories of deity sometimes use multiple criteria for distinguishing the categories. The pantheon of the Tsembaga of New Guinea makes a major division between spirits that live at lower levels of altitude and those at higher levels within Tsembaga territory; the former are more concerned with fertility and with the lower part of the body, the latter with the upper part of the body. Spirits of Tsembaga who have died in battle live at higher altitudes, spirits of others at lower altitudes. The spirits who were never human also differ between the lower and the higher groups. At lower altitudes, for example, dwell spirits that bring illness and death, and at the very highest point the spirits associated with shamanistic ecstasy (Rappaport, 1984, 38-41). Thus, the specific categories thus seem to be based on a variety of related metaphors associating the human body and human activities with physical features of the environment. All these supernaturals of the Tsembaga are localized within the real physical world in which the people live and work. This seems to be true generally of Melanesian societies; supernaturals in the sky or in remote space do not have the importance they do in many Native American societies.

Different emphases appear among the peoples native to the Americas, in view of their being, with few exceptions, predominantly foragers. They obtained meat primarily by hunting, as their only domesticated animals were dogs, guinea pigs, and (in restricted areas of South America) species of llama. Their basic domesticated plants—maize, beans, squash, potatoes, and tobacco—l nt themselves to simple horticultural procedures. They did not have either the grains or the animals that in the other hemisphere led many peoples to find in agriculture and herding a more rewarding way of life.

Among foragers, and most especially in the Americas, the concept expressed in English as guardian spirit is conspicuous. The nature of the guardian spirit is highly variable, and the relation of a person to the spirit may not be as close as the word "guardian" suggests; a person gains power from the spirit but may not be in repeated contact. Among foraging peoples, relation to one's guardian spirit seems especially prone to be close, perhaps because of the absence of the blood sacrifice that, as we will see, herders have available as a means of achieving closeness to the supernatural.

Of great importance where hunting or fishing prevailed rather than gathering were the masters or owners of the prey species, whether thought of as essentially human spirits or as humanized animals who determined the availability of prey. These beings are found among Asian and African peoples as well as those of the Americas. Hallowell (1934) has drawn on his fieldwork with the Saulteaux of Berens River, Canada, to show how direct experience of natural phenomena is joined with the evidence from dreams and conjurings to shape a people's beliefs about owners and masters. The masters sometimes took the form of a major god, as in the case of the Inuit's sea goddess Sedna and the similar Kerekun of the Chukchee.

Success in gathering was less often thought to depend on masters of the plant life, including trees. With masters of either plants or animals, communication was especially by observance of taboos. Faithful observance was expected to evoke a benevolent response from the masters, making their food products available; violation of the taboos would offend the masters and lead them to bring privation or even disaster.

There were also nature spirits, of widely varying importance. Radin, reviewing the religion of Native American societies, concluded that "the sun, moon, and stars are among the most important spirits in America" (1914, 356). In some, the sun seems to have the character of a major god directing the affairs of the world; Robert Lowie, student of the Crow tribe of the western Plains, thought that they probably equated the sun with the One Above, their version of the supreme deity (1935, 252). The religious importance of the heavenly bodies exceeded in the Americas what it possessed in any other large area of the world, unless perhaps in the adjacent area of eastern Siberia.

This seems to be an instance where remote common history may be more important than recent economy in influencing religion. Although most of the Native American societies were foragers, deification of the heavenly bodies also characterized more complex societies of the Americas (as it did the hunter-herders of eastern Siberia, such as the Koryak and Chukchee). In the mythology of the Haida, a complex foraging society of British Columbia, the Raven, a culture hero, placed the stars, moon, and sun in the sky as divinities (Goddard, 1934, 135). The Pawnee, horticulturalists of the southeastern United States, gave special recognition to the morning star (Linton, 1922a), as did the Crow (Lowie, 1935) and some of the eastern Siberian groups (Bogoras, 1907, 313-314). The Hopi, horticulturalists of Arizona, included the sun among the divinities responsible for the crops. The Maya, Aztec, and Incas, complex societies based on horticulture, were sun worshipers, just as were many of the simple hunting societies of the North American Plains. Recent archaeological discoveries in the high Andes of Peru indicate that some of the Incan ceremonies for worshiping the sun took place on mountaintops, suggesting that the mountains themselves were regarded as deities, as they are today by some descendants of the Incas (Reinhard, 1992).

Some foraging groups give the moon a more important place than the sun in their religion. Driver (1972, 425) asserts this of the Inuit. Bleek (1928, 27) seems to imply the same of the San of the central Kalahari of southwestern Africa, in regarding moon worship as their oldest religion, shared with other San and with Khoikoi. For the Siriono, hunters of the Amazon region (who also practice some horticulture), the moon is a culture hero, and is reported to be the only important mystical being (Holmberg, 1950).

Various nature spirits of generally lesser importance were associated with specific places or geographic features; anthropologists often call them "place spirits" or "bush spirits." These spirits in many instances were benevolent, but some were threatening, like disease givers or the man-eating spirits of the Far North of North America.

Among societies that combine foraging with herding, the same range of mystical beings appears. Some—for example, the Koryak of Siberia—add specifically malevolent spirits and the spirits of prey animals they have killed (Jochelson, 1908, 92).

More difference from the foragers is seen in societies that depend principally on horticulture. The most consistent difference lies in the fairly uniform emphasis on ancestors as the mystical beings most conspicuous in daily life. Another difference is found in the greater importance of place spirits or bush spirits, and along with their importance goes an attribution to them of a more human quality. The emphasis on ancestors and that on place spirits both appear generally in a form that means the mystical beings of horticulturalists are closer to people than are the mystical beings of foragers. An extreme of this closeness is seen in the Manus of Melanesia, where the most recently deceased household head, identified by a term translated as "Sir Ghost," is present in the house, his skull being placed in a prominent position. (If the present head of the household feels Sir Ghost has not helped as he should, he may, according to Fortune [1935], banish Sir Ghost by throwing his skull away.)

Guardian spirits are not very likely to appear among horticultural societies, except when an ancestor has that role. Among the Bundi of Papua New Guinea, guardian spirits appear in a different and less individualized form; one spirit is the guardian of all males, and another is the guardian of all females (Fitz-Patrick & Kimbuna, 1983). The guardian spirit of the males has a somewhat punitive role, enforcing the taboos surrounding young men during their initiation period. The guardian spirit of the females is more benevolent, increasing a young woman's attractiveness and helping her in pregnancy and childbirth. Both have roles that are more group-oriented than the typical guardian spirits of Native American foragers (although, as we have discussed in Chapter 2, on power, the more individualized guardian spirit does occur also, though rarely, in Melanesia).

Some herding societies, especially several of mixed economy in East Africa, have well-developed theologies—not necessarily worked out explicitly but clearly implied by the specifics of their beliefs and practices. The one whose ideas have been analyzed in greatest detail is the Nuer, of southern Sudan, studied by Evans-Pritchard beginning in 1930. There is clearly a major god, who is the ultimate cause of everything, both at the original creation and in present day-to-day existence. The same word used as the only name for this major god is also applied to the abstract concept of spirit and, in appropriate contexts, to lesser gods and specific spirits. This Nuer word implies that air and breathing have been taken as a metaphor for spirit, just as in the case of the English word *spirit*, and Evans-Pritchard's analysis of the Nuer concept (1956, 1-27) is remarkably similar to much in Jewish and Christian tradition. Nuer discussions of religion and the associated practices indicate, Evans-Pritchard argues, that the Nuer share with Western theologians a confrontation between the one and the many. There is a sense, he says, in which other mystical beings, and sacred objects, derive their supernatural character from, and thus are *refractions* of, the major god; yet the Nuer never confuse them, he says, with the major god.

The religion of the Nuer's neighbors, the Dinka, also herders, has been reported and analyzed by Evans-Pritchard's student and colleague, Godfrey Lienhardt (1961). The Dinka, too, use a single word for an abstract concept of spirit and for specific beings, including a general creator. Lienhardt finds "divinity" a suitable translation of this word, and for the major god he distinguishes the meaning with a capital letter. Creation is the work of Divinity alone, both the original creation of the world and the creation of new human beings. A man begets a child and a woman gives birth to it; for those two roles the Dinka use a single word, but the word for "create" is reserved for the role of Divinity, without whose participation a sexual relation would be barren.

Dinka dependence on Divinity, expressed in prayer, sacrifice, and respect, is extended also to lesser divinities. Some of these resemble totems, in being attached to particular clans; others are free of any similarity to ancestral figures. The relation of the individual Dinka to all these forms of the divine is very similar to a Dinka's relation to his living father, and doubtless this is especially true as well of a Dinka's relation to his deceased ancestors. A Dinka may be temporarily possessed by any of these divinities or by an ancestral spirit; recurrent possession by one of the "free" divinities is characteristic of respected diviners. All the spirits or powers, together with lesser instances of the uncontrolled or surprising, exemplify the superhuman aspects of the experienced world. Lienhardt considers the term *supernatural* inappropriate, because a Dinka perceives these powers almost as directly in the external world as he does the human powers of the people around him.

Another society near these two and with a similar economy, the Lugbara of northern Uganda, has also been studied by an anthropologist especially interested in religion, John Middleton (1960). Middleton finds a similar range of usage of a single term for a major god, other spirits, and the unpredictable.

In all of these societies, the ethnographers found people able and willing to talk about religious concepts. Here they differ both from the reluctance of many peoples (such as pueblo dwellers of the American Southwest) to reveal religious thoughts to outsiders and from many peoples' lack of interest in theological formulation and discussion. Barth (1961, 152-153), in studying the Basseri, Iranian herders, found so little theological speculation that he was moved to conclude that religious meaning for them lay primarily in their awe-filled orientation toward the annual cycle of movement and the accompanying activities.

CULTURE HEROES

In most societies, people believe in what anthropologists have come to call "culture heroes"—mythological figures involved in the explanation of how the people, their culture, and various other features of the world originated. The Andaman Islanders, for instance, regard fire as the gift long ago of Kingfisher (Radcliffe-Brown, 1922, 201). Important figures in the myths people heard from childhood on, or in the secrecy of initiation rites, the culture heroes were not usually treated as though still alive and active; prayers and other forms of appeal were not generally addressed to them. (This was often true of the major god, too, especially when viewed primarily as a creator rather than a present source of guidance and order in the world.) Exceptions to this remoteness of culture heroes are found principally when they also have the characteristics of some other category of supernatural. Among Australian aborigines, for instance, the culture heroes are also ancestral spirits—distant and mythical, to be sure, but still thought of as active in the current life of their descendants.

SELF AS MYSTICAL BEING

We have presented as mystical those beings believed to exist that are not also natural beings with an existence directly verifiable by ordinary standards of scientific observation. However, our account is incomplete without recognizing that ordinary people are believed capable of being in part mystical beings.

This possibility has already been raised in Chapter 2. A person's possession of mystical power implies that he shares, in the belief of his culture, important characteristics of totally mystical beings. When we turn to the topic of wizardry, in Chapter 6, we will see various specific ways in which mystical power for evil may be believed to characterize some persons. In Chapter 7 we will see examples of mystical power being turned to benevolent uses by healers and diviners. Some of both malevolent and benevolent actions are believed to depend only on a person's gaining the cooperation of a totally mystical being. But many are believed to depend on a person's possession of intrinsic mystical power, on his being at least a semi-supernatural.

These possibilities pertain, usually, only to special persons. But there is a sense in most societies in which everyone is held to be at least a semi-supernatural. As we will see, it is believed that each person will after bodily death continue existence as a spirit or ghost, a totally mystical being. But this spirit or ghost does not come into existence only with the death of the body. It is viewed as a part of the total person already in existence during his entire life (and, in some societies, even before that). This sense in which everyone is believed to be partly supernatural is discussed in Chapter 9.

That in many societies each person is believed to be partly supernatural should caution us further against taking too literally the distinction we so readily make in our culture between natural and supernatural. The potentially supernatural soul may be considered as natural a component of a person as his body; the person's words and actions may yield a perception of his soul as readily as they yield a perception of his body. The evil power of the wizard may be as convincingly felt as Senator Joseph McCarthy and his admirers presumably felt the evil intent of the victims he was denouncing.

CHARACTER OF THE SUPERNATURALS

The gender ascribed to supernatural figures varies by society. In a representative sample of traditional societies, Whyte (1978) found that 13 percent considered all supernaturals to be male. No society was found to have only female supernaturals, but there was wide variation in the relative number and importance of female deities. To what other variations among societies might the degree of emphasis on the two genders be related? Whyte tested the relation of this variable to 51 aspects of the status of women and evidently found no relation (he reports the outcome of a cluster analysis, and this variable is not a part of any of the clusters). If the gender of supernaturals is related to something about the society, it is not as a simple projection (such as Durkheim might have predicted) of the structure of the society.

An ingenious suggestion was made by Guy Swanson (1960). He distinguished two emphases in the way a society might ensure reasonable conformity to its traditional norms of behavior. One is to emphasize childhood socialization—treating young children in ways that motivate them when grown to be good members of the group. The other is to emphasize social control enforced in adulthood by one's peers or by a system of justice. Early socialization is primarily exercised by women; adult social control, Swanson argued, by men. Considering beliefs about the supernatural as devices gradually developed through generations for strengthening established ways of ensuring conformity to norms, then, Swanson concluded that female figures should be more important in the pantheon of societies relying more on socialization and male figures more important in the pantheon of societies relying more on adult social control.

Swanson had no direct way of testing this theory, and the very indirect attempts he made were later shown by Michael Carroll (1979) to be irrelevant. Carroll had available, as Swanson did not, the ratings provided by Whyte (1978) on 51 aspects of the relative status of women. This permitted him to make a less indirect test, but of a modified hypothesis. Rejecting Swanson's assumption that reliance on adult social control implies reliance on males, he agrees that reliance on socialization implies reliance on women. How are societies to be assessed for degree of reliance on socialization? Carroll sees the key to lie in whether a child is viewed as a member of the kin group of both parents (as in our society) or as a member of the kin group of only one parent (as in about half the societies in his sample of 56). Among societies where socialization is conducted primarily by parents (and Carroll considers only those societies), socialization should be especially stressed as the means of ensuring right behavior if both parents have this sense of total kinship with the child. Carroll finds that it is indeed societies with this bilateral rule of descent that are most likely to have a strong emphasis on female deities; 69 percent of them do, as opposed to 22 percent of the societies where children belong to the kin group of only one parent.

This is only a beginning, of course; the test is still somewhat indirect. But in another study, Carroll (1986) shows that similar reasoning contributes to understanding the cult of the Virgin Mary, the timing of its appearance and strengthening, and why it is more important in some Catholic regions than others and virtually absent in Protestant sects. Spontaneous enthusiasm for the cult has in all of these ways been associated with social organization likely to make children experience their father as ineffective and their mother as an object of strongly repressed desire. The role of the mother figure in the pantheon is here as in the cross-cultural studies thus found to be related to the childhood experience of members of the society. Historical study of Western civilization and cross-cultural study of traditional societies come together at this point in suggesting that extremely diverse religions may serve, even in ways that are far from obvious, to promote the integrity of the social order.

Relative emphasis on the feminine or masculine element in the divine can readily shift, as historical evidence shows. So it is easy to suppose that the social conditions are primary, that it is they that influence this aspect of conceptions of the divine, rather than the reverse. For several other qualities of the supernatural that have been subjected to a similar kind of study, the aspects of divinity involved might be thought more resistant to change. Here one may be tempted to consider the supernatural conception to be primary, to be the source that influences the social conditions to which they seem to be related. The information that is available, however, does not indicate in which direction the influence operates, and it may flow in both directions.

Another general aspect of the supernatural that has been studied is the relative benevolence or malevolence a people attribute, on the whole, to the supernatural figures they believe in. Generally, a mixture of good and evil is attributed to the supernatural, and often to the same figure. The Navaho, for example, have supernaturals along the whole range from almost totally malevolent to almost totally benevolent (Sandner, 1979, 137). Yet Lambert and coworkers (1959) found that two different judges, reading the ethnographic data, could agree fairly well on judging the average malevolence or benevolence assigned to the supernatural by each society in their sample. They found that societies with predominantly malevolent conceptions of the divine showed some tendency to treat their children punitively; those with more benevolent conceptions tended toward greater nurturance in their child rearing.

There is an obvious consistency here between the conception children might form about their parents and the conception they later have about the supernatural, however the consistency arises. With a small sample of just 11 societies that afford particularly full information on child-training patterns, Spiro and d'Andrade (1958) did a similar study. Looking at several different aspects of child training, they, too, found some consistency between the way a society conceives of the supernatural and the expectations child training might instill about how people are likely to act.

Lambert et al.'s ratings of benevolence versus malevolence of supernaturals were used by other researchers (Roberts, Arth, & Bush, 1959) in studying the types of games played in the same societies. They distinguish three types of games—those whose outcome is influenced by physical skills, those whose outcome is influenced by strategy (with physical skill irrelevant), and those dependent on chance alone. This last category, games of chance, was most common in societies whose supernatural figures were predominantly benevolent. Here is a consistency between religious conceptions and recreational patterns, in which the religious conceptions seem likely to be primary. Roberts et al. also made use of another aspect of supernatural belief that had been analyzed by Lambert et al.—whether supernatural figures were believed capable of being coerced by human beings. This belief, too, was correlated with the presence of games of chance.

Another general variation among societies lies in the extent to which their supernatural beings are modeled after animals rather than exclusively after human beings. (We know of no systematic study of this variable, but seem to remember that Meyer Fortes made a valuable suggestion that we have not been able to find again in searching his publications.) There are many animal figures in the pantheon of simple North American foragers—the Saulteaux, for instance, have Snapping Turtle, Thunderbird, and Giant Caribou. The tendency is also found in the more complex foragers of the Northwest Coast, where boats in the winter ceremony have at their bow an active impersonator of Thunderbird. In contrast, African societies seem to form their supernaturals almost entirely on the human model.

The suggestion is that the difference arises from the economy, and illustrates the role of religion in increasing people's confidence of surmounting the major uncertainties in their life. The African herders and agriculturalists have a fairly good mastery of nature, and the uncertainties in their life arise in relations among people; for supernatural help in preventing or resolving difficulties in social relations, they look to beings basically like themselves but of greater power. For the foragers, on the other hand, life is at the whim of natural phenomena; it is to the nonhuman world they look for safety, for supernatural control of the risks that confront them, and for them some supernatural beings take animal form.

SUMMARY

Mystical or supernatural beings, who possess and utilize mystical power, may be divided into four general categories:

1. Major gods who either created the world or control everything that happens now. A single major god is found in many simple foraging societies and in complex societies, especially those in active contact with other societies.
2. Spirits of the dead, either the recently deceased or more distant ancestors. Emphasis on ancestral spirits is favored by a settled way of life and by stress on kinship as the basis of social structure.
3. Other gods and spirits. Societies vary greatly in the number and kinds of gods and spirits they recognize. Of special interest are the guardian spirits characteristic of foraging societies that

stress individual achievement, the spirit masters of game species, and nature spirits (personalizations of geographic features or heavenly bodies).

4. Culture heroes, mythical figures said to have created in the distant past various features of the culture.

To these perhaps should be added, as partial supernaturals, individual persons so far as they are considered to have mystical powers.

A beginning has been made in understanding the sources of variation in conceptions about mystical beings: the relative frequency of male versus female figures, their benevolence or malevolence, and their animal versus human character. So far, such features have been related to the general economy and to formative experiences of childhood.

Chapter 5

Communication with Mystical Beings

Human existence is mostly a story of life with people. Loving and hating, laughing and crying are with persons rather than things. Even essential interactions with things—eating food and drinking fluids—we tend to do together rather than alone, and we often convert them into social ceremonies. Our distinctive ways of interacting with our fellow human beings are carried over to some extent to our interaction with animals and plants. We may endow them with human characteristics they do not have, and we may respond to the actions or attitudes we seem to perceive them to display, even if what we seem to perceive is not objectively there. With spirits and gods, we may facilitate communication by identifying them with a shrine, a grave, a monument, a fetish; but what is important is the interaction with the supernatural being so localized, with its mystical power rather than with its physical associations.

Participants in a religious system may experience much of their thought and action as communication with the mystical beings. In attempting to communicate, they are also, just as in talking to their fellows, expressing something of their own characteristics. Cross-cultural studies of religion in traditional societies, such as we have described in recent pages, have concentrated on the expressive aspect. Concentration on the expressive aspect also characterizes Michael Carroll's application of similar reasoning in his study, described in those same pages, of the cult of the Virgin in European societies. The outcome of all this research shows clearly that aspects of religion express, perhaps quite unintentionally, some of the personal characteristics of the participants. But in the conscious experience of the participants, communication with the mystical beings is likely to be deemed much more important than self-expression.

Anthropological fieldworkers constantly find people seeking to communicate with mystical beings. This is the obvious intent in praying, invoking, and thanking mystical figures, in appealing to them to bring curses down upon enemies, in posing questions answers to which will help decide a course of action. All these actions follow the familiar pattern of verbal communication to one's fellows. It is no surprise that in addressing mystical beings one may speak privately, may think rather than speak aloud. And just as communicating with a person sometimes involves more than speech, addressing the supernatural is often accompanied by an act of giving. The sacrifice of an animal, a human captive, or other valuable possession or the offering of something whose value is only symbolic are obviously attempts to communicate by giving, usually as an accompaniment of speech or thought. Many other instances of doing or not doing, considered in the discussion on rites of passage (Chapter 8) and on festivals (Chapter 10), involve communication with mystical beings—the observance of taboos, the performance of rituals, the conformity to other rules when seen as a statement of obedience to mystical beings in expectation of approval.

All these forms of action or thought are readily seen as communication and are often labeled as such in anthropological accounts. It is for reverse communication, from mystical being to person, that this paradigm has been less used in anthropological discussions, and may be quite alien to the thinking of many Westerners not trained in anthropology. This is understandable. Because the Western social scientist does not believe that mystical beings exist, at least not those of traditional peoples, and the Western layperson typically gives no credence to the reality of pagan gods, the idea of communication from them does not readily spring to mind. Yet their mystical beings may be very real to members of a traditional society (as are their own to many members of our own society), and therefore they may experience many occurrences as communications from mystical beings. In looking at modes of communication, we will begin with modes in which communication *to* mystical beings is generally dominant and later proceed to modes in which communication *from* mystical beings is generally dominant. This is a classification of convenience and does not represent an absolute difference.

In any instance communication may be felt to be occurring in both directions, just as in ordinary conversations between two people. That possible communications from mystical beings sometimes have the full psychological reality of normal communication from another person does not, of course, mean that they always do. Of a society Jon Christopher Crocker studied in Brazil, for instance, he reports:

> Ordinary Bororo are quite sure that the shaman's mystical experiences are entirely "real," that no clear distinction can be made between them and ordinary sensate knowing. This does not mean they suspend all judgment and abandon their usual skepticism. There is a continual process of social verification of shamanistic accounts, all the livelier for being partially covert. (1985, 207)

In some societies, there may be general doubters, as well as those who, like some Bororo, question the genuineness of specific messages. There are disagreements about the interpretation of obscure messages.

The degree of uncertainty and the salience of the message may greatly influence what people do and feel in response to any apparent message from mystical beings.

An example of the value of thinking of relation to mystical beings as akin to communication back and forth between two people: Communication from mystical beings might be taken the more seriously, have the more societal value, the more the particular being is like a realistic known authority figure; for this reason, messages from a recently deceased person should be more influential than messages from figures of the distant past—that is, messages from the last head of the household should be more important than messages from more remote ancestors. Messages should be more important the more convincingly they are received; peoples whose recent dead are buried conspicuously in the house or community should give purported messages from ancestors more credence than peoples whose dead are discarded or buried in places that are unmarked and not to be visited again.

COMMUNION VERSUS RECIPROCATION

The sociologist and theologian Martin Buber (1958) distinguished two patterns of personal relationship, which he termed "I-Thou" and "I-It." The first is oriented toward entering into the inner life of the other person, toward sharing experience. The latter is oriented toward getting from others what one's own needs demand, toward treating others externally, like machines to be manipulated. When these two patterns are expressed in relationship with the nonhuman world, the I-Thou pattern leads to a dominant interest in a sense of communion with the nonhuman, whereas the I-It pattern leads to a dominant interest in a reciprocating relation in which one seeks to treat the nonhuman world in a way that will guarantee the response one wants.

The Christian tradition in Western society is often said to stress communion with the divine as the ideal pattern—a pattern conspicuous in the significance for many people of the rite of communion and dominant in the quest for mystical experience. Yet many features of Christian tradition do not depend on such an I-Thou orientation: prayers seeking benefit for oneself or for one's group, for instance, or moral conformity in the expectation of reward in this life or the next. Relation to mystical beings, seeking communion or gain, is mixed and variable among us, and that is likely to be true elsewhere too. But those going from our society to observe others seem constrained by the Christian ideal of communion, or perhaps by the difficulty of sensing a quest for communion by other people in an alien context, and have much more to say about quest for personal and social benefit.

Most of what we can report about communicating with mystical beings, on the basis of ethnographic reports, then, suggests an orientation toward seeking benefits. Raymond Firth (1964, 259), in writing at great length of religion among the Tikopia, says, "Worship was regarded as a two-way relationship, with material offerings as part reciprocity for past and future benefits." The reader may form the same impression of traditional societies in general, from what we will be reporting, for our material is principally concerned with human efforts to gain from relation to mystical beings some measure of practical security rather than of emotional intimacy.

To correct the possible impression that a quest for communion is completely absent in traditional societies, it is appropriate to begin with a few clear instances of its importance. Among the Lovedu, a South African group, ancestral spirits are felt to be present at religious ceremonies and to be

> a part of the living community. They can be given more tangible form (at their own request) by being "brought home" and placed in a living goat, sheep, or beast called by their name, or in having set up, in their name, a shrine or mound of earth, often with a growing plant or tree in it. Like living elders, the ancestors must be given their due and informed of what goes on. (Krige, 1974, 96)

The kachinas, mystical beings of pueblo dwellers of the American Southwest, are thought by the Hopi to be present during the ceremonial season when the dances are performed, although when the season is over "they withdraw to their homes in San Francisco Peaks and elsewhere" (Goddard, 1931, 115). At the potlatch ceremonies of Northwest Coast tribes, the deceased ancestors of the hosts were felt to be present. Of one of those tribes, the Tlingit, Sergei Kan (1986, 198-199) reports that "a small portion of the gifts was burned for the benefit of the donors' matrilineal ancestors," and he argues that in earlier accounts of potlatches the notion that benefit was being sought from the ancestors was given a greater place than it deserves.

Regardless of whether the main aim is to gain practical benefits or to sense communion, a person may seek to comunicate through a specialist or to communicate independently. Sometimes independent communication is not thought possible for the average person or is forbidden. Yet, even in societies where direct communication with mystical beings is open to everyone, some individuals are considered more apt, so that their help is sought by others. In most societies, communication with mystical beings is primarily in the hands of people with special aptitude or skill, even though they may be in other respects typical members of the society, not professionals devoting their working life entirely to their religious activities. The way they communicate varies, and scholars show little agreement in the way they classify such people.

Shaman, priest, diviner, medicine man, healer, sorcerer—all these and other terms have been applied. Sometimes the impression may be created that these terms mark a set of categories among which people who practice communication with mystical beings can be neatly divided. Such a mistake comes naturally to us who live in a society in which rabbi,

Catholic priest, Congregational minister, and the like are clearly distinguishable, with no intermediate categories. In the many worlds of traditional religions there are no uniform rules about the activities of religious practitioners; any categories they are placed in are devised by visitors from our society who carry preconceptions it is difficult to be rid of. The various labels properly distinguish activities rather than persons.

One distinction that can be useful, if not carried too far, is between shaman and priest or, more properly, between shamanic and priestly kinds of activity. The shaman communicates with mystical beings directly, as by visions experienced in trance; the priest communicates through carrying out established rituals and does not necessarily have any vision or other direct communication. By most definitions of shamanism, of course, many specialists in communicating with mystical beings would remain unclassified, for they fit neither the definition of shaman nor that of priest. Shamanism has been much written about in recent decades—sometimes in the course of imaginative attempts to portray the historical development of religion (Eliade, 1964), sometimes in the hope that shamanic traditions can be drawn on for spiritual guidance in our own troubled times (Kalweit, 1988). Both kinds of effort often lead to an exaggerated picture of uniformity of the varied phenomena to which the label of shamanism is attached.

Rather than define categories that inevitably are artificial, we would describe modes of communication, mentioning along the way their typical patterns of appearance in the social structure. We will at times use such terms as shaman and priest, when in their narrow meaning they seem clearly appropriate, but more often we will use terms less tied to the aims or theories of Western observers.

What are the beings with which people seek to communicate? We have seen, in Chapter 4, that the relative importance of various kinds of being may vary according to the economic basis of life and according to the past history of the society (with resulting resemblances to neighbors and to distant speakers of related languages). So, too, does the relative importance of various modes of communication. Thus, in this chapter we will also deal with various types of economy or various regions in turn.

MODES STRESSING COMMUNICATION
TO MYSTICAL BEINGS

Prayers and Offerings

Prayer is often mentioned by itself as an important part of human effort to communicate with mystical beings—the effort to make one's needs known and to receive the help or guidance that would lead to meeting the needs. Among the peoples of the Great Basin in the United States, social get-togethers had, along with their obvious contribution to recreation and the knitting of social ties, an important religious function expressed primarily in prayer. A Paiute healer depended on his spirit helpers for help in diagnosis and therapy and sought their help by praying (Whiting, 1950, 40). In the Southwest, among the Navaho, and to many other North American peoples, prayer was a conspicuous part of curing rituals and of daily household routine (Kluckhohn & Leighton, 1947).

Prayer may sometimes be inferred from observed behavior, as in the case of the Netsilik Inuit ritual in response to success in the seal hunt. The hunter who has harpooned a seal through a hole in the ice divides the liver with his companions, and he kneels on one side of the hole while they kneel on the other. Eskimo familiarity with prayer is suggested by the following account of an observation by Vilhjalmur Stefansson, Arctic explorer and ethnographer:

> Stefansson relates how certain inland Eskimos in northwestern Alaska were deeply impressed by the efficacy of a Christian prayer as an aid in caribou hunting. But the second year it did not work so well, and they decided that white men's prayers, like their rifles and other things, deteriorate with age. (Weyer, 1932, 454)

Two foraging societies at the southern tip of South America, the Ona and the Yahgans, were studied by Martin Gusinde (1917). Both groups addressed in prayer a higher being to whom they attributed illness. Gusinde reported that the Yahgans used ancient formulas in prayers, particularly at times of prolonged illness, with requests such as "You-up-there be good to us." Though illness might generally be expected to be a prime topic of prayer, there are exceptions. The Andamanese, inhabitants of islands between India and the Malay Peninsula, are reported not to pray for good health (Radcliffe-Brown, 1922), though there seems no reason to doubt that prayer is one of their means of seeking to communicate with mystical beings. For another foraging society, the Vedda of Sri Lanka, the specific purpose of prayer mentioned by the ethnographers (Seligmann & Seligmann, 1911) is to gain help in catching game.

Prayer is often linked with offerings. (Offerings is the term used for bloodless sacrifice, in which what is offered is of relatively small value.) In Native American societies, prayer to the sun is often accompanied by offerings of tobacco smoke, while on the same occasion a pinch of tobacco might be placed on the ground as an offering to the earth.

The Russian anthropologist L.I. Shternberg (1933) learned something of the meaning of offerings in a foraging society through his efforts to make his scholarly mission compatible with the demands of the ongoing culture of the Gilyak, the Siberian society he was studying. While traveling with a group of Gilyak, he wanted to climb to the top of a hill that was a sacred place of a certain deity; his companions would not go there and disapproved of his going. When he proposed to go alone, he found that his companions feared the deity's wrath both for his safety and for theirs. His previous analysis of other incidents and statements had led him to the conclusion that offerings or sacrifice were considered by the Gilyak to involve exchange with a mystical being, in which a person offers something the being does not have and receives in return something the being can provide. So he suggested that he would offer some candy at the top of the hill, and his companions were relieved that he had a special food item that might please the deity. On his return, they were satisfied with the account he gave of his offering as a request to the deity for reciprocation in food and safe delivery home for everyone in the party.

Sacrifice

Foragers

Among foragers, blood sacrifice of animals—that is, the killing of animals as a sacrificial offering—seems to be confined to dogs and bears. Some tribes that use dogs in hunting do not use them in sacrifice. Their faithfulness as helpers in hunting was given by the Seneca, an Iroquois tribe of New York State, as especially justifying their use in sacrifice. L. H. Morgan explains the appearance of dog sacrifice in annual Seneca ceremonies of prayer and thanksgiving, as he observed them in the middle of the nineteenth century:

> The simple idea of the sacrifice was, to send up the spirit of the dog as a messenger to the Great Spirit, to announce their continued fidelity to his service, and also to convey to him their united thanks for the blessings of the year. The fidelity of the dog, the companion of the Indian, as a hunter, was emblematical of their fidelity. No messenger so trusty could be found to bear their petitions to the Master of life. The Iroquois believed that the Great Spirit made a covenant with their fathers to the effect, that when they should send up to him the spirit of a dog, of a spotless white, he would receive it as the pledge of their adherence to his worship, and his ears would thus be opened in a special manner to their petitions. (1851, 216-217)

Dog sacrifice is mentioned in accounts of foraging societies in other parts of the world, too.

Bear sacrifice, although very important to some foraging societies, is confined to northern Eurasia; in North America the bear is of great religious significance but not subject to sacrifice.

The Ainu, aboriginal group in northern Japan, and the Gilyak of Siberia had bear festivals that took place at set intervals. The sacrifice was made possible by the capture long in advance of a bear cub, which was caged and tended as a so-called house bear. During this period it was paraded about, honored, fed, and well cared for. When the time for the sacrifice approached, the bear, though tortured, was still fed well, in an attitude of apology and hope that he would report having been well treated. In the case of the Ainu, beer was offered to other deities invited to partake of the feast (Kindaichi, 1949). The Gilyak also sacrificed dogs on the same occasion (Hawes, 1903). The sacrifice of both species was thought of as a way of sending a message to the deities.

Human sacrifice does not seem to have been common among foragers. A major instance was among Northwest Coast tribes, where the favorable environment had led to great class distinction. Slaves were sometimes sacrificed in connection with the building of a large house or totem pole; what the significance of this was, beyond assertion of supreme temporal power by the wealthy man responsible, is not clear from the retrospective accounts. A number of tribes in the eastern part of the United States killed war captives, but again the religious significance is not clear.

Lesser human sacrifice, voluntarily giving up a part of one's own body, was practiced in some foraging societies. Among the Crow it was a common component of the vision quest, common enough so that the anthropologist Robert Lowie found in 1907 that most older men lacked a finger joint. In a description of the quest for a vision or revelation, Lowie describes the preliminary fasting and spending the night almost naked in a rocky place. Then,

> Rising at daybreak, he sat down toward the east. As soon as the sun rose, he laid his left forefinger on a stick and chopped off a joint. This he put on a buffalo chip and held it out towards the Sun, whom he addressed as follows: "Uncle (i.e. Father's clansman), you see me. I am pitiable. Here is a part of my body, I give it you, eat it. Give me something good. Let me live to old age, may I own a horse, may I capture a gun, may I strike a coup. Make me a chief. Let me get good fortune without trouble." (1935, 239-240)

The sacrifice of a finger joint sometimes occurred at the time of the major ceremonial known as the Sun Dance among various Native American foragers of the Great Plains. Another form of self-mortification was, however, more standard at that ceremony. Some young men had skewers pushed through the flesh of their back or chest, by which they were then either suspended from the main Sun Dance pole or linked to a heavy weight they pulled over the ground (until they were torn free, according to some accounts).

As blood sacrifice is a mode of communication with mystical beings little used in Western religions, we deem it especially useful to illustrate the variety of meanings found in it. Beyond foraging societies, which are rare in Africa, we choose African societies for this purpose, for sacrifice has been especially well reported for a number of them. All of those we consider have domestic animals, including cattle. In some, herding is the principal source of subsistence, but in some it is secondary to agriculture, with cereals being the major food.

Herders and Cultivators

Traditional peoples whose economy is based primarily on herding domestic animals are found almost exclusively in Asia and Africa. The northern Asian territory extends into the extreme north of Europe, where the Lapps live with their reindeer herds. But there were no pastoralists in aboriginal North America or Oceania; in South America, herding of llamas

played some part within the Inca Empire, and herding had great importance in a few later societies, especially some derived from segments of
that empire.

Few of the pastoralist societies had remained isolated from the great
religions by the time their cultures were studied by Western ethnographers. Most of the African pastoralists, and many of the Asian, are Muslim.
Some of the northern Eurasian herders are Christian, and some African
herders have become Christian in recent generations. The herding societies that participate in Islam or Christianity show in their version of those
great religions considerable similarity to the religions of those that do not.
Hence we have thought it pertinent to look at all the herding societies
rather than confining ourselves to those whose members do not consider
themselves Muslim or Christian.

Most of the herding societies live a nomadic life, of the pattern called
transhumance, moving from one area to another as seasonal changes make
first one and then another part of their territory the best area for their
animals to graze and find water.

The one society for which there is the fullest report of sacrificial
customs and what they mean to people is the Dinka, herders of Sudan. A
British anthropologist, Godfrey Lienhardt, studying among the Dinka
between 1947 and 1950, concentrated his attention on religion (1961).
Cattle are of great importance in Dinka life. Their milk is a main source
of food; their meat is eaten only when it is available because of a sacrifice.
Millet porridge is also a regular source of nourishment, and all of these are
supplemented by fish and other meat when available.

Individual cattle are highly valued. As we mentioned in Chapter 3,
Dinka men are proud of the cattle they own, and their personal identity is
defined largely by their cattle. The special value of the cattle, beyond the
milk the cows contribute, lies in the potential sacrifice of the steers
(castrated bulls) or, more rarely, of the sexually intact bulls. Though sheep
and goats are also subject to sacrifice, it is usually as a supplement to
sacrifice of cattle. Sacrifice is always for the benefit of someone or some
group, and the owner of the chosen victim may be proud of being able to
provide an animal suitable for the particular purpose, but the personal loss
is often severe. This perhaps balances the animal's loss of life, just as the
gain to the human beneficiaries is thought to be balanced by the gain to
cattle as a whole. "Sacrifice is made equally for the benefit of men and of
cattle, for the whole group, cattle and men together, suffers or thrives"
(Lienhardt, 1961, 21).

Among the Dinka, a sacrifice seems always to be a social occasion,
even when it is performed for the benefit of a single, well-defined individual. Some of its contribution to social life obviously comes from the people's
enjoyment of their roles as participants in the ceremonial acts and in the
surrounding opportunities for communication with each other. But the
purpose of the occasion, justifying and providing the background for all
the rest, is to communicate with mystical beings. Respect for them sets
the general tone of the ceremony, and respect is also shown toward the

victim, which must be treated in proper ways, and toward the human participants. The sacrifice is a gift to the beings who are addressed, an effort to obtain their attention and favorable regard. The message to mystical beings is conveyed in the prayers or even insistent demands uttered by the people officiating at the ceremony, often and eloquently repeated, and perhaps by the unspoken thoughts of the others who are present.

A frequent occasion for a sacrificial ceremony is serious illness. A diviner is first consulted for advice about what in the past of patient or relatives has occasioned the punishment of the patient, and about what beings should be addressed in prayer and sacrifice. Plans are then made for the sacrificial ceremony, and an animal selected as victim. The prayers are directed at persuading the relevant beings to withdraw the punishment, to accept the sacrifice and consider that the misdeed that occasioned it has been sufficiently expiated.

Participants give more attention, Lienhardt says, to the content of the prayers than to the actual killing of the victim. Indeed, a sacrificial ritual may include no killing; the beast may be dedicated rather than killed, and is thereafter reserved for killing at a later ritual. (If a suitable animal is not available, too, a particular variety of cucumber defined as sacred is acceptable as a temporary substitute.) Yet the suffering of the animal is important, Lienhardt concludes. It is tethered during the ceremony and ordinarily becomes quiescent; this is seen as a diminution of its power. If the ritual is one aimed at the recovery of an ill patient, this diminution of the animal victim's power (eventuallly, its loss of life) is seen as a source of the patient's increase in power. It is recognized that the patient's return to full health may be gradual. The sacrifice creates "a moral reality, to which physical facts are hoped eventually to conform" (Lienhardt, 1961, 251). It is also recognized that the patient may not recover; the mystical beings may have decided not to accept the sacrifice, or the source of their punishment may not have been correctly identified.

> It is of particular importance . . . to recognize that the sacrificial rite is first and foremost an act of victimization. A strong and active beast is rendered weak and passive so that the burden of human *passiones* may be transferred to it. It suffers vicariously for those for whom sacrifice is made. (Ibid.)

Sacrifices may be held among the Dinka on various other occasions when a misfortune threatens an individual or group. When someone has died, for example, there is danger that his or her spirit may be hostile toward survivors or their cattle; thus, funeral ceremonies may include a sacrifice to the spirit of the deceased, accompanied by prayers seeking to persuade it to withhold any malevolence.

Sacrifices may also be held to prevent misfortunes from occurring even in the absence of present threat. There are regular sacrifices just after the annual harvest, asking protection during the coming dry season:

> The regular sacrifices of this period anticipate an approaching period of dispersion and danger but also of pleasure (for the Dinka enjoy their

dry-season camps) at a time when social life is in the villages at its most concentrated and intense. People thus sacrifice for prosperity and strength just at the time when they are most experiencing the fullness of social life and, in the temporary abundance of the harvest, are at the peak of their physical well-being. (Lienhardt, 1961, 272)

A sense of the great variation in sacrifice within a single society may be gained from Evans-Pritchard's (1956) detailed account of religion among the Nuer, herders and neighbors of the Dinka in Sudan. Casual minor offerings by an individual may take only a moment; a serious rite may last hours, and its character varies radically according to the occasion and purpose. No single mood, such as awe, predominates. Even at serious rites, the interest and attention of participants may vary widely; only on the most solemn of occasions does everyone remain attentive to the lengthy invocations. There is no prescribed content, little routine. As Evans-Pritchard says, "Nuer are more interested in purpose than in details of procedure" (1956, 212). Though the victim is always referred to as a cow, it may in fact be a sheep, a goat, or even a cucumber.

The invocations are not primarily requests; they more characteristically take the form of affirmative statements (e.g., that the sick man will be healed at the moment of sacrifice). They are thought of as a communication to mystical beings; because the Nuer use the same word for a general concept of deity and for lesser spirits of the air and of the earth (which may be manifestations of deity), it is difficult for an observer to know just how the invoker pictures the object of his address. He does not address ancestral spirits, however; Nuer religion differs from many other African religions in giving no place to ancestral spirits. When the victim is killed, its life is taken by mystical beings. What follows—the allocation, cooking, and eating of the meat—is an important social occasion but not a part of the sacrifice; there is no ceremonial eating together of spirits and people.

And what communication is received from the deity or spirits to whom the sacrifice is made? Evans-Pritchard does not mention advice or information, but there is a clear implication that if a source of frustration, such as illness or threat of illness, disappears or is averted, this is considered a communication from deity or spirit. And everyone hopes that the deity or spirit, having accepted a gift, will feel an obligation to do in return what the giver wanted.

Evans-Pritchard finds in sacrifice still another aspect of interaction between person and deity. The person for whose benefit the sacrifice is performed is, to some extent, he argues, identified with the victim. This is symbolized in many instances by rubbing ashes on the animal's back just before the invocations. It is specifically the evil features of the person, the internal sources of the problems confronting the person, that he or she thus seeks to transfer to the beast. Acceptance of the sacrifice, then, means that the deity is taking the person's evil away with the life of the victim. The evil is "ransomed or expiated or wiped out with the victim" (p. 281). This interpretation of sacrifice, shared by the Tiv of Nigeria (Downes, 1971, 94), is akin to scapegoating.

Sacrifice is practiced widely in African societies, in those depending on crops as well as in herders. From one society to another there are differences in detail, even though the general pattern of communicating to mystical beings and expectation of response from them remains a constant. The main consistent difference is that primarily agricultural societies address their sacrifices to ancestral spirits more than herding societies do. We see this as one more example of how closely religion is tied to the general life of a people. When people are settled in a single place through the generations, generally with graves as constant reminders of grandparents and even remoter forebears, ancestral spirits have a vivid presence they may lack among the more transient herders. Communication with them is thus more actively sought, even though other mystical beings may be addressed at the same or other times.

Reports on sacrifice in specific African societies sometimes bring out features that are not mentioned in many ethnographies of other societies. They may in some instances be unique or rare features; in some other instances they may be features that did not happen to be mentioned in the rather sparse accounts that generally are provided. Nonetheless, they may be taken as representative of the general character of sacrificial practices, as adapted to the specific character and needs of at least one society.

One such instance is the specific report of sacrificial ceremonies as providing an opportunity for people to inform the spirits of their ancestors about events in the living part of their society. Whether this goes with a belief that the ancestral spirits cannot ordinarily see for themselves what is going on or with a belief that they will ordinarily be inattentive, it can be a convincing element in the larger expectation that the ancestral spirits will on this occasion be present and likely to reply with their own messages to the living.

Another instance is the idea that the food and drink provided for the ancestors at the ceremony is itself an important communication, beyond its first value in obtaining the attention of the spirits who are addressed. Sometimes a portion of beer is poured on the ground or into a hole, and sometimes a portion of meat is laid out for the spirits. But such material gifts are symbolic; more often, perhaps, people are explicit that it is the spiritual aspect of the food and drink that spirits are able to absorb, and the material aspect is entirely distributed among the living participants. The occasion for a sacrifice is often a misfortune that is taken to have been brought about by the anger of ancestral spirits. If the angry spirits can be induced to partake of food and drinks (in the sense in which they can be believed to do so), then their anger may be quieted, in just the same way as food and drink may quiet the anger of living persons. This is most clearly brought out in Grace Harris's (1978) study of the Taita.

In some societies, it is believed that the spirit of a dead person needs in the afterlife to have food and drink at hand for its own nourishment (and perhaps the nourishment or entertainment of companions in the spirit world). The prestige of the spirit in that world may depend, just as in this life, on how amply it is supplied. Where the supply is thought to be provided by the sacrifices made in the funeral ceremonies, the family is motivated to be strongly supportive of the interests of its newly deceased member, and large provisions may also yield the family prestige in the living community as well.

The extreme of funeral sacrifice to provide the deceased with supplies for the afterlife is seen in some African kingdoms, strongly stratified societies in which the king has vastly greater power and wealth than other members. The king's funeral among the Dahomeans and the Ganda, for example, included in former times sacrifice of persons whose spirits were to serve the king's spirit in the afterworld. In both these societies, when occasions required that the king himself offer sacrifices to mystical beings, he was likely to offer human rather than animal victims. The reasoning behind this expectation is stated as follows by Herskovits, the anthropologist who has reported most fully on the Dahomeans:

> When any being, human or supernatural, devotes himself to favoring the ventures of a man, that man must make known his gratitude for such service. The tangible way of expressing such gratitude is by gift-giving. Good form demands that a man give according to his means. It follows, therefore, that whereas the destitute man can only offer beans or corn or millet, and the poor man can add to these only a chicken, a man of wealth can also offer sheep and bullocks, while when "blood" offerings are required of a King, then he must offer the costliest of all "blooded" creatures—human beings. Thus the matter of human sacrifice, as viewed by the Dahomean, resolves itself into another example of how in this culture the conspicuous utilisation of wealth offers a means for maintaining prestige. (1967, 55-56)

Communication is in many of the societies in both directions at once, as has been implied in some of the descriptions cited here. This is brought out most clearly in connection with John Middleton's account (1960) of sacrifice among the Lugbara of northwestern Uganda. It is performed in connection with illness, and its main meaning seems to differ from that encountered in any of the other societies we have reviewed. It marks a restoration of a person's former well-integrated position in his lineage, after a period in which he had an illness that was interpreted by oracles as due to some lapse of lineage loyalty on his part. The sacrifice permits him to give up his sense of guilt for the sin he must have committed. The social occasion surrounding the sacrifice may facilitate this; members of the lineage eat cooked portions of the sacrificed animal, and thus share a ceremonial meal with the relevant ancestors. Others present (in-laws, for example, to use Western terminology) are given raw portions to take home with them; Middleton reports that even this form of participation creates a strong sense of commensality. Unlike sacrificial rituals in many other societies, Lugbara sacrifices are not characterized by prayers. Instead, there are addresses, often long, that center on a full account of the circumstances that led up to the ritual and an affirmation that the unity and morality of the lineage are firmly reestablished.

That sacrifice may especially serve to bring together living persons and the spirits of their deceased ancestors is emphasized in Junod's account of ceremonies he witnessed in southern Africa, among the Thonga in the early 1900s. The sacrifices were directed to specific ancestral spirits. The clear directedness is illustrated by his account of a sacrifice by a family who had migrated from the north; care was taken to have the animal pointed toward the north so that its dying cry would be heard by the family's ancestral spirits (Junod, 1962, i, 158). Sacrifices seem intended to establish communication with very specific spirits, the family ancestors who can be named; the channel of communication is then used to plead for the interests of the individual, family, or larger group. Junod describes many sacrificial rituals appropriate to various needs or situations, but the sacrifice is not considered simply as a gift to appease or compel the spirits, to gain specific ends. A Thonga, in sacrificing, "really aims at entering into relationship with those powerful spirits who control his life" (ibid., ii, 420).

In one Thonga ritual that Junod described in detail, separate portions of the meat offering are placed out for the spirits individually as their names are called. The clan chief who conducts the sacrifice speaks to the spirits in a familiar manner, begging them not to be angry with their living descendants and to protect them from various possible evils (ibid., ii, 401-403). The gift does not have to be of great value, and its material aspect is in fact put to use by those present. The ancestral spirits, Junod concluded, are thought to consider the gift "as a token of love from their descendants, and a sign that these have not forgotten them, but will do their duty towards them" (ibid., ii, 415).

The message from mystical beings that sacrifice may evoke is often a long-delayed but very real change in the problem situation—a patient's gradual recovery, for example. But sometimes it is an occurrence superficially unrelated that is given meaning by conventions of interpretation, similar to codebooks for mystical interpretation of dreams. An example is provided by Winter's masterful analysis (1964) of the meaning of a sacrifice among the Iraqw of Tanzania; he first observed it and then interviewed the participants. A widower sacrificed a bull to the spirit of his late wife. Many details of the ritual were performed to ensure acceptance of the sacrifice by the spirit; what is especially valuable in the account, however, is its clarity about communication in each direction. While placing some of the meat on a small altar prepared for the occasion, the widower addressed the spirit of his wife, asking her to forgive him for grievous wrong he had done her while she was alive and to cease the retaliatory evils she had been bringing on him and his household since her death. He then waited quietly for the arrival of a hyena, and spoke in the same vein to the first one to arrive; he was in fact again addressing his wife, knowing that her spirit would have entered the body of the hyena to communicate her response to the sacrifice. The means of communication would be by her then influencing the movement of scavenger birds (kites). The fact that a kite came to the meat, but only after an hour, meant that the wife accepted the sacrifice but with reluctance, so that the widower's troubles were not ended. Thus, a traditional symbolism of natural events permitted the sacrifice to provide two-way communication with the deceased.

Much the same variety of meanings may be presumed in other parts of the world where sacrifice is practiced, though evidence about the meaning is very sparse in comparison with that provided by the thorough studies of religion on which we have been able to draw for many African societies. We already mentioned in Chapter 3 the sacrificial practices of occasional foragers in the Americas and Asia and of the rare herders of the Americas. Sacrifice of reindeer is widespread among Siberian groups where they are domesticated. The multiplicity of meanings of sacrifice in a single society is illustrated for Siberia by what Anisimov (1963, 104-105) witnessed among the Evenk (Tungus) in 1931. A reindeer was sacrificed "to the gods of the above" in the course of obtaining their advice and other help in combating an illness. The spirit that caused the disease was also offered the sacrificed reindeer as a more attractive place to dwell than the body of the patient.

Human sacrifice is found sporadically, and especially often in more complex societies, in other parts of the world. The Pawnee, a horticultural society of the southeastern United States, until the early nineteenth century sacrificed each year a captive maiden (Linton, 1922a). She was captured from another tribe for the express purpose of immolation by bow and arrow at a ceremony in honor of the Morning Star. She was honored in her captivity, as captives of war are sometimes honored before eventually being killed. This practice resembles the Ainu's sacrifice of the house bear. Both suggest that the sacrificial victim must first become symbolically associated with those who are offering it, as though only then could the victim be carrying a message from them.

In the complex kingdoms of Middle and South America, human sacrifice was practiced on a large scale, and there, perhaps, the main message directed to the gods was a demonstration of zeal in devotion to them. Capturing prisoners for sacrifice was, at the time of the Spanish conquest, a main aim of Aztec warfare; the victim's heart was dedicated to mystical beings, and his limbs were used as food. Michael Harner (1977) has assembled impressive evidence that this union of religion and massive cannibalism was a product of population pressure. Natural conditions and agricultural technology had supplied food for population growth in the absence of large animals that could be domesticated and make animal protein abundant. Hence, the established idea that the gods appreciated the spiritual aspect of human blood as food could readily spread, encouraging the eating of the flesh itself by people in a powerful enough position to assert their claim in the face of shortage. The antiquity of human sacrifice in Middle America is indicated by its earlier appearance among the Maya. Self-sacrifice of blood—obviously not with a nutritional intent—was apparently an obligation of royalty among the Maya; carvings record, for instance, the queen's drawing a cord through her tongue to produce bleeding (Schele & Miller, 1986).

MODES STRESSING COMMUNICATION
FROM MYSTICAL BEINGS

Life Events

Anything that happens can be interpreted as a communication from mystical beings, and beliefs about mystical beings guide the interpretation. Abundant crops, a successful hunt, or good health—all may be taken as a sign of approval and assurance of goodwill from whatever mystical beings are thought to take a positive interest in community or individual. Failure of crops or prey, severe storms, disease or death may be signs of disapproval or evidence of malevolence, perhaps on the part of the normally benevolent beings or perhaps of other beings believed to be chronically menacing rather than helping.

How dependably are the mystical beings beings counted on to show their approval or disapproval by what they allow to happen in the course of one's life? Many incidents recounted in ethnographies show that intervention by mystical beings is often a real promise or threat, that events are confidently expected that will be perceived as expressing their approval or disapproval. But the only comparative study we know of, relevant despite its very different orientation, is that by Julia S. Brown (1952). As a part of her study of how 110 societies enforce their sexual mores, she looked at each society's relative dependence on supernatural agents for punishment of each of a number of deviations. Typical of deviations for which mystical sanctions predominate are those that people in the society see as affecting only the participants or their immediate family (such as sexual relations during pregnancy or lactation) and may even be known only within the family. For sexual deviations seen locally as having broader implications for the community, mystical punishment is usually subordinate in importance to punishment by human beings, and mystical punishment may not even be mentioned in the ethnographies. Brown's results suggest a general belief that mystical beings cannot be counted on to punish deviations and are relied on only when human punishment is likely to be unavailable. They do, however, imply a very widespread readiness to perceive misfortunes that do occur as messages from mystical beings.

Some of the interpretation of events may be spontaneous; gross catastrophe might anywhere invite a supposition of divine ill will. But some interpretation depends on cultural guidance, on a sort of lexicon of the meaning of events, that everyone has learned and draws upon. The events that followed a widower's sacrifice among the Iraqw, were interpreted by such a route. But ordinary members of some societies lack a widely known lexicon, or wish to go beyond it; for them, divination may be placed in the hands of specialists. The specialty of divination is in some societies specific; a diviner does not otherwise participate (except in a lay capacity) in communicating with mystical beings. When the divining is finished, others act on the diagnosis. In many societies, on the other hand, the priest, healer, or other person who has done the divining will carry out any other shamanic activities that are indicated by the diagnosis.

Omens

Of life events that may be interpreted as messages from mystical beings, many occur in divinatory sessions, often conducted by specialists. Mystical beings are being invited to communicate by causing a seemingly random event to take one form rather than another.

For at least one foraging society of the western United States, the Crow, the ethnographer reports a complete absence of divination. Yet divination is frequently reported for foraging societies, though perhaps less regularly than for societies with other economies. Generally, it is not possible from the brief descriptions available to tell what rationale, if any, lies behind the divinatory practice or how seriously the outcome is taken.

In some cases, the divination may be entirely mechanical, falling into the traditional category of magic rather than religion. Lorna Marshall (1962), for instance, tells of the Kung San's divining by throwing leather oracle disks on pieces of skin and observing the positions in which they fall. She refers to it as a "secular" matter, evidently implying that it is more a game than a communication from mystical beings. More evidence of sensed communication with mystical beings appears in Coon's account of Ainu divination, in that prayer is mentioned as a part of the procedure:

> If he [the diviner] wishes to predict the outcome of an enterprise, or to determine the guilt or innocence of a person accused of breaking a tabu, he will take the lower jaw of a fox out of his box and place it, teeth up, on top of his head. After appropriate prayers he lets the jaw slide off his forehead onto the mat on which he is sitting. If it comes to rest teeth up, the answer is yes; if down, no. (1971, 372)

Scapulimancy is a common technique of divination, based on observing the visible pattern produced by burning the shoulder bone of an animal. It has often been assumed to be a purely magical procedure in which the diviner interprets the outcome by rules he has learned but gives no thought to why the heat has produced the particular pattern. Hallowell (1942, 44), however, after long contact with the Saulteaux in Manitoba learned that for them a spirit is considered to be involved in determining the outcome.

Communication with spirits is even clearer in an episode among the Akoa Pygmies of Zaire, described by Father Trilles (1932)—again an instance where the information could probably be obtained only after long contact with the society. When word that a troop of elephants was near reached the group Father Trilles was with, the headman wanted to know what the outcome would be if his people ventured out for the dangerous hunt. The headman prayed to certain spirits, and then in a dream was told that several of his men would be killed. The prediction did not seem to be trusted completely, for enthusiasm for the hunt continued, and the head-man invited a neighboring band to join in the hunt. The headman of the neighboring band then took over the auguries. He invoked water spirits while performing an elaborate procedure with bubbling water in a geode. The water made various spots on the ground that when dried were interpreted as predicting that five elephants would be killed along with one hunter. A further divination was performed with the addition of other objects, including a ram's bone that had been stolen from the black group with which these Pygmies had regular social relations. It was this final prediction, that eight elephants and one hunter would be killed, that conformed with the outcome. Clearly, the Pygmies did not rely completely on any one method of divination, but they regarded at least some of them as involving communication with spirits.

In more complex societies, divination sometimes occupies an impor-tant place in the daily activities. An example most fully described is provided by Evans-Pritchard's (1937) account of the Azande of southern Sudan. They rely mostly on divination that depends on the mystical power of a poison forced down the throat of a chick. A question is posed to the poison oracle about the direction of mystical influence on some future event, one direction to be indicated by the death of the chick and the opposite to be indicated by its survival. Evans-Pritchard speaks of such divination as a daily occurrence and a topic of conversation, for, he says:

> No important venture is undertaken without authorization of the poison
> oracle. In important collective undertakings, in all crises of life, in all serious
> legal disputes, in all matters strongly affecting individual welfare, in short,
> on all occasions regarded by Azande as dangerous or socially important, the
> activity is preceded by consultation of the poison oracle. (1937, 261)

Simpler and less trusted types of oracle are consulted for predictions about more trivial issues of everyday life, or as a preliminary to consulting the poison oracle; the nature of the mystical power that is tapped is not clear from Evans-Pritchard's account.

Dreams

All over the world, groups are found for which ethnographic reports mention the religious role of dreaming. We will draw on a few of them to illustrate points likely to be of general significance.

Dreams are an important source of communication with mystical beings among many Native American groups. Ridington (1971, 1988) shows it to be especially true of the peoples of the Athapascan language family, in his effort to make intelligible to Westerners the thought system of the Beaver, or Dunne-za, of British Columbia, who in this respect appear to be typical of Athapascan societies. His own experience among the Beaver, as well as the experiences there of other ethnographers, makes clear that for that society dreaming is an important source of knowledge.

Lack of appreciation of this fact may be a major reason that Westerners feel that Athapascan cultures are individualistic and give little importance to religion. Religion is, in fact, for the Beaver experienced largely through dreams, and only the rare outsider who speaks of his own dreams may begin to have access to this important part of their life.

Among the Ojibwa or Saulteaux, members of the Algonkian language family, Hallowell (1934) finds dreams similarly important, though the communications he mentions are (unlike those that Ridington reports for the Beaver) entirely benign. The guardian spirits who present themselves to boys at puberty and will serve them all their lives come in dreams. The dreams are thought of as very real experiences; Hallowell cites an instance where a description of a particular spirit as seen in a waking vision was not fully trusted until another person reported a similar description from a dream. Among the spirits that might communicate in dreams are the masters of game species, and the hunter who follows up his dream with successful action obviously strengthens general belief in the mystical value of dreams.

Another Native American society where an ethnographer has given special attention to dreaming is the Rarámuri (also known as Tarahumara), of northern Mexico, and here too "dreaming is their principal avenue of communication with beings like God and the devil, who have a substantial impact on their lives" (Merrill, 1987, 200). Sometimes there is felt to be explicit communication from the divinity, who "may simply tell dreamers what he plans to do" or may cause them to experience in a dream an event like one they will encounter in waking life. In other cases, dreams require interpretation, as they so often do in other cultures, and the exact source of the communication from mystical beings is not explicit, as far as one can tell from Merrill's account (p. 206). The Rarámuri consider the dream state to be dangerous. People are exposed there to attack by various malevolent spirits, and also to importuning by spirits of dead relatives who may wish for their company. All this is a form of communication, even if quite unwelcome.

Among the Kagwahiv of Brazilian Amazonia, shamans were believed to commune with spirits during dreams as well as during trances, and even today it is said that anyone who dreams has a little of the mystical power that shamans possess more fully (Kracke, 1987, 33-34). Farther south, among the Avá-Chiripá of eastern Paraguay, Bartolomé (1979) found dreaming to be the main channel of communication from mystical beings. At his shamanic initiation by a distinguished aged shaman, he was told that he could expect the shaman's spirit to continue postmortem instruction via dreams.

> This would be the case until I had enough "wisdom" (lightness, purity) to be able to travel in my dreams to the country of the dead where I would have access to the wisdom of other dead shamans as well as to his. The process would continue through the years until my knowledge was such that I could receive visits from . . . the sacred hummingbird, messenger of the sun. He

would give me still more wisdom until I could communicate with the "spirits of all things" (plants and animals) and have a "helper" (auxiliary spirit) who would collaborate with me. . . . When my knowledge was such that I could act as a healer, I would also employ sleep. For example, if I did not know the right treatment for a sick person, I would have to intone my chant with great sincerity, to the sound of the *mbaraká*, a present from him, before going to sleep. As I slept the treatment would be revealed to me. Should it be necessary to use herbs, the dream would tell me which ones and where they could be found. On the following day, I should go to the place indicated and if I did not find the herb immediately it would be pointed out to me by means of a *sign* of some kind, like a broken branch, or a bird sitting on the plant in question. (Bartolomé, 1979, 127)

Raymond Firth found dreaming to be an important locus of communication with mystical beings in the Polynesian community of Tikopia. A great variety of spirits were thought likely to produce dreams. Among them were malicious spirits who might take the form of relatives or friends, giving dreams that might have damaging effects if taken as helpful advice about future action. This was one important basis for Tikopian recognition of the uncertainty of dream interpretation, and other bases (universally present) lie in the ambiguity of symbolic meaning and dependence on context. Firth concludes, very wisely:

This flexibility of the dream interpretation is one of the factors in preserving the belief in dreams. If a dream makes an impression it is told to the family circle and its meaning sought. At any given time there is a certain background of social interests against which it may be set; a fishing expedition, the future of a newly-married pair, and a quarrel over the boundary of an orchard, for example. The dream is discussed in this general context, and its bearing as an omen decided. But its interpretation is dependent on human fallibility: members of the family circle may disagree regarding it. Hence when its promise as originally understood is not fulfilled, the reason is found in a false attribution. The anticipated result did not follow, it is said, because the dream really referred to another situation. (1934, 74)

The flexibility of dream interpretation also allows for the adjustment of messages to the demands of social and personal conditions. An apt example is provided by Hollan (1989) in a study of dream beliefs among the Toraja of Sulawesi (formerly Celebes). One of the men Hollan interviewed at length told him of dreaming that the spirit of his dead father seized him to bring him to the land of the dead, and of his interpreting the dream as a prediction of his own death. A specialist he consulted, however, persuaded him that it signified that his father's spirit was hungry; the sacrifice he then offered to his father apparently had considerable therapeutic value.

Dreams may themselves—at least, dreams as reported—be flexible in response to expectations established by religious customs. When James Fernandez (1972) interviewed 50 Fang men about their participation in rituals involving occasional use of a hallucinogen, he found that 40 percent of them mentioned, as a reason for their taking the drug, that a dead relative had come to them in their sleep and told them to.

The religious significance of dreaming has also been considered for a Melanesian society, the Foi of the New Guinea highlands. Weiner's account suggests that the Foi regard the entire content of dreams as messages from, or at any rate creations of, mystical beings. "The Foi say that it is ghosts who 'give' people dreams, by which they mean that they expose the soul to these oneiric apperceptions. A Foi man seeking ghostly revelation through dreams must therefore go to those places where ghosts are known to reside" (James Weiner, 1986, 117). Male prestige among the Foi is dependent on revelations obtained in dreams; so men would prepare by fasting, then go alone to a ghost-ridden spot to sleep.

Among the Nalumin, another New Guinea group, dreaming seems to be viewed as the standard route, open to everyone, for messages from mystical beings. There, "dreams are understood as a means by which ordinary people can experience (though with less accurate recall) much the same contact with the hidden world of spirits as shamans do in séances" (Bercovitch, 1989, 138-139).

Trance

Dreaming is an altered state of consciousness that everyone experiences everyday (though not necessarily remembering the experience after waking up). Dream experiences are often interpreted as communications from mystical beings. The same sort of interpretation is made of experiences in other altered states, often referred to as *trances*. The anthropologist Erika Bourguignon (1973a), searching only for trance states that are institutionalized and culturally patterned, surveyed ethnographic data on 488 societies and found them to be reported in 437, or 90 percent, of the societies. In traditional societies, the altered states were "almost without exception sacred states" (ibid., 9). Though she did not put it this way, it appears that any form of trance or altered state of consciousness may be the occasion for an experience that is interpreted as a communication from mystical beings. A more qualitative review of altered states in traditional societies has been provided by the psychologist Edward Kelly and the anthropologist Ralph Locke (1981, 27-41, 53-84). Although oriented toward the possibility that the altered states favor this-worldly psychic events, they, too, find widespread reports that altered states of consciousness induce experiences that are seen as messages from mystical beings. Another anthropologist, Felicitas D. Goodman (1988), sees religious trance as probably basic to religion in all human societies. The evidence she offers is mostly from single ethnographies that have given full attention to religious experience, and we cannot share her conviction about what would be revealed by equally full knowledge about the experiential side of religion in all other societies. But we are persuaded, as she is, that trance plays a much wider role than is suggested by the objectively oriented ethnographies that have so often been produced by Western scholars.

Trance is a term best known in psychology in accounts of hypnosis. It refers to a condition in which a person is relatively cut off from most external stimulation and from conscious memory of the past; often, after the trance, the person may be cut off also from memory of the trance experience itself. Because the term refers to an internal state whose external manifestations can be mimicked, students of hypnosis have difficulty determining in any particular instance whether a person after being subjected to trance induction is reporting actual experience or is pretending. For this and other reasons, some even doubt whether states of consciousness are indeed altered by hypnotic induction (see, e.g., Barber, 1969). We find more convincing the argument presented by Hilgard (1977) that hypnotic trance does occur, differs markedly from person to person and occasion to occasion, and is an instance of human potentiality for dissociation.

Ethnographic fieldworkers who have witnessed shamanistic behavior seem little inclined to doubt the genuineness of some trance experiences. This is especially true of the few anthropologists who have made a serious effort to be trained in shamanic skills. One is Miguel Bartolomé, whose training through dreams we have already mentioned. Another is Michael Harner (1980, 1-19), who was trained by shamans in two Amazonian societies, the Jívaro and the Conibo. Here the trance experience was initially brought about by hallucinogenic drugs, and the genuineness of an alteration of consciousness could not be doubted. Harner seems to have the conviction also of the genuineness—though in an "alternate reality"—of the supernatural figures who appeared in the trance. Larry Peters (1981) is another anthropologist who, in a very different part of the world, also sought shamanistic training. Among the Tamang of Nepal, he found a guru willing to accept him as a disciple. Here no psychedelics were used; instead, induction of trance was facilitated by meditation and the rhythmic beat of drums. Peters was less successful than Harner in attaining a high degree of trance; perhaps related to this, as source and as effect, is the fact that he did not attribute any reality to the supernatural figures encountered by his guru and perhaps by his fellow disciples. But he, too, does not seem to doubt the true alteration of state of consciousness.

Many accounts of shamanistic training and performances have been written by anthropologists who have not themselves been trained as shamans. Audrey Butt Colson (1977), for example, has reported on shamanistic training among the Akawaio of Guiana. S. M. Shirokogoroff (1935) and A. F. Anisimov (1963) wrote in great detail of shamanism among the Tungus (or Evenk), the Siberian group whose practices were the basis of the seventeenth century introduction into European culture of the very name and concept of shamanism. Such accounts tend to use a different vocabulary—of behavior rather than of experience—but they seem consistent with those of Western trainees, who are able to report on relevant experiences they themselves have had.

Accounts of their own training by both Harner and Peters portray the gaining of control over trance as a central part of learning to be a shaman, and the essence of shamanistic behavior as the controlled use of trance in helping others. The shaman, it is believed, becomes able not only to control his entry into trance but also, in local belief, to control the spirits he encounters, to gain their cooperation in benefiting, or at least ceasing to trouble, his fellows. Western observers generally recognize, as do at least some of the shamans they have studied, that practitioners sometimes simulate trance in their efforts to help their fellows and to maintain the reputations upon which their efficacy depends. A detailed account of a shamanistic trance among the Evenk, provided by Anisimov (1963, 100-105), shows the shaman as emphasizing to those present his control of spirits and his having spirit helpers who will supplement his own direct approach to higher gods during trance. The shaman dances frantically in trance, ending with collapse and foaming at the mouth. Anisimov provides no clue as to how much of the information and advice the shaman reported receiving was actual trance experience and how much was conscious fabrication.

Widespread aids to the induction of trance include rhythmic motion, loud percussion, and ingestion of psychedelic plant material. Just as in our society, these plants or their products are much used for relaxation, brief ecstasy, or dulling the sharp edge of troubles. Weston La Barre, who has devoted much of his career to the anthropological study of psychotropic drugs, asserts that "there appears to be no human society so simple in material culture as to lack some sort of mood-altering drug as an escape from the workaday world" (1980, 62).

Unlike our society, most traditional societies use these drugs for religious purposes. This is especially true of the plants that lead to hallucinations. Some of the experiences they induce are of interaction with fantastic beings, and they may be accompanied by a persuasive sense of reality and power. Some are of interaction with persons dead or distant, and the reality of interaction may simply be taken for granted, as it would be in a dream. Consumption of hallucinogens, often in the presence of the teacher or after preparation by the teacher, is in many societies (as among the Jívaro and Conibo, among whom Harner was apprenticed) an important part of training in shamanic activities. The conviction of reality that accompanies many of these experiences must contribute a great deal to belief in reality of the supernatural beings encountered in trance and of the communications with them. La Barre (1972), speculating about the origins of religion in prehistory, has argued that hallucinogenic substances must, through their influence on the experiences of shamans and prophets, have played a major role in giving rise to, and reinforcing, religious beliefs and practices. Certainly the religious use of hallucinogens is not only widespread but very ancient (La Barre, 1980, 37-92; Dobkin de Rios, 1984).

In the following sections we present some modes of communication with mystical beings that occur more readily during trance, though they can also occur in the absence of trance.

Visions

Communication with mystical beings in visions is experienced in many cultures, and in earlier chapters we have given examples of its importance in the vision quest which played a central part in the life of many Native American groups. For Africa, too, many instances of visions could be cited. Here are extracts from an account given to Fernandez by a Fang of a vision induced by ritual consumption of *eboka*, the standard hallucinogen of his society:

> When I ate *eboka* very quickly my grandfather came to me. . . . Because my grandfather was dead before I was born he asked me if I knew how I recognized him. It was through *eboka*. He then seized me by the hand and we found ourselves embarked on a grand route. . . . We came to a table in that road. There we sat and my grandfather asked me all the reasons I had eaten *eboka*. He gave me others. Then my grandfather disappeared and suddenly a white spirit appeared before me. . . . Since then I have seen nothing in *eboka*. But each time I take it I hear the spirits who give the power to play the . . . [harp]. I play what I hear from them. Only if I come into the chapel in a bad heart does *eboka* fail me. (1972, 252)

We use the term *vision* to include experiences in any of the sensory modalities; this man's later visions, he reports, were entirely of music. More often, perhaps, two or more senses contribute to a single vision, as they did in his first experience with the hallucinogen, and as they have in many of the guiding experiences young men and women have obtained in their vision quests, where what they hear may be fully as important as what they see.

Occasional reports are of visions had under conditions that have received much attention recently in our society, near-death experiences. Such visions are characteristically about the afterworld and interaction with ancestral spirits there. Even more than in our society with its strong skeptical traditions, they are often experienced as simple reality. In fact, the accounts we have read in ethnographies seem never to include any doubt on the part of the person reporting.

Instances of visions originating in the setting of a traditional culture have been described as they entered into a setting of Western psychotherapy by W. Scott MacDonald and Chester W. Oden, Jr. (1977). They report on three teenagers of Native Hawaiian background in a job training camp near Honolulu. Each had been referred for counseling because of disruptive or non-conforming behavior, and each was troubled by repeating visions of a deceased relative, visions that were apparently extremely realistic. Attempts at Western-style psychotherapy for the hallucinations were unsuccessful. In each case, the teenager was finally advised to speak at the next opportunity with the beloved relative, and each then received from the apparition a message expressing discontent with the way he or she had been behaving. In each case the outcome was great improvement in constructive behavior and cessation of the hallucination. Presumably this incident, occurring in a setting of wider-community rejection of the traditional religion of an ethnic group, is indicative of even greater constructive value of messages perceived as coming from ancestral spirits in traditional cultural settings where no one denies their mystical origin.

Shamanistic Travel

In many societies shamans are thought to travel mystically to a mystical region and communicate there with spirits. Typically, the shaman did this during a trance characterized by frenzied dancing or during pauses or apparent collapse and would return with messages pertinent to the problem that had occasioned the travel. But sometimes, as we have seen for the Avá-Chiripá of Paraguay, the travel was experienced in dreaming. Some writers have included mystical travel as a part of their definition of shamanism. This seems too restrictive, for such travel was sometimes attributed only to particularly outstanding shamans (e.g., Balikci, 1963, 381, reporting on the Netsilik Inuit), and is sometimes not mentioned in accounts of behavior patterns otherwise clearly deserving to be called shamanistic.

Spirit Possession

An especially striking form of communication with mystical beings is spirit possession, where a spirit is believed to take over control, partial or complete, of a person. Whether there is thought to be communication back and forth between person and spirit may depend on the degree of normal consciousness that the person retains. Where spirit possession is believed to be the cause of illness (considered in Chapter 7), the spirit may be thought to be controlling only the state of health, and the victim may have to depend on a healing specialist for effective communication with the invading spirit.

But spirit possession of a more positive sort involves much more varied communication from a mystical being: Everything the person does, says, and feels during the possession trance is considered to be dictated by the possessing spirit rather than by the person himself or herself; indeed, it is considered to be the spirit who is acting, not the person. Herskovits describes spirit possession as it occurs in various West African societies:

> Under possession the worshiper . . merges his identity in that of the god, losing control of his conscious faculties and knowing nothing of what he does until he comes to himself. This phenomenon, the outstanding manifestation of West African religion, is, for all its hysterical quality, by no means

undisciplined. . . . As a rule, possession comes on at some ceremony where a follower of a god is moved by the singing, dancing, and drumming of a group of which he is a member; the god "comes to his head," he loses consciousness, becomes the deity, and until his release dances or performs after the fashion of the spirit who has taken possession of him. (1941, 215)

Spirit possession seems to depend on the same human capacities that in our society permit the induction of hypnotic trance and, as a deviant adjustment of some people to their life problems, multiple personality (Bourguignon, 1989). Just as those manifestations seem to be possible only for some individuals in our society, so in other societies are there individual differences in ease of becoming possessed. But some provision for spirit possession in religious life is found in a large proportion of societies. Herskovits asserts its presence in West African societies generally (and in American derivatives, such as Haitian vodun religion). Kenneth Stewart (1946), in gathering information about spirit possession throughout North and South America, found that the belief was very widespread yet not present everywhere (and he found the same to be true of the ascription of illness to unwilling possession by ill-intentioned spirits). Bourguignon (1973a), in her survey of almost 500 societies the world over, found belief in spirit possession to be present in more than half.

Behavior of people under spirit possession has been reported in detail especially by observers of religious cults in Africa and in Haiti, Brazil, and other American countries where religious traditions of African origin are widespread. Many of the observers have sought to describe the experiences of the entranced devotees. Painful or unhappy elements are not missing, but the experiences seem predominantly of pleasurable excitement, building up at times to an ecstatic peak. The body of the devotee is often described as the horse, and the possessing spirit or god as the rider who uses the voice and body of the entranced to communicate both with that person and with the others present. Whether the entranced person remembers afterwards or is amnesic, the experience is one many devotees are glad to repeat.

Besides the positive value of the experience itself, of being possessed and acting temporarily as a mystical being, spirit possession in cult members brings other gains. Some are consciously realized and reported by the participants themselves, and some are inferred by outsiders from observation of cult behavior and its setting in the lives of the participants. One notable study that focused on these other gains (though not denying the appeal of the experience itself) was of the Shango cult in Trinidad by Walter and Frances Mischel (1958). Their observations of cult gatherings there led them to formulate six types of gain realized by members through possession trance. The first four are gains attributable to particular aspects of behavior under possession; the remaining two are attributable to more general facts about how the possession experience fits in with the person's normal life. All are worth comparing with gains people may realize from participation in other religious practices, including those of world religions.

1. The person in trance receives full attention of others in the Shango group, and is treated with awe, respect, and indulgence.

2. At times, a spirit is critical and threatening toward its host; though unpleasant, this is an opportunity for penance that may reduce guilt and anxiety.

3. Close physical interaction with the other cult members provides some gratification of sexual and aggressive interests.

4. Women often behave in a masculine manner and men in a feminine manner while possessed, and this permits for some people manifestation of tendencies ordinarily denied expression.

5. Any worrisome features of the normal everyday behavior of a possessed person can be regarded as a part of the personal characteristics that lead up to possession and thus may be justified both to the self and to others.

6. Solution of problems in the individual's life can be made by the possessing spirit, relieving the conscious individual of responsibility for making difficult decisions.

What spirit possession does for people beyond the intrinsic value of the experience itself can also be considered by way of looking objectively at its circumstances or correlates. This has been done in a systematic cross-cultural study of societies in sub-Saharan Africa. Lenora Greenbaum (1973b) looked at 114 societies there for which data permitted a judgment of presence versus absence of possession trance, and found its presence to be positively correlated with indices of social complexity. Specifically, possession trance was found most commonly in societies that had hereditary social classes and in societies that had slavery. In a more detailed study of a much smaller sample within the same region, she found possession trance to be correlated also with rigidity of social structure, with a denial of the individual's "freedom for achievement and personal control over his daily life activities."

> The rationale is that, under rigid systems, simple decision-making is fraught with danger from internal and external social controls. Possession trance relieves the individual of personal responsibility in the decision-making process by temporarily changing the identity of a human being into that of a spirit. The medium, through whom the spirit speaks, and the petitioner, following the spirit's dictates, can thus solve the problem of meeting crucial daily life decisions without either intruding personally into the established order of things. (1973a, 59)

Although Greenbaum refers here only to possession of a spirit medium, her reasoning would apply equally well to possession of a layperson. Her cross-cultural study thus supports the importance of the sixth of the gains outlined by Mischel and Mischel, escape from responsibility for decision making.

Similar interpretation of what a person stands to gain from spirit possession has been made in much broader cross-cultural research by

I. M. Lewis (1966, 1989), who sets it more directly in a context of everyday social relations. He began with intensive study of a single society, the nomadic Somali, and then checked the general applicability of his findings by comparing ethnographic reports from other societies. His general approach was, as he points out, that of epidemiology: Looking at internal differences within a society, he asked in what segments of the population the phenomenon commonly occurred and where it was absent or rare. Concentrating on spirit possession as a presumed source of illness, he found its occurrence among Somali to be especially frequent in married women. Marriage brings severe subordination and deprivation to Somali women; possession illness, for which a woman may find company and support in cult groups, permits some freedom in efforts to alleviate these conditions. Though many a husband shows clear awareness that a wife is using her presumed possession to claim privileges he does not consider justified, he is likely to grant these privileges to some extent under the pressure of the cult group and the religious rationale it presents. The cult group contributes to therapy by encouraging development of the possession into an ecstatic form, which in itself provides new gratification.

The conclusion of Lewis's epidemiological research is supported by a further finding, that the rare men who experience spirit possession are individuals who in their own way are deprived—by low social status or by general maladjustment. Lewis finds that an epidemiological approach to existing ethnographies, both in Africa and elsewhere, leads to the same outcome. No matter in what continent, nor whether the powerful men support an indigenous religion or one of the world religions, any separate religion of women and subordinate males is likely to share the general pattern Lewis found among the Somali, including a dependence on spirit possession to justify and forward rebellious attitudes.

Communication with a mystical being sometimes occurs through gradual transformation—something like progressive possession but apparently thought of as a person's becoming much more thoroughly a mystical being. This is the case of the transformation of individuals into Wechugas, mystical Person Eaters, among the northern Athapascans of Canada. Ridington (1976) heard of only one case among the Beaver where the transformation was believed to have progressed to the point of cannibalism, but he knew people who were believed to have begun the gradual transformation and to have been cured, like the old man whose rescue by his young daughter we discussed in Chapter 2.

Ridington found people took great care, as did their friends on their behalf, to prevent transformation. The threat to each person was of transformation into the mystical animal that was otherwise his personal friend and source of his mystical power. Any event that might strengthen this mystical power could threaten to initiate the transformation. Thus, when Ridington turned his car radio on, one of his passengers quickly turned it off; the reason was that another of the passengers had a kind of power such that the twang of guitar strings was likely to start a process of transformation to the monster whence came his power. As discussed in Chapter 6, on wizardry, in many societies individuals are believed to undergo transformation back and forth, especially at night, between normal human and mystical form and power.

In a specific type of spirit possession called *spirit mediumship*, the spirit seems to take over the voice of the possessed person, or seems in disembodied form to speak in another voice that is either heard by others who are present or is reported by the medium. These are familiar phenomena of the spiritualist séance in our own society, and they are found in many foraging societies. They are often a part of the specialized performance of shamans, found in societies of diverse economy as well as in purely foraging societies. A particular form of shamanistic activity, called *conjuring* by anthropologists, is especially characteristic of some North American foragers.

Conjuring has been most fully described by Hallowell (1942), who observed it at various times during his fieldwork with the Saulteaux, an Ojibwa group in Manitoba. A séance is arranged on plea to a conjurer by an individual who needs his services. A fee is settled on, a special tent or hut is erected, and word of the plan is spread. As dark approaches, the spectators gather around the hut; the conjurer arrives after having purified himself by bathing. The person who requested the séance will probably distribute tobacco among the spectators, for their smoking is believed to encourage the approach of the spirits to the hut. The conjurer is considered to be instrumental in bringing various of his patrons or guardian spirits to the hut. The hut may shake as soon as the conjurer enters it; if not, it shakes as the session proceeds, and the arrival of each spirit is likely to be announced by a thud. Among the Saulteaux, Great Turtle is the being that appears first and serves as intermediary for the other animal spirits, who identify themselves by singing their own distinctive songs. There are moments of joking and repartee, much of which is between spectators and spirits. The more serious communications are in response to queries put to the spirits by the person who arranged the séance or by other spectators. They may concern diagnoses and prognoses of illness, the location of an object that has been lost, the present whereabouts of someone who is away on a trip, or the outcome of proposed ventures.

Conjuring was especially common in the tribes that, like the Saulteaux, spoke Algonkian languages, but occurred in many other foraging societies of North America as well. Some séances conducted by shamans in Siberian tribes (described, e.g., by Anisimov, 1963) were very similar to those of the North American conjuring hut, suggesting a common historical origin in the distant past. Among tribes on the North American Plains, warfare provided a special incentive to elaborate techniques for foretelling the future. Conjuring there differed in various details from that of the Saulteaux. Often the site was part of a dwelling, curtained off and kept dark. The helpers of the conjurer were often ghosts rather than animal spirits. The conjurer sometimes displayed his powers by fantastic tricks, such as getting free after being tied up at the beginning of the session.

SUMMARY

People extend to mystical figures the sense of direct communication that they experience daily with fellow human beings. Like communication with people, communication with mystical beings may be oriented more toward communion for its own sake or more toward communication back and forth for the sake of benefit to the human or mystical figure or both. The latter sort has lent itself more to observation and report. Either sort may be carried out by a person on his or her own or through a specialist. Specialist activities can be usefully classified into shamanic (in which the specialist, often in trance, is believed to be communicating directly with mystical beings) and priestly (in which communication is by performance of ritual).

Communication between person and mystical being is generally thought to occur in both directions. Certain modes of communication, however, stress the one direction or the other. Communication toward mystical beings is stressed in prayers and offerings and in sacrifice. Communication from mystical beings is stressed in the interpretation of life events, omens, dreams, and experiences in trance, vision, and shamanistic travel. The extreme of communication from mystical beings is seen in spirit possession and mediumship, where the mystical figure seems to take direct control of a person's speech and gestures.

The role that specific modes of communication play in the life of various traditional peoples is indicated by fieldwork in a number of societies.

Chapter 6

Wizardry

That mystical power can be used by people to harm their fellows is an idea found almost everywhere. Among the terms that have been applied— black magic, evil eye, witchcraft, and sorcery—the first two have a restricted meaning. Witchcraft and sorcery are more general and are often used interchangeably. However, in recent decades, they, too, have been given more specific meanings by anthropologists. For a more general term, then, we follow Middleton and Winter (1963) and Crawford (1967) in choosing *wizardry*.

Wizardry often involves no mystical beings—just the mystical power of the individual wizard or the automatic effects of magical skills he or she exercises. In this case it falls outside the narrow definition some give to religion as necessarily involving supernatural beings and into the category of magic. But wizardry may have much the same role in the life of society and the life of the individual when spirits are involved and when they are not. Our broader definition of religion, based on mystical power regardless of whether mystical entities are involved, makes it appropriate, of course, to consider wizardry as a whole, whatever the particular pattern of beliefs in which it is set.

Wizardry involves beliefs about how one person may bring harm to another and about how the victim may hope to counter or neutralize the potential damage. It may also involve overt acts, practices rather than mere beliefs—a wizard may actually take steps to harm someone by mystical means. Someone who feels he is a victim may take action against the supposed wizard, either in ways that depend on mystical processes or in ordinary ways such as killing the wizard or initiating legal proceedings. Beliefs and practices may not go hand in hand; for example, in some societies where belief in wizardry is universal and detailed, the anthropological fieldworker may come to doubt whether any of the supposed wizards ever perform any of the acts attributed to them. The psychological and social meaning of wizardry for the persons accused of wizardry, moreover, is likely to be very different from its meaning for the actual or potential victims of wizardry. So we will try to be explicit about belief versus practice and about wizard versus victim or general public.

The basic similarity of wizardry all over the world is a major finding of anthropological fieldwork, but so too is the variation in significant details. We are led to consider wizardry region by region, selecting some of the best studied cases for each broad region, along with some that have special features we will mention for comparison. We will try to indicate not only the form wizardry takes but also something of its role in the general life of the society.

SUB-SAHARAN AFRICA

Sub-Saharan Africa provides a good starting point for a survey of wizardry. It was there, in southern Sudan, that the British anthropologist Edward Evans-Pritchard (1937) began in the 1920s his detailed study of wizardry among the Azande that has widely influenced the way anthropologists classify and label the varieties of wizardry. His work was followed, too, by studies focused on wizardry in many other African societies (in speaking of Africa, we will ordinarily be referring only to regions south of the Sahara), so that pertinent information is more thorough for Africa than for any other region of the world. It is based on fieldwork done mostly from the 1920s through the 1940s. Colonial administrators and Christian missionaries had for some decades attempted to destroy beliefs and practices of wizardry. The descriptions refer to a combination of the indigenous customs that had preceded attempts at interference, as they could be learned about by retrospective accounts, and the very lively survival or modification of some features under outside pressures.

Azande

Wizardry is of prime importance in Zande explanation of events. For a Zande, Evans-Pritchard reports, "Almost every happening which is harmful to him is due to the evil disposition of someone else" (1937, 53). In particular, death is almost always attributed to wizardry; where there is an obvious cause, such as an enemy spear or the claws of a lion, the concatenation of circumstances that led to the fatality is still attributed to wizardry.

Evans-Pritchard found among the Azande two pertinent sets of belief, and he used for them English words that had not previously had such sharply distinguished meaning. One set of beliefs pertained to an inborn capacity and propensity for evil making, needing for its exercise only thought—perhaps unconscious—and no equipment or actions; this he termed *witchcraft*. The other set of beliefs pertained to a person's manipulation of materials or words in order to produce an evil effect, and this he termed *sorcery*. As other anthropologists subsequently made intensive studies in other societies, it turned out that a distinction similar to that of the Azande is made in some other places, but by no means all. Very different distinctions among types of wizardry are made in some societies, and in some, no comparable distinction is to be found. To reduce confusion, we favor the more general *wizardry*. When we speak of witchcraft and sorcery, it is with the intention of being more specific, using the words in a sense close to that given them by Evans-Pritchard, preserving the distinction between producing evil without and with the use of techniques or materials (but not implying detailed similarity to the Zande concepts).

Among the Azande, witchcraft is the most common explanation for misfortune, readily offered both by the victim and by his or her fellows. Sorcery, on the other hand, is appealed to more on the basis of specific evidence (by Zande standards of evidence, of course). There is reluctance to attribute misfortune solely to other sources recognized by the Azande, such as "incompetence, breach of a taboo, or failure to observe a moral rule" (1937, 64). Expectation of witchcraft is so general, indeed, that it is considered in advance as a potential danger in connection with any plan, major or minor, and possible witchcraft is mentioned in conversation many times a day.

How do the Azande conceive of witchcraft? What processes do they believe to be involved? Evans-Pritchard devoted much effort to seeking answers to these questions. Part of the inquiry was simple. Azande agree that witchcraft is an inherited physical substance in the abdomen of some persons, active only at times (and not necessarily active at all). Determining the details, however, was a difficult search, for the Azande do not have clear and consistent theories they can put into words. Their conception of witchcraft had to be inferred from diverse items of behavior and from their answers to specific questions they were evidently not used to considering. Though witchcraft is said to be hereditary, men inheriting it from the male line and women from the female line, the implications of this view are not pursued consistently. And there is little interest in general identification of the persons who have witchcraft; instead, interest focuses on which person's witchcraft is active at a particular time, toward a particular victim.

Witchcraft is sometimes taken to operate impersonally, its spirit or essence leaving the witch's body. But witches are more generally thought to attack their victims personally. Their spirit makes repeated visits to the victim and eats a bit of some vital organ, eventually bringing about death. Azande say that witches perform their evil acts consciously and intentionally. Yet, when people are themselves identified as witches (as most Azande eventually are; see pp. 118–119), they presumably have no awareness of the evil acts convincingly ascribed to them. If they cannot persuade themselves the accusation is mistaken, they seem to consider themselves exceptions to the general rule of awareness.

The Azande have a number of other beliefs about witches, not entirely consistent with these more basic beliefs. Witches are sometimes thought to be malevolent persons rather than ordinary people with an inborn substance that is temporarily activated. They are sometimes held to form a brotherhood, engaging in nocturnal expeditions. They are said to use an ointment that makes them invisible on these expeditions. These are all, presumably, beliefs held by people who do not consider themselves possible witches. Evans-Pritchard never had an opportunity to hear anyone confess to witchcraft or to learn what beliefs might be held by those—if they exist—who believe themselves to be witches.

Disruption of anyone's plans by witchcraft is thought so likely that divination is regularly used as a help in planning. If the outcome of the divination indicates that a trip today will be frustrated by witchcraft, it will be postponed until a day on which divination indicates witchcraft will not interfere.

Divination is also resorted to when misfortune has occurred. It is used to identify any witch who may have been responsible and thus permit punishment or an attempt to make the witch desist. The various techniques of divination often yield contradictory outcomes; the trust placed in them depends on the reputation of the technique and of its practitioner and on the social status of the practitioner or his employer (divination performed at the direction of the king cannot be challenged). If the misfortune is a serious illness, the person identified as the source of witchcraft is confronted with the accusation and usually promises, while denying any knowledge of being the source, to halt any witchcraft that may have been proceeding from him or her. The fact that witchcraft may be unconscious and might be in anyone makes such a response, despite its apparent acceptance of possible responsibility, not excessively threatening to the supposed witch. If, however, the misfortune is of a kind that cannot be undone or stopped, an already fatal illness, for instance, the situation of the accused witch is more perilous. In pre-colonial days, heavy reparations might be exacted, and the witch might even be killed. At the time of the fieldwork, the witch became the object of vengeance sorcery arranged for by the relatives of the deceased (p. 544).

Sorcery techniques among the Azande combine a variety of material substances with verbal spells, and they are said to be used for a variety of evil purposes. (Similar and even identical techniques can also be used for good purposes, such as countering the evil effects of witchcraft; they are then not regarded as sorcery, but as good magic.) A person convicted of sorcery is likely to be treated more severely than one convicted of witchcraft, perhaps because deliberate intention is necessarily involved. But conviction must ordinarily depend on divination rather than on direct evidence, for sorcery is held to be conducted strictly in private. Evans-Pritchard was even led to doubt whether sorcery is ever actually practiced, though good magic is common. Good magic is practiced to some extent by all adults, but especially by male specialists.

Other Sub-Saharan Groups

Inspired by Evans-Pritchard's example, a number of anthropologists, during the succeeding decades of colonial rule, studied wizardry in other African societies. In some, wizardry is obviously important and had been described at length even before Evans-Pritchard's work. Further, it has continued to appear in detailed studies of societies all over sub-Saharan Africa on into the period of national independence. In some societies, general concern with wizardry was immediately apparent to the researcher; in others, only after an extended period of study was the importance of wizardry perceived. But in no African society, except perhaps among Pygmies, does a belief in wizardry seem to be absent or completely trivial.

Almost everywhere, different categories of wizardry are recognized; rarely, if ever, are the categories exactly those portrayed by Evans-Pritchard for the Azande. Witchcraft, for example, is often said to be inborn in most witches, but acquired by some through training. Witchcraft is not often described elsewhere as an anatomical feature of the body, recognizable on autopsy; but it is, however, among the Ibo of Nigeria (Jones, 1970, 324), the Nyakyusa of Tanzania (Wilson, 1951b, 308), and the Tiv of central Sudan (Bohannon, 1958).

If the essence of witchcraft belief is the possibility of injury by malice alone, with no assistance from materials, verbal spells, or other behavior, it is found almost everywhere in sub-Saharan Africa but varies greatly in importance. The same is true of sorcery, involving the deliberate use of medicines or spells. Sometimes, if both forms of wizardry are present, one form is more important, sometimes the other, or they may be assigned different roles. The Lugbara, for instance, believe that witchcraft rarely kills anyone but that sorcery often kills (Middleton, 1963a, 269). Either or both, moreover, may predominate over other ways of explaining illness or death—the influence of ancestral spirits, especially—or may be less conspicuous. Among the Gisu of Uganda, for example, all deaths are attributed to wizardry, though some say the ancestors must give their consent (La Fontaine, 1963, 189).

Societies differ, too, in the outcomes ascribed to wizardry. Sometimes human sickness and death are the only misfortunes mentioned. At the other extreme are the Wambugwe of Tanzania (Gray, 1963, 144–157), who depend on the wizardry and good magic of the chief for success in competition with rival chiefdoms, in bringing rain at the right time in their own region, and in carrying locust plagues and cattle diseases to their rivals.

How wizards are believed to bring harm varies widely. In general, the procedures attributed to sorcerers are ones that persons could actually perform, though it is uncertain how many actually do so. Materials used include animal parts, exuviae from the intended victim (hair, nail parings, excrement), and various artifacts and plant products. In Nigeria, Yakö wizards depended especially on materials associated with evil spirits, whose assistance could thus be enlisted (Forde, 1964, 227). The materials may be planted in or near the victim's dwelling, or merely stirred or looked at to the accompaniment of a verbal spell. Such procedures are sometimes attributed not only to mere sorcerers but also to wizards whose powers are believed to include those of witchcraft.

A witch may need only to wish evil in order to expect it to happen. But, in many African societies, witches are also believed to engage in a great many activities that, unlike mere wishing, seem to us improbable or impossible. In southern Africa the Thonga believe a witch leaves its body at night, acts alone or with other witches, and when awake may have no memory of what has happened (Junod, 1962). In some societies, witches are at times believed to kill a victim by gradual eating away of his or her internal organs, at other times by eating the victim's reflection or shadow (Ardener, 1970, 145). They are often believed to eat human corpses, perhaps during nighttime meetings with fellow witches, and to wander about at night and engage in naked dancing and various obscene acts. Incest and killing of a close relative are often believed to be requirements for full membership in the witchcraft fraternity. Many of these acts are the reverse of normal human behavior, and witches are sometimes portrayed more literally as inverted physically—walking at night on their hands, feet high in the air—and inverted morally, the incarnation of evil. Unlike the devil, who is given this role in Western tradition, the witch, who is pure evil, may in many societies be any of one's relatives, friends, or neighbors.

Impossible speed is sometimes attributed to the nocturnal movements of witches; in more than one society, it is said to be attained by riding on hyenas. Other animals, too, often enter into witchcraft beliefs. A witch may be thought to operate through a special animal, either by transformation into that animal or by owning the animal and ordering it to perform mystical acts—as do the were-animals described by Ruel (1970) for the Banyang of West Cameroon.

Sorcerers are less likely than witches to be considered totally evil, because they are merely doing with magical acts what might be done ordinarily by any person who has been sufficiently angered to violate usual norms of restraint on aggression. On the other hand, though, the element of voluntary action in the sorcerer's conduct leads sometimes, as among the Azande, to more blame than is placed on a witch.

In some societies, a conspicuous reaction to people suspected of wizardry consists of protective measures that have a great impact on the general character of social relations. In Zaire, among the Amba (Winter, 1963, 290–291), a family may move to another village in an effort to escape dangerous neighbors. Gisu avoid walking alone at night; company protects them against wizards while also reducing the chance they will themselves be suspected of wizardly wanderings (La Fontaine, 1963, 198). In South Africa, the Tswanas' main protective device is to have a specialist make tiny cuts on all the bodily joints and rub in a magic salve, not only to protect the person but to reflect the attack back upon the sorcerer (Schapera, 1952, 46). Among the Wambugwe, who believe daytime wizards operate by casting an evil eye on the food one is eating, extreme privacy is observed for meals. Each family eats alone, with no visitors, in their house well separated from all other houses (Gray, 1963, 162–165). Among the South African Thonga studied early in this century by Junod (1962, 535), it was reported that recent increases in wizardry had led families to build their huts in isolation rather than in compact villages. Similar scattering of dwellings to distance each family from possible wizards is reported for the

Bakweri and Kpe of Cameroon (Ardener, 1970, 145; 1956, 51) and for the Lovedu of the Transvaal (Krige & Krige, 1943, 259).

In some societies, when a particular person is suspected of wizardry (having perhaps been identified with the help of a diviner), the victim will approach the wizard and ask him or her to desist. As is said among the Lugbara (Middleton, 1963a, 265), the victim may be partly to blame, because he or she in the past may have been rude and insolent to the suspected bewitcher, and a polite approach may help remove the motivation. Among the Lovedu (Krige & Krige, 1943, 259), the approach to the suspect was less direct: Without naming anyone, the victim would shout loud complaints or threats.

When a person or family become persuaded they are victims of a particular wizard—again, very likely after consulting a diviner who may have confirmed their suspicions—reaction in other societies may be stronger. Rather than approaching the wizard, the victims may inform relatives and friends about their suspicions and gain support for action, if power relations within the community make it feasible. In precolonial days, the local legal system might deal with the case; in later years, a decision might be reached more informally. If the community agreed on identifying a wizard, the wizard might be severely punished. Sometimes an ordeal was a final part of the decision process. The ordeal was often cruel in itself (taking poison, for instance) and likely to be damaging even to the lucky person for whom the outcome was a finding of innocence. Conviction in some instances might lead to requirement of reparation to the victim or to expulsion; in former times, expulsion sometimes took the form of being sold into slavery (Goody, 1970, 214). More often, however, the convicted wizard was killed. Among the Bakweri of West Cameroon, execution of wizards was so regular a part of life that each village had its own hanging tree (Ardener, 1956, 105). The methods of execution were in many societies extremely cruel, as though the degree of punishment should be proportional to the severity of the crime.

The consequences of being considered a wizard are not everywhere, though, uniformly bad. The power of the wizard may be thought capable of being turned to clearly good purposes as well, so in some societies the wizard is in demand as a diviner or as a healer. The evil power may itself, moreover, be put to uses considered socially desirable even if at a cost to someone. A sorcerer may be employed, for instance, for magical attack on a witch. Or, as already mentioned, the wizardry of a group's leader may be part of a sort of psychic warfare against other groups. For a family head, wizardry may be seen as a valuable contribution to his ability to protect family members against magical attack by others (Goody, 1970, 212). Within the larger local group, an acknowledged wizard may gain real social power because of everyone's fear of his or her mystical power. Ethnographies include reports that some individuals welcome a reputation for wizardry. They may be walking a knife-edge path between power and disaster, but the choice of such a path is not unlike the choices some adventurous people among us make in sports, in business, or in crime.

Periodically, in many African societies, fears of wizardry seem to become so prevalent and so strong that a social movement arises directed at total elimination of wizardry. These "witch-cleansing" movements have been observed by Westerners during and after the colonial period, but oral tradition suggests they also occurred earlier (Willis, 1970). They involve specific rituals to identify wizards and make them confess, and medicine administered to the entire community. The medicine is generally "credited with the dual power of protecting the innocent against mystical attack and killing any who attempt to revert to their evil ways" (Willis, 1970, 131). The relief experienced by the community seems never to be more than temporary; new cleansing movements arise on the average about every ten years in parts of Central Africa, according to Willis. This recurrence suggests strongly that the conditions of ordinary life in these societies create a need to believe in wizardry. To members of the societies, the confessions occurring during the cleansing procedure confirm the truth of the fantastic beliefs; to the outsider, they suggest that the fantastic beliefs do serve in some compelling ways to satisfy the needs of individuals or of the group as a whole. What those needs may be, we consider in the latter part of this chapter.

NORTH AMERICA

Navaho

The North American people whose wizardry seems to have been the most intensively studied are the Navaho, who live in Arizona and New Mexico. Clyde Kluckhohn (1962), in the course of fieldwork conducted for 20 years up to 1941, gave special attention to wizardry. He found the Navaho distinguished among four major categories of wizardry. All would fall in Evans-Pritchard's category of sorcery, as all are believed to involve the use of materials or verbal spells or both. Some of Kluckhohn's informants mentioned other forms of wizardry, dependent only upon mystical power in the person or in the outside world, but such witchcraft (as Evans-Pritchard might have called it) was clearly not the common Navaho pattern, and it seems possibly to have resulted from outside contact.

The types of Navaho sorcery differ from each other in several ways. For example, the materials are supposed to vary: Exuviae of the victim are used in one type, plants in another; in a third, powder made from corpses; in the fourth category, any of a number of small objects or particles are magically shot into the victim. The types vary as well in the importance of verbal spells. They also differ to some extent in the usual age and sex of the supposed participants, and in the particular kinds of evil they seek to encompass. But all require training or initiation, and at the cost of killing a near relative, preferably a sibling. All but one type involve nocturnal meetings, a sort of witches' sabbath; almost as frequent is mention of incest. In some, wizards are believed to travel at night at great speed, dressed in the skins of wolves, coyotes, bears, or other wild animal.

As in Africa, the beliefs about what wizards do are a compound of the possible and the impossible. Kluckhohn reports abundant evidence that these beliefs are held widely and seriously among the Navaho; protective measures are common, and accusations of sorcery are made, sometimes leading to killing the accused. But concern with sorcery appears to be less ubiquitous than in many African societies. Kluckhohn reports that of more than a thousand cases of illness and how it was interpreted, in his records, wizardry was blamed in only eight instances (1962, 54); though he assumes such an interpretation was sometimes concealed from him, it is doubtful that wizardry was the usual interpretation of illness. In a group of 500 living Navaho, only 19 were known ever to have been accused in gossip; in 30 years, this group had seen only six public accusations and only two persons had been killed as sorcerers. Do acts of sorcery actually occur? Kluckhohn's judgment is, though without conclusive evidence, that at least some people attempt to practice some types of sorcery.

Other North American Groups

To the south of Navaho country live the Western Apache; their languages are of the same Athabascan family, and the two peoples may have had a common origin many centuries before or during a southward migration from what is now western Canada. The Western Apache have also been studied by an anthropologist who gave special attention to wizardry and to religion in general, Keith Basso (1969). There are differences in emphasis: The Western Apache apparently make less of initiation into wizardry and more of specific training in techniques, for instance, and less of animal disguise. Yet the general picture of wizardry is similar—many of the same techniques for harming others and for warding off harm, similar ideas about the antisocial behavior of wizards in their nocturnal gatherings, similar patterns of suspicion and accusation and of retaliation against wizards.

Rather different beliefs about wizardry were found by Beatrice Whiting (1950) among the Harney Valley Paiute of Oregon, in fieldwork done from 1936 to 1938. Possession of general mystical power was conspicuous in Paiute beliefs, and wizardry was believed to depend on power conferred by spirit helpers in dreams. The wizard brought evil on his victim either by direct action of his thoughts or by calling on his spirit helper. The beliefs were in these respects close to what Evans-Pritchard called witchcraft. The Paiute did not, however, regard wizardry powers as inborn, though Whiting's data showed such powers to run in families, probably because young people were encouraged to dream of acquiring powers like those claimed by their parents. Illness attributed to wizardry also was believed to involve, at least sometimes, intrusion of alien objects into the victim, and in this respect Paiute beliefs, like those of the Navaho and Western Apache, resembled Evans-Pritchard's category of sorcery. As among the Navaho and Western Apache, wizardry did not appear to be the most frequent explanation of illness for the Paiute. Competing with it were the idea of deterioration of the blood, of being made ill by a ghost, or of suffering from withdrawal of one's own mystical powers by the spirit helper who had given them. Whiting learned that at least 7 percent of the community she studied had at some time been accused of wizardry. These accusations played an important part in social relations in the community.

Although considered more briefly in many general ethnographies for other North American tribes, wizardry seems to be present almost everywhere. For some societies where it is not reported, its presence in closely related societies gives grounds to suspect that it is present there too but not conspicuous enough to have come to the ethnographer's attention. There is certainly variation in the importance of wizardry. In some societies it seems to be more important than among the Navaho, Western Apache, or Paiute. Of the Cochiti Pueblo, for instance, Fox (1964) says that while wizardry is blamed only for illness of sudden onset, not for accidents or slowly developing illness, practically everyone is suspected at some time, by someone, of wizardry. And in some societies almost all illness is blamed on wizardry.

Two features are especially common in the wizardry beliefs of groups in what is now the United States and Canada. One is the stress on guardian spirits as the source of the power exerted by the wizard. The other is the idea that power gained from one's guardian spirit may be exerted either for good or for evil. Shamans, then—people normally looked to for beneficent application of mystical power to the diagnosis and healing of illness—are also potentially to be feared for possible wizardly misuse of the power.

Further south in North America and in Central America, wizardry beliefs are described in many ethnographies. In some instances, details are similar enough to southern European beliefs—for example, ascribing the wizard's malevolence and power to a compact with the devil (Saler, 1964)—so that European influence through recent centuries is clear. On the other hand, many of the details are similar to features found in more remote parts of the world and serve to confirm the universality of tendencies expressed in wizardry. However distant their origin, the traditions remain strong in many places. In one community, in the Mexican state of Chiapas, for instance, the ethnographer reports that in the year for which information was available, a man was killed as a witch about every two months. After each killing, the community would quickly hold an informal trial of the killer to reach a consensus about the justification for the killing; if he was exonerated, the police were able to learn nothing about the killing, which remained officially an unexplained death (Nash, 1961).

SOUTH AMERICA

In South America, as in North America, wizardry is an important feature of the indigenous cultures. In the Inca empire, not only was a man convicted of causing death by sorcery subject to execution but all his descendants were also killed (Kendall, 1973, 94). Recent ethnographies indicate the seriousness with which wizardry beliefs are still taken in modern times.

Rivière (1970) shows for two societies (the Trio of the Brazil-Surinam frontier and the Shavante of central Brazil) that wizardry beliefs are involved in the basic structure of the community or of intercommunity relations. Among the Trio, wizards are considered to attack members of other villages, not of their own. Fear of wizardry is a reason given for locating villages far apart from each other and for avoiding contact; yet, when there is occasion for contact, the same fear motivates outward cordiality and the offering of hospitality. Among the Shavante, wizardry is feared within the community; accusations of wizardry, and attempts to practice it, are a tool of political action, of the struggle among local factions for power and prestige. In both societies, wizardry is a common explanation of death, and death is considered an appropriate punishment for wizardry—though power differences among Shavante factions influence whether the punishment occurs, and the Trio are satisfied with revenge wizardry, which is considered responsible for the next death that occurs in the village of the enemy.

Equally serious is the attitude of the Mehinaku of central Brazil to wizardry. When a death is confidently attributed to the wizardry of a particular man, he is exposed to the possibility of being ambushed and killed. Gregor (1977, 205–209) reported four such killings in 80 years in the village he studied.

An intimate relation between wizardry and general view of the world is seen in another group of forest dwellers, the Jívaro of Amazonian Ecuador (Harner, 1973). Wizardry depends on spirit helpers, which have a semi-physical form as small objects in the body. They are part of the unseen world that is held to be more real than the world of ordinary experience. Hallucinogenic drugs give access to the unseen world, and one becomes a wizard by ingesting them for this purpose, by being provided with spirit helpers by a person already endowed with them, and then by abstaining from sexual intercourse for a period of months. Essentially the same procedure is required to become either a healer or a wizard; the outcome depends on whether initiation is by one who is primarily a healer or a wizard and on the initiate's own choices and self-control. A healer can also harm, as in many other societies, but a wizard's power is restricted to harming. The power of both healer and wizard weakens in time, and renewed contact with the unseen world, facilitated by hallucinogens, is necessary.

OCEANIA

From Oceania—Melanesia in particular—came one of the first detailed accounts by a modern anthropologist of wizardry as it appeared in the life of a preliterate society little touched by contact with the outside world. In

1927–28, Reo Fortune studied the Dobuans, residents of islands off New Guinea, just south of the Trobriand Islands where Malinowski had worked less than two decades earlier. Fortune found wizardry so important that in the title of his book he characterized the people as "sorcerers of Dobu" (1932).

Sorcery was practiced by the men of Dobu. Fortune was convinced that its actual practice was widespread, and serious belief in it—with consequent fear—universal. One basic method was to chant a verbal spell into some material object and then place that object where the intended victim would come into contact with it. In another method, the sorcerer obtained hair, nail parings, or other exuviae of his victim and chanted a spell over them. The spells were specific to each disease traditionally recognized by the Dobuans; each man owned a few spells, and their distribution was widely known or at least rumored. All sickness was attributed to sorcery, except for the epidemics introduced by outsiders in recent decades. Accidents, on the other hand, were attributed to witchcraft, believed to be practiced by women. The belief was that a woman, during sleep, traveled in spirit to seize the soul of her victim; whether any women in fact believed they engaged in witchcraft, Fortune did not report. The fear of wizardry was heightened by fear of poisoning, and some of the same precautions were prompted by both. The paranoid character of social relations in Dobu was confirmed by the reputation of Dobuans among neighboring peoples, and by Malinowski's report (in his introduction to Fortune's book) of his earlier experience with Dobuan visitors to the Trobriands.

A half-century later, Morren (1986) has described wizardry fear in a Melanesian society remote from the Dobuans—the Miyanmin of the West Sepik region, inland in Papua New Guinea. Here, sickness has other sources too, and if not fatal, may be ascribed only to taboo violation, menstrual blood, or worms. But all deaths are attributed to wizardry— some to a form of sorcery believed to be practiced by a neighboring tribe, some to sorcery the Miyanmin believe they can perform themselves with the aid of ancestral spirits. Funeral ceremonies are an occasion for accusation and violence, sometimes physical as well as verbal, for the death is confidently believed to have been brought about by an enemy.

In the years between the fieldwork of Fortune and Morren, many other anthropologists have studied Melanesian communities—in recent decades the prime region for access to societies within a few years of their first contact with the literate world. Repeatedly, wizardry emerges as a significant element in Melanesian cultures, though varying in its degree of dominance. Among the Kwaio of the Solomon Islands, for example, Keesing (1982, 52) reports little concern about wizardry despite belief in it; the Kwaio eat together at feasts and do not seem worried about their exuviae. For another people of the Solomon Islands, on the other hand, Hogbin reports that all deaths except those of young children are ascribed to wizardry, and that anyone who becomes ill "takes for granted that he has been bewitched" (1964, 51), suggesting a degree of concern similar to that of the Dobuans or the Miyanmin. The Fore of the New Guinea highlands are an intermediate example. They attribute about 50 percent of deaths to sorcery. This attribution is, however, very persistent: Lindenbaum (1979) found their major cause of death (*kuru*) confidently ascribed to sorcery long after medical research on the site had clearly established it as a neural disease transmitted by cannibalism.

In many New Guinea communities, belief in sorcery plays an important part in political competition. Power as a sorcerer is one of the attributes admired and feared in the "big men" of the community, so that reputation for sorcery is sometimes sought rather than avoided by would-be leaders (cf. various papers in Berndt & Lawrence, 1971, and in Stephen, 1987b).

Other parts of Oceania vary much more widely in the importance of wizardry. Some local groups among the Murngin of Australia ascribe all deaths and sicknesses, as well as some other misfortunes, to wizardry (Warner, 1958, 193). At the other extreme, Spiro (1952) seems to imply a complete absence of wizardry belief among the Ifaluk, a Micronesian people who live on a small atoll in the Caroline Islands, remote from any other community.

THE SETTING AND MEANING OF WIZARDRY

For other aspects of religion, many anthropologists are content to report as accurately as possible the beliefs and practices of the society they are studying. For wizardry, often reports are accompanied by special attempts to explain or understand. Whatever the reasons for this, the result has been a great variety of theories about wizardry. A theory often seems to be presented as a candidate for acceptance as an exclusive single theory about wizardry (or about magic, which includes similar procedures not aimed at harming people). To us, it seems unlikely that any single theory of wizardry applies to all its occurrences. Rather, all, or most, of the theories may have valid application to the understanding of wizardry in some of its occurrences. We will try to give something of the flavor of some of the theories.

In seeking to understand any society's religious practices and beliefs, we are inclined to attend respectfully to the explanations offered by its members. In many societies, the local explanation for belief in wizardry is that wizardry is in fact present and effective and is a real threat to health and life, and the explanation for countermeasures is that they can be successful in averting the danger. Most of the fieldworkers on whose reports we depend seem to reject these explanations altogether. These explanations imply, in modern terms, the reality of psi processes, especially of psychokinesis, and the fieldworkers, like many of their fellow scientists back home, deny all possibility that psi processes really occur. Recent research in parapsychology provides grounds for questioning this total denial (see, for example, Krippner, 1977). Yet even the strongest reasonable interpretation of this research does not justify the supposition that wizardry is satisfactorily explained by realistic efficacy alone. At most it would justify the supposition that wizardry belief and practice are supported partly by realistic fact, but leave fully open the expectation that wizardry has other important sources too. Into these we propose to inquire here.

A distinction is often made between explanations based on the individual and explanations based on the social group, psychological versus sociological explanations. Reasoning in one case is about processes going on in the many individual persons who make up the society. Reasoning in the other case is about processes of group formation and interaction. Personal preferences or professional background can lead to rephrasing the one kind of explanation so that it has more obviously the character of the other kind. But the difference seems to us worth preserving, as a contribution to clarity.

WIZARDRY AND THE INDIVIDUAL

Emotional Expression

Scholars who have given thought to the role of wizardry in the life of the individual have generally stressed its expressive function. Some have stressed its role in facilitating expression of some particular motive, such as those we will go on to consider. But some have presented, instead, a general argument, that expression of personal feelings is the prime nature of what wizardry does for people. The British anthropologist John Beattie (1964, 204), for example, says that what distinguishes an act of wizardry from ordinary instrumental activity is that though it may be aimed at specific goals (such as injuring an enemy), its essential character is symbolic, an expression of feeling. The wizard may believe in the real efficacy of his acts, but he will be much less concerned about proof of their efficacy than he would be about everyday acts whose function is more purely instrumental; the expression of the wizard's feeling provides in itself very considerable satisfaction.

Beattie's argument refers to *acts* of wizardry. An Italian anthropologist, Vinigi Grottanelli (1976), takes a similar position while considering the whole complex, including beliefs as well as acts. He bases his view on fieldwork with the Nzema of West Africa and on an account of their witchcraft written and published by a member of the society, P. A. K. Aboagye. Although Aboagye asserts the reality of witchcraft events, he distinguishes it from the everyday reality on which Nzema and Westerners agree, and in effect is presenting the witchcraft complex as a set of symbols, as metaphors. In arguing that witchcraft is to be understood as metaphor, he is implying that its function is expressive, like the metaphors of art.

Of course, the social and personal context of an expressive act, either of wizardry or of accusation, gives the emotional expression added meaning. To the routine of everyday life it may bring drama and excitement; to a person in a subordinate position it may bring attention and response such as he or she does not ordinarily receive. These values were noted by Kluckhohn (1962) in his study of accusations of wizardry among the Navaho.

Aggression

Acts of wizardry are all directed at hurting people, even in those instances where the acts are socially justified, aimed at protecting the wizard's group from external dangers. Accusations of wizardry also bring damage to other people. If an accusation is accepted by others, it may lead to the killing or ostracizing of the accused. If not altogether accepted, it may still weaken the confident trust others have placed in the virtue of the accused. Wizardry is obviously concerned, then, with aggression. This salient fact is perhaps the one point on which everyone who has written about wizardry would agree. Members of societies where wizardry is rampant may also be quite explicit in their agreement on this point. As La Fontaine (1963, 192) reports, "All witchcraft and sorcery comes, say Gisu, from the jealousy, anger and spite of men towards one another." Equally explicit are the Lugbara, who say witches and sorcerers are both motivated by the feeling of *ole*, which seems translatable as envy or resentment (Middleton, 1955). An inference from this point, with which not everyone would agree, is that a main function of wizardry is to permit, and to facilitate, the expression of aggression by members of a society. As Kluckhohn (1962, 90) put it, actual practice of wizardry offers a channel for direct aggression, whereas wizardry beliefs provide a channel for displaced aggression.

Impressive evidence relating variations in wizardry to variations in aggression was obtained in a cross-cultural study by John Whiting and Irvin Child (1953, 263–304). They employed judges to read, for each of a number of societies, pertinent extracts from ethnographies and then rate for each society the amount of concern people had about the danger of wizardry. For the same societies they employed other judges to read ethnographers' reports about child-training practices and rate the degree to which lasting anxiety about each of several motivational themes should result from the way children were treated. Concern with sorcery turned out to be markedly related to anxiety about aggression (resulting, for example, from severe punishment for aggression in childhood).

Similar evidence was obtained by Robert LeVine (1962) in two kinds of cross-cultural study. Of three neighboring polygynous societies in East Africa, the Kipsigis had a man's co-wives living far apart, and were little troubled by accusations of wizardry; Luo co-wives lived close together, and wizardry was of great concern to the Luo; the Gusii were intermediate in both respects. LeVine attributed this to the fact that rivalry between co-wives is a major potential source of friction and of hostility, exacerbated by proximity, and that accusations of wizardry are especially likely to come from tension between co-wives. He then verified this general reasoning in a broader cross-cultural study of many societies.

Some of the aggression associated with belief in wizardry is quite realistic and severe—causing the death of another person, at the extreme— but especially distinctive here is aggression that may have no realistic consequences for other persons. Acts of wizardry may have no effect on the intended victim and never be known to that person or to anyone else but the wizard; yet the wizard may believe ill effects to be certain or at least likely, and gain satisfaction from what to us seems mere fantasy. Similarly, a person's belief that he or she is the intended victim of wizardry may permit that person to fantasy retaliating, or to imagine disaster spontaneously coming upon the supposed wizard. When a sorcerer leaves traces of his acts, so that the victim is alerted to his danger and may be made sick from worry, or when the accuser tries to persuade others that he is the object of attack and that the wizard merits punishment, the fantasy of aggression merges into direct instrumental attack, and a motive for aggression may be satisfied in more than one way by community acceptance of the reality of wizardry.

Anxiety

Another motive to whose management wizardry is relevant is that of anxiety. Social life, for a variety of reasons, gives rise to anxiety which may be vague and little understood and which a person is unable to adjust to by realistic interaction with the environment. Belief in wizardry may be useful here. A person who claims wizardly skills may like anyone else feel vague anxiety. By blaming it on the machinations of another person and directing his skills at that person as a target, he can do something to channel the anxiety and make it more endurable, perhaps actually reducing the strength of the anxiety. For the nonwizard, similarly, it may be possible to attribute vague anxiety to the evil effects of someone else's sorcery or witchcraft. Accusing the supposed wizard, or even private fantasies placing blame on him, may channel and reduce the anxiety. This is one of the advantages of wizardry that Kluckhohn (1962) reported for the Navaho. Belief in wizardry can even be used to relieve the anxiety a person may feel because of his own misbehavior; Beidelman (1963, 85) reported for the Kaguru (an agricultural people of Tanzania), what must be true in many societies, that one may excuse his misbehavior by saying it was a result of his being bewitched.

A special instance of a similar use of wizardry beliefs was uncovered by Roberts and Nutini (1988) in an analysis of events centering on child-hood deaths in rural Tlaxcala, Mexico. Parental negligence, perhaps even infanticide, may be implicated in some deaths, and gossip may enlarge on the possibility. Death may also be ascribed to bloodsucking wizards; and by describing the circumstances of the death in ways especially suggestive of this source, the parents may divert gossip away from blaming them-selves. Apparently, wizardry is believed to be entirely supernatural, so that the bloodsucking witches are not considered to be actual persons of the community and new hostilities are not likely to be aroused by blaming children's death on wizardry.

Sexuality

A frequent element in witchcraft belief is the attribution to witches of participation in nighttime revels that involve forbidden sexual activities. Quite apart from supposed orgies, the belief that each witch has a "familiar" as a sexual partner as well as helper may encourage sexual fantasies. Monica Wilson (1951b) finds an important sexual element of this sort in the Pondo and not in the Nyakyusa, two African peoples she studied. She traces the difference to the much broader sexual taboos to which the Pondo are subjected, viewing witchcraft beliefs as a medium for sexual fantasies among the Pondo and not among the Nyakyusa.

Less frequently a sexual element is manifested in sorcery, in a belief that incestuous acts are required before one is privileged to begin training. Both witches and sorcerers, thus, are at times fantasied to engage in forbidden sexual acts. Conceivably, some persons may be freed by these beliefs to widen their sexual activity from the permitted to the forbidden, as a part of their life as witches or sorcerers. But even more important may be the opportunity for ordinary people to revel in fantasies about the forbidden sexual activity of wizards and gain a kind of indirect pleasure from it, a kind of pleasure often in our own society ascribed to those who take an intense interest in the sexual life of people they disapprove of. This indirect or displaced expression of sexual interest is comparable to the displaced aggression permitted by wizardry beliefs.

Mastery

Need for mastery is a basic human motive. We have alluded already to the satisfaction that may be gained, in connection with anxiety, by finding a means of action believed effective. The same point applies more broadly in connection with any need, general or specific. The absence of any way of coping may be a source of worry and of wish to find some means of coping. Where no realistic way of coping is available, belief in wizardry may provide a useful substitute.

A generalized need for mastery may be what is involved in curiosity, in attempts at understanding. Beliefs about wizardry may be seen as part of the effort in every society to explain the facts of the world and of human life. These beliefs may be selected for emphasis in a particular society because of special circumstances—a generally exaggerated need for aggression or anxiety about aggression, for example. Once selected, they may be adhered to because they offer individuals a sense of understanding, of being able to explain what is happening to them and their fellows. This view of religion in traditional societies has been most strongly advocated by Horton (1960). The special contribution of wizardry belief, as Evans-Pritchard (1937) demonstrated so well for the Azande, is that it offers an explanation for what lies behind misfortunes. Like us, the believer in wizardry may understand very well the physical events involved in an accident. But in addition to explaining *how* the accident happened, the believer also can explain *why* it happened, and is not left with the empty explanation of chance occurrence (Gluckman, 1944). Wilson (1951b, 313) quotes the impressive way a Pondo put this point: "It may be quite true that typhus is carried by lice, but who sent the infected louse? Why did it bite one man and not another?"

WIZARDRY AND SOCIETY

Social Control

Beatrice Whiting (1950) convincingly stressed the enforcement of social norms as a main function of wizardry. She emphasized the role of accusations rather than the role of acts of wizardry or fear of wizardry. Studying a Paiute community in Oregon, Whiting found a clear tendency for accusations of wizardry to be directed against persons who were deviant in some way that elicited disapproval. Fear of being accused of wizardry, she argued, serves to inhibit people from deviating from social norms. Thus, the social need for wizardry to be employed for social control should be greatest in societies relatively lacking in other techniques for enforcing social conformity—that is, in societies with no formal political structure. Whiting checked this prediction by a cross-cultural study. In each of a sample of societies, she read relevant ethnographic data and rated two variables—importance of wizardry and presence of superordinate social control—and found these two variables were inversely related, as she had predicted.

This function of wizardry beliefs in supporting conformity has been noted by various ethnographers. Rappaport (1984, 131–132) suggests that Tsembaga norms of equality are maintained in part by giving wealthy men reason to fear being suspected of wizardry and hence exposed to heightened danger in warfare. Wolf (1955, 460) reports that this economic leveling effect of witchcraft fear is characteristic of the peasant communities of the Latin American highlands, whose reliance on subsistence farming is associated with a conservative intolerance of individual wealth. Kluckhohn (1962), while giving special attention to psychological functions of wizardry, also points out that the Navaho are especially likely to direct their accusations toward the wealthiest individuals, who by their accumulation of property are violating the communal norms of Navaho life. A Navaho leader a century ago brought about the execution as wizards of his rivals who threatened his peace-oriented policy in relation to whites; less consciously, Kluckhohn (1962, 122) concludes, accusation of wizardry is a threat regularly used to check "all individuals who threaten to disrupt the smooth functioning of the community." Basso (1970) makes a similar observation about the Western Apache.

All of these cases illustrate the convergence of individual and social functions of the same behavior. Accusing the wealthy of wizardry, for example, gives the accuser the gratification of direct and realistic aggression against the very persons whose lack of generosity he resents. At the same time, the accusations may serve as displaced expression of hostility really felt toward forbidden targets, reducing the burden of resentment one may feel toward friends and relatives for quite other reasons but cannot act on. Thus, the same accusations that relieve personal tension help maintain social norms of equality and of family integrity.

In some societies, the bad consequences of being considered a wizard may be mild enough so that people in a secure position who dare to be independent can risk accusation, and only the less secure experience pressures toward social conformity from fear of being accused of wizardry. This is the situation Beidelman (1963, 96–97) reports for the Kaguru of Tanzania.

The dramatization function for the individual also is relevant to the social control function. As Marwick (1965) points out, the drama of accusation and resultant controversy, perhaps culminating in punishment of the supposed wizard, may be especially effective in reinforcing social norms because the mode of enforcement is more exciting than the highly regulated courtroom drama of our society.

Wizardry itself, as well as accusations, may play an important role in social control. Bronislaw Malinowski (1926) reported that in the Trobriand Islands the local chief relied largely on wizardry to enforce his power and authority. He did so by employing the best sorcerers in his district to work for the death of his intended victims and letting it be known that he was doing so. Apparently generalizing to other traditional societies, Malinowski (1926, 93) said of wizardry that it supports law and order and "is always a conservative force, and it furnishes really the main source of the wholesome fear of punishment and retribution indispensable in any orderly society." If Malinowski was guessing that chiefs in most traditional societies depend for social control mostly on their people's fear of sorcery, he was probably mistaken. But, at any rate, the Trobrianders are not unique in this respect; Michele Stephen (1987a) reports that various Melanesian societies share this sort of positive function of the sorcery of "big men." More diffuse fear of wizardry is also ascribed a role in social control by Kluckhohn, in his interpretation of Navaho wizardry.

Appeal to fear of wizardry itself in enforcing conformity to social norms is, of course, likely to appear explicitly in the socialization of children. The Nyakyusa of Tanzania provide an example; as Wilson (1951b, 308) says, "Children are warned not to be quarrelsome or boastful or brusque in their manners, lest they arouse the anger of witches."

Redirecting Aggression within the Group

Among the Navaho, Kluckhohn found a tendency for accusations to be directed at the wealthy and powerful, a tendency that works toward controlling the amassing of wealth and enforcing the distributional norms of the Navaho. This suggests in part a redirecting of hostility originally felt toward peers, heightening the hostility also engendered directly by envy of the wealthy. In some societies elsewhere, in contrast, the wealthy and powerful, notably royalty, are exempt from accusations. Yet the king, at the peak of wealth and power, may be the most envied man in the society, a natural target of hostility however much he may also be revered. This situation suggests that in such societies wizardry may serve to strengthen the position of the ruler by directing toward other people the hostility felt toward him. Marvin Harris (1974, 207–221) has put forward the thesis that the witch mania in Europe during the fifteenth to seventeenth centuries, in which thousands of people were burned to death as wizards (Larner, 1984, 36), was a device of the ruling classes to lead the masses to blame their misery on witches among themselves, diverting the aggression they justifiably felt toward government, clergy, and the wealthy. A comparable thesis may well apply to some of the stratified traditional societies.

Segmentation of the Community

Several students of African societies have been impressed by the contribution wizardry beliefs make to the needed breakup of social units that have become too large or too conflicted. Accusations, counteraccusations, and their hateful consequences, though unpleasant at the time, may smooth the way toward forming smaller and tighter groups. Persons accused of wizardry, or fearing wizardry from their neighbors, may actually move and form a new, smaller village. Or, without moving, they may alter their social interactions so that what was a single large kinship group is broken into two smaller and more harmonious groups.

Mary Douglas (1963) refers to this as the "obstetric" function of wizardry beliefs. She has portrayed the disruptive effects of wizardry among the Lele (a people of Zaire) as severe enough to induce social splitting. Yet she feels that wizardry is so painful for the Lele and so vigorously combated as to cast doubt on whether it can reasonably be thought to have this positive function. An obstetric function in giving birth to new groupings is, on the other hand, given a major place in Gray's (1963, 157–161) account of wizardry in the Wambugwe of Tanzania, as it is in Marwick's (1952) account among the Cewa. For the Gusii of Kenya, Mayer (1970, 56) reports that "the parties to a witchcraft case do not want to be reconciled. What they want is an excuse for rupture."

In-Group versus Out-Group

In some Melanesian societies, accusations of wizardry are most often directed at outsiders, members of nearby tribes. This has led to the suggestion that wizardry beliefs serve there to facilitate tribal cohesion, by displacing to other communities the hatred and fears engendered by social life within one's own community. But not even in Melanesia does this tendency always occur; the Dobuans, for instance, are portrayed by Fortune (1932) as dominated by fears of wizardry by members of their own community. And in Africa, ethnographers rarely emphasize suspicions of outsiders; accusations are usually made within the community, though to be sure they remain relevant to defining in-group and out-group on a smaller scale. Perhaps there may be a characteristic difference here between large societies such as many of those in Africa (where even the local community may far exceed the size of an entire Melanesian society) and societies that consist of only one or two small villages.

Maintaining Social Structure

Several British anthropologists have related wizardry to the particular social structure of an African society they had studied, and Gluckman (1972, 17–33) has extracted from these efforts a general view of wizardry as a way of making more tolerable some major ambiguity or incompatibility intrinsic to the social structure.

The Pondo social system in South Africa, for example, stresses loyalty to descent group, and associated with this is great sexual restraint by men (in that a large proportion of the women in their vicinity are sexually tabooed to them). Ascribing wizardry to people suffering from this conflict shifts awareness to their presumed evil intent, away from the conflict itself. Among the Yao of Malawi the social structure places high value both on the family loyalty of brothers and on competition among them for power and prestige. Sorcery accusations are especially often directed at a brother, and they distract attention from the underlying conflict created by the Yao social system. Somewhat similar circumstances among the Cewa lead accusations of wizardry to be concentrated on fellow members of the matrilineal lineage.

In all these and similar instances, Gluckman argues, the social structure tends to develop some particular form of moral crisis, involving courses of action that are incompatible but both highly valued. Wizardry beliefs, and their outcome in accusations, divinations, and further action, are shaped by the character of this moral crisis. They serve, Gluckman suggests, to conceal the conflict and the disharmony it produces, and thus permit maintenance of the incompatible ideals and the social structure that produces them by attributing the discomfort or tension to someone's moral lapse rather than to the social structure itself.

In a rare study of wizardry in a segment of modern European society, and of what it does for people there, Jeanne Favret-Saada (1989) similarly interprets it in relation to strains in the social system. We go out of our way to mention her work despite its modern European reference because it so clearly illustrates how important values for the individual and for the social structure may reside in the same behavior and beliefs. She studied wizardry in a rural region of France where a family enterprise (typically a farm) retains some integrity from one generation to the next through concentration of property and power in a single successor (typically the oldest son) at the expense of all his relatives. The concentration is supported by custom but violates standards of fairness and decency and even, at times, national law. If the family sees its business declining, it is likely to attribute the trouble to wizardry. Favret-Saada studied in detail the therapy conducted by specialists at "unbewitching." The family head tends initially to accuse relatives of bewitching him, but the unbewitcher gradually shifts the accusations to neighbors, and trains the family head to take various steps of aggressive defense. The family heads most likely to feel bewitched, Favret-Saada suggests, are those least able to play without remorse the mean, self-centered role required for financial success and most aware of the damage done to their close relatives by the concentration of property and power in their own person. The intrafamily hostilities are deflected, by the unbewitching, toward neighbors, and the family head is likely to become more effective in directing and controlling the family unit. This reduction of individual tension facilitates the continuation of the traditional pattern of family enterprise in the face of pressures for change.

Restoring Social Equilibrium

When a society is disorganized because of rapid social change, Basso (1969, 59) argues, wizardry beliefs and the resulting accusations can help restore equilibrium. On a smaller scale, in many a community wizardry may help restore social equilibrium when disruption occurs in the multiple interacting groups that make it up. Jean La Fontaine finds this value in the ideology of wizardry among the Gisu, which

> accepts the fact of conflict and explains it in terms of dyadic relationships which Christianity does not do. An accusation of witchcraft places responsibility for conflict on both accuser and accused, for the accuser must accept the fact that he has incurred someone's enmity before accusing him. The accusation precipitates a crisis in their bad relations and sets in motion the process which will restore harmony. It also enables the individual to transform and release his feelings in aggression. Christianity, whose primary concern is the soul and its relation to God, dismisses conflict as the inevitable result of man's sinfulness, whereas the pagan "doctrine" of witchcraft dramatically states the joint responsibility of individuals in a dyadic relationship to maintain amity by right behavior. (1963, 219)

The restoration of social equilibrium portrayed by La Fontaine is one solution of conflict—the complement to segmentation, where conflict is resolved by termination of the relationship.

Supporting the Worldview

Wizardry beliefs may serve a society by providing support for accepted views of the social and physical world, views that work well enough to be worth sustaining and might be threatened by unexplained failure of confirmation. Any action that conventional wisdom suggests should be successful may on occasion fail; if failure can be confidently attributed to interference by the evil intent of some wizard, the conventional wisdom is not threatened.

A special case of this, applicable so far as a society's worldview is concerned with such abstract or general issues as the problem of evil, is the fact that wizardry offers a solution to the problem of reconciling the existence of evil with a view of the world as otherwise benevolent. Whereas some Christian traditions ascribe evil to the machinations of the devil, wizardry beliefs permit its ascription to deviant individuals dominated by evil intent toward their fellows. Mayer (1970, 52) points out, for instance, that the Gusii of Kenya are able to maintain that spirits are uniformly good because misfortunes can be confidently attributed to living persons.

The ascription of all evil to wizardry is facilitated in some societies by elaboration of a symbolism of evil, and some of the details may be distinctive. Among the Amba, Winter (1963) shows how the witch must be identified as a member of the local community, so that he or she is guilty of traitorous villainy, and the witch is in various other ways imagined as the reverse of normal humanity—responding to thirst, for example, by eating salt, and remaining active all night instead of sleeping. The Gisu of Uganda, while likewise portraying wizards as inhuman in various ways, symbolize this by imagining them to be members of some other community where worse evil occurs than is imaginable in one's own village (La Fontaine, 1963, 214–215). As mentioned earlier, wizards are often pictured as the opposite of normal humanity.

Not only a sense of the benevolence of the world may be preserved by established recourse to wizardry as an explanation of misfortune; a sense of predictability may be preserved in the same way. This point is eloquently made by S. F. Nadel in his account of religion among the Nupe, a tribe of Nigeria. He had earlier (1935) proposed that Nupe belief in wizardry served to permit a belief in benevolence. Later (1954, 202–206), in considering the whole of Nupe religion, he had to reject that explanation, for the Nupe have no belief in a benevolent world. They view the world, rather, as subject at all points to accident and evil. The function of wizardry belief, for the Nupe, he then proposed, is to increase a sense of predictability by providing specific explanations of evil occurrences, and offering the possibility of taking action to forestall or undo them—explanation and action that yet, by its narrowly focusing or channeling hatred and fear, would permit the continued functioning of society.

PSYCHOLOGICAL AND SOCIETAL COSTS OF WIZARDRY

Each of the various gains, to individuals or to the functioning of society, offered by wizardry may bring with it potential disadvantages. Basso (1970, 61) found that of 27 cases of accusations of wizardry by Western Apache individuals, two had led the accuser to such discomfort that he later withdrew the accusation. A member of the Nalumin, a New Guinea group, told a fieldworker that "living with witchcraft is like living in the midst of an unending hidden war" (Bercovitch, 1989, 140). Spiro (1952), seeking to explain why wizardry is absent on the island of Ifaluk, concluded that the intragroup suspicions and hostility that it would bring could not be tolerated in a small society living on an isolated island, where removal to some other nearby site is not available as a solution to severe conflict. The implication is, of course, that heightening of social tension is everywhere a consequence of wizardry beliefs, the very consequence that in other situations (as Douglas, 1963, argues) may be a real advantage through facilitating a splitting up of groups that have grown too large.

In both its personal and its societal consequences, then, wizardry is parallel to neurotic symptoms in that it provides a solution to conflicts but does so at great cost.

SUMMARY

Wizardry is a general term that includes sorcery (the deliberate use of the mystical power of words, procedures, and devices, to harm other persons), witchcraft (the direct but often unconscious use of personal mystical power to harm others), and various mixed or ill-defined ways of seeking mystically the same hostile end. In some societies, attempts are apparently made to engage in wizardry, though good evidence of actual practice is often lacking. In many societies, however, there is no doubt that fear of becoming a victim of wizardry is very widespread. Individuals suspected of practicing wizardry are subjected to consequences of widely varying nature—from cruel execution through milder hostility to actual gain in prestige.

Fear of wizardry leads to protective measures such as care not to offend potential wizards, or avoiding contact with them—effects that may have positive value in facilitating breakdown of a single contentious group into smaller and more compatible groups. But fear of wizardry may interfere seriously with effective functioning of the community, and this suggests that belief in wizardry has other strong countervailing values. These can be expressed with reference to individual members of society, and effects of sorcery on their emotional and cognitive life. It can also be expressed with reference to the structure of the community and how it serves the emotional and cognitive life of its members.

Chapter 7

Illness and Healing

Injury and disease pose threats to livelihood and to life itself. In traditional societies realistic means of fighting against them are even more limited than they were in our society a few generations ago. Traditional societies rely greatly, then, on religion in seeking to account for sickness and injury and to prevent or cure them. We will consider in this chapter the religious aspect of their coping with these dangers. We must recognize, though, that in looking at reactions to illness as a part of the religions of traditional peoples, we may risk in several ways a serious departure from those peoples' modes of thought.

1. Traditional peoples may distinguish less sharply than we do between illness and other kinds of misfortune. All undesirable events may be grouped together, both in a theory about why they occur and in practices directed at alleviating or preventing them.

2. As we have said in other contexts, the distinction between realistic and unrealistic, in theory and in practice, may also be much less sharp than among us. To concentrate on what we would consider unrealistic theories of illness and on unrealistic efforts at cure, as is dictated by our focus on religion rather than on medicine, should not blind us to the important role of realistic medical practices among traditional peoples. Of the plant medicines in standard use among them, for instance, some have been validated and adopted by Western scientific medicine. Many others may have valuable placebo effects that do not depend in any way on religious concepts.

3. Therapeutic procedures often involve activities that serve other purposes as well; in discussing them solely as therapy we may neglect these other purposes.

More than on other topics, then, in our discussion of illness and healing, we are taking behavior and ideas out of context; we will try to minimize this effect by occasional reminders.

REACTIONS TO ILLNESS

For some traditional societies, pieces of information on reactions to illness are available in general ethnographies or in ethnographies directed primarily at other problems. For a few societies, fieldworkers have concentrated on reactions to illness and thus have provided especially rich information. We are going to start by reviewing reactions to illness in several of these societies, to sample the diversity and the broad similarities that emerge.

Kalahari (San)

The San of the Kalahari Desert are foragers whose responses to illness, especially their therapy, are known in some detail (see Marshall, 1962, and Katz, 1982, on the Kung; and Barnard, 1979, on the neighboring Nharo). They conceive each kind of illness as a specific substance that somehow gets into a person—sometimes put there by spirits or by a wizard, but often not. The illness may develop out of the potential for illness that everyone has, a potential that makes everyone a glad recipient of preventive therapy (Katz, 1982, 53). The spirits involved are sometimes of specific ancestors, wanting the company of their loved ones; often they are remoter and not identified, and may even be the great god or the lesser god. In these latter cases, the motive is not clear, but the illness seems not to have been brought on as punishment for moral infractions.

Therapy involves, in part, drawing any illness substance out of the patient. This may be done by a therapist (any of about half the male population or 10 percent of the women) in an individual session. More conspicuous in San life, however, are group sessions at which several people may seek relief from illness. A session generally lasts through a whole night, with a number of people crowded around a campfire. The women are most active in singing. Men (and sometimes women) dance around the outer circle. In the course of dancing, one or more go into a trance in which they sense energy to boil up within them and their healing power to be heightened. Some descriptions of the experience closely resemble accounts, in a Hindu tradition, of the rising of the Kundalini from the base of the spine to the top of the head (Katz, 1982, 165). The entranced therapist touches everyone present, being especially attentive to those currently ill; the touch draws the illness substance out of the person and is thought to be beneficial to all, so much so that sessions are often held even though no specific complaints of illness occasion them. The therapist is himself (or, less often, herself) endangered by the substance and strives vigorously to throw it out at the spirits that are felt to be gathered around the campfire. Another process is also recognized: The entranced therapist transmits to the patient some of the energy boiling up within, and the energy can then also work against the disease directly within the patient (Katz, 1982, 42).

Another process involved in therapy is the helper's active effort to get back the patient's soul, which a spirit or god may have taken away. For this, the healer may at the height of ecstasy experience traveling to the place of gods and spirits, where he confronts and argues with these mystical beings at the risk of his own life. If his own mystical power is strong enough, he is successful in this struggle and brings the missing soul back to the patient (Katz, 1982, 43).

The more general aim of Kung therapy is reported (Katz, 1982, 53–54) to be the reestablishment of a balance among individual, culture, and environment. As this implies, illness is seen as destroying a gestalt, or order, in the person's relation to group and total environment. If the patient dies, order may still be restored through realization that, despite devoted efforts at healing, this was the outcome ordained by the spirits.

Ojibwa

Irving Hallowell studied over several decades a more complex foraging society, the Saulteaux, an Ojibwa community in Manitoba. In reporting their response to illness, he stresses that it is an integral part of their general worldview. The Ojibwa personalize the parts of the universe that they recognize as important causal influences. The winds, the sun and moon, the masters of various species of plants and animals—all are seen as initiating and controlling events, and in that respect they are like the individual human person, but much more powerful. Noting that the term "supernaturals" does not well express the Ojibwa conception, Hallowell instead calls them "other-than-human persons." They are responsible for illness and other major events. The crucial question for Ojibwa, in confronting illness, as in confronting other disturbing events, is who did it or who is responsible (Hallowell, 1976, 403).

For Ojibwa, what distinguishes persons from other animate beings is the capacity to transform the self, and this capacity is greater for persons with greater power. Wizards, when actively harming others, may change in appearance, and may even take animal form. Other-than-human persons may transform themselves into apparent human beings. Even the real identity of a person causing illness may thus be suspect. It can be guessed at, though, when someone gets sick after refusing hospitality or failing to share what he has and another needs; the illness is likely to be attributed to retaliation through wizardry by the person who had been spurned. Departure from proper sexual behavior, deceit, and violation of taboos imposed on one in a dream or vision are also likely sources of illness; action by other-than-human persons is suspected here, although such mystical entities are conceived by Ojibwa to be mostly helpful rather than mischievous or cruel.

The way for an Ojibwa to seek recovery from serious illness agrees with these theories of the sources of illness. Reliance is placed on confession of the misdeeds to which the illness is attributed. The feelings of guilt that prompt the confession, and the shame to which this public exposure leads, are the way by which reaction to illness plays an important role in motivating adherence to the moral traditions of the Ojibwa. When confession fails to produce a cure, and an expert healer must be appealed to, the healer must work through his established relation with one or more other-than-human persons.

The American anthropologist Ruth Landes (1968) studied reactions to illness in other Ojibwa communities living in Ontario and Minnesota. Her report gives special attention to the group ceremonies greatly elaborated among them and added to the individual work of healers. For cure from a serious illness, an Ojibwa could pay qualified specialists to perform one of various rites. Each occupied several evenings, and brought to bear on the illness the prior visionary experiences of the healer and myths about distant ancestors and about creation. Such rites were graded, each level adding recondite knowledge not included at lower levels, and participation in them conferred membership in the healing society, though special instruction and visions were necessary to go further and become a healer.

Gnau

Gilbert Lewis, physician as well as anthropologist, spent 22 months among the Gnau, a horticultural people of the Sepik River area of New Guinea, studying their reactions to illness. His report (1975) analyzes more thoroughly than almost any on other peoples how sickness and injuries are classified and conceptualized by the people studied. Major illness, though not distinguished by a name, brings behavior and attitudes similar to what might be expected anywhere, rooted in universals of physiology but elaborated by Gnau cultural tradition. These reactions seem to be elicited at times, however, in persons not physically ill in a Western sense. (Lewis was not permitted to make Western-style medical examinations, and could judge the illness only by obvious symptoms and eventual outcome.) Lewis tries to summarize as follows the attitude of a Gnau who is ill:

> If you are ill you are in danger of continued or aggravated illness from which you could die. You are in danger of attracting the attention of many spirits, and you are weak....Once ill you are in greater danger of further and cumulative attack. You must appear wretched for in this way you may deceive a spirit into thinking its aim, which is your bodily ruin, accomplished and it may leave you. (1975, 139–140)

Explanation of illness is especially important for the Gnau. It is essential for classifying the illness and indicating the proper therapy, for classification of an illness is based on what cause it is finally attributed to rather than on the symptoms it presents. Yet Lewis was struck by how much illness is simply accepted, without being explained or treated (pp. 359–360). The Gnau seem satisfied by the obvious naturalistic explanations for wounds, burns, and the like (p. 249). For other illness, explanations are diverse. Spirits are ascribed the main causal role. When some-one dies, his or her spirit is a source of danger for at least a day or two, as it may want to take the spirit of a close relative or friend for companionship. Longer after their death, a person's own ancestral spirits are benevolent, but other persons' are a potential danger, as are various "great spirits" that never were living persons. A dangerous spirit of whatever kind is likely to bring illness by way of food—sometimes because the spirit resents the patient's eating a food toward whose source the spirit is protective, but sometimes just because the spirit enters the patient's body along with the food—but spirits also bring about illness by other means (p. 216). Living persons may also be involved in causing illness, mostly because they may be accompanied by spirits that would otherwise not notice the potential victim, but occasionally by acting through wizardry to bring on or exacer-bate illness. The patient is at times judged to be completely responsible for the illness through having broken a taboo, with neither spirits nor persons taking part in bringing about the illness, and some taboo breaking brings about illness in persons other than the violator (pp. 185–186).

Therapeutic steps the Gnau patient can take include withdrawing from company, appearing wretched (so aggressive spirits will feel they have already accomplished their aim), and avoiding all foods especially associated with the spirits to whom the illness is ascribed. The patient, relatives, and friends may speculate about recent acts of the patient that may have provoked a spirit; if rituals appealing to that spirit lead to no improvement, then another hypothesis will be substituted and dictate the next step in therapy. Where unintended effects of wizardry are suggested, counterwizardry may be attempted.

If the patient recovers, the ritual of return to normal life is bathing to "wash away the filth" of the illness. The whole sequence of activity, Lewis points out, closely resembles the general pattern of "rites of passage" except that here the person returns to the old status of health rather than advancing to a new status. Divination directed at identifying a person who has maliciously directed wizardry at the patient is used only in case of death; it is thought useless while the patient is alive, as there are believed to be no countermeasures for this type of sorcery (p. 228).

Navaho

The Navaho of Arizona and New Mexico, the largest Native American society, have a complex mythology, pantheon, and cosmology; and ideas about illness and therapy are central to its elaboration. Indeed, it has been said that Navaho religion is a set of ceremonies whose explicit purpose is the curing of the sick. The Navaho attribute illness to a great diversity of causes, from wizardry by evil persons to action by any of numerous gods and natural phenomena and to innumerable actions or inactions of the afflicted person. Through many of the specific causes, however, run certain broad tendencies:

1. There is order in the universe and society. Actions that depart from the orderly pattern may put the person out of harmony with his world, and this disharmony may be expressed in illness. Therapy, then, is directed at restoring order.

2. Badness or evil may be placed in one by the gods, by wizards, or by one's own actions; therapy is directed at expelling the badness, leaving a gap into which goodness may come instead.

3. Mystical power inheres in the gods, in the myths, in natural phenomena, and in rituals, and contact with any of these is capable of a good influence or a bad influence; they may all be appealed to in appropriate ways in explaining misfortune or in curing it by transmission of mystical power.

There are about 36 traditional rituals (called, in English, chants, sings, or ways), each lasting anywhere from one to nine nights and the intervening days. Which one is appropriate is decided with the help of diviners—diagnostic specialists who work either through stargazing or through hand trembling, two procedures for inducing a state evidently believed favorable for clairvoyance and wise decision or advice. A chant

> is communion with the supernatural world; it is drama; it is medicine and a fight against both physical disease and mental anxiety; it is a vital group activity which demands participation from all those who attend; and, due to accident or misconduct, it may even become one cause of further anxiety and illness which will, in turn, be treated by ceremonial procedures. (Leighton & Leighton, 1949, 145)

The importance of chants in Navaho social life is apparent in nineteenth-century material provided in an autobiography recorded in minute detail by twentieth-century fieldworkers (Dyk, 1938; Dyk & Dyk, 1980). The accompanying ideas about causes and cures of illness are also similar to what emerges in recent Navaho studies. Departure from orderly patterns was dangerous; an epidemic of mumps, for example, was blamed on one man's wearing a mask at an inappropriate time, when a ritual was in progress (Dyk & Dyk, 1980, 352). In addition to the group rituals, a variety of other therapeutic procedures are also mentioned, such as sprinkling cornmeal and individual praying and singing (Dyk & Dyk, 1980, 353).

In twentieth-century ethnographies, illness is blamed by diviners on various specific sources. One man's careless loss of a flint from his medicine bundle was said to be the source of the serious illness and death of his wife and a grandchild (Reichard, 1970, 85). A man studying to perform Night Chant made mistakes that led to paralysis, so that he had to abandon the training (ibid., 94). A woman's breast cancer was blamed on her having incorporated sand-painting designs in her weaving, violating the rule that the designs should never be given permanent form (ibid., 95–96). Another woman's migraine headaches, endured over 17 years, were believed to have been initiated by a stroke of lightning (ibid., 97).

The cause ascribed by the diviner helps in deciding what chant is likely to provide a cure. Each of the various chants has its own set of traditional songs and appropriate sand paintings. The sand paintings must carefully follow traditional patterns that

> recall significant episodes of mythical drama....The patient in his or her
> plight is identified with the cultural hero who contracted a similar disease
> or plight in the same way the patient did....From the myth the patient learns
> that his or her plight and illness is not new, and that both its cause and
> treatment are known. To be cured, all the patient has to do is to repeat what
> has been done before. It has to be done sincerely, however, and this sincerity
> is expressed in concentration and dedication. The sandpainting depicts the
> desired order of things, and places the patient in this beautiful and ordered
> world. The patient thus becomes completely identified with the powerful and
> curing agents of the universe. (Witherspoon, 1977, 167–168)

The patient literally enters this ordered world by sitting on the sand painting, and is sprinkled with appropriate bits of the sacred image. A sand painting characteristically portrays mystical beings enclosed within a circular or rectangular frame. The visual pattern is regarded by Jung and Jungians (e.g., Sandner, 1979) as a mandala, symbolizing both the centeredness of the individual and the oneness of individual and world. The Navaho pattern differs from mandalas standard in other cultures in usually having a clear opening in its boundary, which the Navaho see as expressing the possibility of evil escaping and being replaced by the entrance of good.

In the minority of illnesses attributed by the Navaho to wizardry, the wizard's confession or death offers the best promise of cure. Otherwise, hopelessness may prevail, but a great variety of therapeutic techniques may be tried. Protection from wizardry is one of the gains from participation in chants, and it may be strengthened by preventive use of medicine made from animal gall and by private production of sand or pollen paintings (Kluckhohn, 1962, 46–56).

The potential consequences of being accused of wizardry are so serious that the wizardry explanation of illness plays an important part in the regulation of social behavior of the Navaho. Accumulation of wealth, reluctance to share goods, is a frequent source of suspicion, and creates the risk of denunciation and execution or expulsion (Kluckhohn, 1962, 49). One who escapes such extremes may still suffer in his relation with the community. An episode from the nineteenth-century material recorded by Dyk presents an example of the consequences of being stingy and reluctant to share one's wealth and possessions. When Old Man Hat was gravely ill his wife suggested that they get a singer to treat him, and his response was "How will we put up some kind of doings? There isn't anybody around to help us. If somebody were around then, perhaps, we could put up some kind of doing. But like this, when we're all alone, we can't do anything. So let the things that are bothering me kill me" (Dyk, 1938, 251). Inasmuch as Old Man Hat had just previously responded to a relative's request for a new buckskin by throwing him his old, used leggings, it is evident that he knew it was hopeless to appeal to this relative for help. Stinginess in the past had led him at various times to be considered a wizard (though he blamed his illness on other less reprehensible deeds of the distant past), and the singer finally called in now told him, in effect, that he had bewitched himself and his case was hopeless (Dyk, 1938, 272–273).

The theme that underlies both explanation and treatment of illness among the Navaho is that illness is one aspect of disorder, of lack of suitable connectedness among people, between people and animals and between people and the rest of the vividly animated world. Recovery from illness depends on reestablishing the proper order and connectedness.

Murngin

The Murngin, or Yolngu, are a group of tribes in the extreme north of Australia (northeastern Arnhem Land). Their religion received major attention in fieldwork in the 1920s by the American anthropologist William Lloyd Warner (1958); he reported reactions to illness most fully where relevant to religion, but to some extent even when not. Fifty years later the Australian anthropologist Janice Reid (1983) centered her Murngin fieldwork on health, illness, and death. In the 1920s Murngin religion and medicine had been little influenced from outside. In the 1970s, scientific medicine had wide influence, but traditional medicine remained viable alongside it. Other traditional religious beliefs and practices had also survived alongside the alien teachings of Christianity.

Warner reported a special set of beliefs about wizardry as an explanation of mortal illness. Sorcerers, it was believed, exert mystical power to abduct a victim, cut him or her open, remove the heart's blood and thus the soul, and finally restore the body to its normal appearance. The victim then was believed to die in three days, and there was no way to avoid this outcome. (Illness brought about by some of the other procedures of sorcery, it was believed, could be undone by the wizard should he change his mind.) But some illness was explained in quite different ways. Spirits of the dead were often thought responsible; sometimes a misdeed of the victim was thought to be punished in this way. Breaking tribal laws during the annual great ceremonies, or participating only incompletely in the ceremonies, might also be blamed. Many minor ailments and wounds would seem from Warner's account (pp. 219–222) to have been explained naturalistically or not at all, and to have had folk remedies that were not associated with ideas of mystical power.

Some techniques of therapy described by Warner, such as removing a foreign object from the body, were closely tied to particular explanations of illness, but many were not. Purification by painting the body with red ocher, for example, was believed to be beneficial. Certain wizards, whom Warner called "white magicians," were able to draw on their mystical power to fight the mystical power applied to evil purpose by "black magicians," but for soul-loss cases the white magicians were helpless. The white magicians depended on spirit helpers who inhabited their medicine bags, and the performance of rituals was thought to be itself a curative and preventive. The curative activities of white magicians served, Warner concluded, to give the patient "a sense of well-being and adjustment to his community." In particular, relation to the community was involved in a curing ritual in which the patient was placed within a representation of his clan's "totemic well," especially constructed for the ritual. Male clan members gathered around and sang songs pertinent to the clan and to the well that represented it. This ritual "averts illness from anyone who participates in it and from the group generally; on the contrary, anyone who does not participate in it will be ill" (p. 228).

Fifty years later, Reid found the patterns of explanation basically similar to Warner's description. Her information is fuller, however, because of her concentration on response to illness. She found that practice of the special fatal form of wizardry discovered by Warner was attributed almost exclusively to strangers. She reports additional wizardry techniques that might be practiced by anyone, but finds that here, too, there are pressures against accusations within the community, and that fellow clan members in particular are rarely accused. The various forms of wizardry, she reports, are "considered to be the causes of many serious illnesses and of almost all, if not all, deaths" (p. 44).

But the Murngin go beyond the notion of wizardry as the proximate cause, to ask about the ultimate cause—that is, what led to the use of wizardry. Reid found a variety of motives believed to lead other people or spirits to call on wizards—jealousy, adultery, broken marriage contracts, retaliation for murder, for example. But especially prominent here, as in Warner's account of explanations of illness, are violation of religious rules and failure to meet reciprocal ritual and economic obligations. Ordinary people or wizards or both are generally involved in the causal chain, yet at times the violation of religious rules seems to be considered a cause of illness without human mediation. The spirits associated with the myths of the Dreamtime, and with the places sacred to their celebration, seem to be the sources here; spirits of recent ancestors are very rarely blamed.

In the treatment, by contrast with the explanation, of illness, Reid finds the last half century to have brought great change. Hospitals, physicians, and aborigine assistants with some training in scientific medicine are available and are commonly the first resort of the seriously ill. But traditional medicine remains very active. Skepticism is expressed more often than before about some traditional techniques, for example, the removal of an alien object from the patient's body. It is as though the treatment of proximate causes and of the resulting symptoms had been largely turned over to scientific medicine, but for the treatment of ultimate causes reliance is placed on traditional medicine. (The same sequence can be observed in our own society, of course; as scientific advances clarify natural processes in disease, moral blame and prayer do not necessarily disappear.)

Healers are ordinary members of the local community with special reputations for effectiveness in putting mystical power to beneficent use, whereas sorcerers are unidentified outsiders thought to make evil use of mystical power. The two remain quite distinct, as Warner had reported with the terms "white magician" and "black magician." The healer, especially called on when wizardry is suspected, acts first as diviner, not only to identify any human involvement in the proximate cause but also to probe the ultimate cause. The healer joins then with relatives, friends, and neighbors in singing for the patient sacred songs celebrating the Dreaming. People thus show that they care for the patient and seek to heal by orienting him toward the ancestors, the land, and the sacred heritage.

A joint reliance on physician and healer parallels what has been reported for some Navaho, among whom it has been encouraged by some of the representatives of both medical traditions (Bergman, 1973). The orientation of Murngin traditional therapy, finding healing power in community participation—in harmony with living fellow members, with the mythical figures of the Dreamtime, and with the land and life that link the two—is also extended to preventive medicine. Recent decades have seen a movement from the modern towns back to "homeland centers" in the countryside.

> The leader of one homeland centre told me that, when his family first went to live there, they were skinny. After some time, though, they had shiny hair and round faces. This, he maintained, was due to the supernatural power inherent in the area and in some of the foods, such as the rock oysters. (Reid, 1983, 156)

Akawaio

The Akawaio are one of the small groups in northern South America that are survivors of the largely extinct aboriginal population of the Caribbean region, speakers of languages of the Carib family. The Akawaio live in the western part of Guiana (the former British Guiana). The British anthropologist Audrey J. Butt (later, Colson), in fieldwork there in 1951–1952 and in 1957, gave special attention to the explanation and treatment of illness.

The Akawaio well illustrate a general point: Careful inquiry into a people's explanations of illness almost always uncovers a diversity of explanations. The Akawaio share many of the explanations found in other parts of the world. They generally attribute illness to the evil activity of malevolent persons, but believe that various processes may be involved. The victim's soul may have been enticed to leave the body; if it is prevented from returning, death will result. Alien spirits may have entered the body; indeed, soul loss and spirit possession may occur together, the departure of the person's own soul having left room for the alien spirits. The spirits that may enter include spirits of specific diseases, the spirits of various plants, and even the spirit of the person bringing about the illness (Colson,

1976). A person is in some danger from what may be done with his exuviae; though such fears are less extreme than in some societies, they extend even to footprints, which may be burned to do one harm.

More unusual is the Akawaio emphasis upon blowing in a ritualized manner—"short sharp gusts" accompanied by a verbal spell or command. It is believed that by blowing appropriately on some small object, one may send its spirit into the body of an intended victim and produce illness, but apparently blowing alone is also thought capable of a similar effect (Butt, 1956). The fieldworker had no opportunity to observe blowing for evil purposes, for her informants denied doing it or even knowing how; consistent with this is their general tendency to blame outsiders for illness. Yet Akawaio conceptions of life after death suggest some fear that illness might be brought about by fellow Akawaio; a likely source of illness is said to be the "shade" of a deceased person, which wanders in the forest, whereas the person's "spirit" returns after death to the sky whence it had originally come (Butt, 1954, 54).

Death after brief illness has a special explanation that again suggests some fear of fellow Akawaio as well as of members of other tribes. The word *Edodo* "is used throughout British Guiana for 'a secret killer' who is said to catch his victim when he is alone, and to break his bones and poison him. On recovering consciousness the victim returns to his village not knowing what has happened; he falls ill and dies within a short time" (Butt, 1956, 55).

The victim of such an attack, like the victim of serious sorcery in northeastern Arnhem Land, cannot be helped; his death is inevitable. But for other diseases a variety of therapeutic techniques are used by the Akawaio shaman or by the patient. Most of these have a specific fit to the explanation of the illness. If malevolent blowing is blamed, well-intentioned blowing is used to cure the illness. If the explanation stresses soul loss, attempts are made to coax the victim's soul back. If spirit possession is instead stressed, then therapy is especially directed at frightening the alien spirits away or at getting stronger benevolent spirits to chase them away. Many influences on health are categorized as hot or cold or bitter or sweet. Illness tends to be blamed on extremes, and therapy aims at restoring balance by use of the opposite extreme. If illness is blamed on a substance or action that is classified as hot, for example, then its effect is countered by something cold.

Some therapeutic acts may be effective regardless of the cause ascribed to the illness. Ritualized blowing is the prime example; it sends the blower's spirit out to do what the blower intends, and if strong enough the spirit will complete its mission while away, perhaps helped by spirits invoked by the verbal spell. Ritualized blowing can be done by anyone, but most effectively by shamans or by old people who know best the traditional spells. Blowing is also thought to be done by nature spirits—sometimes with evil intent as the source of illness, sometimes with good intent by spirits called up by a shaman who is trying to cure a patient (Butt, 1956, 1961).

Some of the Akawaio therapeutic practices, and the explanations given for their efficacy, illustrate nicely a general point about traditional societies—that our culture's distinction between natural and supernatural cannot be used to classify their reactions to illness neatly into these two categories. The same reaction often has both natural and supernatural (i.e., mystical) aspects. The most basic and seemingly natural therapy of resting at home in one's hammock is explained partly as avoidance of exposure to dangerous spirits outside. Infusions of certain barks have therapeutic value; the reason lies partly in their attractiveness to spirits. One of these barks may be lit and carried around the village so that the smoke will pull an invalid's missing soul away from its captor and restore it to its proper place in the invalid's body (Colson, 1977, 51). Some of the plants that have therapeutic value are known in a rather personal way because their spirits appear in séances among the spirits that speak through the medium or help in his shamanistic flight (Colson, 1977, 51). The ant cure (making ants sting the patient) may have realistic value through distracting the patient's attention from other pains, but is explained as serving to drive away the spirit of the disease (Colson, 1976, 453–454). The mixture of what Westerners would consider natural and supernatural may of course also be seen in the explanations of illness; whooping cough, for example, is recognized as a distinct disease entity, but it is thought to be brought about by a specific spirit, and this spirit is likely to have been sent by a sorcerer from another tribe (Colson, 1976, 446).

The first reaction of Akawaio to illness is rest and restriction of eating—sometimes fasting and sometimes only avoidance of certain foods. Family responsibility is very conspicuous in response to illness, for both rest and food restrictions are observed by relatives as well as by the patient. The responsibility of relatives often extends to siblings and cousins, but is especially important for spouse and parent. Colson (1976, 433–435) describes cases of parents starving themselves for fear of harming a desperately sick child. Among the reasons cited were that if the parents ate, the spirit of the child's sickness might share the food, get stronger, and thus kill the child. In other ways, too, imprudent behavior may be threatening to relatives. Colson (1976, 480–481) cites a child's death from whooping cough as believed to be retaliation by powerful jaguar spirits for the father's having recently hunted and killed a jaguar.

SIMILARITIES AND DIFFERENCES

Bewildering variation appears among these six societies, and even within a single one. Yet there are uniformities as well. All have some mystical explanations and treatments. Naturalistic explanations of illness are often present too, though some societies seem to lack them. All societies probably have some naturalistic treatments, too. Our concern here is with the mystical aspect of explanation and treatment and its relation to the rest of religion.

Do mystical explanations of illness and mystical approaches to healing show some similarity all over the world? The six societies we have
looked at suggest some possibilities. There seem always to be some
tendency to blame oneself for getting sick and some tendency to blame
others. The others who are blamed characteristically include real, living
people, whether they be relatives, village mates, or foreigners. They also
typically include some "persons" who are not real, living people—the spirits
of the dead, nature spirits, or gods. There is a uniform tendency, too, for
methods of healing to be reasonably related to explanations of illness, to
be attempts to reverse or undo the sources to which illness is attributed.
But societies vary in the importance they assign to each cause.

Regional Variation

Earlier in this century a major interest of many anthropologists was
how culture traits spread from one society to others; from the facts about
how a trait was distributed over the earth, they made inferences about
where and when it had originated. This interest guided the research that
produced the first major monograph on customs concerning illness. Forrest E. Clements (1932) reviewed and classified explanations of illness all
over the world; working from his findings about their geographic distribution, he ventured to guess approximately where and when each explanation had originated. Attribution of illness to soul loss or to magical
intrusion of a foreign object, he concluded, had only a single point of origin
and spread from there over the rest of the world. Attributing illness to
violation of a taboo, on the other hand, he thought had probably started
independently in three different places (Middle America, the Arctic region,
and southern Asia).

More recently, Murdock (1980) has argued in a similar vein that
regional variations indicate an important influence of diffusion of ancient ideas, gradually through the passing centuries and millennia; he
was impressed by the failure of some explanations to appear in places
isolated from the societies that already share them. But anthropologists in recent decades devote less energy to largely unverifiable speculation about remote history, and are more interested in the way culture
traits function in societies in which they are present. They are more
willing, moreover, to credit the creative potential of people, in being
capable of independent invention or elaboration of explanatory ideas
and of therapies. Murdock points out, for example, that attribution of
illness to the action of spirits is almost universal (being clearly present
in all but two of a world sample of 139 societies). Understanding of the
wide variations found in the importance and elaboration of that explanation must then be sought in the way it fits into, or is used, in one or
another culture, and Murdock made a start at testing the relation
between importance of spirit explanation and several variables of general societal characteristics.

Place in the Total Culture

One of us, together with the anthropologist John Whiting, some years ago found evidence that theories of illness were to some extent consistent with motivational themes characterizing the life of a people (Whiting & Child, 1953). Our research was concerned with several broad motives to which psychoanalytic theory had directed the attention of psychologists: oral pleasure, dependence, sexuality, excretory need, and aggression. We were interested in whether the way a child's social environment treated these needs would, as psychoanalysis led us to expect, shape lasting personality to a sufficient extent to be expressed in aspects of adult life capable of subtle influence from within. Explanations of illness occurred to us as an aspect of adult life not, under primitive conditions, open to much influence from realistic knowledge, yet emotionally important and therefore open to influence by motivational themes. For this reason, we were not surveying all possible explanations of illness but were analyzing only those that seemed likely to be well suited to express one or another of these motivational themes.

We found little or no evidence that any explanations of illness were related to residues of childhood experience with excretory or sexual needs. But we found very substantial evidence of a relation for the other needs. Explanations that looked capable of expressing oral anxiety—such as attributing illness to something swallowed or words spoken—were found especially often in societies where children were deprived of early oral pleasure or were severely weaned. Explanations that suggested anxiety about close interdependence—such as attributing illness to an alien spirit's entering one's body or to one's soul's wandering—were found especially often in societies where infantile dependence was frustrated or even punished. Explanations attributing illness to foreign objects or other forms of attack by wizards or spirits, or to earlier aggression by the patient, were found most often in societies that demonstrated special concern with aggression in their socialization of children.

This aspect of religion, then, the nonrealistic explanation of illness, appears to be in part consistent with major worries and wishes of the members of a society. Just how great an influence this is, the research does not permit us to judge. The correlations on which we based our conclusions certainly are not strong enough to suggest that explanations of illness are influenced only in this way. Yet the influence may be strong enough to play an important part in understanding any single case.

Shirley Lindenbaum (1972), for example, in seeking to understand how ecological conditions were relevant to explanations of illness in New Guinea, appealed to motivational factors just such as Whiting and Child had tested in their more superficial cross-cultural study. Her work illustrates how broad correlations about single variables give way, in detailed analysis of particular societies, to a richer account of how explanations of illness relate to the whole culture. Melanesian societies in New Guinea vary in whether illness is attributed primarily to sorcery or to ancestral spirits, and Lindenbaum takes the Fore and the Enga to represent the two extremes.

The Enga attribute illness mostly to ancestral spirits, the Fore mostly to sorcery (and thus, of course, to living persons). She finds a clue in the relation between the sexes and the ecological conditions associated with it. The Enga have a population that approaches crowding (not by urban standards, but in relation to their mode of living off the land); they reduce sexual relations to a minimum as a way of controlling population growth, and teach men to fear their own sexuality even in adulthood. They can readily accept the idea that ancestral spirits would enforce population control by threatening to bring mortal diseases; hence when serious diseases occur, they are blamed on ancestral spirits. In contrast, the Fore feel their land to be adequate, and they even welcome settlers from outside. Fore men, far from viewing their own sexual activity as dangerous, feel threatened in their sexual adequacy and fear sexual competition from other men. This provides the setting for an aggressive rivalry of which sorcery fears are one expression. Lindenbaum does not imply conscious planning and decision, but argues in effect that this description is a verbal approximation to complex series of events that shape the interaction of these several aspects of culture.

Specific Theories of Illness, and their Relation to Other Aspects of Religion

Finally, we will look at a number of the principal mystical explanations of illness (and the therapies associated with them) that are repeatedly found, and consider them in relation to other aspects of religion. A more general inquiry into traditional medicine might consider mystical explanations and therapies in relation also to other features of culture. So far, though, there has been little systematic study on which to draw.

Soul Loss

Soul loss as an explanation of illness is widespread in western North America, and Elmendorf (1952) has surveyed it in detail. He found three large areas in which it was conspicuous, from northern Mexico up to western Canada, and great variation in the form this explanation took. What was believed to be lost was generally what might everywhere be called the soul—a psychical part of the person believed to survive bodily death. But in some societies it was, instead, the guardian spirit, or something called the heart, or luck, whose loss was responsible for illness. The cause of the loss was diverse. Sometimes it was spontaneous, either in a dream or in waking life, but sometimes the loss was by theft. Still other causes were fright or a fall. Where an agent was responsible for the soul loss, it might be a wizard, a ghost, or any of various mystical beings. The soul in some cases was believed to remain in the vicinity, but in other cases, to be in the land of the dead, on the way there, or in various other places not quite in this world. Generally, recovery of the soul was thought possible, but in some societies not, so that if this was declared the source of the illness all hope was gone. Elmendorf's analysis shows effectively what a wide range of explanations, and of implications for action, may be concealed under a simple label such as "soul loss."

This western North American variation in the form taken by a soul-loss explanation of illness is duplicated the world over, with variation conspicuous also in its importance and even its presence. Perhaps its absence in some societies may conceal traces of an ancient presence. In our society the tradition of saying "Bless you!" when someone sneezes is often supposed to have originated in fear that the person's soul might escape; the relation to an explanation of illness is more strongly suggested by the German "Gesundheit!" which means "Health!" Among traditional societies the soul-loss explanation of illness is often explicit, but its relation to other aspects of religion varies. Sometimes the soul goes off on its own—a possibility often thought, as we will see in Chapter 8, to be a special danger in the case of infants. Sometimes the soul is enticed away by the ghosts of recently deceased relatives who crave the companionship they have lost. Often the soul is in danger of unfriendly attack, or theft, by wizards or spirits. Preventive measures, and therapy for serious illness, are appropriate to the form of the soul-loss explanations. Much of the activity of shamans and of mediums is pertinent. The medium, communicating in trance with spirits, tries to enlist their support in securing the return of the patient's soul by the spirits who have stolen it. The shaman, in out-of-body travel to the spirit world, seeks to wrest the soul from its captors and return it to the patient's body.

Spirit Possession

Disease may be caused by the entry of a spirit into the person for malevolent purposes. In some instances, the spirit may be thought to take full command of the person, a notion that seems most likely where the disease is totally incapacitating, and this may be associated with the idea that the person's own soul has been lost or is now pushed out by the invading spirit. Often, however, the invading spirit causes illness while still coexisting with the person's own soul, and this theory may, for convenience, also be called "possession"; as with "soul loss" the local terms all translated as "possession" may cover many specific ideas.

Possession may be brought about in a variety of ways. The spirit may enter of its own volition, it may be sent by higher spirits or gods, or it may be sent by a wizard. In some societies, anyone may be thought capable of sending an invading spirit; among the Akawaio, for instance, even material objects have souls, and anyone may by blowing on an object in the right way send its soul to possess a victim.

For therapy, this theory dictates efforts to rid the victim of the possessing spirit. Rituals of exorcism are required in some societies; in some, practical measures obnoxious to the spirit may be sufficient, such as surrounding the patient with smoke or bad odors. Another device is to enlist the help of friendly spirits; among the Yanoama, for example, a friendly spirit may be sent to enter the patient to destroy the malevolent spirit or to persuade it to get out (Taylor, 1976, 28). Among the Lovedu of Southern Africa, where illness may be explained as due to possession by an ancestral spirit, exorcism is not the cure. The spirits in this case are basically benevolent, and are causing trouble because their wants are not known and being met. A group ceremony, guided by a specialist, relies on protracted dancing to lead the spirit to make its wants known. Subsequently, the patient is able to be an untroubled home for the spirit (Krige & Krige, 1943, 242–249).

Material or Object Intrusion

Illness is sometimes thought to be caused by alien material rather than an alien spirit. The distinction may not be perfectly clear, for the spirit may be that of a material object, as among the Akawaio, or the intruding object may be of a spiritual character and not visible to ordinary people even when supposedly extracted. The material may sometimes be a powder or fluid thought to be mixed in with food or drink; in this case, the theory may be confused with the administration of realistic poison, yet retain a mystical character in that wizards are thought responsible for the poisoning. There may be no very sharp distinction between poisons we would think realistically effective and poisons we would consider imaginary; similarly, there may be no very sharp distinction between a physical object a healer exhibits after supposedly sucking or squeezing it out of a patient and the invisible object or spirit on which he or she can only report.

The principal device of therapy here is, obviously, the removal of the intruding material. Well known to Western observers is the practice of healers in some societies of seeming to remove a physical object, deceiving patient and bystanders. This is a case where the Western observer is almost inevitably convinced that the healer is deceiving his fellows, and in some instances healers are found quite willing, in talking with outsiders or in describing the process of learning to be a healer, to admit their deception. Westerners may be too ready to suppose that healers are equally deceiving their fellows in their other therapeutic acts. This seems too facile an extension to members of other cultures of the skeptical attitude Western scientists tend to share about religious therapy as practiced in our own society. Western observers who do not share this skeptical attitude and become intimately acquainted with healers in other societies are likely to remain convinced that some, at least, of the healers are as sincere, as lacking in hypocrisy, as the most serious healing priests or Christian Science practitioners in our own society. In many of the more thoroughly psychological acts of healers, it may be generally true that the healer believes in the real efficacy of the procedures just as the patients do.

Intrusion by Disease Entity

Close to the naturalistic contagion theory of modern medicine is the explanation of illness as due to intrusion by a particular disease entity. We have seen an example of this in the Kung belief in a substance responsible for each recognized type of disease. The cure is to draw the substance out, and among the Kung this may occur through physical contact with an entranced healer. Among the Lunda, who have a similar theory, the disease entity is personalized in such a way that obnoxious herbs are thought capable of driving it away (Turner, 1967, 300–301). This explanation of illness lends itself to development of fear of contagion. When a Papago is suffering from a disease that is explained in this way, others are likely to keep their distance; proximity to the patient may draw a person to the attention of the disease, which is thought of as a personalized entity that may enter anyone at its choice (Bahr et al., 1974). In some societies, intrusion is by something less specific, a generalized badness, which may be sent by gods or wizards or be brought on by one's own actions. This is especially common in African societies, but is also a part of the Navaho theory of illness. Here, too, the cure is expulsion, and the lengthy sings of the Navaho are thought to act partly by ridding the person of badness and making room for goodness to take its place.

Violation of Taboos

Doing what is strictly forbidden is often thought to cause illness. This mystical retribution, as Murdock (1980) calls it, is sometimes considered to be automatic but sometimes to require mediation by one or more spirits. The two explanations may be found in the same society, as we noted for the Murngin and as Kennedy (1967, 186) reports for the Nubians of Egypt. Sometimes, as among the Navaho, violations that seem very minor to the outsider are regarded as sources of serious illness. Sometimes, too, the retribution may not be visited on the violator himself but on a relative; thus, the mystical theory of illness serves to increase group responsibility, as among the Gnau.

Confession is a frequent form of therapy for disease that is ascribed to violation of taboos, and the confession is often expected to be public. An instance where this therapeutic role of confession has been amply described is provided by the Ojibwa (Hallowell, 1963).

Spirit Attack

Already implied is that sickness may be brought about by a spirit, as an aggressive attack on the person. The attack may take one of the forms already indicated—stealing the person's soul, for example, or entering the person's body. But it may also be by unspecified processes, and for that reason it is useful to recognize spirit aggression as a separate possibility. The attack may be considered to be justifiable punishment, or a part of one's fate, or an arbitrary and perhaps whimsical act by a spirit. One can hope to prevent whimsical attacks by avoiding being noticed by spirits, a preventive practiced by the Gnau. Where the spirit aggression is thought to be motivated, steps are in order to avoid or stop annoying the spirits. Ancestral spirits are especially likely to be the source of aggression, and we have seen that sacrifice, prayer, and other efforts to satisfy ancestral spirits form a good part of religious observance in many societies. Spirits are often associated with place (as in the belief in haunted houses), and for a localized epidemic a therapy and preventive is to move the entire village to a new site, leaving the ghosts behind, a device reported from Melanesia for the Manus (Romanucci-Ross, 1979, 131).

Homeopathic and Contagious Magic

James Frazer (1922, 11–45) distinguished two types of magic. According to belief in homeopathic magic, a person can be affected by what happens to objects similar to himself or herself. If a sorcerer shapes a doll to represent a victim and plunges a needle into the doll's breast, the victim may die of a heart attack. According to belief in contagious magic, a person could be affected by what happened to objects connected with the self by closeness or contiguity. If a sorcerer destroys some clothing, or some nail parings, of an enemy, the latter will suffer. As Frazer put it, homeopathic magic involves thinking based on the law of similarity, contagious magic upon the law of contact. Some later writers have used "sympathetic" for Frazer's "homeopathic"; he preferred to apply "sympathetic" to both types of thinking, on the grounds that "both assume that things act on each other at a distance through a secret sympathy."

Frazer sought to understand the varied ways in which health and welfare, sickness and other misfortune, could be believed to be influenced by events occurring at a distance, with no possibility of a causal influence. Not every instance of magic can be fitted neatly into his classificatory scheme, but a very great many can, as is well illustrated by his voluminous presentation of examples. His distinction between similarity and contiguity is familiar in other contexts. It corresponds exactly to the distinction made by literary critics, in analyzing poetic language, between metaphor and metonymy. It corresponds approximately to the distinction made by Freud, in discussing how we create our dreams and how psychoanalysis may lay bare their meaning, between symbolism and association. Thus, Frazer's study of primitive magic was getting at fundamentals of human thought.

The same sorts of magical connection between events at a distance may be thought to give rise to illness without the action of a sorcerer. Accidental as well as deliberate damage to symbols or property of a person could endanger him. As Frazer showed by many examples (ibid., 19ff), taboos are a sort of negative magic, prohibiting certain actions because of the bad magical effect they might have. Taboos on the behavior of wives whose husbands are away at war or on the hunt, for instance, are often based on magical effects: The wife must not empty the dish lest her distant husband find himself starving.

Magic may also serve benevolent purposes, healing rather than injuring. In the therapeutic procedures that the Lunda use in treating leprosy, for example, "the main principle underlying the treatment is to collect a number of substances that exhibit sympathetic associations with leprosy ... and to incinerate these, thereby destroying the disease (by sympathetic magic)" (Turner, 1967, 309).

Disturbance of Social Relationships

Underlying many of the explanations of illness, as we have seen among the Navaho, is a core allusion to the patient's relations with other people, and this is sometimes quite explicit. Another very apt example is offered by the Fipa of southwestern Tanzania. R. G. Willis reports on two Fipa theories of illness causation, one the simpler folk theory and the other a more complex theory held by the medical specialists. The folk theory "sees sickness as the manifestation of a kind of injurious communication between human beings. The theory is understandable as the logical complement, ... of the Fipa perception of the self as emerging from a continuing process of constructive interaction with others" (1972, 376).

In this folk theory, the blame is placed on sorcerers, who have presumably contaminated the victim's food or drink—often the very beer that normally plays a central role in positive social interaction. The second theory, that of medical specialists, is a complicated development and supplementation of the folk theory, apparently more clearly mystical but still built on social relations. The most serious disease, according to this second theory, comes from pollution brought about by social interaction with someone "who has recently had secret, adulterous sexual relations" (Willis, 1972, 374).

Both the folk and the specialist theories summarize a great variety of specific explanations, tracing the illness to various agents. Ancestral or other spirits, or a specific sorcerer, may be responsible. Divination identifies the specific source and points to the locus of disturbance in the patient's social relations. If ancestral spirits or apprentice sorcerers are responsible, the disturbance is in the patient's kin group. If an established sorcerer or a nonancestral spirit is responsible, the disturbance is in "the wider, communal sphere of village society" (Willis, 1968, 143).

Victor Turner, discussing healing among the Ndembu of Zambia, implies that the healer is similarly aware of the importance of social relations in disease and in therapy:

> It seems that the Ndembu "doctor" sees his task less as curing an individual patient than as remedying the ills of a corporate group. The sickness of a patient is mainly a sign that "something is rotten" in the corporate body. The patient will not get better until all the tensions and aggressions in the group's

interrelations have been brought to light and exposed to ritual treatment. (1967, 392)

A similar stress on social relations is apparent in several of the societies we considered at the beginning of this chapter. Generalizing about therapies, both the traditional and those associated with scientific medicine, Arthur Kleinman says:

> The healing dialectic has been considered effective when the bonds between the sick individual and the group, weakened by disease, are strengthened, social values reaffirmed, and the notion of social order no longer threatened by illness and death; or when the individual experience of illness has been made meaningful, personal suffering shared, and the individual leaves the marginal situation of sickness and has been reincorporated in health or even death back into the social body. (1973, 210)

SUMMARY

Religious conceptions are everywhere in traditional societies drawn on in seeking to understand the sources of illness and to prevent or cure it. In some societies, response to illness and its threat is the main concern of religion. Typically, a traditional society exhibits a variety of mystical explanations of illness and a variety of mystical procedures for healing. Procedures for healing are mostly attempts to undo the processes to which the illness is attributed. Underlying many of the specific mystical explanations and treatments of illness may be a basic concern, explicit in some societies, with the strength and integrity of the patient's relation to the social and cosmic order. Cross-cultural research indicates that illness tends to evoke responses consistent with motives predominant in its members. More important may be the influence of economy and social structure, but this awaits future study.

Chapter 8

Rites of Passage, and Relation between the Sexes

Emphasis on creed in the history of Christianity might suggest to some that belief is the core of religion. But in seeking to understand the religions of traditional peoples, ritual seems more basic. That has been the opinion of many scholars, beginning with those who had little to work with but the ancient history of Near Eastern religions (Smith, 1889). The Christian emphasis on creed was favored by Christianity's arising in an era of literacy, among peoples with professional clergy and philosophers. Emphasis on ritual performance, in traditional religions, was favored by the absence of writing during their formative period and by the close involvement of religion in the everyday life of the whole population.

The rituals found in traditional religions are enormously varied, and available knowledge for some is rich in detail. Malinowski (1935) devoted two volumes to the agricultural rituals of the Trobriand Islanders in Melanesia; Monica Wilson (1957, 1959) wrote one volume on the kinship rituals and another on the communal rituals of the Nyakyusa; and James Fernandez (1982) has devoted a very large book to the Bwiti rituals developed by the Fang in response to the pressures of change.

Adequate understanding of the religious life of a particular society may require mastery of such full accounts. But broad understanding of religious life at large can hardly encompass the details from the hundreds of societies for which we have fairly adequate information about rituals. How can we generalize? How can we consider what, in general, rituals contribute to the life of all societies and all individuals? One way is to confine ourselves to one type of ritual at a time, rather than all types at once, and look more closely at how that type appears in the life of various societies. We undertake to do so in this and the two succeeding chapters. With less concentration on ritual, too, we have looked in earlier chapters at the rituals involved in attempting to cause and to cure illness and at the rituals through which people seek to communicate with mystical beings or to obtain mystical power themselves.

An early student of ritual, A. Van Gennep (1909/1960) distinguished a type found in all cultures that he labeled *rites of passage*. His label has come into common use, in ordinary speech as well as in anthropology, so we adopt it generally in this chapter. We intend, however, no distinction between "rite" and "ritual," nor between either of these terms and "ceremony," and occasionally use all of these terms. Scholars have sought to extend and improve our understanding of rites of passage and of the form they take in specific societies. These rituals are the central topic of the present chapter and of the discussion of mortuary rituals in Chapter 9. The rites of passage most uniformly found throughout the world are those that mark transition points in the life history of the individual, and we will focus our discussion in this chapter on rites associated with the beginnings of the individual life and progression on toward adulthood. Many of these rituals differ markedly between the two sexes, and we will therefore take this as an occasion to consider related aspects of the religious significance of gender and magico-religious practices related to sexuality. We will be selective, omitting rites of marriage, which often have less religious significance than in the West. Rites of passage associated with the end of life, we consider in Chapter 9.

(How far the category of rites of passage is spread, beyond rites marking major transition points in the life of the individual, varies among authors. So do the definitions of other categories to be contrasted with this one. Chapple and Coon [1942] use "rites of intensification" to label rituals that intensify feelings about group life and values. Titiev [1960] has a similar category called "calendrical rites." These are the main subject matter of Chapter 10, on festivals. Honko [1979] notes that these typologies attend mostly to rituals for the regularly recurring events of individual and group life. Honko gives explicit recognition to rituals that cope with more unpredictable problems, labeling them "crisis rites." These would include many of the rituals that we consider in various other chapters. Other rituals, such as those arising in the less crucial contexts of everyday life, do not fall neatly into any of these categories. The important thing to recognize about typologies of ritual is that they classify purposes or occasions, and that a single ritual performance may serve two or more purposes or occasions.)

RITUALS OF PREGNANCY AND BIRTH

In many societies, mystical beliefs and practices appear at the earliest possible time in the life cycle, in the very effort to increase or to decrease the likelihood that a new life will start, and then as in other parts of the life cycle they are mingled with customs of more realistic character.

Traditional societies have developed many techniques to control fertility. So thoroughly realistic as hardly to merit attention here are the promotion of sexual intercourse for purposes of fertility as well as pleasure, or sexual abstinence, contraception, abortion, and infanticide as devices for limiting the number of new members added to family and community. These are often accompanied by practices based on erroneous beliefs about natural processes. The essential role of semen in human fertility, for example, in many Melanesian societies is misjudged to be continuous, so that intercourse during pregnancy is required as a male contribution to proper development of the fetus. Nor does timing of intercourse in relation to the menstrual cycle, in attempts to achieve or avoid conception, show any conspicuous tendency to be based on correct beliefs (Montgomery, 1974, 145–146).

The mystical beliefs and practices concerned with pregnancy are also numerous. An example is provided by taboos on a woman's eating certain foods while pregnant. Barbara Ayres (1967) conjectured that food cravings in pregnancy are partly motivated by a woman's desire to be dependent on others at this critical period, a desire echoing her own experience in childhood. Ayres confirmed this idea in a comparative study of a worldwide sample of 40 societies. Food taboos for pregnant women were present in all but four, and the number of such taboos in any single society was found to be related positively to the encouragement there of dependency in childhood. The severity of punishment for violating the taboos, moreover, was found to be related to the severity of punishment for dependency in childhood. Ayres concluded that these taboos serve to control the widespread threat of expressing emotional dependence at the expense of overeating and excessive weight gain in pregnancy; thus, the taboos provide mystical support for maternal health. (Many societies, she found, permit pregnant women to be indulged in their cravings for unusual or scarce foods, a permissiveness that poses no dangers of overeating but might contribute to a sense of being loved and cared for.) Food taboos of the pregnancy period must in some societies, such as several Chaco tribes and the Yanoama of South America, be observed by the father; this custom foreshadows more extensive male participation in the rituals surrounding childbirth itself (Vinci, 1959, 76; Métraux, 1963).

Early Western writers on traditional peoples were impressed by occasional reports of what seemed a strange custom of male behavior in connection with childbirth, a ritual whose significance was generally obscure to outsiders. A man whose wife is about to give birth, it was reported, would take to bed, perhaps act as though suffering the pains of giving birth, and in other respects seem to imitate the role of his wife. This custom, which some of the early writers believed to have characterized some European groups as well, was termed *couvade*. The element of clear imitation of the female role was exaggerated in early reports, and as more and more traditional societies came to be known, the term was extended in its meaning (Munroe, Munroe, & Whiting, 1973).

Many societies, while having little or none of the specific custom of the father clearly imitating the mother, still required that the father mark his participation in childbirth, interrupting the usual routine of his life in ways that were less disruptive yet had a symbolic, a religious, significance rather than a purely practical one. (In our society at present, for example, for a father to take over some of the cooking might be a purely realistic adjustment to the isolation of the nuclear family. For him to distribute cigars to his friends is a purely symbolic act, and if this custom were given a mystical significance, it would clearly fall within the broader definition of couvade.)

Typical of couvade ritual in the broader sense is the following description by the American anthropologist Leopold Pospisil of relevant practices and beliefs of the Kapauku, a Melanesian people of West Irian (the Indonesian part of New Guinea):

> The birth imposes only a few restrictions on the parents. The mother is forbidden to leave her room for about three to five days. For about seven days it is taboo for her spouse to fell trees, burn them, plant sugar cane, build fences, or take a long walk. There are no food restrictions for either spouse. All these taboos have been set by ... [the creator] and their neglect would cause the newly born child to become sick. (1958, 37)

Couvade, in its original, narrow sense, although definitely occurring in some societies, is rare. In a worldwide sample of 44 societies, Montgomery (1974, 161–162) seems to have found none in which the father's behavior around the time of childbirth was imitative of the female role in any further sense than observing the same taboos as his wife. Couvade in the broader sense is much more common and—often in a mild form—characterizes about 45 percent of peoples the world over (Paige & Paige, 1981, 286–288). The frequency of such rituals should not be surprising; behavior and physiological symptoms reminiscent of couvade occur in our own society on an unconscious basis, in a frequency that appears to be somewhere between 10 percent and 50 percent (Lipkin & Lamb, 1982).

Many attempts to explain couvade have been made. Like other rites of passage, it may "provide a buffer which absorbs the shock and emotional agitation inherent in a delicate transitional situation" (Coelho, 1949, 53). But just why is it successful in doing so? Some theories have stressed its functional value for the social group, and others have emphasized what it does for the individual.

A notable psychological theory of couvade was presented by Munroe, Munroe, and Whiting (1973); they considered couvade to be a way that psychological conflicts characteristic of men in certain societies might be resolved. In some societies, they argued, men have an especially strong identification with the female role because of their being associated in early life primarily with their mothers rather than with their fathers. In such societies the demands of the adult male role place men into conflict about their sexual identity. In some societies where men face this dilemma, it is resolved by strengthening the masculine tendencies through initiation rituals (discussed later in this chapter); in others, it is resolved by permitting or even requiring men to express their feminine side in connection with the birth of their children. This psychological theory predicts that couvade should be especially common in societies where young children are treated in a femininizing manner—as, for example, by mother and child forming a tight social group with the father little in evidence. That is exactly what Munroe, Munroe, and Whiting found in their comparative cross-cultural study.

A very different theory of couvade, based on sociological considerations, was presented by Karen and Jeffrey Paige (1981, 198–199). The motivation for couvade, they propose, is the desire of a man to make a firm public announcement that he is the father and has the rights of a father to control the child's destiny. In societies where men are bonded together in groups based on kinship, such public claims are not necessary; the social structure makes clear the position and rights of the father and the enforcement power of his male relatives. In a comparative cross-cultural study, Paige and Paige found that in societies that have "strong fraternal interest groups" couvade tends to be absent; in societies that lack them, couvade tends to be present. The motivation stressed by Paige and Paige thus arises from the circumstances of adult life and looks toward maintaining a predictable social structure, rather than from personality characteristics originating in the experiences of early childhood.

Munroe, Munroe, and Whiting (1981, 624–628) later took account of both sets of facts in an expansion of their psychological theory. An initial motivational basis for couvade is laid, they argue, in any society in which strong identification with the feminine role is induced in young boys. If the society is so organized that adult men have high solidarity, that identification will generally be changed before a boy becomes fully adult (with the help of initiation rites, considered later in this chapter), and motivation for couvade is removed. But if the society is not so organized, the feminine identification will continue and lead to couvade.

The researchers proceeded to test this combined theory. The index they used for social structure favoring male solidarity was patrilocal residence, as opposed to all other residence rules. Patrilocal residence means that married couples live with the husband's family, so that closely related men are lifelong residents of the same large household whereas women are separated from their own close relatives. They found that practice of couvade was primarily found in societies that had an initial close tie between mother and child and did not have patrilocal residence. Thus, the rituals of couvade seem to satisfy a subtle motive for expression by men of a feminine side of their identity, and are not needed if that side of their identity has been reduced or eliminated in adolescence or early adulthood.

This theory embraces two points about couvade that had long been recognized by earlier writers and that are at least implicit in the two separate theories that it brings together. One is that in couvade practices a man seems to be expressing a sense of closeness and participation with his wife, perhaps a mystical feeling of oneness. The other is that in couvade a husband is marking himself out as the father of the child in a sociological sense. Thus a man who believes the child to spring from an adulterous union may still, if he accepts the child, engage in the same practices as though he were also the biological father. (In some few societies of South America, couvade can serve also as an acknowledgment of possible biological paternity alone, and thus may be shared by the sociological father with any other men who have had intercourse with his wife at relevant times. Paige and Paige [1981, 192–194] interpret such instances as assertions of competing claims to the rights of fatherhood.)

Another point long recognized is that the actions of the father in following the rules of couvade are at least partly motivated by concern for the health of the child. This point about couvade is not incompatible with the theories we have reviewed, and is supported by the explanations offered by the people themselves in various societies. A mystical relationship between father and child, making the child's welfare dependent on the activities of its father, is explicit in the Melanesian case quoted earlier from Pospisil, as well as in many others. It is particularly conspicuous in peoples of the Caribbean area and parts of South America (Rivière, 1974; Métraux, 1963). As a Yanoama man said to Vinci: "the man must stay in the hammock without stirring, because any strain on his part, or any mishap that came his way, would affect the child and might have dire results" (1959, 76).

However, the child's health may well be at least equally dependent on mystical relation with its mother (as among the Kapauku), and the taboos that must be observed may apply equally to both parents. At the extreme, among the Waiwai of Amazonian Brazil and Guiana, dietary restrictions for both mother and father often last for three years after the birth of the child (Fock, 1960).

Parental concern for the health of a baby often seems to be expressed in, or exacerbated by, a blaming of disease and death on loss of the soul. At birth, the soul is widely thought to be only lightly associated with the body, and parental action may help prevent its wandering off. If an adult's soul wanders, it can find its way back, but an infant's soul may not be able to return on its own. Among the Aranda of Australia, the soul of the child is thought likely to follow either the mother or the father, even partaking in activities of the father that could bring the infant harm; here is a powerful motivation for restricting parental activity. The Aymara mother, likewise, believes her baby's soul is likely to follow when she goes abroad, and she must be sure it does not get left behind. In some societies, the fear is not so much of the soul's wandering as of its being seized; it may be stolen or devoured by malignant beings, either human, animal, or mystical. Among the Tzeltal of Middle America, for example, it is evil spirits that may seize the child's soul. Tzeltal mothers mark the child or its path to help its soul get back quickly if it starts wandering, and Tzeltal fathers perform the ritual called "sowing the soul of the child" as soon as possible, to ensure the baby's survival (Villa Rojas, 1969, 224).

The relation of couvade to belief in soul loss as a cause of disease or death appears to be very close. We checked this on the sample of societies that had been used by Munroe, Munroe, and Whiting (1973). We began by adopting their ratings on the presence or absence of couvade. For each society we sought evidence on belief in soul loss as an explanation for illness and death. For some of these societies, Murdock (1980) had rated presence or absence of one type of belief in soul loss—voluntary departure of the soul from the body—and we accepted his positive judgments of presence as clearly pertinent to our broader definition. Murdock apparently had not looked specifically at beliefs about infancy and had not considered seizure or seduction of the soul by outside agents, so we searched the ethnographic reports for these possibilities in the remaining societies. The outcome was that of 36 societies with belief in soul loss 32 (89 percent) practiced couvade, whereas of the 30 societies lacking belief in soul loss only 11 (37 percent) practiced couvade.

This relation appears to be independent of the relation of couvade to feminine identification and to absence of fraternal interest groups. Neither of these conditions, as they were measured by Munroe, Munroe, and Whiting (1973), showed any substantial relation to belief in soul loss. And when we divided the sample into societies having at least one of the two conditions and those having neither, there remained a substantial relation in each group between soul loss and couvade. Of societies having at least one of these two predisposing conditions, couvade was found in 93 percent (26 out of 28) of those believing in soul loss and 53 percent (10 out of 19) of those lacking a belief in soul loss. In those lacking both predisposing conditions, the percentages were 75 percent (6 out of 8) and 9 percent (1 out of 11).

Concern for the health of the newborn is also concern for its spiritual well-being. Often, the two are not sharply distinguished; explanations of physical illness often appeal to spiritual defects as the source. Some writers on couvade, and many of the indigenous descriptions on which they rely, stress its role in providing firm development of the soul—the positive side of the concern expressed negatively in fear of soul loss. As Rivière (1974) points out, couvade customs in this way parallel the Christian ritual of baptism and the customs of godparenthood. Emphasis on the father's role in rituals surrounding childbirth may then express a common idea that spiritual growth must be promoted by men, in parallel with women's provision in pregnancy and later of conditions for physical growth.

Rituals surrounding childbirth include a great variety of other rules commonly stated to be followed for the benefit of the child. Very often justifications given exemplify the magical principle of like causing like. Among the Karen of Burma, for instance, if the afterbirth is disposed of by hanging it in a tree, "a large tree of one of the hardiest varieties is selected for the purpose, in order that the babe may gain strength therefrom" (Marshall, 1922, 169).

To summarize: Couvade rituals help solve for individuals problems arising from gender identity, and thus help the society maintain its established pattern of differentiating between the roles of male and female. They also alleviate anxiety about the physical survival and spiritual development of the infant and thus, in the long run, reduce anxiety about the survival of the society. In the face of the dangers that lurk in societies with high infant mortality, then, couvade rituals may contribute to the optimism essential for effective social life.

RITUALS OF ADVANCEMENT TOWARD ADULTHOOD

Human transformation from infant to adult is a gradual process. Even menarche, an abrupt and critical event in the female, is but one point in a generally smooth series of changes. Societies differ widely in how they divide the total period of development into categories, and at what points they facilitate a person's transition from one category to the next by ceremonies that place the change in a context of social values and worldview. Scholarly attempts to generalize about rites of passage vary, too. Some scholars have looked at all forms of initiation, some have focused only on rites that include genital operations, and some have considered for each society the one transition rite most emphasized there. Yehudi Cohen (1964b), on the other hand, treats separately rites in the prepubertal period and those in the pubertal period. We will begin simply with an example for each sex of initiation ceremonies most thoroughly studied by anthropologists.

Girls' Initiation Rites

A very full account is available of girls' initiation ceremonies among the Bemba, a tribe in Zambia. Audrey Richards (1956), doing fieldwork there in 1931, had an opportunity to be present at the many sessions of two young girls' joint initiation, under conditions favorable for understanding and recording what went on. The ceremony lasted 23 days, considerably abbreviated from the many months over which it would have extended in earlier generations. For the most part, the two initiates just watched, listened, and did what they were told (beginning with entering the hut crawling backward under blankets). The most active participants were close female relatives, and especially one woman with recognized skills that qualified her to be mistress of initiation rites. Ritual activity occupied a large part of some days, a few hours on others, and apparently none on a few days. It included a great deal of dancing and singing, activities at once ritually important and a source of enjoyment. The texts of the songs, the paintings and sculptures made at some sessions, and a variety of small objects (figurines) symbolized various cultural values, especially those pertaining most distinctively to the role of adult woman. They were used to provide reminders and emotional meaning, rather than teaching ideas completely unknown to the initiates. There were only moderate teasing and little physical discomfort.

The particular procedures used are specific to the Bemba (except for some shared with closely related tribes). But much of their general nature is found in most of the societies elsewhere that initiate girls. The initiation occurs somewhere around the girl's first menstruation (often much more precisely than among the Bemba). One girl (or a small group reaching menarche at about the same time) is separated from normal life—rigidly, in many societies—and undergoes various experiences under the charge of older women. The experiences usually include some degree of hazing and considerable rehearsal of the role of adult woman in the particular society. Psychological preparation for childbearing, and quest for mystical support for fertility, are generally conspicuous. The effect on the initiate seems itself to be considered in part a mystical effect.

A number of societies in Africa and a few elsewhere include in girls' initiation some form of genital mutilation, felt to be justified by custom and mystical beliefs. Often inaccurately referred to by Western writers as female circumcision, the operation is most often partial or complete removal of the clitoris or a partial sewing together of the vulva (infibulation). Removal of the clitoris may be thought of as increasing the distinctiveness of the female, by removing the part of the genitals that most resemble the male genitals. (Janice Boddy [1982] confirms this as one element in the symbolic significance of a complicated female mutilation performed in a rural group of northern Sudan.) Infibulation seems, rather, to be a device for ensuring virginity or for asserting exclusive sexual rights of a particular male. These mutilations are absent in the Bemba and in most other societies that, like the Bemba, trace descent through the mother rather than through the father.

Boys' Initiation Rites

Victor Turner (1962, 1967, 151–279) has reported in depth on a male initiation he witnessed among the Ndembu, in Zambia, and has used it as a prime example in analyzing the symbolism of ritual. It was the first time in ten years that the ceremony had been performed in the particular set of villages, and 29 boys ranging in age from about 6 to 16 were ready for initiation. The importance of the event is indicated in the intense maneuvering Turner reports about who should fill the various official positions, and in the fact that many adults devoted much time and effort to the rites over a period of about two months. The novices seemed clearly aware of the critical meaning of the ceremony as a turning point in their lives. They felt, on the one hand, some danger of castration or death from circumcision, but on the other hand, the absolute necessity of taking part, in order to shift from one mode of life to another.

> From being "unclean" children, partially effeminized by constant contact with their mothers and other women, boys are converted by the mystical efficacy of ritual into purified members of a male moral community, able to begin to take their part in the jural, political, and ritual affairs of Ndembu society. (Turner, 1967, 265–266)

The novices spent the weeks of the ceremony in places specially prepared for each phase, isolated most of the time from their families (to which they would at the end return). Circumcision came on the second day, and healing was completed by the end of the ceremony, about two months later. The novices' behavior, clothing, seating, eating—all were regulated in great detail by custom, and their families were at various times also subject to many taboos and positive requirements. Sanctions for departure from the rules were severe, including diminished prestige and the threat that ancestral spirits, already lively presences to participants through the prayers addressed to them, would punish deviants with leprosy. Novices eventually see some of the long-dead ancestors dancing, and learn only later that living men are impersonating them, unknown to women and to uninitiated males. The sounds of a bull-roarer similarly shift from providing fearful evidence that mystical beings are present to being a secret shared with all initiated males. During the weeks of healing, much time is devoted to tutoring in the adult male role and in issues of morality. Dancing and singing are conspicuous, and on some days involve relatives and even visitors from other communities. The final return to family is itself impressively ritualized, as though to ensure that the whole community recognizes in all future actions the transformation that has occurred.

Initiation Rites across Societies

As with the example of girls' initiation rites, much in this example of boys' initiation rites is typical of many other societies as well. Turner was especially interested in the particularities, seeking to understand Ndembu rites most thoroughly in the context in which they occurred. Our interest here is in a comparison among societies, in seeking to understand broad similarities and major differences.

Our reading of ethnographic reports on religion in societies all over the world leads us to complete agreement with conclusions that had already been reached by Schlegel and Barry (1979, 1980) through a systematic analysis of initiation ceremonies in a worldwide sample of societies (excluding modern industrial societies).

1. More societies have initiation ceremonies for girls than do for boys. Schlegel and Barry find that the societies initiating girls alone are more than twice as numerous as those initiating boys alone. Taking into account those that initiate both sexes, girls are initiated in 35 percent more societies than are boys.

2. There is a widespread, though not universal, difference between ceremonies for the two sexes, in that boys tend to be initiated in groups, at times not precisely related to any specific step in physical maturity, whereas girls tend to be initiated singly, at each girl's first menstruation. This difference is doubtless in large part due to the lack in males of any developmental change as dramatic and conspicuous as menarche, but it is consistent with another general point we will present below.

3. A ceremony is almost never for boys and girls together. In the many societies that initiate both, the rites are almost always separate and held at different times. This fact suggests that most societies give overwhelming importance to gender in defining social status; they do not initiate into adult personhood but specifically into manhood or womanhood. The distinction is sharpened by the fact that for a society to initiate one gender by

no means implies initiation of the other. Schlegel and Barry's sample contains more societies that initiate only one gender than societies that initiate both genders. It is clear that initiation is not thought of as necessary for becoming simply an adult.

(We have found very few instances of joint initiation of boys and girls, and in no instance is an identical rite performed for the two indiscriminately. The closest approach is found in the Yahgan of Tierra del Fuego [Gusinde, 1917]; but there the boys go on later to a further ceremony for them alone. Among the Mundugumor [Mead, 1935], a tribe in the Sepik area of New Guinea, initiation is required for boys but optional for girls, and the girls who elect to take part are exempt from the physical ordeals the boys go through. For the Orokaiva, also in New Guinea, several differences in treatment of the two genders are described both within and beyond the joint ceremonies; in at least one of their villages [Chinnery & Beaver, 1915], boys and girls are separated for several weeks after the joint ceremonies, and apparently have very different programs for that period.)

4. Ceremonies vary with economy and social complexity. Schlegel and Barry (1980) report that ceremonies for girls predominate in the simpler societies, that ceremonies for boys become equally frequent at a middle range of complexity, and that with greater complexity both ceremonies tend to disappear. They interpret these differences very skillfully as a consequence of the fact that the social significance of gender varies with the level of social complexity. Our detailed study of individual cultures leads us to make more explicit within the general variable of complexity the specific variable of economy as a direct influence on the social significance of gender.

The predominance of girls' initiation in the simpler societies, we believe, is attributable to the fact that these societies are foragers—that is, they depend on hunting and gathering. This type of economy leads to concern with female pollution as a threat to the food supply (Schlegel & Barry, 1980; Child & Child, 1985). It is significant that girls' initiation in these societies generally involves seclusion and imposition of food taboos— two features that also appear repeatedly among foraging societies as aspects of sex differentiation in other contexts than initiation. Societies in the middle range of complexity, on the other hand, include many herding societies; here the animals that provide food are under control, so that fear of their being scared off is less likely to arise. An important motive for girls' initiation as ensuring food supply through imposition of taboos is thus absent, and the presence or absence of initiation ceremonies is free to be influenced by other variables. In still more complex societies, people develop many specialized interests, and religion is likely to be built around specific cults or around prestige and social stratification rather than around the basic distinction between men and women—a point that has been made very effectively by Allen (1967) in a systematic comparison of initiation rites in various Melanesian societies.

Initiation ceremonies are generally linked to age or biological maturity. In some societies, though, rites of comparable significance are performed on the occasion of specific achievement. Some North American foragers have as rites of passage a first game-kill rite for an individual boy and a first fruit or wild plant rite for a girl (Driver, 1972, 98, 101). A similar type of rite is found among the San of southern Africa on the occasion of a boy's first killing an eland (Lewis-Williams & Biesele, 1948). A somewhat comparable ritual in a much more complex culture is the famous Naven ritual of the Iatmul, in the Sepik area of New Guinea (Bateson, 1958). When an Iatmul boy or girl accomplished for the first time something notable, the achievement might be celebrated with a Naven ceremony during which the mother's brother treated his nephew or niece to a kind of "shaming" behavior. The uncle's behavior commonly included transvestism and imitation of a decrepit elderly woman; to stop such a bizarre exhibition the nephew or niece had to give the uncle something of value. The Naven ceremonies were expensive to perform and seem to have been given only at times when the situation was just right and there was an audience to enjoy the fun.

WHY INITIATION RITES?

The differences between the sexes in initiation ceremonies are so great as to suggest that the conditions leading to the adoption of ceremonies may be quite different for the two sexes. Several cross-cultural studies, in addition to those already mentioned, have been directed at revealing the conditions for male initiations; fewer such studies have been concerned with female initiations.

Frank Young (1965) has presented the most notable theory attributing male initiation rites to the influence of adult social relations. In societies where adult men have high solidarity, functioning in various ways as an exclusive group, the entrance of youths may be disruptive of established ways. This disruption can be reduced or prevented by dramatizing the change from boyhood to manhood, facilitating the smooth and full participation of the newly adult in his unaccustomed role. Young thus predicted the degree of dramatization of male initiation would be positively correlated with degree of male solidarity, and found this to be so. A more complicated theory of how initiation facilitates transition from one age status to another has been given in a cross-cultural study by Cohen (1964a). Paige and Paige (1981), looking only at rites involving circumcision, attribute their occurrence to their value in reducing conflict among adult male groups, with the needs of the initiate being relatively unimportant.

Just as in the case of couvade, explanations appealing only to adult male interaction may be contrasted with explanations appealing also to needs, perhaps unconscious, in the initiates. The two types of explanation are sometimes labeled as sociogenic versus psychogenic, but to us this labeling seems inappropriate, as both types do, at least implicitly, refer both to individual feelings and the social conditions from which they spring. Explanations appealing to needs in the initiate for which cross-cultural evidence has been adduced have already been mentioned in our account of couvade. (Munroe, Munroe, & Whiting, 1981). These studies are restricted to initiation rites that include circumcision, and relate them to early childhood conditions that might produce in boys a feminine identification. The presence of these conditions (sleeping with the mother or being carried close to the mother's body) is indeed found to be correlated with such initiation rites. But, as we mentioned earlier, this correlation is found primarily in societies that have strong adult male solidarity. Thus, as in the case of couvade theory, Whiting and his associates present an integrated theory that takes account of both kinds of condition that make for male initiations.

Less effort has been directed at the question of why some societies initiate girls and some do not. An excellent summary and evaluation of the evidence has been presented by Judith Brown (1981, 582–587). The various studies are more diverse and more difficult to integrate than those on male initiation. They do confirm that for women, as for men, initiation rites are related to social conditions that seem to give the rites special value in resolving conflicts within the person and conflicts between persons.

A suggestion made by James Brain relates the severity of female initiation to men's motivation to maintain a dominance that they feel to be threatened: "We shall probably find long, painful, or harsh initiation rites for women in those societies in which there is a possibility that women for economic reasons might achieve a position of dominance" (1977, 197). Brain offers as a specific case to suggest this principle the Luguru, a Tanzanian people. Luguru women's rights to land equal those of men, he reports; the children belong to the women, and "women traditionally chose and could depose the head of the subclan, the autonomous land-holding unit" (ibid.). Sufficient threat appears here to suggest that Luguru men might support a tradition of punitive initiations of women, and the female initiation rites are indeed such as result "in girls' beginning their married life in a condition of physical and psychological weakness" (ibid.).

MALES AS AGENTS OF SOCIAL CONTINUITY

We have mentioned Schlegel and Barry's (1979) finding that initiation rites for the sexes differ in time of occurrence and in tendency to be held for an individual or a group. Related to these two facts is another difference that is also expressed in other contexts than that of initiation. As Schlegel and Barry point out, girls' ceremonies generally focus on fertility and sexuality, whereas boys' ceremonies often focus on spiritual change. This difference was very apparent in our less systematic survey of many societies.

It would be easy to misinterpret "fertility" and suppose girls' ceremonies to be uniformly concerned with maximizing human fertility, as in some instances they are. They may equally be concerned with teaching girls techniques of birth control and abortion, as they are especially in foraging societies where large families are not generally considered desirable. But the emphasis in girls' initiations, even in the foraging societies, seems characteristically to be on the recognition and celebration of the girl's having reached sufficient maturity for marriage, and of course sexuality and childbearing are a part of this even if in the particular society not confined to marriage.

Although comparable recognition of maturity is involved in boys' ceremonies, there is often a strong emphasis on what may be characterized as a spiritual change. This change is probably facilitated by the fact that a group rather than an individual is being initiated, for the change is in the direction of identification with the society as a whole and its continuity through time. This meaning is especially clear in one feature that characterizes many male initiation ceremonies: that they involve the introduction of youth to the deceased ancestors of the society. Very frequent, for instance, in Melanesia, is conspicuous use in the male initiations of sacred musical instruments that are explicitly said to represent the ancestors. Musical instruments play the same role in some South American societies. Among the Hopi, in Arizona, some of the kachinas (masked dancers), to whom novices are introduced at the central point of an initiation, represent ancestors. Among the Kiwai Papuans (Riley, 1925, 196), initiation is the occasion on which a boy learns that adult men, of whom he will now be one, have the duty of representing the ancestors to all females and uninitiated males; just as for an Ndembu youth, what he had previously believed, in common with all the uninitiated, to be literally the ancestors are now revealed to him in solemn secrecy to be men of the community in masks and costumes.

These features of initiation rites suggest that it is males who are especially concerned with religious expression or promotion of social continuity. This is consistent with the general tendency for the priesthood, if present, to be almost entirely occupied by men. In several Melanesian societies where important foods are divided into male and female items (with the male crops—such as yams, taro, sugarcane, and bananas—suggestive of phallic symbols), the major cult activities are centered on the male foods. More generally, men seem to be the keepers of sacred tradition, which comes from the ancestors and must be transmitted to the new generation.

This gender difference in religion may be contrasted with the reverse difference in immediacy or obviousness of contribution to social continuity. It is women alone who give birth to the children, who ensure the continued existence of the society. Perhaps for girls it is sufficient at puberty to celebrate their readiness for this all-important role. A more abstract and spiritual contribution to social continuity may be needed more by the male sex. Irving Goldman has expressed this difference well in a discussion focused on the Cubeo tribe of Colombia.

> The distinction between masculine and feminine generative functions is made by all societies that have developed a masculine "making of men" cult and employ ritual rebirth imagery. In such cults specifically, and in initiation cults generally, men have the ritual responsibility for completing by

themselves what was begun by birth. Within this broad tradition, Cubeo give to men primary responsibility for a second and equally important generative process, namely that of infusing the body, which is delivered by women, with the spirits and powers of their male ancestors. (1976, 291)

MALE ENVY OF WOMEN

We have considered two general kinds of religious practice (with associated beliefs) that either seem on the surface or have been plausibly interpreted to arise from male interest in imitating the role of women. In the case of couvade, some aspects are obviously imitative of the female role, and the correlation of couvade with conditions making for feminine identification in males strengthens the argument for that interpretation.

In the case of initiation rites, the argument is less direct. It begins with the fact that circumcision increases the distinctiveness of the male genitals, removing that portion that most clearly resembles the female genitals. T is is a point that is consciously recognized in some traditional societies. Of the Bambara and Dogon of Mali it is said:

> The notion of the bisexuality of human beings is fundamental: the spiritual principles are sexed like the body, whose ambivalence is evident during childhood: the boy is feminine in his foreskin; the girl is masculine in her clitoris. One of the aims of circumcision and excision is to help the child attain the sex to which it is apparently destined by removing the organ of the opposite sex. (Dieterlen, 1951, 70–71)

Burton and Whiting (1961) proposed that male adolescent initiation rites that include circumcision are an aid in terminating boys' identification with the female role. This hypothesis led them to predict that such rites would be found principally in societies where boys in their earliest years are exclusively nurtured by their mothers and come to envy women as controlling and providing resources, but where in the later years of childhood boys see men as the controllers and providers. They took exclusive mother-infant sleeping arrangements as an index of the former condition, which would make for a continuing unconscious envy of femininity, and patrilocal residence (in which a married couple live with the husband's relatives, not the wife's) as an index of the latter condition, which would make for a conscious need for masculinity. In a sample of 64 societies, Burton and Whiting found that of the 13 having adolescent male initiation with circumcision, all but one shared both conditions. This finding suggests that male initiation rites most obviously stressing adult male identity are partly motivated by an effort to undo a latent envy of women. (By contrast, the much rarer operation of subincision, practiced by some Australian aborigines, might be directly motivated by an envy of women because it greatly increases the resemblance of the male genitals to those of the female.)

A third aspect of religion we have considered, the role of men in providing spiritual continuity of the society, might well be a sort of imitation of women, who have a more obvious role in providing biological continuity. We now turn to a variety of other aspects of religious belief and practice that seem relevant to this same general theme.

Most important are a group of features that have provided the basis for Margaret Mead's concept of "womb envy" and Bruno Bettelheim's similar concept of "vagina envy," presented, respectively, in *Male and Female* (1949) and *Symbolic Wounds* (1954). Both authors have principally stressed aspects of male initiation rites in various New Guinea and Australian societies, and Bettelheim has also stressed rites of purification that adult men in some of the same societies carry out repeatedly. In reading the detailed ethnographic material, we have been impressed by the acuity of these authors in discerning a pattern whose presence has also been confirmed by later fieldwork in societies little known at the time of their writing.

The pattern may be summarized as envy by men of the reproductive role of women. Bettelheim calls attention to it in the obvious but rare form we mentioned earlier, the genital operation of subincision, found only in Australia. This operation feminizes the male genitals and usually results in men's squatting to urinate, in what is generally the female manner (Bettelheim, 1954, 112–114). Both Bettelheim and Mead call attention to an expression of the pattern that turns out to be more widespread—periodic bleeding from the genital region, produced in men by deliberately cutting or otherwise wounding the genitals, and often explicitly referred to as a kind of menstruation (Wogeo, Kwoma, Arapesh, and many central highland New Guinea groups).

Beginning with this more widespread pattern noted by Bettelheim and Mead, we will report briefly on the following beliefs and practices that suggest conflict in males about their gender identification: forms of male pseudomenstruation; purification rites for males; beliefs of men that seem to claim for them a more important role than that of women in human conception; beliefs in semen as an important factor in both fetal and adolescent growth; ideas about the male role in causing girls to begin menstruating; myths about men having had menstruation; myths about men having taught women how to have babies; myths about men having stolen sacred musical instruments and rites from women; ideas about male pregnancy, lactation, and defecation; and the ritual rebirth of males (and in some cases of females, too) through men's rituals. These beliefs and practices seem in some instances oriented toward strengthening male feelings of superiority and dominance, and in other instances toward direct expression of male envy of females. They suggest a potential ubiquity of conflict in males about their sexual identity, even though some manifestations of the conflict are rare, and the rituals of some societies may show little or no evidence of the conflict.

Male Pseudomenstruation

During initiation, Arapesh, Kwoma, and Busana boys (Tuzin, 1980; Whiting, 1941; Hogbin, 1951) are taught to bleed their genitals from time to time, and the same is doubtless true in many other Melanesian societies. Kwoma males believe that women can stay healthy through menstruation but that men must depend on bleeding their genitals to promote growth and health (Whiting, 1941, 211). Thus, the Kwoma use of bleeding as a cure for illness at other parts of the body may have a latent genital significance. The Barasana of the Amazon area of South America claim that women, because of their menstruation, are semi-immortal, the ability to menstruate being compared to the ability to change one's skin (S. Hugh-Jones, 1979, 185). Gregor (1977, 254) reports that during two ceremonies of the South American Mehinaku, "men shed 'menstrual' blood by scarifying their bodies and piercing their ears." Some of the highland New Guinea groups also practice bleeding the nose—an instance where the nose seems clearly to be a phallic symbol. Of one of these groups, the Gahuku-Gama, Read reports that the men

> did not hesitate (without any prompting) to liken the nose-bleeding rites of the *nama* cult to menstruation, explaining that both were necessary to complete the processes of maturation and also acknowledging that men had to simulate (ritually induce) an event that occurred naturally in women. (1986, 197)

Purification Rites

Avoidance of menstrual blood by males is fairly widespread. Its most usual appearance, in hunting societies, seems to have primarily another significance than the one we are considering here. It protects the hunters and their success by ensuring that simply as men they will have avoided menstrual blood. The purification rites we are considering here are of another sort. An example is provided by the Gururumba of the New Guinea central highlands (Newman, 1965, 79–80); here, boys practice self-induced nose-bleeding, cane-swallowing, and vomiting. These acts are said to be necessary to rid them of the menstrual blood and fluids that are thought of as sources of female pollution coming from the mother—in infancy through mother's milk and in early childhood from other food the mother has provided. Pseudomenstruation rites are also often given this meaning.

Beliefs about the Male's More Important Role in Conception

Reports of the belief that men are more important than women in procreation are hard to find in the ethnographic data; there is rarely any account of ideas about human conception. The facts assembled by Ford (1945) by Broude and Greene (1976), as well as our own reading in the ethnographic literature, make clear that many peoples in South America (Jívaro, Cubeo, Tupinamba, Shavante, Nambicuara, Mundurucú), Oceania (Truk, Tikopia), and Africa (Hausa, Mbundu, Ndembu) share the idea that in some way the man's role in conception is the more important one. At least two Melanesian groups—the Rossel Islanders (Armstrong, 1928, 100) and the Umeda (Gell, 1975, 94)—believe that the fetus is essentially an "egg" placed in the mother by the father. The first Europeans to view semen through a microscope were evidently set to invent the same idea, so that they saw the spermatozoon as containing a little human being. To the Rossel Islanders and some other groups the mother is merely a "passive receptacle."

The function of the father was very important in many Australian groups (such as the Arunta and Walbiri) because he was considered to have helped the mother become pregnant through his efforts in seeing that she became the recipient of a "spirit child" (Arunta and Walbiri). This spiritual role of the father was especially stressed in some Australian and Melanesian societies for which Malinowski (1929), Montagu (1974), and Spiro (1968) have been able to argue (with the support of other evidence) that they lacked all recognition of the physiological role of semen in bringing about conception. (Against their view, Leach [1969] and the Berndts [1951, 80–83] argue, instead, that Australian groups had separate beliefs about the spiritual and physiological roles of the father in conception; when questioned in detail, they report, informants were likely to acknowledge that semen is essential. The spiritual function of the father, then, may represent merely a claim of a special additional role, rather than a denial of what seems to most peoples obvious reality.)

The Importance of Semen in Fetal and Adolescent Growth

Some women anthropologists have pointed out that while menstrual blood is often considered dangerous to men, it is in fact considered intrinsically dangerous and hence a threat to women as well. Semen, too, in some societies, is considered a threat to both men and women, a locus of mystical danger (Faithorn, 1975, 136–137). In addition, for men in some New Guinea societies, such as Faithorn studied, the loss of semen is considered debilitating. Perhaps because men cannot claim for themselves the powers of women in giving birth, they need to show that semen is very powerful, whether for good or for bad. Conception in many groups is thought to take place when menstrual blood is dammed up through contact with semen. A good supply of semen is claimed by the men to be needed to nourish the fetus during its development; hence, intercourse must take place regularly, at least in early pregnancy.

Because men in many central highland groups of New Guinea are aware that females develop and grow more rapidly than males, they feed or inject or smear male initiates with semen in order to make up for their naturally slow rate of growth. Among the Kimam of West Irian (Serpenti, 1965), the initiates are coated with semen. Homosexual acts involving initiates are performed in order to feed or inject the valued semen into the initiates, who later in their turn serve as initiators and give semen to the next lot of novices. Oral or anal sexuality is given this significance in the rituals of the Sambia (Herdt, 1981), the Keraki Papuans (Williams, 1936), and the Marind-anim (Baal, 1966).

Male Role in Causing Girls to Menstruate

Some Melanesian, Australian, and South American groups and the Asian Lepchas share the idea that men cause girls to start menstruating. Some Australian groups practice the deflowering of girls who are approaching maturity. Among the South American Cubeo this is done by a shaman or an old man (Goldman, 1963, 179–180). Myth may help maintain this practice and the accompanying beliefs. Hugh-Jones (1979) reports that the moon also plays a role in causing the "opening up" of girls of the Cubeo and Barasana; and the Berndts (1951) mention a similar belief among New Guinea groups. The availability of this alternative explanation may leave belief in a usual necessity for male participation still tenable when it is challenged by some girl's starting to menstruate while known to be a virgin.

Myths about Men Having Experienced Menstruation

Two of the cases that we can cite as examples of peoples who have a myth or legend about men having formerly had menstruation are from parts of the world that we have not yet considered and that do not seem to be characterized by extreme antagonism between the sexes. They are the Hill Maria Gond (Grigson, 1949, 362) and the Lepcha (Gorer, 1938, 226), peoples of Asia. In both groups the inconvenience of menstruation, rather than its danger, seems to be involved in a mythical history that assigns menstruation to men for a portion of the past. In the Lepcha account, women's vulvas were once located on the top of their heads; recognizing the unpleasantness of this situation, the gods transferred this source of bleeding to the men's knees. A hidden envy of women's procreative powers is an explanation that Gorer felt would fit this Lepcha myth. He also offers the same explanation for the Lepcha belief that sexual intercourse with a male is a normal prerequisite for first menstruation (though the male may be a mystical being). The Barasana of South America also have mythological references to males having had menstruation at some time in the past, as we will indicate later.

Myths about Men Having Taught Women
How to Have Babies

Here we have just two examples of this myth, both from Oceania. Both the Arapesh and the Tikopia tell of a time when people did not know how to deliver babies without slitting open and hence killing the mother. The hero of both tales is a man who was reported to have taught his wife and then all the other women how to deliver a baby from the vagina. (See Mead [1940, 245–246] and Tuzin [1978, 63] for the Arapesh and Firth, [1956, 20] for the Tikopia.)

Myths about Men Having Stolen Sacred Instruments and Rites from Women

These myths take various forms, but for some time they have been known to exist in both Melanesia (Gourlay, 1975) and South America. In most instances it is the women who had the musical instruments and/or sacred rites first and the men who usurped them. Sometimes there are explicit statements about a switch in dominance or other aspects of sex role as a consequence of the women's loss. In the case of the Barasana (Hugh-Jones, 1979, 127), the story is more complicated. There, whichever sex lacked the instruments at a given period was the sex that at that time menstruated. The first theft was carried out by the women, who got the instruments and rites from the men, who then menstruated. The men eventually stole back both rites and instruments, and then the women menstruated and have done so ever since. Another version, also suggesting male envy of women, is that of the Soromaja of West Irian. Here the men stole the flutes from the women. For Soromaja men, flutes represent fertility; they are symbols of creative power. The myth seems to be about men's gaining a kind of power that they envy women for possessing exclusively (Oosterwal, 1976, 325).

Ideas about Male Pregnancy, Lactation, and Defecation

We have found sporadic occurrences of bizarre notions that may be rare expressions in men of a common conflict between a latent desire to be more feminine and a conscious wish to be even more masculine. Among the most extreme misconceptions about human anatomy and physiology is that from New Guinea underlying the Hua male's fear of becoming pregnant. Meigs (1976) reports that the Hua find the idea of pregnancy and other normally female states abhorrent and a real possibility for men. They are not the only New Guinea people for whom belief in male pregnancy has been reported; Meigs cites Hayano's report (1974, 20) of such a belief elsewhere in the eastern highlands of New Guinea. The high incidence of kwashiorkor (a protein deficiency disease) in this region may favor the development of such beliefs, for the distended abdomen it causes might simulate a state of pregnancy in males.

The possibility of male lactation is reported to be taken seriously in at least one society, where it is said that in case a baby cannot be nursed by its mother, a grandfather can induce lactation in himself. The Baroya, of New Guinea, while not claiming that men themselves can produce milk, believe women capable of producing milk only by transforming the semen they have received in intercourse (Godelier, 1986, 57). A similar belief is reported (Traube, 1986, 94) for the Mambai of East Timor; they hold that semen is the source of the bones in fetal development, and that the leftover semen gives rise to the woman's milk.

Another mythical approach to the male body, rendering it distinctively superior to the female rather than simulating the female, is exhibited in two widely separated groups. Lindenbaum (1976, 58) reports that Fore males "maintain the pretense that they do not defecate." Included in young boys' initiation in this New Guinea society is instruction on the location of the hidden male latrines, to be kept secret from all females. A group in east Africa, the Chaga, have a similar fiction: "The central teaching of the [boys'] camp was the 'stopping up of the anus'....The plug ... supposed to have been used for this, represents in a concrete manner male superiority" (Raum, 1940, 318). An Australian group, the Wik-mungkan, have a strange way of stating the contrast between male and female anatomy, a way that seems to exaggerate the contrast. According to them, "Anatomically men have the same sexual and excretory organs, and in the same order, as male flying foxes; while women, it is claimed, have a different reproductive and excretory system" (McKnight, 1975, 95).

Ritual Rebirth through Male Rituals

Gennep (1960) proposed the general notion that imagery of rebirth is characteristic of a certain phase in all rites of passage. Like other brilliant inferences by Gennep (whose book was first published early in the century), this suggestion is probably exaggerated. Yet, in many societies the rebirth of males through exclusively male activities has a distinctively important place in initiation ceremonies. It asserts the superiority of men over women, through symbolically denying the distinctiveness of women's unique and essential contribution to society, and establishes men's dominance in ritual life. One out of innumerable examples is provided by Hiatt (1971). Some of the male rites he reviews use phallic symbolism in attributing to male influence the fertility of humans, animals, and plants. But it is with uterine symbolism, emulating the role of women, that men perform the ritual that "finalizes the separation of boys from their mothers and 'reproduces' them as men" (p. 77).

Though an extreme pattern of sex antagonism and envy of women's fertility seems very clear in the ethnographies of many New Guinea and Australian societies, a minority of anthropological writers disagree with its interpretation as expressing male envy of women. Langness (1974) presents a detailed argument against that interpretation. He finds it impossible to believe, in view of the extremely low status of women in the New Guinea highlands, that men there could envy women. He argues that the pattern should be interpreted merely as the affirmation and enforcement that it certainly is of male superiority. It seems to us that this argument does not sufficiently acknowledge the multiplicity of meaning that characterizes human thought and the ambivalence that is everywhere found in important personal relationships. For our part, we find it difficult to believe that such a wealth of female symbolism could be repeatedly invented and regularly sustained by males, at such cost to their comfort, without direct motivational support.

This general pattern has been most consistently found in New Guinea and Australia. But it appears with less regularity in two other regions— tropical regions of Africa and of South America—leading at times to similar summary statement by informants or by ethnographers. Among the Central African Luguru, Brain says, "Though women may have the babies only men can give birth to adults" (1978, 185). The Wiko of Zimbabwe have similar ideas about the way circumcision rites alter the status of boys; Gluckman says that the boys become "people, they are born again" (1949, 157). Writing about the Barasana of Western Amazonia, Hugh-Jones argues that "the rites imply that whereas women create children, it is men who create adult men and the society they represent" (1979, 13).

These three groups of societies generally share the characteristic of extreme antagonism between male and female. Most of these societies, in all three regions, are warlike (Langness has stressed this feature), and the need for male solidarity in warfare has been asserted to be an important source of the sharp separation and antagonism of the sexes. Many other societies, however, provide evidence that the demands of warfare are not a sufficient condition for extreme hostility between the sexes. An example is provided by the warrior-pastoral Masai of Kenya (Llewellyn-Davies, 1979). The inferiority of females is very clear among the Masai, from exclusive male ownership of cattle (even though women must tend them) to many details of daily life. Men have great control over the sexuality and fertility of their females; for instance, intercourse with a man is believed necessary for a girl's breast development to start. Yet the relationship between the sexes is not characterized by extreme antagonism and hostility. Certainly one does not read about the Masai, as about some of the other societies we have cited, of gang rape as a punishment for erring women. Masai women as a group have a clear solidarity of their own. This solidarity is permitted by a pattern of mutual "respect" enforced by each sex, and officially encouraged by a ritual performed at four-year intervals, the blessing of the "fertility of the female." The blessing is done by a man chosen by the women. The men, moreover, are expected to contribute food and drink for this ceremony. It is of interest to find that the Masai look back in myth to a time when there was no fertility and no human reproduction, and men and women were equal, all of them warriors. According to this myth, this period was brought to an end when the men caused the women to have vaginas and bleed and the women became fertile; women then lost their bravery and became inferior to men.

In each of these features of religious practice and belief that we have reviewed, we may, upon reflection, see some parallels within our own society, though we will be less inclined to regard them in any sense as religious. They are not among us, as in these traditional societies, closely related to the more systematic or basic features to which some people might wish to restrict the term *religion*. We would be more certain, too, in looking at our own society, to ask about female envy of the male. It is partly, but only partly, because of the contrast with our own society that we have stressed, and ethnographers have stressed, for such societies as we have been considering, the opposite pattern; the pattern more familiar to us, female envy of the male role, seems always to be present, too. And so may we expect that the less familiar pattern is also present in our society.

But both patterns are less conspicuous among us, and for a reason that cross-cultural study helps illuminate. We may ask which societies, among the traditional ones studied by ethnographers, show most strongly the features we have portrayed. We have mentioned the influence of type of economy and also the influence of general complexity. As societies become more complex, differences other than gender become more important. Various ethnographers (e.g., Lawrence & Meggitt, 1965b; Allen, 1967) have pointed out that gender differentiation becomes less important in societies that divide people sharply into age grades and in societies that emphasize other structures that cut across gender lines. Our society is one that for long has had complex, diverse structures relatively independent of gender, and this independence has been increasing in recent years. If occupational and leisure-time activities continue to become increasingly shared by men and women, we may expect that envy of each gender by the other will diminish. The envy seems sufficiently rooted in the biological differences between the sexes so that we cannot expect it to disappear completely. The religious practices and symbolism of traditional peoples can help us understand some of the subtler universal trends in human thought and behavior.

Initiation ceremonies, then, have similar functions to those found for couvade rituals. They play an important part in maintaining the society's traditional pattern of gender role. They thus provide religious support for the traditional birth rate and for the male role in continuing the spiritual traditions. A variety of indirect evidence suggests that an envy of women underlies the sometimes superficial priority of the male role.

SUMMARY

Major points in biological development are marked in many societies by rituals that are an important part of the religious life, bringing mystical beliefs and practices to bear on the transmission, to each new generation, of the traditional role of each sex and age group. Realistic attempts to increase or to decrease fertility are often accompanied by rituals that seek mystical help. Childbirth is the occasion in many societies for ritualized participation by the father, termed *couvade*. Competing explanations for its presence or absence agree in finding that it satisfies diverse needs derived from the customary roles of the two sexes, and that it is also oriented toward mystical protection of the infant's health. The progression from childhood to adolescence or adulthood is marked, for the most part separately for each sex, by initiation ceremonies oriented toward preparation for the adult sex role. A variety of facts from a number of societies suggest that underlying the content of many rites of passage there is a very widespread male envy of women, which has been given the name *womb envy*. Theories about social influences on rites of passage help explain the aspects of mystical belief and practice that support and accompany those rites.

In Chapter 9 we consider rites of passage associated with the end of life, and in other chapters we consider rituals that form other aspects of the religious life.

Chapter 9

Death and the Afterlife

A speech made by a LoDagaa youth at his friend's funeral:

I've come for no bad reason.
Just that you and I were inseparable
and went everywhere without any trouble.
But it was God's will
that this morning
people should say you were dead.
But you and I
used to walk together
and all men knew it.
Then God came to take you.
So I said to myself
I would bring
that pot of beer.
Thus we used to do
for everyone to see.
So I brought along
this beer to give you
to drink.
Have a good journey
and may nothing trouble you.
And this cock,
take it
along with you.
If you want to go anywhere,
the cock will always get up at dawn,
and crow,
and you'll get up too
and set off again.

Look after the fowl well
as you go on your way.
If it crows, get up.
Every man who sets off
takes a cock with him.
And when you reach your house,
greet all your people warmly.
May there be nothing wrong there
and may they look after the place well.
Whether it was that somebody
killed you
because you and I went together
and people were angry;
whether it was because of this you were killed,
or because you yourself wanted (to eat) somebody
and God took you away,
go ahead
and I will follow you.
And these twenty cowries I give you
so you may pay
at the River
and get across.
Have a good journey
and go to see your people.
And this arrow,
take it along
and shoot the witch.
As for the beer,
and the fowl,
if there is anyone
who will be to me
as my friend was,
let him take the beer and fowl.
But if there's no one,
let me drink and weep,
and know that the friendship dies today.

(Goody, 1962, 134–135)

The LoDagaa are a people of mixed economy (horticulture, herding, and gathering) in northwestern Ghana and nearby areas of Burkina Faso. They are the subject of a uniquely full account of practices and beliefs related to death by the British anthropologist Jack Goody (1962). He selected the funeral speech with which we have opened this chapter as illustrating most succinctly many aspects of LoDagaa mortuary customs. Of these, many are in spirit, though not in concrete detail, shared with most societies around the world.

Anyone's death poses three problems that are more or less universal, regardless of religion, but whose resolutions are related to religion. It poses a fourth problem that is created by a nearly universal religious response to death, the belief that something of the deceased continues to exist after bodily death.

1. Where there was a living person, people now find themselves, in the typical death, in the presence of a dead body. What to do with it? In some few societies, this problem seems to be dealt with independently of religion. Some nomadic societies must keep on the move, because all members may be threatened if kept in one spot by the mortal illness or death of just one. Here the corpse, or even the moribund, may be abandoned, and in some instances without ceremony or obvious religious involvement. Examples are provided by the Siriono of Amazonia (Holmberg, 1950) and some Inuit groups in the Arctic (Jenness, 1922). In some Vedda groups in Sri Lanka, the corpse is abandoned where the death occurred, perhaps covered with branches, and the rest of the small community moves to another dwelling (Seligmann & Seligmann, 1911, 122).

It remains possible that in these examples there is still important religious involvement that has eluded ethnographers. For almost all societies mode of disposition of the body is associated with religious beliefs and practices. It may well be influenced by realistic factors, too (burial in deeply frozen soil being impossible, for example), but religious involvement is likely to remain conspicuous.

2. The dead person's accustomed interaction with others is severed; a gap is created in the life of surviving friends and relations. Among those closely dependent emotionally on the deceased, and among many whose relation may have been more formal, grief seems to appear in some form everywhere. Even specific expressions are very nearly universal. Crying is reported among the bereaved in all but one of 73 societies for which Rosenblatt et al. (1976) obtained a relevant account; in Bali alone did they find no published evidence of crying occasioned by death. The problem for the grief-stricken is how to bridge the gap, work through the grief, return to whatever is possible of normal life. Rosenblatt et al. report for some societies customs that need have no relation to religion—for example, the bereaved family lessening reminders of the loss by moving to a new location and perhaps destroying the dwelling in which their relation with the deceased had been centered. Though these features might well comprise a perfectly realistic mode of coping with loss and grief, the bereaved persons are likely to view them in the light of their religious beliefs and place them in a context of other customs whose meaning is even more dependent on religious beliefs.

3. The third problem is explaining the death. Basic inquisitiveness of human beings might be sufficient to make this a universal problem, but the fact that competing explanations may dictate competing courses of future action (revenge versus prayer versus improved sanitation, for example) often makes the problem an urgent one. Though the problem is not created by religion, its solution is mediated largely by religion; even in recent times among us, despite the great advance of medical science, people often seek through religion an answer to such questions as "Why were our family the chosen victims of this calamity?"

4. Belief in some kind of afterlife is almost universal, and anyone's death thus poses a fourth set of problems: What actions should the living take in relation to the surviving spirit of the deceased?

The speech by the LoDagaa youth whose friend has died illustrates all these problems and the way they are solved by a particular culture and person. The speech is addressed to a dead friend whose body is about to be placed in the ground as dictated by the ceremonial practices of the LoDagaa. The severing of the friendship is recognized, and the ritual includes an invitation for its renewal by a suitable volunteer, whose acceptance of the relationship would be recognized by his taking the material aspect of the beer and fowl brought as offerings to the deceased.

Two explanations of the death are considered, one in which the deceased would be to blame and one in which others would be. In case the latter explanation is correct, the spirit of the deceased is provided with the spirit of an arrow (which has been broken, presumably to release its spirit or power for use in the afterlife), so that the deceased may revenge himself on the wizard who killed him. Most of the speech is concerned with the afterlife. In accordance with the beliefs and practices with which his culture provides him, the bereaved provides the fowl and drink whose nonmaterial aspect will awaken and nourish the deceased on the trip he must make to the afterworld, the shells he must pay the ferryman to cross the river boundary, the arrow for revenge, and best wishes for the life and the company he will find on the other side. At the end, the bereaved acknowledges that the friend may be irreplaceable and he will be left in his grief.

SURVIVAL OF THE SOUL

Belief in Survival

So far as we have been able to determine, a belief that some part of a person survives beyond bodily death is present in almost every society. There may be societies in which the belief is completely absent, but the ethnographer has not looked for it and has made no report. Definite statements that the belief is absent are, however, rare. For the Hadza of Tanzania, Woodburn (1982, 192) reports that many people "are quite explicit that when one dies, one rots and that is that," and that statements by others alluding to an afterlife may be just euphemisms. He also cites (p. 195) unpublished observations by Robert Dodd on the Baka Pygmies, indicating that the idea of an afterlife has only been introduced to them from outside, and that conservative Baka say, "When you're dead, you're dead and that's the end of you." A close approach to declared absence of an afterlife is provided by the Dinka of Sudan. Francis M. Deng (1972, 136), who is himself a Dinka, reports that the people "view death as a dreadful end mitigated only by the immortality of procreation." Yet the idea of survival is not completely absent among the Dinka; the stress, Deng reports elsewhere (1978, 46–47), is on immortality in this world, through progeny, but ideas of an afterlife are nebulous rather than nonexistent; and another ethnographer definitely implies a belief in survival (Lienhardt, 1961, 289–290).

Exactly what survives is conceived in various ways, but we will use the single word *soul* to cover the various possibilities. Readers should guard against reading into that term the particular meaning it has for them. English speakers tend to think their word *soul* has a clear and universal meaning, referring to a reality that any language must be expected to recognize. Wierzbicka (1989) has shown that there is no precisely corresponding term in other European languages, and even greater variation is to be expected in languages unrelated to them. We use the word *soul* here in its most general sense, for any nonbodily part ascribed to a person, regardless of what distinctions a particular people may make. For the soul that survives bodily death, we will also use the word *spirit* (especially in the familiar phrase *ancestral spirit*), but with no intention of distinguishing it from *soul* beyond confining its usage to a postmortem period.

Frequently, a single soul is considered intrinsic to each living person and is held to survive when the person's body dies; it may be conceived by analogy to breath, or to shadow, or to the body itself (in any case being invisible to ordinary people). Many societies have a more complex view, assigning to each person several things that might be called souls; one or more of these may survive bodily death. One of the more extreme cases is provided by the Dogon, of Mali, who

> attribute eight souls to the person, four having reference to the body and four to sexuality and reproduction. It is only the latter that become enshrined as the ancestor spirit, whereas the body souls return to God when a person dies. More particularly, only two of the sex-linked souls eventually become the ancestor spirit. These two are associated with the reproductive faculty upon which the perpetuation of the lineage depends. (Fortes [1965a, 18–19], summarizing oral statements by the ethnographer G. Dieterlen)

An even greater extreme in number of souls is found in the Rarámuri of northern Mexico, where a principal soul is accompanied by many souls of varied sizes, "with at least one soul located at each part of the body that can move" (Merrill, 1987, 199). A different classification of the individual's immaterial essences is found in the Lugbara. Middleton (1982, 137–141) translates as "soul" the word for what the Lugbara consider the most important element, which is found almost exclusively in males and pertains to the continuity of the lineage. Another element whose name Middleton translates as "spirit" has to do with behavior irrelevant or antagonistic to lineage responsibility. A third element pertains to personality and social influence. Each of these three has a separate postmortem existence. Two other elements, breath and shadow, disappear when the body dies. Variations are found all over the world in the number and character of what might be called souls, and in just what is conceived to survive beyond bodily death. Hultkrantz (1953) has devoted a large volume to conceptions of the soul in aboriginal North America alone.

Support for the Belief in Survival

Early students of the religions of traditional societies speculated about how the idea of the soul and its survival beyond death originated, and many of their suggestions might, on the whole, seem as reasonable today as when they were first proposed. Since, however, there seems in principle to be no satisfactory test for the validity of such speculations, the effort has been abandoned by scholars even if the question continues to arouse interest. What sustains or supports belief in the survival of the soul, though, is a question that might permit of empirical test, and it has a number of potentially valid answers.

One answer that has actually been tested by anthropological field-work in a traditional society is that belief in survival is supported by the training of children, adolescents, and even adults by their fellows and especially their elders. For our own society, the common experience of everyone provides sufficient evidence for this source of support. Survival of the soul beyond bodily death is one of the beliefs taught by the clergy and the scriptures of various denominations. The fact that a large majority of the general population assert, in public opinion polls, a belief in immortality suggests that pressure from parents and peers is also an important influence toward implanting or sustaining the belief. A widely publicized instance of the pressure occurred some years ago when, if we remember the incident accurately, a U.S. senator declared Eleanor Roosevelt unfit to represent her country at the United Nations because she had expressed uncertainty about personal immortality.

However, this might all result from the professionalization of religion in our complex society. Would a similar process be found in a simple nonliterate society? John Whiting included this among the questions he sought to test in New Guinea, in fieldwork with the Kwoma in 1936–1937 (1941, 202–221).

Adult Kwoma fear the ghosts of dead relatives, and children's observations of this fear in their parents might provide sufficient training. Whiting also noted, however, that children were very specifically warned about places and circumstances that might expose them to hostile attack by ghosts. Nocturnal sounds of bird and animals, moreover, were often interpreted to children as ghosts in disguise. In all these and other ways, a Kwoma could hardly arrive at adulthood without a strong belief that spirits of the dead remain alive and active.

However, if nothing else sustained the belief, it might eventually die out. Whiting observed and recorded various other sources of strengthening. To his observations we can add suggestions made a century ago by E. B. Tylor (1891), an analysis by Rosenblatt et al. (1976a), for which they draw on a variety of sources, and our own reading of many ethnographies.

Here are the major kinds of experience that in any society might serve to maintain or strengthen the belief in survival beyond bodily death:

1. Dreaming about a person who is dead may be taken as a very real contact with the spirit of the deceased. A Kwoma child who reports such a dream is in fact given that explanation. It is obvious from reports of interviews and conversations in many societies that adults as well as children encounter this interpretation frequently when they report their dreams. Dream contact with deceased persons may be especially important because it occurs embedded in a context of impressive evidence for the reality of soul and its independence of the body.

2. As just stated, dreaming in itself offers (in a prescientific setting) impressive evidence for the reality of soul and its independence of the body. The Polynesian inhabitants of Bellona Island, for instance, consider night-time travel of their soul responsible for dreams not only about the deceased but also about living persons or distant places. When one of the best Bellona informants was brought to Denmark for extended work with anthropologists there,

> he used to tell about his dreams in the mornings. Once when he dreamed that he was back on Bellona, he said: "I'm surprised how fast the ... [soul] ... can travel. Much faster than an aeroplane. Last night I was on Bellona, and then I wake up. I'm in Denmark." (Monberg, 1966, 97)

3. A person may be troubled on recognizing irrational behavior in himself or herself, actions against the best interests of self, family, or group. Belief that one is under the control of a spirit (even totally possessed by a spirit), including the spirit of a dead human being, can greatly reduce this anxiety, making one blameless. This can be a powerful strengthener of belief in the reality of survival. For a particular society—the Ifaluk of the Caroline Islands—Spiro (1953) argues that this is the main source of support for belief in malevolent ghosts (and thus, one might infer, for the general belief in survival). Ifaluk culture places a very high value on nonaggression, yet Spiro's observations of their life, in infancy and in adulthood, give strong evidence of aggressive motivation. Projection of this motive onto evil ghosts (whose power over each person would be thought sufficient to permit the ghosts to implant aggression) makes the aggressive feelings more tolerable by letting each person attribute them to an external source and thus consider them alien to his or her real self.

4. A bereaved person may be surrounded by cues to which he or she has repeatedly in the past responded in the company of the deceased, and they may powerfully evoke, as they have correctly in the past, a sense of presence of the other person.

5. Often a death will have left survivors with unfinished activities that had been planned with the dead person, and this can create in the bereaved a motive for fantasying the presence of the deceased for carrying out the cooperative interaction.

6. More generally, in waking life as in dreaming, the bereaved is likely to have fantasies about the deceased, and a ready explanation for them is that the continuing spirit of the deceased is interacting with the bereaved in a way that brings these thoughts about. As in the case of possession, belief in spirits thus provides an explanation for one's own thoughts or behavior.

7. In waking life as in dreams, a person may have the experience of seeming to hear or see the deceased. Such visions are not uncommon in Western society, as shown in various collections of seemingly psychic experiences (e.g., Myers, 1903, vol. 2, 1–80). We tend to call such visions hallucinations, with the implication that they correspond to no external reality. But unless one has been trained to explain them in some such way, they may powerfully support the idea of survival; they are, after all, very real experiences.

8. Spirit mediumship, as we have seen in Chapter 5, is found in many societies. Where it is widespread, many individuals have direct experience, presumably convincing to them, of being temporarily possessed by the spirit of someone who is dead, and other persons present are likely to feel they are actually witnessing an instance of possession. Even where spirit mediumship is restricted to a few individuals, all or most members of the society are likely to attend séances at some time and to have indirect experience of the presence of spirits, including those of deceased relatives and friends. The scientific tradition in our society does not prevent among us a frequent acceptance of this experience as convincing evidence of survival, and in pre-scientific societies acceptance must be much more general.

9. Continued existence of the deceased's spirit plays in most societies an essential part in funeral rites. Belief in survival is thus supported by the variety of advantages that may be brought about by those ceremonies.

10. Belief in survival is likely to be integrated not only into the pattern of funeral rites but also into many other aspects of the culture. In every chapter we have seen instances—for example, that personal power may be derived from spirits of the deceased, that sorcery and healing may be thought to work through them, and so on. In this chapter we will see how belief in ancestral spirits expresses and supports the structure of power and authority, the basic organization of a society. The reality of the spirits cannot be challenged, therefore, without a threat to the survival of the whole pattern of the culture by which people live. Some individuals, moreover, will always have a special dependence on belief in survival. A spirit medium, for instance, is likely to believe he or she is in direct contact with spirits of the dead, and the respect accorded the medium depends on others holding this belief. A healer may interpret apparent successes or failures as reflecting decisions by ancestral spirits, and thereby have a plausibility and freedom from personal blame that might not be possible otherwise. Persons with these special skills, and those who make use of their skills, have special reason to adhere to belief in the reality of spirits of the dead.

11. What have come in our society of late to be called "near-death experiences" provide another significant source of belief in survival, in traditional societies as well as in our own. People who are desperately ill but recover, and people who come near death in accidents, sometimes report vivid experiences that they can interpret as an approach to the afterlife (e.g., Ring, 1980). Researchers find that people in our society who have such experiences often do not report them for fear of being considered insane, but such reluctance is less likely in traditional societies. Ethnographers have sometimes recorded accounts of such experiences even when not actively seeking them out, and it is reasonable to assume that in many societies knowledge of their occurrence is very general. In our society, of course, the scientific tradition leads to a search for purely naturalistic explanation of such experiences, reducing their impact on belief in survival. But their impact is not likely to be attenuated to any such degree in traditional societies.

12. A broad assemblage of experiences is implicitly appealed to in the "sociological" explanation offered by Goody (1959) for the apparent universality of belief in survival. He sees the belief as arising

> from the basic contradiction which exists between the continuity of the social system—the relative perpetuity of the constituent groups and of their corpus of norms—and the impermanence of its personnel. This conflict between the mortality of the human body and the immortality of the body politic is resolved by the belief in a future life. Perhaps only situations of rapid social change can admit widespread skepticism in this field. (p. 135)

To us it seems improbable that this kind of support for the belief could be nearly as widespread in most societies as some of the supports we have adduced earlier. It seems likely to be confined to the more philosophically inclined people that Radin (1927) argued are to be found in any society. Even if so restricted, it could be an important influence, for the philosophers of any society are likely to be especially important shapers of its general worldview.

13. A wish that one's life could go on, reluctance to accept the finality of death, is a common experience that might motivate belief in survival beyond death. In our society, this wishful-thinking hypothesis is widely assumed to provide the principal explanation (other than religious training) of belief in survival. At least one anthropologist seems to propose it as an important influence in most societies: "The certainty of the individual's extinction as a human being contradicts so outrageously the value and effort of living that most cultures minimize the confrontation with this certainty, or cushion it with assurances of some form of immortality" (Morton-Williams, 1960, 34).

This statement appears in a discussion of Yoruba responses to the fear of death. That individual survival is not assured to Yoruba women might throw some doubt on the hypothesis, but Morton-Williams suggests that the wish is weaker in them because they find a realistic immortality in their own lifetime through bearing children. That some individuals look forward hopefully to extinction, rather than dreading it, need not invalidate the wish-fulfillment hypothesis, which requires only that many persons want to avoid viewing death as an end to their existence. There may be a relationship, not yet explored, between satisfaction in this life and strength of interest in an afterlife, either in comparing individuals or in comparing societies. It is possible, too, that wish fulfillment is more significant by way of supporting belief about survival of others than about one's own survival.

Character of the Afterlife

Of the nineteenth-century Englishmen curious about the religion of traditional peoples, Everard im Thurn was one who was not satisfied to speculate on the reports of others but was himself an early collector of ethnographic data. He studied the Indians of British Guiana, trying to separate carefully his own religious conceptions and the thought of the Indians. There are no recorded facts, he wrote, to "indicate that the Indians realize that the existence of the spirit is everlasting" (1882, 374). Many Western visitors to various native groups had been impressed by the clear evidence of belief in a life beyond the grave and had projected into this their own conception of immortality, of life into eternity. Close attention to what the Guianan natives did and said (or to what other native groups did and said, he implied) would reveal that their ideas pertain only to a continuity of the life of the soul on both sides of death, not to a conception of everlasting life.

A century and more of later fieldwork shows that im Thurn was right. When Raymond Firth reviewed the variety of beliefs about the afterlife, the first conclusion he stated was that "in most primitive communities it is continuity rather than immortality that is assumed. In some societies, like the Manus, there is provision for termination of the soul. In most, it is believed to endure, but there is no positive notion of eternity as such" (1967a, 331).

Survival beyond bodily death is no guarantee of longevity for the soul. The soul of a Manus man has a period of importance during the life of his immediate heir. But then it becomes a wanderer, and eventually a sea slug (Fortune, 1935, 6). Similar decline from human status forms the belief of some other societies as well. Among the Zuni of the American Southwest, souls must die three more deaths in the afterlife and then become some animal "for which they had an affinity in life" (Tedlock, 1975, 269). The Krahó of Brazil also view the soul as dying several times after bodily death, each time becoming a smaller and smaller animal, to end as a stone, a root, or a tree stump (Cunha, 1981, 163–164).

More frequently there is no mention of either extinction or immortality, and the description of the afterlife alludes principally to those who died within the memory of those still living. The afterlife thus seems to be conceived in relation to the personal interests and memory of living persons rather than as an abstract doctrine. The recently dead may be thought of as the persons they were known to be and as continuing somewhat the kind of life they had before. About the more remote dead there may be vague general ideas, and some mythical distant ancestors may be given names. But "in an oral tradition the simple process of forgetting destroys links in the chain that are no longer required" (Goody, 1962, 388).

Though belief in an afterlife may perhaps be found in all human societies, there is no approach to universality in ideas about the character of the surviving soul, the circumstances of its existence, or its relation to the people who remain alive. In all of these, there is great diversity. Many ethnographies, in reporting ideas about postmortem existence, speak principally about the significance of the dead for those still living; others speak principally about the postmortem life for its own sake, as though the concern of those living were with their own future or with achieving a valid empathy with their departed relatives. This difference in what is reported probably reflects in part a real cultural variation. This was the inference of the British anthropologist Max Gluckman, and our reading of ethnographies confirms it.

> There are, it seems to me, two aspects of survival after death: the journey of the spirit to and its continued existence in another sphere of living, and the relations of the dead with the living. Most people pay attention to both of these aspects. But it also seems that social attention when directed to the second emphatically in the form of an ancestral cult tends to exclude any emphasis on the first.... I think it will be found in general that people with a well developed cult of tendence on the ghosts have a very inchoate picture of the afterlife, which will depend on individual imagination rather than cultural dogma. (Gluckman, 1937, 125–126)

Where details of the afterlife are recounted, they tend to be based on simple extension of normal life. In a hunting society, the spirits hunt; in an agricultural society, they are cultivators. They live in dwellings such as they occupied in life; they continue the familiar social structure and patterns of interaction with others. A special version of such a view appears in the Kaluli of Papua New Guinea. The unseen world of the afterlife has continuous reality in the same place as the ordinary life, and each living person has a place-holder there in the form of a shadow animal, which will be replaced by his own shadow self when he dies.

> When asked what the people of the unseen look like, Kaluli will point to a reflection in a pool or a mirror and say, "They are not like you or me. They are like that." In the same way, our human appearance stands as a reflection to them. This is not a "supernatural" world, for to the Kaluli it is perfectly natural. Neither is it a "sacred world," for it is virtually coextensive with and exactly like the world the Kaluli inhabit, subject to the same forces of mortality.... In the unseen world, every man has a reflection in the form of a wild pig (women appear as cassowaries) that roams invisibly on the slopes of Mt. Bosavi.... When a person dies, his wild pig aspect disappears from the

> *mama* [unseen] world. His personal life virtue, which animates his living body and is manifested in his breathing and conscious awareness, escapes with his last breath and takes on human form in the *mama* world where it continues a life very much like the one he left. In the visible world, the person now usually appears in the form of a bird or a fish, and his longhouse as a tree or river pool. (Schieffelin, 1976, 97)

Not all societies where statements about the afterlife have been recorded claim much knowledge about its character. The Kaguru of Tanzania seem to assume an existence much like the life they know, but their ideas are vague (Beidelman, 1964, 116); they do, however, recognize death as leading to an increase in "supernatural power and rectitude" (Beidelman, 1966, 370), thus making explicit what is implied by the widespread role of ancestral spirits in enforcing moral rules. The Lugbara do not profess to know the details of life beyond the grave, but they locate an ancestral spirit at first under the living compound, then in more remote places underground as younger generations take its place, until it is finally absorbed into Divinity (Middleton, 1982, 151). The Nyakyusa generally profess no definite knowledge, but look to the afterlife with fear. For them, "the place of the shades [somewhere underground] is a vague and shadowy land where no certain happiness is traditionally believed to be" (Wilson, 1957, 17). Some of the younger Nyakyusa express confidence in finding the afterlife happy, but their elders are skeptical, attributing this idea to missionaries, who after all can cite no evidence for this view (Wilson, 1939, 10). In some societies, such as the Krahó (Cunha, 1981, 172) or the LoDagaa (Goody, 1962, 371), different individuals give differing accounts of the afterlife, there being evidently no version that is traditionally agreed upon.

Sometimes the afterlife is modeled after the present life but is improved. The Cocopa, for example, who live in the desert of the American Southwest, picture the souls of their dead as going to a region a little to the south, where it is never too hot or too cold, where horses and their fodder are plentiful, and where life can be devoted to feasting, dancing, and singing (Kelly, 1949, 152). In a shorter time perspective, the Gebusi of New Guinea portray the freeing of the soul from the body as leading first of all to the immediate enjoyment of making love with a spirit in the treetops (Knauft, 1985, 86–87). The Mambila report postmortem life to be familiar in kind but more prosperous and happier (Rehfisch, 1969, 308, 310). The Toraja of Sulawesi, on the other hand, complain that the afterlife is dull (Downs, 1956, 44).

A Western background leads one to expect that the afterlife might be thought to vary from one individual to another as punishment or reward for behavior during this life. Striking differences of opinion are to be found in general discussions of this question by anthropologists. At one extreme, Goody suggests

> that retribution is to some degree an essential feature of all beliefs in a future life. For whether the Other World is seen as a continuance or as a reversal

of this, its whole conception must necessarily reflect the ideas of the living, ideas that are always tinged with moral undertones, even if they fail to make explicit provision for a judicial process in the Land of the Dead. In other words, the idea of rewards and punishments after death appears to be an inevitable extension to the supernatural plane of the system of social control that obtains upon earth, no less so if the next world is seen as making up for the inadequacies and inconsistencies of this. (1962, 375)

Goody's view emerged from a detailed study of the LoDagaa, where he found ample evidence of postmortem punishment for misbehavior in this life. At the beginning of this chapter we quoted a LoDagaa funeral speech, during which the speaker gave cowrie shells with which his dead friend could pay the boatman to ferry him across the river to the Land of the Dead. The cowrie shells would have been thought a futile gift if the friend's evil deeds had outweighed his good; the boatman might have let him aboard, but then, as one young man pictured it to the anthropologist:

If you've done wrong, when you enter the boat you'll drop through the bottom into the water.... If you fall in the water, you won't drown, but will just have to go on swimming for a long, long time; it'll take you some three years to cross. You'll suffer a great deal on the way and you'll have nothing to eat. (1962, 372)

After getting across, the miscreant might have a thousand years of suffering before being allowed to farm once more and get food. Virtuous LoDagaa dead, on the other hand, after a period of farming, eventually are able to get food by just thinking of what they want.

Postmortem punishment and reward are sometimes not elaborated even though they clearly are believed to occur, as among the South African Swazi, where

the ancestors are not prepared to accept all and sundry into their fold: they reject ("close the road to") the undiscovered murderer, the woman who has a child by a secret lover, and the man who commits incest. The belief in punishment after death is, however, not very highly developed" (Kuper, 1947, 190).

At the opposite extreme from Goody's view, Firth says that

"as a rule the fate of the soul is not associated with any concept of rewards or punishments after death. The doctrine of retribution on a moral basis after death is generally lacking. In this there is a strong contrast to the beliefs of followers of most of the major religions" (1967a, 331)

Our own reading of many ethnographies fully supports Firth's statement. Anticipations of reward and punishment in the afterlife, as among the LoDagaa, are exceptions rather than the rule. Among the Pueblo societies of the United States, for instance, Parsons (1939, 216) reports that the Hopi are unusual in expecting punishment in the afterworld for witches and some other serious offenders; and we have a similar impression of rarity in our worldwide reading. Specific denial of such a belief is found in some ethnographies, and to them must be added the many in which the vagueness of beliefs about the afterlife indicates the absence of any definite expectation of reward or punishment.

We may conjecture that the relative unimportance of postmortem rewards and punishments results from the lack of opportunity for confirmation of their occurrence. Rewards and punishments that are said to occur during a person's lifetime may refer to events actually experienced by a person directly or witnessed in others, giving their threatened occurrence a vividness and realism not shared by threats of what may happen in an afterworld of which one has no direct experience. Beliefs about the afterlife do, however, play a major role in many societies in the enforcement of moral rules. The relevant aspects of these beliefs have to do with the relation of ancestral spirits to the living, as we have shown in Chapter 4; the rewards and punishments that ancestral spirits are believed to bring consist of the very real pleasures and pains, hopes and fears, of everyday life in this world.

The afterlife is often expected to vary from one individual to another on other bases than rewards or punishments for behavior during this life. Most conspicuous are the variations implied by the assumption of continuity of social status before and after death. The soul continues the gender of its earthly life. Men and women continue to follow distinct patterns of occupation and recreation; in stratified societies, class position tends to be maintained, and so on. However, some societies introduce distinctions that seem to be made at random or are determined by events in this life that are morally neutral or over which the person has no control.

The Mundurucú, of tropical South America, hold that there are three underworlds, each with its own dominant activity. One is for those who at ceremonies have played the sacred trumpets; they can continue their trumpet playing. A second is for those "who know the ceremonial dances for the spirit mothers of the game"; they can continue dancing. The third is for those whose death happened to be brought about by demons; life in that world is less pleasant and ends with a transformation from human spirit to demon (Murphy, 1958, 23–24). The Tsembaga of New Guinea assign the afterlife to two separate regions, both of them real parts of the tribal territory. The spirits of Tsembaga who die of accident or illness live in the lower-altitude portion, whereas spirits of those killed in battle live in the higher-altitude portion. The two have somewhat different activities and are appealed to for different kinds of help to the living (Rappaport, 1984, 38–40). The 'Aré'Aré, of the Solomon Islands (Coppet, 1981, 178), look forward to a different afterlife according to whether they happen to be killed by a living person (i.e., are murdered) or by a spirit (i.e., die of illness). The Dogon, a tribe in Mali, provide an African example of a similar kind. If a Dogon dies while pregnant, for instance, or from illness suffered from falling asleep near certain dangerous stones, her or his soul must, unlike other souls, wander forever in the bush (Dieterlen, 1941, 193, 197).

The varieties of afterlife we have been presenting are beliefs about the eventual life the soul of a deceased person enters into for the long run. The afterlife may be different for the first few days or months. These temporal variations are related to the ceremonies that follow upon a death and to variation in how the spirit of the deceased is conceived to interact with the living. We turn next to those more general facts.

MORTUARY RITES, AND BECOMING AN ANCESTOR

An important and revealing fact about mortuary rites in traditional societies the world over is their very strong tendency to be multiple: one set of ceremonies immediately or soon after death and other ceremonies later, perhaps months or even years, after the death. Rosenblatt et al. (1976, 92) found that of 61 societies in their sample for which information indicated whether there was some later funeral ceremony (at least ten days after the initial ceremony), 46 (75 percent) do indeed have at least one, and a number of these have more than one. The fact of frequent delay in completing rituals occasioned by a death helps to understand what such rituals do even in societies where the rituals are completed expeditiously.

The fact that funeral ceremonies are in most societies at least dual was first noted and elaborated early in this century by a French sociologist, Robert Hertz (1960). He was best acquainted with data that were already available to him about funeral customs in some Malaysian or Indonesian societies, in which the duality of the ceremonies is especially pronounced. But he correctly noted evidence of it in many other societies as well. Hertz concluded that the splitting of mortuary rites, with a considerable period between, was appropriate in relation both to the body and the soul of the deceased and to the survivors. In many societies, the mode of disposal of the corpse is one that requires a delay; the flesh must decompose, for example, so that the bones may be easily separated and cleaned. The soul may need to undergo some preparation for its great transition from normal life to an afterlife; an initial ceremony may start this process, but much time may be required for completing it. The survivors may need support of others in an initial ceremony, but then require a period of working through their grief, and of adjusting to the practical consequences of their loss, before they are ready for a final farewell to the deceased.

Fieldwork in recent decades (e.g., Metcalf, 1982; Huntington & Metcalf, 1979) has given a very detailed picture of the dual ceremonies in some tribes in Malaysia and Madagascar (whose culture bears in this respect as in many others traces of its origins in a migratory flow from Malaysia or Indonesia, perhaps by way of slow movement down the eastern coast of Africa). Goody (1962) gives a very full account of a four-part series of funeral ceremonies in an African society. Satisfactory detail is available on secondary or multiple ceremonies in a number of societies elsewhere in the world. But first we will consider what may be said about the initial funeral rites regardless of whether they are succeeded by later, final rites.

The initial ceremony is generally built around the disposition of the body. Though a universal necessity, the disposition takes many forms. Burial in the ground is most common, but various other practices are standard in some societies. The body may be exposed on a platform or in a tree, for the flesh to be eaten by wild animals or birds. Alternatively, it may be dressed and seated in a place of honor to receive visits while decay begins. It may be packed into a large jar in which the flesh will disintegrate. The body may be treated with fear and avoidance, disposed of promptly and with finality—or, at the other extreme, portions may be eaten by relatives as a part of the funeral ritual or the bones kept and worn as constant reminders of the deceased.

The treatment of a person's body may be different according to age, sex, social status, and circumstances of death. In many societies, for example, a man's body is buried with the left side up and a woman's with the right side up, or vice versa. The number of categorical distinctions made has been found to vary with the complexity of the society (Binford, 1971); recognition of different roles among the living carries over, to some extent, to differences in burial. An occasional society goes beyond distinction by category, making some aspect of the treatment of a person's body unique to the individual. The Gusii of Kenya bury each person in a distinctive place, which, by its relation to the person's residence, symbolizes and perpetuates individual identity (LeVine, 1982b, 33).

In most societies, the initial ceremony is a group activity that brings together not only the immediate family but neighbors and other relatives who live near enough to be notified in time. ("Relatives" is defined by the kinship structure of the society.) Funeral ceremonies may be one of the few occasions on which the members of an important social grouping come together (though final ceremonies may be even more significant in this respect than the initial ones, as advance notice can permit attendance by those more distant). Funeral ceremonies thus serve not only to recognize the diminution of social ties by death but also to renew other social ties and reinforce the basic social structure of the society. A detailed analysis of ritual wailing at funerals of several tribes of central Brazil led to the conclusion that it has this kind of significance:

> It may be proposed that ritual wailing represents not simply the feeling of loss but, in a more complex way, the desire for sociability that is the inverse side of loss. Loss occasions the wish to overcome loss through sociability, and it is this sociability that is signaled through adherence to a culturally specific form of expression of grief. (Urban, 1988, 393)

Emotions distinctively appropriate to the occasion may be expressed, then, in ways that renew or reassert the ties implied by the basic pattern of the society, by the way kinship is reckoned, and by the system of neighborhood relations, prestige and power, and economic exchange. But the ties of which weeping and commiseration provide a special reminder may also be renewed by making a funeral the occasion for interacting in the same way as at other times of meeting. Thus, in New Guinea, where social relationships are largely defined by rules of property exchange, giving and receiving are a major part of the activity at funerals; people's chosen participation or absence renews old relationships, modifies them, or establishes new relationships within the limits set by the social order (Strathern, 1981).

Some writers have seen funerals as gaining their principal value precisely in this way—from their bringing people together to interact in their accustomed ways. Funeral ceremonies have been interpreted as response to a threat posed to society by the death of one member: If each person in a group must die, can the group survive? Bringing people together for their accustomed mode of interaction provides reassurance. An occasional ethnography cites evidence that such thoughts are embodied in the ritual or are expressed by informants in discussing funerals. The symbolism of funerals may in more subtle ways express a struggle against extinction, an assertion of continuity, a faith in the regeneration of life. Bloch and Parry (1982b), in their introduction to a volume on this theme, cite a variety of ways in which rituals symbolize the struggle.

If positive interaction and the mutual solace of sharing grief are characteristic of initial funerals, so is an undercurrent, sometimes the open expression, of fear and hostility. It is an occasion in most societies for people to wonder and perhaps to discuss why the person died. The blame may be laid on ancestral spirits (who are likely to be thought present at the funeral) or on living members of the family. Why should such thoughts or open accusations accompany the mutual nurturance expressed at a funeral?

M. E. Opler (1936b) offered an interpretation of the fear of the dead for particular societies he had studied, and suggested it might apply to many others as well. He had studied three Apache tribes of the American Southwest and found similar emotional conditions in all three. The Apache, like many other hunter-gatherers, stress in their child training the development of independent skills and self-reliance, yet they live in the intimacy of extended family groups that even in adult life greatly restrict the expression of independence. The contrary feelings of love and resentment that result are associated with fears of wizardry from intimates; almost everyone has at some time received a grant of mystical power, yet might be called upon in return to use that power to kill a relative. Everyone has cause, therefore, to fear his or her relatives.

The mixture of love and fear continues, Opler reasonably supposes, upon death of a relative, and each emotion is heightened. Expressions of grief are often extreme, but fear of the deceased is equally conspicuous and even more lasting, centering on expectations that the soul of the deceased will bring serious disease. Burial is speedy, and the bereaved attempt to avoid being reminded of the deceased, for thinking of the deceased is likely to bring the spirit back to threaten, perhaps to kill. Opler assembled numerous observations he had made among the Apache that argued for the validity of his interpretation, tracing the grief-fear ambivalence about the dead to a continuation of the love-hate ambivalence about living intimates.

A different view of ambivalence toward the spirits of recently deceased relatives was put forth by Radcliffe-Brown (1922) in his work on the Andaman Islanders. He traces it to the mixture of attachment to the deceased and attachment to life. Because the dead spirit remains emotionally attached to the living relatives, it may seek their company even if this means bringing them to the land of the dead, and the living relatives may experience some wish to join the deceased no matter how much they value life. While Radcliffe-Brown reports that the Andamanese consider the general relation between living and dead to be dominated always by hostility, he seems to trace the hostility only to the threat death poses to individual and community, not to a view that dead spirits are evil in intent. This social-structural view of the sources of fear of the dead need not be incompatible with Opler's view that traces the fear to hostility originating in family relationships. Both sources might be present in a single society or single individual, and to varying degrees.

The LoDagaa youth, in his funeral speech, speculates on why his friend had died, and such speculations are sometimes the only way this question appears in the funeral ceremonies. But in many societies the question is pursued more systematically. Either in the initial ceremonies or in the period that follows, one or more diviners may be called on to seek the answer (see Chapter 5). The LoDagaa provide a prime example. Two different types of skilled divination are called on, one depending on the help of nature spirits, the other involving communication from the deities via the manipulation of cowrie shells. In addition, funeral speeches may include a request to the spirit of the deceased to reveal through dreams the cause of the death, and the behavior of family members may give clues to their possible complicity. Agreement needs to be reached on the various aspects of causation (the immediate physical instrument, the human beings who may have been involved, the mystical figures who may have been appealed to or may themselves have initiated events, the motives of both human and mystical sources) before the later ceremonies can be properly planned (Goody, 1962, 208–219). Goody speculates on what is gained by divination:

> First, the very discussion of intimate details of past events with an "expert" has some cathartic effect for the client in cases in which he is seeking advice on his own behalf. Second, the diviner reinforces the social mores by a firm restatement of what ought to be done; characteristically, he speaks in highly standardized forms of speech, in riddles, proverbs, and short pithy sayings, which embody the traditional standards of the society. Third, and most important, the diviner formulates a "rational" course of action in anxiety situations. (1962, 211)

During the period immediately following the death, and including the initial funeral, grief may be the principal emotion. We may reasonably infer that in many societies it is accompanied by fear of being accused of having taken some part in bringing about the death. We know very definitely that it is commonly accompanied by fear of the spirit of the deceased. The spirit is sometimes supposed to be angered by the frustration of dying and thus being deprived of all the positive values of life. In particular, it is often, as among the Andamanese, thought of as feeling lonely, wishing to have again the company of family members, and having the power to bring about their death and a reunion. The spirit is often pictured as being at this period in the immediate vicinity, perhaps in the treetops or even in the family dwelling, not yet qualified for movement toward the eventual afterlife, or not yet oriented toward accepting it instead of the life just left.

In some societies, fear may be expressed in the feeling that contact with death is polluting. The Kota of India are reported (Mandelbaum, 1965) to consider polluted everyone who is associated with a death, and even the spirit of the deceased. Funeral rites of the Kota seem largely directed at removing the pollution. A more extreme case is found in the Sebei, an East African group studied by Goldschmidt (1973). Here the emphasis is on pollution of the survivors, and the soul of the deceased receives so little attention, Goldschmidt says, that an observer might not guess that the Sebei even believe in a soul. A rite to purify all the survivors normally occurs on the fourth day after the death. The widow, in particular, must have ritual intercourse about this time with the man who has inherited her as spouse, and this ceremony is regarded as purifying her.

The final ceremony, or series culminating in the final ceremony, marks a clear transition for soul and for survivors, and usually for the body of the deceased. It is often timed to be held in the period most convenient for the economic cycle of the year. Because the participants are usually numerous and the ceremony may last many days, it is often community-wide, concluding the farewell to all members who have died since the previous ceremony of this kind but long enough in the past to make a final ceremony appropriate.

The body of the deceased may be left where it was first placed (as among the LoDagaa). But often it is moved at the time of the final ceremony; hence writers often speak of *secondary burial*. Removed from its temporary location, the body may be cleaned and reduced to bones, or prepared for cremation or for reburial. The final disposition of the remains may then be the central event of the ceremony. Among the Bara of Madagascar (Huntington & Metcalf, 1979, 107–109), the bones are carried in a boisterous procession to the mausoleum of the lineage, which is opened no more than once a year, and is placed with the remains of the previously deceased. The ceremony is conceived to be a social occasion for the dead as well as the living; the new spirit is introduced to the family spirits already resident in the mausoleum, with whom it is seen as continuing an active life. In Borneo, initial burial, by placing in a mausoleum the jar or coffin containing the corpse, is for most persons the final burial. But for some few persons, the corpse is cleaned at a later ceremony, and only then placed in a mausoleum (Metcalf, 1982).

Outsiders can most readily understand the physical aspects of funeral proceedings, and may exaggerate their role. Metcalf has shown, for example, that contrary to the belief of many outsiders, the Berawan of Borneo do not consider that the physical changes in the corpse dictate the schedule of mortuary ceremonies. Circumstances sometimes permit the Berawan to hold a lavish community ceremony in the days after the death, and in that case there is no later ceremony. Often, the state of agriculture prevents many people from taking part at that time in a major ceremony (which may last up to ten days), and finds many people unable to provide the funds needed for a major initial ceremony; in that event, the later ceremony takes its place, and initially there is only a smaller, more intimate funeral. The corpse does not need to await being reduced to bone, and the soul is not impeded in its progress toward ghostly status. A separate final ceremony, Metcalf reports, has probably always been rare, and it is especially rare in recent times when the advent of commercial credit has removed some of the economic barrier to lavish initial ceremony. Formerly, a death that called for a large ceremony had to be delayed until family and others obliged to contribute had in hand their next harvest, and many months' accumulation of other resources, to defray expenses; now the necessary food and drink could be bought immediately and paid for later.

For the survivors, the final ceremony generally marks the end of mourning, the period during which various taboos must be observed by individuals of varying kinship relation to the deceased. It generally marks, too, the end of special temporary danger to survivors from the soul of the deceased. These religious implications of the final ceremony are accompaniments of the realistic implications: that the property, responsibilities, and privileges of the deceased have been redistributed.

For the soul, the final ceremony completes (if the initial ceremony has not already completed) the transition from a special temporary status of recently deceased (sometimes distinguished by a special term such as ghost) to a more permanent status. In almost all societies, as we indicated earlier, everyone's soul survives the death of the body, but the status of ancestral spirit is in some societies reserved for only a few.

In the first place, of course, only the spirit of a mother or father can become an ancestral spirit, and in some societies it seems to be only the spirit of a father. Social parenthood is more relevant than biological parenthood; in some societies, for instance, a childless young widow may still be able to give her deceased husband children by permitted intercourse with other men, and the deceased husband may thus become eligible for ancestorhood. Men who are lineage heads are more likely than others to be recognized as ancestral spirits. Condition at the time of death is sometimes relevant, as among the Shona of Zimbabwe, where potency at the time of death is a requirement (Jacobson-Widding, 1986). More often, certain categories of death (such as suicide or by particular diseases) may preclude ancestorhood. In any event, ancestral spirit is a status to which the deceased may be advanced, usually by appropriate ritual procedures. Thus, the sequence of rites of passage through which a person's development is shaped does not necessarily end with a farewell to life; for many individuals, further advancement lies ahead.

REINCARNATION

Belief in reincarnation is standard in many societies around the world, and in some it is an integral part of the life cycle of the individual. In the Trobriand Islands, Malinowski (1916) found that after death the spirits were believed to go to a nearby island (Baloma) and live in villages of the dead. A spirit continued aging there, and eventually became a spirit embryo, ready for transplanting into the womb of a woman of the same subclan in its native village. Conception could not occur without this reincarnation. (Whether the Trobrianders recognized that conception also requires semen is the subject of controversy, as we mention in Chapter 7.)

Reincarnation fits, for the Kaguru of Tanzania, into a picture of life and death as alternating periods, each bringing advantages. Death brings to the spirit "a strengthening of certain ghostly aspects that provide supernatural power and rectitude which a man could never possess in life" (Beidelman, 1966, 376). Entry into life is thus a close parallel to entry into death:

> When a child is born, the ghosts it left behind miss it and try to draw it back. A newborn infant is in danger for this reason and is not wholly part of the living. Grieving ghosts frequently cause infants to sicken and die, but ghosts may be consoled by having their names (called the names of "grandparents") given to infants. Thus, the birth of a living child is mourned as a kind of death by the ghosts of the other world. It represents the loss of certain supernatural forces held by spirits in exchange for vital forces of the living. (Beidelman, 1966, 376)

A very different picture of reincarnation is found among the Aranda of central Australia. Here conception depends not on the spirit of a deceased person of some recent generation but on the spirit of a remote mythical ancestor. Aranda mythology portrays such a spirit as divisible; a part can become the germinating soul of one person, other parts can play a similar role for other persons, while the spirit remains still intact. According to the fullest account available of these beliefs (Strehlow, 1964), a person has two souls: a mortal soul that comes into being as the embryo develops from the mating of man and woman and an immortal soul that enters after pregnancy is clearly present. The immortal soul is a reborn part of the mythical ancestor associated with or dwelling at the place where the woman is located at the time of the incarnation. This soul affects the appearance and character of the person, making it resemble the animal species that also derives from the same mythical ancestor and that constitutes the person's individual totem. It is this soul, or personal totem, of a person that "mainly determined the nature of his rights, duties, and functions in the religious sphere" (Strehlow, 1964, 733). Kangaroo men, for example, were the exclusive officiants at all rituals pertaining to kangaroos. When a person died, his mortal soul survived only for a while; his immortal soul, however, returned to its source, becoming once more a part of the mythical ancestor still existent in a particular sacred spot. Thus,

> the true home of every man is the site where he once lived and moved without fetters in a more glorious age than the present, at a time when the world had first become awakened out of eternal sleep in the thick, silent darkness that had encompassed the earth ever from the beginning of time. (Strehlow, 1947, 91)

SUMMARY

The belief that a person has one or more souls that survive bodily death apparently occurs everywhere, and a number of more or less universal kinds of experience would seem to reinforce the belief. Notions about the afterlife vary, but generally have in common that they are based on the present life of the society. Death occasions ceremonies, usually a sequence of two or more for each person; from one society to another, these are enormously diverse in detail but they have almost uniform basic functions:

1. To dispose of the body of the deceased in a manner feasible in the physical setting and appropriate to the society's belief system
2. To help the survivors adjust emotionally to their loss
3. To facilitate any replacement that may be dictated by the kinship customs of the society
4. To renew commitment to the established patterns of relation among kin, neighbors, and so on
5. To recognize the new status of the deceased person as spirit
6. To relate to the spirit in whatever ways customs may dictate: protect from its attack, aid it on its way in the afterlife, for example.

Chapter 10

Festivals

Festivals are rituals that are open to the whole community or large segments of it. Some festivals focus on particular individuals, as when a group of young people are initiated or an invalid is the object of a healing ceremony and the event is open to all who wish to take part. More characteristic of festivals is a focus on concerns of the whole community, especially on the supply of food. In most regions, the sources of food and the activities that procure it vary with the season. Pastoral peoples often add to the variation of weather a variation of place, as they move from one area to another in adaptation to the use they make of the land. For all these societies, festivals are generally timed in relation to the annual cycle; hence anthropologists have often called them calendrical ceremonies, though the calendar may be the variable one of plant growth or weather changes rather than a fixed one based on astronomical observations. Even in the rare tropical areas where conditions are fairly constant through the year, particular crops may be planted and harvested at a conventional time, or particular wild game or fruits may be most available at a fairly uniform time; so even here where the timing is largely conventional there may be a calendrical aspect to festivals.

The amount of information available about festivals varies a great deal among societies. Some anthropologists, or whole schools of anthropology, have greatly interested in this aspect of social life, and others not. In addition, there may be real differences among regions in the extent to which conditions tended to induce an elaboration of calendrical ceremonies. Some of the best information is about native North American societies, and we will begin with them.

FESTIVALS IN NORTH AMERICA

From northern California through Oregon, Washington, British Columbia, and southern Alaska, many societies depend on salmon as their main source of protein. People can eat salmon fresh for many months, as the salmon are in the coastal waters or swimming upstream for spawning, and some of the catch can be dried for use the rest of the year. For each tribe this basic economic condition divides the year into two parts. As the Bella Coola express it metaphorically, "During nine months the canoe of the salmon was in the Bella Coola country. As it departed, another canoe bringing the winter ceremony arrived, and remained four months" (Goddard, 1934, 128).

In most of these societies, the beginning of the salmon season was marked by the first-salmon ceremony, a ceremony distinguished by its serving the interests of the entire community. Other festivals among these peoples conspicuously served the interests of particular individuals, increasing the prestige of the person in charge and his family or social group. The first-salmon ceremony seemed to be directed only at ensuring the continued supply of this essential food.

The ceremony was based on the view that the salmon willed themselves to be caught, were potentially immortal, and must be treated in such a way that they would continue to cooperate in the human food quest in years to come. These basic elements were a constant, but the particulars of the ceremony varied from one society to another. Some groups emphasized taboos to be observed in order not to offend the salmon—requiring, for instance, that any person who was ritually unclean (by local definition) must stay away from the first-salmon ceremony. The taboos were sometimes given strength by being embodied in mythology, as in retelling how Coyote, long ago, in establishing many features of the culture, laid down the rules for this ceremony.

Sometimes practical acts were emphasized. Thus, the Chinook buried the heart of the first salmon, making sure that the dogs could not mutilate it. Others cast bones and heart into the water, to encourage reincarnation of the salmon. The Tsimshian sought the favor of the first salmon caught, which had given up its present life for the sake of the people, by addressing it with honorific titles.

For some tribes, the first-salmon ceremony marked the beginning of the new year. And regardless of whether it was given this position in the calendar, it was often incorporated in a vision of *world renewal*. World renewal is the underlying theme that Kroeber and Gifford (1949) detected in complex festivals of several small tribes in northwestern California. Some were associated with first-salmon ceremonies, but some were separate. They included dances, feasting, offerings to mystical beings, and recitations and meditation by the priests of the cult. The festivals seemed directed at ensuring the renewal of a productive relationship with the natural world. To that end, they were built around recall of the life of the spirits that in ancient times had preceded humankind and dedication to patterning human life after their model. Thus, maintenance of the tribal economy was linked with the traditional cosmic view.

Comparable festivals, with similar significance, occurred in societies not dependent on salmon. The Creek, horticulturalists of the Southeast, had a rite lasting four to eight days, timed to mark the ripening of corn. Fire was newly made, providing a fresh source of fire for each family. Purgatives, emetics, and fasting prepared each person for bodily renewal through first tasting of the new corn and subsequent feasting. This main calendrical ceremony of the year was preceded by several "stomp dances," variously timed in relation to earlier events in the growing season; the dances were described by one informant as a feast of renewing love, of confirming friendship.

The myths of how the festivals originated portrayed them as established for the survival and health of the tribe. Participation in them was taken seriously as a community obligation. Whatever ceremony was the largest in a society showed some tendency for other ceremonies to be merged with it. In northern California,

> the great Annual Mourning Ceremony combined two ritual series for Yokuts and Western Mono: basically it was an exaggerated form of the private or family mourning ceremony, but because of its size and consequent dependence upon adequate food supply it necessarily occurred in a season of abundance. Thus the seasonal, public or community ceremonial series, and the non-timed, private, or familial series were combined in the Annual Mourning Ceremony. (Gayton, 1946, 264)

The Pueblo tribes of the American Southwest had an especially rich ceremonial life, described by many ethnographers who have been able to observe the continuance of festivals even after four and a half centuries of contact with Spaniards, Mexicans, and Americans. Some ethnographers of special skill have also been able to study the meaning of the rituals and accompanying beliefs, despite the general secrecy and reserve that have facilitated their retention. Many descriptions of Pueblo festivals have been summarized by Elsie Parsons (1939), who also exhibits the complicated ways in which responsibility for the festivals is integrated with the whole social structure of each pueblo. This diffusion of responsibility for religious practice and the participation of so large a proportion of the community in the singing and dancing may be reasons for the remarkably persistent integrity of these societies.

For interpretation of Pueblo ceremonies, we have drawn especially on Ford (1972), Harvey (1972), and Ortiz (1972b). The calendrical festivals are portrayed by these anthropologists as having a useful practical function. The explicit function of many, especially of ceremonies during the growing season, is to control the spirits responsible for the weather and thus for crop yield. Increase in public confidence that the harvest will be good may itself be a valuable result. But Ford (1972) reports a subtler result as well. The festivals involve large accumulations of food, which is redistributed ceremonially in a way that alleviates the suffering of poor families. The undernourished gain from the well nourished without the indignity of begging or accepting gifts from identified donors.

In the close tie of Pueblo ceremonies to the calendar and to the significance of seasonal changes in the life of the community, a theme of cosmic regeneration again appears. Ortiz suggests that

> the major rituals of violence or rebellion, occurring as they do at changes of season, are in major part intended for societal and cosmic regeneration and renewal. Indeed, Stephen's Hopi informant actually told him that the mock battle at the winter solstice was supposed to "represent" the sun's journey across the sky. . . Relay races throughout the pueblos have also been explained as intended to give the sun strength for this journey, and they almost always occur at actual or culturally construed changes of season. Other symbolic acts which often accompany war ceremonies, such as the making up of new songs (Santo Domingo and Tewa), the village-wide distribution of seeds and/or prayer sticks (Hopi and Zuni), the giving out of new fire and/or water (Tewa, Zuni, and Acoma), bathing, and games like shinny are also intended to renew and regenerate nature. (1972b, 152-153)

Ceremonies that occur only at certain seasons may have little direct religious relation to the economic calendar. An instance is to be found in the potlatch ceremonies of various tribes of the Northwest Coast. They are held in the winter season, not because they relate to the activities of that period but because, requiring an accumulation of food and other goods, they are possible only after a period of maximum economic productivity. Potlatch hosts feed their numerous guests for many days, and distribute gifts of great total value. The relation between groups in these societies is in large part regulated by the obligation of chiefs and the groups they represent to give potlatches and the obligation of their guests to accept their gifts and to offer gifts in turn at some future potlatch of their own.

Competition for status through the amount of wealth accumulated and then given away in potlatches has been stressed in many accounts of these ceremonies, especially accounts based on potlatching practices after the great increase in wealth brought about by Europeans' purchase of furs. The redistribution of property doubtless served a useful social purpose at all times, too, aside from the status gain for the hosts and the maintenance of intergroup relations. Indeed, evidence from the days before the fur trade suggests that potlatches tended to be given by communities at times when they had an excess of food accumulated, for the benefit of nearby communities whose food supply was deficient (Suttles, 1960; Vayda, 1961; Piddocke, 1965). Perhaps for all these reasons the potlatch custom is supported by the mystical beliefs of these tribes and has been maintained (even if in altered form) up to the present. In some societies the principal purpose that determines when a person or group will offer a potlatch lies in its character as a funeral ceremony (Lantis, 1947, 110-111; Kan, 1986).

FESTIVALS IN OCEANIA

In 1928, a young British anthropologist, Raymond Firth, arrived at the tiny Pacific island of Tikopia. Brought up in New Zealand, he had developed early a fascination with the culture of the Polynesians, and his doctoral dissertation under Bronislaw Malinowski had been devoted to the Maori, the Polynesians of New Zealand. Most Polynesian societies, and especially their religions, had been greatly altered by that time. His aim in going to Tikopia was to study a Polynesian group whose aboriginal culture was still largely intact. His choice was sound. Tikopia is a small and remote island with nothing to tempt commercial exploiters, and the one missionary who had been there for some decades lived largely as a Tikopian and had caused little disruption of the social order. During the year Firth spent in Tikopia (1928-1929) and in subsequent visits in 1952 and 1966, he achieved the knowledge and understanding from which came a series of publications (1967a, 1967b, 1970) that give perhaps the best account of a traditional system of religious belief and practice and of its eventual breakdown under alien influence.

At the heart of Tikopian religion were two sets of calendrical ceremonies, one in the period of the trade wind and one in the period of the monsoon. Each set lasted more than a month, and the entire body of ceremonies was known by a name that Firth translated as "The Work of the Gods." Some ceremonies were general community festivals; in some, more restricted groups participated. Firth has recorded very full descriptions of the rituals, and summarizes in this way their overall meaning to the Tikopia:

> The performances were a formal traditionalized means of maintaining contact with powerful spiritual beings and inducing them to look with favour upon the Tikopia by the grant of food and health. The spiritual beings were conceived as being in reciprocal relationship with the leaders of particular lineages and clans, though the benefits to be derived from them were regarded as spread rather indifferently over the whole population. Contact with them was to be maintained partly on the same pattern as contact with powerful human beings, that is, by presentation of gifts and conduct of abasement. But they had to be treated with even more deference and even more formality. In particular, they had to be addressed by special titles not necessarily known to ordinary men and in much more elaborate set phraseology. (1967b, 6)

One component of the Work of the Gods (and of other Tikopia ceremonies) was the kava ritual, so frequently performed that Firth took part on 170 occasions. Kava is a plant from which a psychotropic beverage is made. A chief, acting in a priestly role, presided over the Tikopia kava ritual; the kava drink was prepared by one elder and dispensed by another. Rarely did any of the people present taste the kava. It was poured out as an offering to the spirits at appropriate points in the ritual: Because it was thought that most spirits like to drink the spiritual essence of kava, these libations were a way of establishing communication between the chief and the spirits he was addressing. (In many other societies of the Pacific [J. W. Turner, 1986], some of the human participants drank the kava, and the altered state of consciousness that resulted was evidently considered to facilitate communication with the spirits.) The chief's repeated prayers were generally for the benefit of his lineage group (most heavily represented among participants in the rite) and for the community at large, the entire population of 1,200.

The specific content of the chief's prayers, and the particular deities invoked, varied with the set pattern of each of the two series of Work of the Gods; the emphasis for each day was established by tradition. At one time, concern would be directed primarily at the refurbishing of canoes and other equipment necessary for fishing and supplementing material readiness of the canoes with mystical power granted by spirits. At another time, the focus would be on yam culture or on the dangers of high wind. Throughout, the rituals seemed to Firth to be directed at confirming and strengthening the traditional relationships among individuals and among lineages and thus bringing mystical support to the normal functioning of the society. On many days, some participants had the responsibility of bringing appropriate food, and a part of the ceremony involved the distribution of the food to all present—including, in some instances, food for them to take home for use there or for further distribution.

Another Polynesian society whose religion remained fairly intact at the time of anthropological study is that of Ontong Java, a group of small islands northeast of the Solomon Islands, visited by the Australian anthropologist Ian Hogbin in 1927 and 1928. The Ontong Javanese had only one set of calendrical ceremonies, lasting somewhat over a month. As in Tikopia, each day in the set had its own name and traditional rites. There was more emphasis than in Tikopia on ritual exchanges. On certain days, men gave coconuts to their wives' sisters, and women in return gave puddings; on some days there was a more elaborate pattern of exchanges. There was no precise rule about equivalence of gifts, but a gift considered inappropriately small or large led to criticism, as indicating either stinginess or ostentation. These exchanges, Hogbin felt, served to strengthen the interdependence of people. The very existence of the annual ceremonies and the required participation had the same effect, in view of shared beliefs about them; anyone's failure to participate fully might lead to punishment by mystical beings not only of the errant person but of the whole community. The ceremonies also reiterated the dependence of everyone on the chiefs of lineages, who, as in Tikopia, led the ceremonies and communicated with the spirits. During the rest of the year, dependence on the chiefs for continued relation to mystical beings had, Hogbin concluded, a similar effect. Universal awareness that everyone's welfare depended on the priest-chiefs' maintaining the goodwill of the spirits apparently increased the sense of tribal unity (Hogbin, 1931).

In both Tikopia and Ontong Java, ceremonial exchange was not confined to a community itself but also involved relations among communities, and this is an important feature of many Melanesian religions as well. The extension is especially clear in an incident witnessed by James Turner during fieldwork in Nairukuruku, a Fijian village. (Fiji is primarily Melanesian, but shares aspects of Polynesian culture as well, being located on the border of the two areas.) A village some distance upriver suffered several misfortunes and consulted a seer. The ancestors of these villagers had, in the 1870s, found refuge in Nairukuruku, and the seer suggested a relationship:

> The troubles may have been due to their unpaid debt to the descendants of the people who had sheltered their ancestors. This imbalance in the relations between the two groups was evidently distressful to the ancestors. The people living upriver presented a feast and yaqona [kava] to the people of Nairukuruku and the troubles came to an end. (Turner, 1987, 212)

Turner found ceremonial exchange to be of great importance within the community, too:

> The very act of giving is itself productive, efficacious, or a source of power. For in the act of giving and in the fulfillment of traditional obligations, one pleases the ancestors and secures their blessing. Conversely, failure to fulfill traditional exchange obligations can provoke their wrath. (1987, 218)

The Trobriand Islanders are a Melanesian society for which the sequence of calendrical ceremonies, including exchanges among communities, was charted by Bronislaw Malinowski on the basis of his fieldwork during the First World War. In *Coral Gardens and Their Magic* (1935) he focused on the horticultural cycle. The tubers produced are disposed of in complicated gift exchanges; each person's best produce is given to other households, and only the poorest is kept for use in the immediate family. For each stage of work, from preparation of the soil to harvest and distribution, the practical work was intertwined with magical procedures. Malinowski found the Trobrianders well aware of the distinction between practical and magical, but confident of the importance of both. Magical procedures were mostly conducted by the village specialist, often witnessed by the general public. The procedures do not seem generally to allude to mystical beings, nor do the punishments feared for violation of accompanying taboos and other rules. Fear of sorcery is another sanction for deviation. Again it does not appear that sorcerers depended on spirits; precise performance of a magical procedure was what would produce the victim's illness or bad luck. Among the Trobrianders, festivals were not communal banquets but, rather, occasions of ritual giving of food for storage. In some ceremonies, however, some of the food was set out briefly as an offering for ancestral spirits, and at one part of the horticultural cycle a return of the spirits played a major part in the ceremonies.

Inserted into relaxed periods in the horticultural cycle were the *kula* voyages that became world renowned through Malinowski's *Argonauts of the Western Pacific* (1922). The attendant ceremonies were tied to the calendar only in an approximate way; they took place, of course, whenever the voyages occurred. The kula was (and is still) an exchange system in which men of island societies to the east and north of New Guinea participate, forming roughly a ring several hundred miles in circumference. Around this ring circulate, in opposite direction, two kinds of valued objects: armlets and necklaces, both made of shell. Individual men may have kula partners in one or more societies in each direction from their own. In an expedition in the clockwise direction, they visit a community in which they receive from their partners kula necklaces; in the counterclockwise direction they receive kula armlets. They, in turn, are the hosts for expeditions to their own community, when gifts will be solicited from them.

The kula objects differ widely in fineness, beauty, and history. There is great interest in what pieces will come to each person on an expedition, to hold for a while until they must be given to partners from the other direction. Rumor may trace the movement of the most distinguished pieces as they move around the circle, giving a basis for speculation about who in this community will have them next. There is great interest, too, in how many kula objects a person will receive, both a consequence and a source of general prestige. The kula expeditions are the occasion also for practical trade between communities, though this is not carried out between kula partners. (In later decades, ordinary trade has been greatly facilitated by government motor vessels that link the islands, but the kula system has not withered from the great reduction of its practical accompaniment [Leach, 1983, 16]).

A kula expedition may be seen as one protracted communal ceremony; ritual traditions specify the procedures at each point, from initial planning of the trip to celebration upon return. As with Trobriand horticulture, magic is conspicuous and mystical beings play a minor role. (This may be partly a misconception based on the fact that Malinowski and subsequent investigators seem to have been little interested in some aspects of religion. Some Trobrianders have criticized Malinowski's account of the kula for failing to note that great success in the kula might permit a man to be released from the cycle of reincarnation [Leach, 1983, 12]).

When a new canoe must be built, the felling of a tree is preceded by a ritual to expel the wood sprite that occupies the tree, and various stages in the canoe making are accompanied by magic to make the canoe light, strong, and swift or by rituals of exorcism. Loading the canoes, setting off, and stops along the way are accompanied by magic to ensure speed. As the destination is approached, personal grooming is accompanied by beauty magic and followed by magic intended to influence the kula partners toward generosity. Magic is also employed in a man's interaction with his kula partner, as he offers minor gifts before and after receiving the kula objects that are the central aim of the expedition. The greatest danger feared on the voyage out and back is attack by flying witches from other communities, and safety magic is counted on for protection from them.

Along the shores of the Gulf of Papua (on the southern side of the mainland of Papua New Guinea) men of the Motu tribe make trading expeditions each year, in the period between the trade winds and the monsoon season. The main activity is practical: obtaining sago to supplement their own meager food production, in return for the pots made by Motu women. But the voyages are described as "the most important event in the social life of the Motu" (Williams, 1932, 139). Like the kula voyages of the Trobrianders, they are accompanied at all stages by magical procedures, beginning with the construction of the dugout canoes. The magic is related to Motu mythology; mystical power resides largely in the magician's citing correctly the names of mythical figures of long ago and in how well he impersonates these primeval figures, renowned for their unrivaled strength.

Various other regions in Melanesia have systematic trade or ceremonial exchange between communities, generally requiring canoe voyages at a time of year favored by climate and the horticultural cycle (Harding, 1967, 244). Ethnographic reports on them, however, have not been oriented toward their relation to religion, even though the relation may well be as close as in the Trobriands or the Gulf of Papua.

In much of Melanesia, ceremonial exchange, or ceremonial distribution with expectation of future reciprocation, is important quite apart from distant voyages. The fullest account is Roy Rappaport's (1984) description and analysis of pig ceremonies among the Tsembaga, in the Bismarck Mountains of the eastern highlands of Papua New Guinea. The Tsembaga are one of 20 communities that speak the Maring language, each with a population under 1,000. The ceremony of special interest is the *kaiko*, a series of events lasting about a year, given by one of these communities with participation at various points by other invited groups.

The kaiko is a festival directed, like other Maring ceremonies, at the relation of the living community to the spirit world. The kaiko requires sacrificing to the ancestral spirits a large number of pigs, and a community holds a kaiko only every few years, when the natural increase of domestic pigs has reached a point where their care becomes burdensome and their numbers promise to provide sufficient evidence of generosity to the ancestors and to the festival guests. The cycle of ceremony and of pig population is also a cycle of peace versus potential warfare. During the years of accumulation, a community does not initiate attacks on enemy groups; only after completion of its kaiko is it again free to be an aggressor.

The series of rituals making up the kaiko are adapted to the yearly cycle of horticulture and plant and animal life, and the details are worked out on the basis of advice shamans obtain from the ancestral spirits. Various rituals in the early months involve sacrifice of a few pigs, always to feed spirits and living people, the latter on some occasions being confined to the community itself but on others including communities that are allies in wartime. Other events are entertainments, centered on nightlong dances and distribution of food to guests; many of the guests bring objects or materials for trade, and intergroup marriages may have their inception here. Toward the end of the year, much practical work, and rituals and taboo observances prepare for the culmination of the kaiko in large-scale pig sacrifice (96 were sacrificed in two days when Rappaport was there), directed partly at ancestors who had been killed in battle and partly at the larger number of peacefully deceased. About a third of the meat was divided among Tsembaga; the rest was ceremonially presented to guests from several allied communities and was eventually divided among 2,000 or 3,000 persons.

Pork is a major source of protein in the Maring diet, and is available almost exclusively from ceremonial sacrifice of domestic pigs. The kaiko ceremonies and lesser rituals, and the spirit beliefs that sustain and justify them, thus provide an effective system of distribution of protein that at the same time ensures economic and social interaction between communities and helps cement military alliances on which tribal security depends.

Umeda village, in the far western part of Papua New Guinea, illustrates complex communal ceremonies less related to commodities and exchange. Their *ida* ceremony is concentrated in two days and nights, but preparation begins about nine months earlier, with a day and night of trumpet playing during which assignment of roles and other details are planned. In the following months, the men who are to have major roles must live a very restricted life while the rest of the community carry on their normal activities except for minor food taboos. In the month before the ida, the entire community is preoccupied with preparing the abundant special foods and the costumes that will be required. The ethnographer (Gell, 1975) was told that in the rare year when sago was not available in abundance, the ceremony would not be held; ida seems to be a celebration of the bounty of nature, rather than an appeal for help to cope with shortages.

The ida ceremonies center on a series of dances performed by men in elaborately prepared costumes, attended by nearby communities as well as the Umeda, and accompanied by feasting. Early in the series, the principal figure is the cassowary (an ostrich-like bird), and late in the series the human hunter. The Umeda do not express in words the significance of the complex symbolism, but their actions implied to the ethnographer an understanding and appreciation of it. The ethnographer interprets the ceremonies as symbolizing (among much else) the metamorphosis of wild nature into cultured humanity, and an extolling of the Umeda way of life.

Festivals have been well described, too, for a people living to the west of the Pacific, on the island of Timor, in the Indian Ocean. An American anthropologist, Elizabeth Traube, visited the Mambai there in the years just before their life was disturbed by the Indonesian annexation of what had been Portuguese Timor. Her report (1986) focuses primarily on the understanding of Mambai ceremonies and of the mythology and cosmology to which they relate.

The Mambai are an agricultural people; their festivals are organized around the cycle of planting and growth and the seasonal changes on which the cycle is based. One major ceremony comes around planting time, toward the end of the dry season, and a second marks an early stage in the development of major crops. These are described and interpreted in detail by Traube, who witnessed them directly and had a good relationship with two of the Mambai most knowledgeable about their meaning. A third ceremony, when harvest is completed and the dry season begins, she treats more briefly because she was not present during its performance. Her account of the ceremonies is an extraordinarily vivid attempt at leading a Western reader into at least a minimum sense of the experience of a religion very different from our own.

These calendrical ceremonies bring people together in ways reflecting the patrilineal structure of the Mambai. In the festival at planting time members of a descent group from various villages celebrate together. The next festival brings entire villages together, with clear distinction among descent groups embedded in the rituals. In both cases deceased members of a descent group are felt to be present along with the living members. The ceremonies are intended to influence what we would call physical events in the environment, and a major objective is "to regulate the rains that govern agricultural growth." Exchange or reciprocity is an underlying theme of the ceremonies. Allusion is made to the origins of the Mambai world in the back-and-forth interaction of Mother Earth and Father Heaven. Ancestral spirits and the living give to each other, both in the activity of the ceremony itself and in the way the ritual utterances express the Mambai conception of the yearlong relationship. Even the plants enter into exchange; the people give them (through the early ritual) the rain they need to grow; now at the time of the later ritual the plants must prepare, in return, to give themselves up to the people as food. The people reciprocate among themselves, and this seems to be expressed metaphorically in what is said about the cosmos, the ancestors, and the plants. All these relationships are expressed in a variety of ways—speeches, songs, dances, giving and deferring, eating together—and Traube argues that the living participants "emerge from ritual performances with a heightened consciousness of the meaning of their ties to one another" (p. 21).

FESTIVALS IN AFRICA

African religions are less dominated by economic concerns and more by concern for social relations. Before contact with Europeans, the herding and agriculture characterizing much of Africa may well have given people a greater sense of control over sources of food than did the simpler horticulture and foraging typical of the other regions we have been considering. Perhaps more important is the greater density of population, the often larger size of communities, bringing people into such constant interaction that rivalries and interpersonal frustrations may be more frequent.

This emphasis on social relations is to be seen even in a society whose ceremonies are largely organized around the calendar of food production:

the Yakö of eastern Nigeria, studied by Daryll Forde (1964). The Yakö live in villages with populations between 1,000 and 10,000, and the ceremonial life of each village is separate. There are three annual periods of ceremony in the village Forde studied (and probably in each of the other villages), defined by the horticultural cycle. One is around planting time at the beginning of the rainy season, probably in January. In the second period come the First Fruits Ceremonies, typically occupying approximately the month of July, and in the third period, in mid-November, fall the Harvest Rites. Forde has described in greatest detail the First Fruits Ceremonies. As one might expect from the name, ritual consumption of the first yield—early-maturing yams and okra—is conspicuous in the calendar of events. But Forde finds other aspects of the festival more significant.

The Yakö village is divided into groups in many cross-cutting ways. Adult men are a formal group, and so are adult women. People are divided by clan, by ward of residence, and by age within the ward; some groups are based on prestige. Ward leaders form a group. Some groups are defined by religious function—the Council of Village Priests and the Corporation of Diviners, for example. Each of the groups has some defined role in the First Fruits Ceremonies, and many of the events are private; in some cases, indeed, everyone but the few participants must stay indoors. But even private rites in which the small groups take part stress the role of the groups in the community, and there are also events in which large segments of the community actively participate. On the main day of general public celebration, the chief village spirit is reminded of the tasks the community has accomplished and is asked to let fertility, health, and peace continue. Various groups and individuals, in turn, are then blessed and receive gifts of food. The net effect of the ceremonies, Forde (1964, 235, 253) judges, is to inculcate in an emotional setting "the value of harmony and solidarity within the village" and thus contribute to "integrating a very large and complexly organized community."

Ceremonies are obviously important for solidarity and harmony in an agricultural society studied in the 1930s—the Tallensi of northern Ghana, reported on by the British anthropologist Meyer Fortes (1936, 1945). The Tallensi do not live in villages; their houses are scattered individually throughout the land, with no definite recognition of spatial units. The prime unit of social organization is the lineage, based on shared descent through the male line; a group of lineages that claim a common distant ancestor form a clan. The head of a lineage represents the group in relation to ancestral spirits and other divinities, as does for a larger group the head of a clan. The ultimate test of a person's place in the society is provided by his participation in the rituals of a kinship group, and most keenly by his sharing the meat distributed after a ritual sacrifice. Belief is that ancestral spirits would be gravely upset by signs of hostility among co-communicants, for that hostility would suggest hostility among the ancestors themselves. And other divinities would on other grounds be affronted; there is, for example, nothing that "the Earth abhors so greatly as strife between those who worship it together at the same shrine" (Fortes,

1945, 113). Thus, the ceremonies in which fellow clan members take part are a powerful force for social cohesion; disruption would be blasphemous.

Similar considerations apply to the integration of Tallensi society as a whole. There are two large segments of the society, the Tali and the Namoo, and festivals play an important part in preserving a sense of unity. Members of the two segments are brought together—many in person, others through spiritual representation by their clan or lineage heads—at great calendrical festivals. The rituals are performed by only one segment, either the Talis or the Namoos; members of the other segment do not take part directly in them but are present as spectators of the accompanying dances. Most important, perhaps, for integration of the Tali and the Namoo is that part of the ritual of one segment absolutely requires cooperation from the head of the other (Fortes, 1936, 162). Every society is divided into segments, which have both competing and complementary relations. Fortes notes the remarkable similarity between the Tallensi and the much smaller Polynesian society studied by Firth, in the way festivals relate to this segmentation. Generalizing beyond these two societies, he says that the seasonal festivals mobilize "the oppositions and rivalries in such a way as to display and evoke the sense of the inescapable interdependence of the different elements of the society on one another for the attainment of the common good of all" (1987, 40).

Religious concern with social relations is also conspicuous in the Nyakyusa, a people of Tanzania whose rituals and beliefs have been reported in great detail by Monica Wilson (1951a, 1957, 1959). One ceremony of major importance occurred at intervals of about 30 years. The Nyakyusa lived in separate chiefdoms, each embracing a number of villages. The villages were organized by age group, rather than by family or clan, and in each an appointed headman held considerable authority over his fellow commoners. The headship of the entire chiefdom, however, was hereditary, and the ceremony in question centered on the transfer of authority from the old chief to his heirs—generally, his two oldest sons by the wives he married during the ceremony of his taking office. As the chief grows older, he prepares, often under pressure, to give way to his heirs, and a "coming-out" ceremony effects the transfer.

The coming-out ceremony begins with the new chief's ending a period of seclusion. The activities, in which everyone participates, include much feasting and dancing, the naming by the old headman of a a new headman for each village, and food-seizing raids (or mock raids) on villages of other tribes and on the old chief's village. Conspicuous religious elements are various rituals to increase the mystical power of the new chiefs, for general strengthening but also specifically to enable them to counter the mystical power of sorcerers and witches. Half the villages will be under each of the two new chiefs, and two trees are planted to mark the boundary between chiefdoms; the future health of these trees is symptomatic of the health or strength of the chiefs. All fires are put out, and new fire is kindled for distribution throughout; this is part of a general renewal, as villages are constructed on sites not previously occupied. Each new chief marries two new wives, who will be his principal wives regardless of his previous marriages.

Calendrical ceremonies among the Nyakyusa did not include first-fruit rites, except for a minor ritual for the millet crop, where a small amount from each household was collected and kept in a pot of mystical power, to be brewed next year for a beer offering to spirits of the chief's ancestors. The important annual event was the new year ceremony of cleansing the country, participated in by everyone. The cleansing was partly material—throwing out old ashes, for example—but also social. Emphasis was on getting rid of anger, partly by confessing to anger that had been felt but perhaps not expressed.

The cleansing ceremony was likely to be preceded or followed by sacrificing cattle to the ancestors. Sacrificial rituals were the center of the ceremonies on which the Nyakyusa seem to have laid most stress. Though thought of as for the common good, they took place in private, at the sacred groves associated with the mythical founders of the society (the "divine kings"). Only the chiefs, with some close relatives, and priests were present. Sacrifices were held for a variety of reasons—plagues or epidemics, droughts, poor crops. Although they involved appeals to the ancestral spirits for help, they seemed also directed at the quieting or elimination of the anger that must be disturbing the integrity of society.

SUMMARY

In many parts of the world, societies are found where religious concerns are expressed in ceremonies in which a large segment of the community takes part. Whether such festivals are found in all parts of the world, we don't know; for many societies we lack the full knowledge of religious practices that would enable us to be sure that ceremonies were absent.

For many societies, festivals are major markers on the calendar, events absorbing attention and effort at particular periods of the year and prepared for at others. They often are related to the economic cycle—fitted in when the pressures of food getting permit, celebrating the success of the food quest in providing security for the period just ahead, seeking mystical support for future success. They often are accompanied by exchange of food or other goods—exchange within the community, reducing inequalities and preventing starvation of some families while others have a surplus, and exchange with other communities, broadening the variety of available goods beyond what the community normally produces for itself. The sense of mystical support for these activities strengthens the peaceful interaction with other communities and the harmonious ties within the community.

Chapter 11

Religion in Societies Undergoing Rapid Change

What does religion do for people? Members of any religious group, if they give thought to this question, may have specific answers. But answers are more likely to come to conscious awareness in people living at a time of great change, change that may make the values of their religion especially prominent. No general consideration of the question can do justice to the particularities of each time and place, but it can yield an overall picture that may help in understanding any particular instance.

Anthropological fieldworkers were once primarily concerned with trying to record the character of a culture as it was before contact with the alien influence of the Western world. Yet this contact began, in many parts of the world, long before the development of anthropology, and of course has proceeded so far that even persons with memories of precontact cultures have for some time been practically unavailable. So, in the case of religion, as for other features of culture, the attempt to portray the culture as it was has been accompanied by a running account of what it is becoming under acculturation. A look at the process of religious change under the joint influence of alien religion, other alien customs, and alien power is what we are undertaking here.

CARGO CULTS

In the early 1940s, the Admiralty Islands, north of eastern New Guinea, were occupied first by Japanese, then by American and Australian troops. When the war ended in 1945, the Melanesian peoples of the islands reverted to their earlier status of subordination to the Australian government as a part of the Territory of New Guinea. In this status their customs had been changing already through the prewar years; the war and its aftermath accelerated the changes. The American anthropologist Margaret Mead had studied a Melanesian village in the Admiralty Islands toward the end of the 1920s, and in 1953 she returned to observe the changes a quarter of a century had brought. A colleague, Theodore Schwartz, joined in this field trip, concentrating on another village and on the religious aspect of culture. Together they offer an unusually intimate and personalized account of religious change as part of the more general transformation of a society (Mead, 1956; Schwartz, 1962).

Especially influential in the postwar change was a charismatic individual named Paliau. A native of one of the villages in the Admiralties, he had been orphaned at the age of seven and had grown up with considerable independence from the community. Such a history is not unusual among leaders of change in various parts of the world. Orphanhood is found in the story of Moses, and mythology in many countries revolves around heroes who either were orphans or, like Oedipus, seemed to be. Without formal schooling, Paliau yet learned to read and write neo-Melanesian (the language formerly known as Pidgin English, later officially recognized in Papua New Guinea as Tok Pisin) and perhaps English. He had much experience outside the Admiralties, having been employed in the native constabulary before and during the war in other parts of Melanesia. He had been detained in Rabaul, the major city of New Britain, for a year after the war for possible trial as a collaborator with the Japanese occupation (he pleaded that he had collaborated only to the extent that had been directed in advance by the retreating Australians). After his return to the Admiralties, he became a leader in a movement for social reform and progress. The movement was aimed primarily at improving the economic status of the Melanesians, but the way seen as leading there involved many other changes, including modifications of religion. Various communities had their own versions of the movement, and the religious aspect at times developed into a frenzied expectation of rapid change mediated by mystical beings and processes.

The religious movement stressed respect for the dead ancestors and their reburial in cemeteries constructed with new symbolism. Here there was a combination of the old Melanesian religion and of the Christianity which everyone shared. The missionary churches that had brought the Christian message were not, however, its locus; the Christian symbolism was incorporated into a new religion whose participants met elsewhere, though they might well be continuing also as Christian communicants. At the two periods of frenzy (1947 and 1953-1954), people expected the ancestors to come to life again and to be accompanied by material goods such as white men were seen to possess. Sometimes a definite date was confidently predicted for the arrival of the ancestors and the cargo, and this date was identified by some with the return of Christ promised by missionaries and the New Testament texts. Altered states of consciousness, such as characterized mediums in the old religion, were common. Here, too, there was a creative synthesis of the old religion and Christianity and of practical concern for material welfare with reliance on mystical means for attaining it.

In other parts of Melanesia, at this same period and also earlier and later, similar religious developments have occurred. They have come to be known by the general term *cargo cults*, because they all include the element of expecting mystical delivery of material goods. The persistent intrusion of unrealistic cargo expectations into Paliau's movement is indicative of how readily such expectations arise in Melanesian culture. Paliau's movement was, for the most part, a fairly realistic program for social reform, and he had difficulty restraining unrealistic accretions in his followers. In some other parts of Melanesia, cargo beliefs were the main focus of a religious movement.

Much publicized as a response to the high technology of the armed forces sent into their lands during World War II, cargo cults had actually appeared long before that time. Witnessing the canned food and efficient weapons the aliens brought to their land, and the ships and planes that brought them, but lacking any knowledge of how they had come into existence, Melanesians might well spontaneously fantasy their origin to lie in magic. Various prophets vivified these fantasies with specific predictions about when such cargo would be miraculously delivered, and about the beliefs that should be held and the rituals that must be performed in order for the mystical beings to turn those predictions into reality. The cults that developed around these magical expectations of cargo were complex blends of the old religion with its reliance on ancestors, new fantasies, and elements of the Christian religion, which was another alien intrusion. As each prophecy failed, it might lead to a new blend.

The history of the Melanesian cargo cults indicates the importance of charismatic individuals as instigators and guides of religious movements. But it also suggests some uniformities in what their leadership provides to the followers. Times of great uncertainty, of insecurity about continuation of the old social order, and, of reliance on its religious and other customs provide the background. Various religious movements offer various routes to gain security once more. Some emphasize return to the old-time religion and veneration of the ancestors who had been happy with it. Some emphasize adoption of the ways of the aliens. Because neither of these can realistically go very far, it may generate unrealistic hopes and beliefs that merge fantasies from both alternatives, and a social movement may give it a social reality.

PROPHET DANCE AND GHOST DANCE

Through the centuries in which Europeans and their descendants gradually took over their land, Native Americans generally lacked any broad admiration, such as Melanesians had, for the technology the intruders brought with them. During most of this period of history, Native Americans were confronted by a much simpler alien culture than what the twentieth-century Melanesians were to encounter. The foreign elements most attractive to Native Americans—horses and rifles—were accessible to them. The major impact of the aliens otherwise lay in pushing the natives out of their agricultural and hunting lands and, throughout the Plains, destroying the buffalo herds that were the basis of the Plains economy. For religion, a prime outcome was a series of movements looking toward restoration of the pre-invasion life.

Around 1800, a prophet named Handsome Lake preached to the Iroquois of New York State a doctrine that emphasized the moral superiority of their earlier life. White civilization had brought vices, and the Iroquois should return to the life and values they had known before contact (Spier, 1935, 36, citing Parker, 1913). Later movements looked to mystical beings for more direct action against the whites, and these movements, while most obviously derived from the aboriginal culture they sought to rebuild, included also a blend of influence from the traditions of other tribes and perhaps even from Christianity.

Most nearly of pure aboriginal origin were the various revivalistic movements of the northwestern United States and western Canada that Leslie Spier called the *Prophet Dance*. They had begun in the early part of the nineteenth century, and at various later periods they gained vigor and spread from tribe to tribe with slight alterations. Typical of the Prophet Dance are all of the major elements in this summary of the form it took in one tribe:

> Falling-stars, earthquakes, and other strange happenings in nature portended the destruction of the world; certain prophets having communicated with God in their dreams, or having gone to the land of the dead and returned, predicted doomsday when they would rejoin the dead, and preached a more righteous and God-fearing life; and these prophets led special dances and songs concerning the salvation of mankind. (Spier 1935, 7, quoting from manuscript by Cline et al., "The Sinkaietk or Southern Okanagon of Washington")

The doomsday prophecy often came to be directed at the whites. Destruction of the earth and the return of the dead for a new beginning were old doctrine in some tribes. New was a modification that provided permanent destruction of the whites, whereas Native Americans by going to high land would be saved. Aboriginal doctrine could be appealed to against the invaders' agricultural economy; God, or the Earth-Woman, had formed the earth, and its cultivation was an unacceptable interference with the divine.

In the 1870s and the 1890s there were religious outbursts that derived from the Prophet Dance and were commonly recognized under the label of Ghost Dance (Spier, 1927; Lesser, 1933). They started in the Northwest, the region of the earlier Prophet Dance, but spread eastward to many other tribes as well. Here was an even clearer appeal for supernatural aid in the struggle to restore the old life that was crumbling. Mystical beings came nearer to everyone's personal experience. Aboriginally, in some tribes, healing had been the province of shamans. Now anyone who joined in the prescribed dance could hope to gain mystical power through the ghosts encountered in a vision. If the dancing was done just right and on a large enough scale, the ghosts would return to life, and with them would come the animals and fish, the foods of old that had become scarce. With the renewal of the old life, the white invaders would somehow disappear, in a natural cataclysm or, more rarely, in combat in which the native warriors would be magically protected.

The various forms of the Ghost Dance emerged from an inventive adaptation of a medley of elements. The destruction of the whites, for example, was among some Pawnee seen as a selective effect of the second coming of Christ, and Christian elements apparently were emphasized at times specifically to make the movement more acceptable to whites. The Pawnee incorporated a hand game that they had used earlier in gambling; by modifying it and setting it in a Ghost Dance context, they may have reduced the fears of whites that the Ghost Dance was a prelude to real assault, and they clearly enriched their own ceremonial life. The hand game drew on their aboriginal view that luck is deliberately assigned by the supernatural forces, and permitted expression in the Ghost Dance tradition of optimism that luck was now shifting in their favor (Lesser, 1978).

A COMPARISON

The religious movements of the Melanesians and of the Native Americans on the surface seem radically different. The Melanesian movements display an enthusiastic acceptance of the alien culture, and concentrate on seeking quantities of the cargo distinctive of white culture. Movements among Native Americans display a rejection of the alien culture; they are directed at the disappearance of the white enemy and a return to the past with its hunting and gathering mode of life (Mair, 1958, 114). The difference seems reasonable in relation to the threat or promise afforded by experience of the alien white culture. The Melanesians were not ejected from their homelands, were in general not altogether prevented from continuing their traditional mode of life, and yet were exposed to the sight of whites living a life of apparently great leisure in enjoyment of material goods originating from unknown places at a great distance. Native Americans, on the other hand, had their traditional life grossly disturbed—their land taken over by white farmers, the wild plants replaced by crops, the game destroyed by white hunters and trappers—all with such ruthlessness that the whites were likely to be more hated than envied.

This superficial contrast conceals great similarity underneath. Not only the Native Americans turned to their ancestors. While awaiting the cargo, or when the cargo failed to appear, the Manus and their neighbors looked to their ancestors for help. A part of the practices urged by Melanesian cargo cults was the construction of fine cemeteries for the reburial of the ancestors, in the hope of their interceding for the benefit of their descendants (Schwartz, 1962, 303, 332, 335). One Melanesian group, in the Sepik River area of New Guinea, were told by their prophet to expect the appearance of the dead after an earthquake for which they would be prepared in advance, and that it was the dead who would provide them with food, tobacco, rice, and rifles that "would be more powerful than any the government possessed" (Worsley, 1957, 102). Resurrection of the dead was predicted both in the cargo cults and in Native American revivalist cults, and various aspects of return to the past were implied.

On the other hand, there was also rejection of the past. The Manus, as a part of their cargo cult activity, destroyed or threw into the sea useful tools and honored ritual objects, such as ancestral skulls that had served as household protectors (Mead, 1956, 93). Other Melanesian groups threw away quantities of basic foods and killed their pigs, or consumed them along with quantities of other foods in festivities that were expected to end with the arrival of the preferred foods of the Whites. Less obvious, but clearly present, was some rejection of the past in the Native American cults.

In both areas most religious movements were first associated with some sort of prophet, though a single charismatic leader such as Paliau does not appear to be absolutely essential (Guiart, 1952, 1956). In both areas the aboriginal culture favored this dependence on a leader. Among many Native American groups, the vision quest embodied a tradition of mystical power attained by individuals. Similar in effect, without the element of quest, was the Melanesian Big Man cult with its deference to individuals possessing mystical power (Cochrane, 1970).

Another similarity between these two areas is that the societies in which these religious movements developed were simple in social structure and economy, so different from the society and economy of the whites that a general adoption of the alien way of life was hardly a possibility. The Melanesian and North American groups lived by hunting and gathering, in some instances by simple horticulture as well, without dependence on herding or complex agriculture.

For the Melanesians, an implication of this vast difference from the aliens is that in general they had a very limited understanding of the culture of the whites they came in contact with, of the origin of their possessions and the social structure and manner of life that made their production possible. The Melanesians had understood their own traditional religious beliefs and practices as an integral part of their mode of life. Raising pigs and yams depended on the proper performance of the rituals that would ensure the cooperation of the deities. Seeing the material possessions of the whites—whose missionaries, even, seemed enormously wealthy by local standards—they supposed the economy of the whites to be dependent on performance of the rituals that would gain the cooperation of Jehovah. From the early missionary days on through the wartime period of contact with seemingly unlimited wealth of military personnel, adoption of Christianity was seen as a route to acquiring the wealth that it seemed to bring to the whites. Missionaries seemed always to withhold the rituals essential to bring the cargo, but there could still be hope (Guiart, 1970).

This lack of realization was facilitated by the fact that the whites showed little understanding of the Melanesian societies. They often did not recognize the status of the "big men" in a Melanesian group, and treated all as "rubbish men"—to use terms from the neo-Melanesian language (Cochrane, 1970). Native Americans may have had a better understanding of the culture with which they were confronted, but not in any full way that would have made it easy to adopt it as a way of life. Any attempt to cope with the alien culture as a whole might of necessity, then, be unrealistic and call upon the religious traditions of the group. As Lawrence pointed out in 1963, religion had been and at that time still remained more pervasive in Melanesians' thinking than people from Western societies might have guessed.

> The cosmos is still a finite, anthropocentric, physical realm, inhabited by both human and extra-human beings. In order to ensure the smooth working of the cosmic order, men have still to maintain proper relationships with gods and spirits of some sort by means of ritual, which is still seen as part of the technology. Religion still dominates men's thinking in the economic, socio-political, and intellectual fields. For the economic and intellectual fields, this is abundantly clear in the persistence of the cargo belief to the present time. A very great deal of the natives' intellectual effort has been expended in the attempt to solve the problem of adjustment to the new economic order by discovering the true identity of the cargo deity and the correct ritual with which to approach him. (1963, 8)

The Melanesian and the Native American religious movements had in common then, not only a quest for security but also a quest for understanding. Each offered a view of the world that, however unrealistic, seemed to give an acceptable place to the native, to the foreigner, and to the customs and material equipment of both.

OTHER SYNCRETISM IN THE AMERICAS

Two religious movements among Native Americans are especially noteworthy as a creative blend of influences from Christianity and the aboriginal traditions; they became recognized churches even though not established within a Christian church tradition—the Shaker religion (Gunther, 1949; Smith, 1954; Collins, 1950) and the peyote religion (La Barre, 1975; Slotkin, 1956). In both cases there is a strong element of inspirational, individualistic experiences, of altered states of consciousness brought about either by psychedelic drugs or by repetitive movement. (In the other cases we have reviewed, mutual enthusiasm in a social enterprise was the main source of a possible altered state of consciousness).

With difficulty, both religions eventually achieved official standing within the U.S. legal system.

Shaker Religion

The Shaker religion received its name from the shaking characteristic of some members' trances and from the important role of a sort of dance in its ceremonies. (Apparently, it was long after this Shaker religion was established that anyone noted the same name had been applied to a sect in Britain and the northeastern United States that similarly emphasized the dance. As far as we know, neither movement influenced the other.) Originating in the state of Washington in the 1880s, the Shaker religion spread to nearby states and British Columbia. Its origins can be traced to white reaction to a nativistic cult of about 1870 that expected the return of the dead ancestors and the destruction of the whites. The whites feared possible attack, and saw the ritual dancing of the native religious ceremonies as preparation for it. The ceremonies were forbidden by the Superintendent of Indian Affairs. Now ceremonial dancing, and the entire religious event of which it was a part, could take place only in secret. This was the context in which the Shaker religion developed.

Each of the indigenous dances had been sponsored by one or more owners of a guardian spirit, and a person's success in either religious or lay occupation was considered to depend on his relation to his guardian spirit. In the Shaker religion, relation to a Shaker spirit was substituted; vaguely defined, the Shaker spirit might function as a continuation of a person's earlier guardian spirit, whether thought of as a renaming of the earlier spirit or as a more general and different mystical being. Where the earlier guardian spirits were the source of inspiration for a person's "hearing a song," direct contact with the Christian God might now be considered the source. In this changed form, Shakers could continue the earlier emphasis on individual powers to be gained through inspiration by direct contact with a supernatural source. The shaking bore some similarity to earlier shamanistic behavior, and played a similarly important role in the healing that characterized both the indigenous religion and the Shaker churches.

The Shakers accepted the Bible as a sacred text, and their services were a blend of earlier ceremonies and Christian church services. Drinking, smoking, and gambling were forbidden to members. These characteristics enlisted the support of many in the white community, who were able to stop the initial imprisonment of early Shaker leaders. Shakers met in buildings that closely resembled ordinary Christian churches, and in time they adopted an organizational structure, with a bishop in each state, that followed a Christian pattern. By its synthesis of Native American and white beliefs and practices, the Shaker religion gained a wide membership and the respect of the potential enemy, and for many decades it was a thriving movement.

Peyote Religion

The peyote religion is so called because it centers on the ceremonial use of buds of the peyote cactus, capable of psychedelic effects when ingested. The initial spread of this religion in the late nineteenth century illustrates syncretism in the relation between the earlier religion of a tribe and new elements introduced from other tribes; its later development involves a blend with Christian elements taken over from the white community. Peyote offered to many societies some enrichment of their religious practices, but each assimilated it in its own way. The Huichol of northern Mexico, for example, were traditionally a hunting people who had been forced to adopt an agricultural economy; their use of peyote included an annual hunt for the peyote itself, accompanied by symbolism of deer and corn, representing their old and their new economy (Myerhoff, 1974). The Mescalero Apache of the American Southwest found in peyote ceremonies a means for the individual to search for and gain mystical power, as they had formerly done in isolated vision experiences (Opler, 1936a).

In the twentieth century, in many other tribes, peyote religion came to absorb many features of Christian churches and to be officially recognized under the name of Native American Church. Like the Shaker religion, the peyote religion became an instrument for effective continuation of some of the aboriginal religion through fusion with aspects of Christianity and with political and legal aspects of the intruding culture, and in this way assisted in the maintenance of each tribe as a distinct ethnic group with an identity separating it from the surrounding community.

Other Syntheses

Earlier Native American progress toward accommodation is represented in an article entitled "Hoax Nativism at Caughnawaga: A Control Case for the Theory of Revitalization" by Susan Postal (1965). The leader of this movement to promote the rights of a Mohawk Indian group was an outsider, a black American known as Chief Thunderwater. Unlike other Iroquois groups, the Caughnawaga did not adopt the new religion of Handsome Lake. The movement of Chief Thunderwater appealed to the Mohawk group more than the nativistic religion of the Seneca because they were so steeped in Catholicism and because of an "unbalanced continuation of cultural features which laid the groundwork for a positive reception of Thunderwater's ideas" (Postal, 1965, 277). The political significance of the Caughnawaga enlistment in this movement, as viewed by Fred Voget, is summarized here:

> The Indian attains a living awareness of his place as a minority group in the wider society and organizes his life in accordance with this new orientation. In this view the conception of Indian-White difference still is a real factor, as is discrimination, but the leader is no longer the prophet—rather he is the

better-educated knowing person who works to protect and expand Indian rights and privileges by means of the legal-political arsenal supplied by the dominant society. (1959, 27)

The various Pueblo societies of the southwestern United States have achieved a somewhat distinctive combination of their aboriginal religion and the Catholicism brought by missionaries centuries ago. Religious activities had two central foci aboriginally, and both remain strong in a number of pueblos. One focus comprises the dance festivals attuned to the natural calendar. The other distinctive focus is the kiva.

The kiva is a sunken room where men, members of the medicine society associated with the particular kiva, meet periodically. The meetings involve ceremonies, training and initiation of the young, and planning for the more public ceremonies for which the particular kiva group is responsible. These activities were disapproved by the Catholic church during the Spanish regime, but not entirely repressed, and at times the U.S. Bureau of Indian Affairs criticized them. But they have continued, and in general coexist with Catholicism, with the same persons participating and sometimes leading in both.

For one pueblo, Taos, for which John Collins (1967) reported on the relation among various religious organizations, there had been no real difficulties between church and kiva within the memory of his oldest informants. Yet some minor evidence of tension could be seen. Participation in a kiva was symbolic of identification with Indian culture, and social pressure was often exerted to enforce regular attendance. Regular attendance at mass, on the other hand, was for many (and especially at that time the young) symbolic of wishing to be less Indian. Collins reported that the two types of religious activity were often compartmentalized, a person carrying on each with little consideration of possible implications for the other. But the two had not remained totally independent; the kiva activities showed influences from the Christian tradition.

The survival of these major aspects of the aboriginal religion must be attributed to the complexity of the Pueblo cultures, with a political organization, a specialized priesthood, and detailed rituals that could be carried out regardless of what other rituals and beliefs were required by other aspects of life. The syncretism of the Pueblo religions seems to have been satisfying to the members of these tribes. The peyote movement, in its wide diffusion throughout the West, was not adopted by most of the pueblos. The only pueblo to adopt it, according to Collins (1967), was Taos—and Taos lacked the organization of masked dancers and the medicine societies that characterized the other pueblos.

If complexity of the aboriginal culture generally, and of its religion in particular, favors the development of a rich syncretism, it might be expected that the Aztec, Mayan, and Inca empires would have gone further than the small pueblo tribes of the United States. And this seems to be the case, at least in the degree of blending achieved.

The Spanish conquest and rule of Middle America and the Andean region involved a deliberate effort to destroy the aboriginal religions. Religious reasons were adduced as part of the justification for the conquest, and the civil and military authorities supported the work of the Catholic priests. Their enthusiasm was doubtless increased by the peculiarly repugnant character, to Europeans, of the Aztec and Mayan religions, with their very conspicuous practice of human sacrifice. (The absence of human sacrifice doubtless had much to do with the tolerance of the Spanish invaders toward Pueblo religions.) Though the indigenous religions of the Aztecs and Maya were directly attacked by the conquerors, the people themselves and their general culture were not so brutally treated as in much of the area to the north invaded by the British and French; and in the continuing life of the people there developed a true blend of religions.

In the first half century after the Spanish conquest, before Catholic traditions had been much integrated with indigenous religion, nativistic movements appeared in both Mexico and Peru. Both looked toward political power and revival of aspects of the earlier religion, and both included a strong emphasis on physical expression in singing and dancing. Both aroused opposition from the Spanish clergy and administrators, and suppression was especially ruthless in Peru. (For a brief account and references, see Bierhorst [1985].)

Human sacrifice was so important to Mayan tradition that it occasionally recurred for several generations after the conquest but in a form sometimes modified by Catholicism which by then was universal. The victim was, in some instances, nailed to a cross, rather than just being held firmly, before his heart was ripped out. The cross had been an important symbol in the indigenous religion of the Mayas, though not as an instrument of sacrifice. Its continuing use was itself a syncretic development, as its meaning was derived partly from each of the competing traditions. Other elements were shared as well, notably confession. In adopting Catholicism, moreover, additional similarities were created. Aspects or features of divinity in the Christian religion were fused with particular gods in the indigenous pantheon. The moon goddess, for example, came to be fused with the Virgin, and the maize god with Jesus (Thompson, 1954, 13-14).

The recurrence of human sacrifice, and the sporadic religious support of political resistance to domination by whites and Ladinos, were vigorously opposed by the Catholic clergy. But the clergy apparently were little concerned with other aboriginal practices or beliefs that could coexist with the formal requirements of Catholicism. The religion of the descendants of the Maya and Aztecs remains today a blend, the Christian beliefs and practices being no simple acceptance of a European tradition and response to current social structure, but also a product of preconquest religion. June Nash (1968), for example, in a close analysis of the passion play as given in contemporary Mayan communities, finds that the chief figures in the story of Jesus are interpreted in ways based on identifying them "with preconquest Maya cosmological figures."

In Brazil, a wealth of messianic movements have developed. Here, though, the ground was laid before the arrival of Europeans. The traditional religion of the Tupi-Guarani—a large group of mostly populous tribes—included belief in a Land without Evil, toward which whole populations might move by long migration. Population movements guided by this millenarian tradition were under way at the time of colonization and continued sporadically even into the twentieth century. This tradition, in the judgment of René Ribeiro (1970), facilitated the development of a variety of movements, in various parts of the heterogeneous Brazilian population, that drew also on the apocalyptic tradition of Christianity and on specific millenarian myths introduced from Portugal.

The early movements among indigenous groups in Brazil seem not to have been dominated by wishes for adoption of European technology; they were more oriented toward bringing back the good old times or toward maintaining the current culture. As early as the sixteenth century, however, movements in Brazil shared with cargo cults and the Ghost Dance fantasies of inverting the social system: Europeans would disappear or be enslaved to a resurgent indigenous population. From pre-Columbian tradition these movements drew the prediction of imminent change, with abandonment of work and substitution of dancing, but these elements came to be fused with such new elements as believing the leader to be a reincarnation of Christ (Pereira de Queiroz, 1958, 6-7; Métraux, 1941). The opportunity to join with others in a free expression of religious fervor is judged by Ribeiro (1970, 64) to have been a main source of satisfaction for converts. Elements of indigenous and Christian traditions were fused in these movements to produce a dream of eliminating a servile or subordinate position in the world.

RELIGIOUS CHANGE IN AFRICA

For Africa south of the Sahara a wealth of information about religious change is available. The picture is complicated by the diversity and wide time spread of contacts with outside religions—many centuries of gradual spread of Islam across the land before the more recent missionary efforts of Catholics and diverse Protestant groups. The advance of Islam was generally an accompaniment of trade penetration or political domination, rather than proselytizing for its own sake. Christian proselytizing was carried out by professional missionaries, but in various places it preceded, followed, or accompanied political and economic colonialization with its varied effects on a culture. In both cases, then, religious change resulted not only from contact with an alien religion but from other profound social changes as well. Many African societies have been studied by British (and a few by American) anthropologists during periods of religious change, and several missionaries have provided useful reports of their experience and observations.

Missionary efforts are likely to be thought of as leading, whether gradually or suddenly, to disappearance of the old religion as it is replaced by the new. The simple concept of acculturation, as it appeared in anthropology in the 1930s, might encourage the same expectation. Africa is a region where events show clearly a greater complexity. Several observers have noted, for various parts of the continent, that the new religion actually seemed to increase the importance of one part of the old religion: wizardry, in belief and perhaps practice. In Nigeria, for example, Duru (1983) interviewed Igbo adults of varying ages about their impressions of cultural changes through recent generations. Sorcery was the one aspect of religious belief that showed no weakening even among young adults.

Booth (1977, 337) suggests that "dislocation associated with Islamization (though not necessarily caused by it) creates new fears which are expressed and dealt with" through witchcraft, divination, and magical practices. Marwick (1958), writing about Bantu-speaking peoples in the southern countries of Africa, suggests that Christianity and other aspects of Western civilization have increased "preoccupation with beliefs in magic, witchcraft and sorcery" as a means of adjustment to a variety of frustrations. A detailed analysis by Fernandez (1961, 249) of a specific instance—wizardry among the Fang, in Gabon—indicates additional reasons for such an effect. Missionaries there were able to interfere with the ancestor cult and with the antiwizardry societies—aspects of indigenous religion that involved overt behavior of groups of people. They could not attack wizardry so effectively because it is carried out largely in private and in fantasy rather than overt behavior. But the two aspects they could suppress had served as indigenous controls on wizardry, and their removal opened the way to freer practice of it.

These observations about wizardry make very clear that the outcome of contact was not simply the adoption of Islam or Christianity in the form in which they were introduced but the emergence of something new. This is comparable to the emergence of cargo cults in Oceania, yet what emerged in Africa was characteristically very different from cargo cults. To be sure, some movements in Africa included elements identical with main features of cargo cults. As early as the 1850s, many Xhosa, in South Africa, slaughtered their cattle and destroyed their crops, anticipating the return of their ancestors, who would rid the land of Europeans. A century later, among another South African society, the Pende, the belief arose that the ancestors would return and the Europeans would vanish. Various African religious movements in the twentieth century preached the invulnerability of natives to the bullets Europeans would fire at them (see, for example, Davidson [1969]; Middleton [1963b]).

Despite such similarities to the cargo cults of Melanesia, the similarity has never been detailed enough to lead to application of the same label for any African movement as a whole. In one paper it is said: "Despite the interest in wealth, no religious movement that was primarily a cargo cult has ever existed in Central Africa" (Craemer, Vansina, & Fox, 1976, 469), and the same could be said of other regions. Perhaps even more significant is the same authors' finding that many religious movements that did take place "were not purely or even primarily reactions to the stresses of colonial experiences or modernization" (ibid., 265). As Herskovits puts it, "Many of the separatist groups are to be thought of as reinterpretations of the prophet movements widely prevalent in Africa long before European control" (1962, 418). This is parallel to some developments in North America: The Prophet Dance, as Spier pointed out, preceded the Ghost Dance—both of them revitalization movements of indigenous religion—at a time before direct contact with whites (Spier, 1935; Spier, Suttles, & Herskovits, 1959).

Not only in prophet movements but also in less dramatic aspects of religion the Africa of precolonial days showed a disposition toward change and merging of traditions. Herskovits (1962, 419) says that "African peoples . . . in pre-European times took over deities and other supernatural agents and the rites associated with them from societies, friendly or hostile, with whom they came into contact." It may be especially important from the Africans' point of view that the Christian missionaries were members of the conquering society. So far as a people's gods are the source of strength and security, being conquered is a sign that their gods are less effective than those of the conquerors. So the gods of a conquering people are often taken over by the vanquished. The Anang Ibibio of Nigeria are one people among whom various informants gave this as a reason for conversion to Christianity (Messenger, 1959, 290).

More generally, too, receptivity to the influence of alien religions may depend on how a people perceive the agents through whom that religion comes to them. In Indonesia (to which we will soon turn), Christianity was brought by missionaries associated with the European powers that were taking over political control, whereas Islam appeared in (or was associated with) traders from the Asian mainland who were connected with no threat to Indonesian integrity. It is hardly surprising that conversion to Islam was a more spontaneous occurrence than conversion to Christianity. Similar factors have been appealed to in asking why Christian missionaries in East Africa had much more influence on cultivators than on pastoralists. The missionaries' position could be seen as collusion with the white settlers and the colonial administration, in enforcing a restriction of natives to smaller areas of land than before. This view was more likely to develop in pastoralists, who were more immediately and drastically affected by the enforced changes. The collusion with the interests of the white settlers and administrators seemed incompatible with the missionaries' declaration of prime interest in the natives' welfare, and this was, according to Rigby (1981), a principal source of pastoralists' rejection of the religious message brought by the missionaries.

If the indigenous religion is strongly practical or this-worldly, powerful aliens, once their dominance is accepted, may be viewed with special favor and their religion be readily tolerated or even embraced with enthusiasm. Peel (1968a, 290) says this to have been true of the Yoruba, whose aboriginal religion was very tolerant of diversity.

Deference to the religion of conquerors was already found in Africa in precolonial days. Messenger quotes Herskovits's (1948, 552) report that it had long been an important factor in the spread of indigenous West African gods from one people to another. A clear example of the syncretism of the aboriginal religions of two African groups may be found in Fortes's (1936b) account, "Ritual Festivals and Social Cohesion in the Hinterland of the Gold Coast" among the Tallensi. Two subgroups, the Tales and Namoos, make up the Tallensi of the present day. These two groups joined several generations ago to form a single complex society. They had already shared a common language, but in religion they had differed—and still differ—in symbols, in taboos, and particularly in the cult of the ancestors. However, their religious rites have now so developed that each group is dependent on the other in carrying out its respective calendrical rituals (see Chapter 10). As Fortes puts it, "It is notable how these rituals vividly insulate each group from the other, while at the same time uniting them in common responsibility for the welfare of the country" (1970, 161).

This syncretic tradition continued very strongly as African societies became subordinated to colonial powers and suffered threats to their traditional life. Fernandez (1964, 531) says of African religious movements that they have been basically protest movements, "acting to restore to their participants autonomy and integrity in their social and cultural life." Many religious movements in other parts of the world, too, have been nationalistic, but it is in Africa that the connection between religion and politics has been particularly evident, especially throughout the colonial period. Africans, though adept at syncretistic inventions, were also insistent in some cases on continuing their own ritual procedures regardless of disapproval by colonial administrators. They adapted from Christianity the symbolism that appealed to them but retained their own traditional symbolism where it expressed what they continued to favor.

Fernandez studied intensively the Bwiti movement among the Fang of northern Gabon. The Bwiti is directed both at reviving the traditional culture and at reforming it to meet the demands of survival under new conditions; it is relatively moderate in the strength of the political assertiveness accompanying it. The Bwiti leadership has made "a deliberate, organized, conscious effort to construct a more satisfying culture" (Fernandez, 1965, 903). Bwiti ritual procedures show a clear intent of reform; they attempt to increase the solidarity of a group that has, through contact and changed economic conditions, been tending strongly toward individualism. Solidarity is achieved for Bwiti members not by the external activism of many other syncretic movements, but rather, by participating together in beliefs and rituals that unify the two principal religious traditions the Fang have encountered. The Bwiti used much Christian symbolism, and from the traditional Fang religion they selected, then "accentuated and enriched those aspects or ideas that appeared to have parallels in the Christian religion" (Balandier, 1970, 275). A sense of unity was also achieved by fusing riddle and myth, facial decoration and dance, words and drug-induced ecstasy: "In the truly satisfying night-long ritual the living become the dead and the dead become the living, confounding in that paradox the somber inexplicability of death, which no amount of coherence in cosmology could explain away" (Fernandez, 1982, 573).

Of the hundreds, or even thousands, of Christian sects that have arisen in Africa, even those that formally are strictly Christian inevitably seem to show some influence of the culture in which they have developed. An example is provided by the True Church of God, described by Curley (1983) as an evangelical, fundamentalist Christian church, with 125 branches in Nigeria and Cameroon. A major influence of the indigenous culture is seen in the this-worldliness of the sect. Though sharing the literal belief in the Bible, including the concern with the afterlife, of fundamentalist sects worldwide, the major emphasis is on rewards to be obtained in this life, and especially that of good health. The only form of therapy allowed is prayer; all forms of medicine are strictly prohibited. This development is consistent with traditional African emphasis on spiritual or religious explanation of natural phenomena, and carries it further than almost any Western sect. To the Bible, the True Church of God adds, as a sort of religious text, the accumulated knowledge of members' dreams, as interpreted spiritually within the context of the church; this, too, links an indigenous tradition with the fundamentalism the church shares with its Western cousins.

An emphasis on prayer as a practical technique to attain health and prosperity is a fundamental feature of the Aladura churches (Peel, 1968a), widespread among the Yoruba of Nigeria and nearby countries. Here, too, though this element may be shared with fundamentalist churches in other parts of the world, its great strength seems to derive from indigenous sources, from the very serious use of religious conceptions in explaining the natural phenomena of the human body and the economy. A different influence of indigenous traditions on the form Christianity took is seen in a religious movement of the 1930s among the Anang Ibibio of southeastern Nigeria (Messenger, 1959). The Holy Spirit was the most important member of the Trinity in this movement (and indeed was separated from the Trinity). The reason seemed to lie in the Anang tradition of spirits as the only route of access to the supreme deity of their traditional religion (which they identified with the Christian divinity) and the ready interpretation of the Holy Spirit as the most effective of these channels of communication.

A different element in Christianity was stressed in many syncretistic movements in Central Africa—millenialism, the expectation that the present social order will soon come to an end, to be replaced by a new order, whether on the earth or out of it, for which members of the movement would be prepared. This element is in the New Testament texts that became available to all who had learned to read, but it was singled out as a main point of doctrine by the Watchtower Society (later called Jehovah's Witnesses). The society's British and American missionaries were very active, beginning in the late nineteenth century, especially in the eastern parts of Central Africa, and they were joined by leaders from among the black converts. Some of the native preachers founded new millenial movements, as did others whose message did not come by way of the Watchtower Society, and some became martyrs to their faith. The millenialist preachers varied widely in whether they saw their teachings as a form of political revolt against the colonial powers, but the colonial administrators seem uniformly to have felt a threat. At various times and places, the followers of millenialist doctrines took the predictions seriously and precisely enough to stop work and even destroy crops; the desperation of the downtrodden helped shape the particular form taken by the recurrent story of the second coming.

Southern Africa has been the locus of a great variety of syncretistic movements fusing Christian elements with the traditions of the Bantu-speaking peoples who had migrated into this area from East Africa, displacing the earlier Khoisan-speaking population. Wilson (1971), who has done fieldwork in East Africa and among the Pondo of South Africa and the Nyakyusa of Zimbabwe, has summarized the aboriginal religion of all these societies as having four general features in common:

1. Communication with ancestral spirits through sacrifice, prayer, and confession, providing a religious basis for the moral order
2. An idea of the supreme deity, also a support of morality, this idea somewhat vague in the south though more developed in the north (possibly through Islamic contacts along the coast in past centuries)
3. Mystical power in various substances or objects, susceptible to human manipulation, as in sorcery and healing
4. Fear of witchcraft, the power for evil believed to be inborn in some persons.

Wilson sees the changes of recent generations as an outcome not only of interaction with Christianity and with the Europeans who brought that religion but also of the change from small community to participation in a large society. A changed situation makes for changes in religious thought and action; Christianity, present in the religion of the European settlers and in missionary pressures, influences the direction some of the changes take.

Belief in the ancestral spirits continues, but attitudes and actions shift. Continuity is greatest in the attitude of reverence; it becomes perhaps even more conspicuous as fear of the spirits diminishes. The fear lessens because of increasing tendency to adopt what Westerners would consider natural, rather than supernatural, explanations of illness and other misfortunes; hospitals and clinics are increasingly appealed to, rather than the help of the ancestors. Rituals that were formerly aimed at bringing back the ancestral spirits to communicate with them gradually acquire the character more of commemorative dinners.

The Christian idea of God the Father fits well with traditional reverence for ancestral spirits, and the somewhat vague traditional idea of God is moved toward a paternal image. Christian formulations gradually shift the location of God from below the earth, where ancestral spirits dwell, to above the earth. Fear of the power of God, conspicuous in aboriginal tradition, becomes less conspicuous as the approachability of God gradually takes over. The idea of God becomes more clearly monotheistic.

Belief in and use of "medicines"—the mystical power in various objects and materials—undergo both increase and decrease. There is some diminution in their importance as people increase their use of the realistic techniques of cosmopolitan medicine and also increase their reliance on prayer in the search for supernatural support. But the variety of materials to which mystical power is ascribed increases. New materials introduced by Europeans—automobile grease, for one—may gain a reputation; and Wilson reports that South African newspapers have even carried advertisements of "powa pills" for sale.

Continued importance of belief in the power of medicines and of wizardry is evidenced, Wilson reports, by recurrence of revival movements designed, in a traditional pattern, to counter sorcery and witchcraft. But the changed situation leads the revival movements to be directed in part at the Europeans as the new source of evil. And Christianity provides a messianic tradition that is drawn on to give the revival movements a new political character, as we have already seen in Central and East Africa.

The influence of Islam is found, of course, in the more northerly parts of sub-Saharan Africa. One society that has been studied while only in part Islamicized are the Nupe of northern Nigeria. Nadel (1954) was able from his fieldwork in the 1930s to prepare a comprehensive account of their pre-Islamic religion and to study the changes Islam brought to various parts of Nupe society and specific aspects of the culture. A difference from the Christian influence on many African societies was that Islam had arrived by slow diffusion, so that it came to the Nupe already greatly remolded in the pattern of neighboring cultures similar to their own. Christianity, on the other hand, arrived at most African peoples as a religion adjusted to the customs of the distant countries from which the missionaries came.

Islamic beliefs and practices too, as Nadel found them among the Nupe, had been considerably modified by the Nupe; one might almost say that a new religion had been created (as could be said also of many of the African churches built on Christian influence). Elements of the aboriginal religion seemed especially important as marks of identity. Members of the Nupe colony in the Nigerian capital of Lagos, for example, separated from the homeland for several generations, were all Muslims, yet aboriginal ceremonies were greatly valued and were an essential part of what it meant to be a Nupe in Lagos.

At the same time that the Nupe were under Islamic influence, and earlier too, they were also being exposed to the aboriginal religions of the various peoples that surrounded their region in northern Nigeria. Nadel considers the changes arising from all these influences and suggests that some elements are adopted, others modified or rejected, for intelligible motives, and he draws on his general understanding of the Nupe to describe some of those motives. He suggests that to be adopted the novel elements offered by alien religions "must bear some affinity to the traditional pattern; or . . . serve to redress some pre-existing inadequacy; or . . . offer a chance of expression to some new trend, say, a changed outlook of the people, which the traditional beliefs and practices failed to satisfy" (1954, 207). A religion that claims possession of exclusive truth and righteousness might change slowly even in the presence of strong motives; the Nupe had a tolerant and open attitude, and could change more readily.

INDONESIA AND ASIA

Many societies in Indonesia and Asia have been studied by anthropologists especially interested in religion. More uniformly involved here, perhaps, than in other areas is a long history of coexistence of one or more of the world religions and a continuing strong tradition of earlier local religions. Repeatedly, the traces of local religions are found to be strengthened by their contribution to a sense of identity. While this is true as well of other areas we have considered, a couple of examples from Indonesia and Asia bring out this function especially clearly.

Javanese migrants to the Pacific island of New Caledonia find themselves urban residents in neighborhoods of very mixed ethnicity. A community festival of distant pre-Hindu origin in Java had been usually a neighborhood affair that brought religious tradition to the strengthening of neighborly relations. In New Caledonia this festival was adapted to bringing together Javanese immigrants from disparate neighborhoods, and the same religious traditions strengthened the ethnic identity of the Javanese as a group despite their being interlaced with neighbors of very different ethnic background (Dewey, 1970).

A similar function for religion was found by Marjorie Balzer (1980) in a Siberian people, the Khanty, whom she studied during the Soviet period. Here the combined pressures from outside came from the cultural traditions of the Russians, with whom they had dealt for several generations, and from the demands posed by Soviet policy, especially in its opposition to religion itself. Balzer found the Khanty to be in some contexts good Soviet citizens and in other contexts good Khanty. The survival of their distinctive religion gave them a sense of continuity with the pre-Soviet past and security in conforming in necessary ways to Soviet demands without feeling completely lost.

SUMMARY

Traditional peoples in various parts of the world have been subjected to especially severe pressures as a result of contact with outside forces, and they have responded with great and often rapid change. Religious practices and beliefs are among the social institutions that have been affected. Religious movements under these conditions vary, yet show some remarkable similarities from one part of the world to another. They are a rich source of information about the diverse benefits people derive from religion. Among the benefits displayed in many instances are the following:

1. A feeling of continuity with a past now threatened with extinction

2. A fantasy of solutions to problems that may lack any realistic solutions

3. A strengthened sense of identity with the society that has been threatened, or with a specific cult

4. The satisfaction of company in the fantasy of aggressive retaliation against the aliens seen as responsible for the threat to their society

5. Ecstatic experiences attained in group participation itself or with the help of psychotropic drugs associated with the religious movement.

Some of these benefits are of doubtful value, if they reduce the chance that realistic solutions to problems will be found. Some of the movements illustrate, indeed, that religious enthusiasm can worsen people's life situations, leading them to abandon all they have in the vain hope of its being replaced by something much better.

Chapter 12

What Traditional Religions Do for People

GAINS AND LOSSES

In every society some aspects of religious beliefs or practices have obvious intrinsic value. The sense of closeness to ancestors or to divinity a person may experience while immersed in prayer or sacrifice, the deeper absorption in religious ecstasy, the excitement of joining with one's fellows in a community festival—all these may have a positive value of their own quite apart from what else they may do for individual or society. The social scientist's attempt to understand how the religious beliefs and practices serve the other interests of individual and society is often felt to be an attempt to explain away this intrinsic value, to deny that religion has any value of its own. This feeling may be appropriate as a response to some of the attempts of social scientists, viewing religion as nothing but the sources to whose influence it is ascribed (considering the mystical beings, for example, as nothing but a projection of infantile fantasies or of the power structure of society). But, more properly, the social scientist seeks to understand how religion fits into the rest of life, how the experience that has a value of its own also contributes to or interferes with, and thus is influenced by, the other interests of the individual and society. We aim in this book to ask this question of traditional religions. We hope the reader will find the discussion relevant to world religions as well.

Some of the ways the various religions of traditional peoples serve other interests can perhaps be best expressed as benefits to the individual. We have noted many of these benefits, and here we simply recall a few as examples to keep in mind.

1. Various religious practices have therapeutic value, helping to mend disturbances in an individual's relation to self and to others, and also contributing to the cure of physical diseases, at least those that are of psychosomatic origin.

2. Individuals often gain an increment of realistic power—that is, ability to influence others and thus determine the course of events in their own lives—through religious practices. For example, a shaman may, through recognition of success in curing, gain prestige and appreciation. A wizard may be deferred to by others lest they become targets for the wizard's malevolence.

3. A hunter or warrior, through performance of appropriate rituals, may gain confidence and with it a greater chance of success in practical undertakings.

4. A pregnant woman, observing food taboos or requirements that are supported by mystical beliefs but also have realistic value, may increase the probability of giving birth to a viable child and of maintaining her own health.

5. Initiation rites, by informing initiates of what is expected of them in the status to which they are advancing, and of the importance of these expectations, provide a setting in which the more mature behavior and attitudes come to be adopted.

6. A bereaved person, overcome by grief and the loss of accustomed ways, may in numerous ways be helped back to normal life by the mortuary rituals specified in the community's religious traditions.

7. Individuals threatened with an inadequate food supply may be prevented from starvation by their fellows' conformity to rules of sharing established in the community's religious traditions.

Gains such as these are not the only effect of traditional religions on the lives of individuals. The very same features of religion that produce such gains as these for some persons may at the same time have opposite effects in them and, even more, in other people—an unwelcome loss of power, for example, or discomforting fear. But these points, positive and negative, well illustrate that religion in traditional societies is not an isolated part of life, that it is an intimate part of everyone's existence.

Both the gains and losses that traditional religions bring to the individual have their effects on the community as a whole. The pattern of power relationships, brought about in part by sorcery and shamanism, helps define the social structure of the society. The system of food distribution, sanctioned by mystical conceptions, is one part of a more general system of reciprocities that likewise help define the social structure. But some of the gains and losses are more readily expressible in terms of the group itself (though they, too, have implications for the lives of individuals). Here are some examples:

1. Where misfortunes are attributed to wizardry from within (from close relatives, from fellow members of larger kin group or community), this aspect of relation threatens the solidarity of the in-group. Where they are attributed to wizardry from outside, the solidarity of the in-group may be strengthened.

2. The projection of the social system onto a cosmic level, the placement of the society in a framework of mystical conceptions, strengthens

the power relations upon which the smooth functioning of the society depends. Religion here, as Ian Lewis (1989, 130) says, serves to legitimize secular authority.

3. Ceremonies that bring people together, and the gift exchanges that often form part of the ceremonies, heighten the unity and cohesiveness of the community or of whatever segment of it is involved in the ceremonies.

4. The control of antisocial tendencies by wizardry and by beliefs about the afterlife may permit great looseness in nonreligious control. Courts and powerful chiefs or kings may not be needed. But dependence on wizardry for social control may challenge the unity of the society, by giving everyone reason to mistrust others and fear their malice.

In earlier chapters we have elaborated on most of these, and many other, gains and losses to individual and society and on the relation among them, with particular societies providing examples. There, as in what we have thus far said in this chapter, we have stayed close to the concrete data. Our aim has been to be more factual, less theoretical, than many earlier general treatments of the religions of traditional societies. While still retaining this factual orientation, placing religion in the context of everyday life, can we reach a broader statement? It seems to us that the most valuable way of doing so is by considering some of the universal themes of human life that are represented in traditional religions and how they are represented.

Here we take off from an excellent framework for classifying psychological functions of ritual, offered by Robert LeVine (1982a) under the influence of psychoanalytic thought. He suggests a threefold classification of functions. In each category ritual is seen as contributing to the control, and yet to the expression, of some basic motive whose satisfaction may be essential to individual welfare and yet be surrounded by, or lead to, consequences that interfere with smooth functioning of the society.

In drawing upon LeVine's classification of functions, we will modify his general outline in two ways. First, we apply it not only to rituals but to the rest of religion as well—to the beliefs that justify and dictate the rituals and to the experiences yielded by the rituals and beliefs. Second, we expand the list of basic motives or interests. We will begin with the two motives on which we agree thoroughly with LeVine's classification: sexuality and aggression. For one thing, then, religion contributes to the regulation of the sexual motive and its expression. For another, it contributes to the control of aggression.

The third category offered by LeVine we are broadening. He states it as the maintenance of norms of *humility* through control of self-assertive tendencies. At first, we had thought to place beside this as a fourth category the maintenance of norms of *competence* through the control of dependent tendencies. But it seems to us now that these are better combined as a single category, norms of humility and competence. Self-assertion implies a sort of independence (accompanied, to be sure, by assertive dominance over other people), and may well be regarded as a polar opposite of dependence. Normal and satisfactory social interaction requires on the part of each person some measure of dependence upon others and, on the other hand, some measure of independence and self-assertion. Norms of humility may necessarily be imposed in order to prevent some individuals from going to the extreme of self-assertion without regard to the interest of others. On the other hand, norms of competence may need to be enforced in order to prevent some persons from going to an extreme of dependence on others, an extreme incompatible with even that degree of self-assertion and cooperation with others that makes possible contributing one's fair share to the ongoing activities of the society.

Even with this modification, it seems to us that the classification LeVine has introduced remains excessively oriented toward motivations concerned with the biological sources of interpersonal behavior. It is, in short, too exclusively based on early psychoanalytic theory. We would add to it a fourth basic motive to which Freud also gave prime attention, but primarily in his later writings, the motive of *anxiety*. Moreover, the development of psychological theory within the neopsychoanalytic framework, as well as the whole development of academic psychology and of cultural anthropology in this century, confirms the equal importance of another kind of motive, less obviously related to the biological underpinning of human behavior, a motive for *cognition*, understanding, or experience. Rituals seem sometimes to offer satisfaction of desires for novelty and excitement, and at other times of desires for relaxation in the familiar, and in doing so they help sustain norms of *routine* and of *novelty*. Here, as in the case of humility and competence, there are somewhat conflicting norms between which a balance needs to be achieved. (The same is true, if less obviously, for sexuality and aggression.)

NORMS OF SEXUALITY

Religion aids in the control of sexual impulse, directing sexual expression into channels not disruptive of the many other interactions that help form the complex structure of social life. Perhaps the best evidence for this function of religion is supplied by some of the systematic cross-cultural research of G. P. Murdock reported in his book *Social Structure* (1949). Most relevant is his analysis of the ritualized avoidance, joking, and license between certain pairs of opposite-sexed relatives. Relationships between successive generations are particularly noteworthy. Avoidance is especially common, for instance, in the relation between a man and his mother-in-law, and Murdock plausibly interprets this as a device for preventing a sexual relationship that would be peculiarly threatening to the integrity and effective functioning of the two interacting and overlapping nuclear families involved. Avoidance by a man of his paternal aunt, Murdock found, is almost limited to societies in which that aunt is likely to become the man's mother-in-law (because of a cultural preference for cross-cousin marriage in which a man weds his paternal aunt's daughter). The opposite of avoidance—ritualized license, in the sense of sexually tinged joking and other freedom of sexual reference in the relation between two people—Murdock finds almost exclusively between those types of siblings-in-law who are potential secondary spouses (and, often, also currently accessible as an extramarital partner). Here the ritual helps channel sexual impulses in a direction favored or permitted in the particular society.

However, jesting may not always be in a direction where overt sexuality is also acceptable. Under adequate control, jesting may accompany avoidance, as a way of making the avoidance more tolerable. Gorer calls attention to the "verbal preoccupation with sex" of mixed-sex groups among the Himalayan Lepcha and says,

> I think one of the reasons for this constant verbal preoccupation with the comic aspects of sex is the fact that at any village gathering or feast the great majority of the people present are, owing to the stringent incest laws, forbidden sexual partners; there is a release from tension in thus jesting about these dangerous subjects, although even in jest direct invitations are not made to people who would count as incestuous. (1938, 262-263)

Methods for controlling adulterous behavior are diverse, and many involve ritual and associated aspects of religion. Among the Azande the poison oracle is used to detect adultery; this ritual (whether actually carried out or merely threatened) is a device men use to control their wives; whether or not the oracle is believed to be perfectly accurate, the threat of being subjected to it may be a powerful deterrent. A Chaga woman must confess infidelity if she is having a difficult childbirth; the birth will be quicker if she names the seducer to the midwife. A Chaga man, moreover, has available a ritual he can perform to keep seducers away from his wife. As these cases suggest, there is a tendency for ritual, like other aspects of social control, to be directed at restricting women more than men. But the difference is not absolute. Among the matrilineal Bemba, for example, a man who has committed adultery must look to his wife for protection from mystical punishment, as she is the only one who can carry out the ritual that is needed. Such a necessity must serve to discourage men from adultery.

As we have already suggested, ritual is not simply inhibitory of sexual expression. Many societies have periods when sexual relations ordinarily forbidden are temporarily permitted. Such license comes usually as part of a series of rituals, either at the end or at some definite earlier time. This type of public mass license is found in many African groups, among the Lepchas and Ifugao of Asia, some New Guinea groups, and some South American societies, particularly in the Amazon area. We noted only two cases of license among the Plains groups of North America. Among the Arapaho, license is part of the Sun Dance ceremony. Among the Pawnee, it comes after the annual Sacrifice to the Morning Star and is apparently believed to help ensure the continuity of the society.

This theme of relieving anxiety about survival of the group is suggested also by a fact observed for both the Ifugao of the Philippines and
the Cubeo of South America: In these two cases, at least, license often
comes at the end of a very serious and solemn complex of ritual observances
occasioned by death. Of the Cubeo mourning ceremonies Goldman says:

> The final sexual event in this ritual sequence is to be understood as somewhat
> more than sexual consummation. It is also an act of mass adultery, as the
> Indians are only too well aware. In this act, the adulterous longings of the
> people are given expression without any real suppression of the stormy
> feelings of jealousy that adultery provokes among them. The adulterous act
> adds still another modality of sexual passion. (1963, 239)

Indications of the significance of sexual license are not confined to
suggestions of desire for continuity of the society, as this passage about the
Cubeo shows. Permission or encouragement of sexual release, and a
suggestion that this helps people accept the restraint demanded at other
times, appear in Nadel's interpretation of sexual license among the Nupe
of Nigeria. For the "rather prudish Nupe," Nadel has this to say about the
license at a particular dance, a dance unusual in that both sexes take part:
"we may call the *gunnu* . . .a safety-valve, a licensed compensation for
otherwise rigid self-control; certainly, it puts a premium on a mode of
behaviour otherwise not only improper but unthinkable" (1954, 113).

Not only in unusual situations does religious tradition of a society
serve to promote as well as to control sexual satisfaction. The customs we
have considered in discussing initiation, with their separate emphasis on
preparation of male and female for their adult role, are decidedly oriented
toward maintaining a pattern of sexual behavior that will ensure the
continuity of the society. Religious pressure toward sexual enjoyment is
not concentrated in a marriage ceremony, as among us; it is generally a
conspicuous element in rituals preparing the young man or woman for
adulthood.

NORMS OF AGGRESSION CONTROL

The varied patterns of social interaction on which any society depends
would be directly threatened by excessive, inappropriate aggression, yet
may require that people have some degree of freedom to express aggression
in socially useful ways. One very important role of religion here is the
actual resolution of specific conflicts through the use of rituals appropriate
to that purpose.

An extreme example of ritualized solution of aggressive conflict is
provided by an incident among the Comanche of the western United States
although the account is not full enough for us to judge what role religion
may have played. Two bitter enemies were forced into a destructive public
form of duel; they were tied together and equipped with implements with

which to kill each other, and neither man was to be allowed to survive (Lee, 1957, 151-153). Here, obviously, benefit was only to the rest of the community. A more constructive way to allow individuals to work out their hostility without killing each other is found in the Inuit "song duel," a way of giving a clever person, perhaps less physically capable than his rival, a chance to draw on his creative skill in a ritualized and public contest (Hoebel, 1954, 93). Here a more group-oriented society uses ritual to resolve conflicts by other means than brute aggression. Lorna Marshall's "Sharing, Talking, and Giving: Relief of Social Tensions among the !Kung Bushmen" indicates how seriously the Kung view any signs of friction between individuals. As she puts it, "Occasions when temper has got out of control are remembered with awe" (1961, 231-232). The Kung, like the Inuit, use songs as social discipline, though talking is an even more common way for them to settle differences. Kung rituals for sharing meat—the most prized food—and for greeting strangers and for welcoming visitors to their small huts all seem to bring rewards of avoiding hostility.

In the more complex of our traditional societies, the role of rituals in drawing individuals and groups together in performances that call for harmony and peaceful cooperation is especially apparent. This is clear in Turner's analysis (1968) of the "rituals of affliction" among the Ndembu of Zambia and in many accounts of harvest and first-fruit rites in diverse societies.

Rituals also provide for expression of aggression under conditions where its intensity or direction can be controlled. Discussing one ceremony in southern Africa, Wilson says: "So far from rituals having the sole function of promoting social integration, as some would have us believe, the burial rites of the Nyakyusa were occasions on which existing antipathies arose; but the quarrels were not within the mourning lineage" (1957, 25). These fights were between villages or chiefdoms. The impression we get from her accounts is that emotions were heightened by the ritualized display of destructive acts by the dancers; in the past this might have resulted in warlike display and some actual fighting, though by the time of her study sexual display and lovemaking were more characteristic outcomes.

The mortuary rituals of the pastoral Sebei of East Africa present another instance of controlled expression, the quarrels in this instance being confined to the kin group. The mortuary rituals provide a setting for discussion of the various sources of friction that arise in the distribution of debts and possessions left by the deceased and in the assumption of obligations created by the death. Among the Sebei, as among the Nyakyusa, the rituals seem generally appropriate for allaying feelings of guilt that the death may arouse, for reducing everyone's emotional burden. Yet, in this very setting, as Goldschmidt reports for a case he observed in detail, there developed " openly displayed hostility, the evocation of ancient quarrels, accusations, and intimations of engaging in sorcery, adultery, family disloyalty, and other dishonest and reprehensible acts" (1973, 95-96).

In many societies, few deaths are ascribed to natural causes, and many are ascribed to the ill will of members of the community. In this case one function of mortuary rituals may be to defuse the intragroup hostility that could lead to violent revenge. A study of New Guinea tribes in the Sepik region, by Tuzin (1974), illustrates this function; once a satisfactory explanation of a death is arrived at, no retaliatory action is taken.

The importance of rituals in control of aggression is especially apparent in intergenerational hostility. As Murdock (1971) and other anthropologists have pointed out, the relationship between alternate generations is frequently easier than that between successive generations. Tension between father and son has been particularly reported in tribes having patrilineal descent and patrilocal residence. For example, father-son antagonism among the Gisu of Uganda related to patrilineal inheritance and especially to the father's having to give up a parcel of land to his son following the son's circumcision. Delay in letting their sons be circumcised is then a part of the harsh treatment by some Gisu fathers. Turner (1971) contrasts with this the situation among the matrilineal Ndembu, where a youth's conflict is more likely to be with his maternal uncle; here the father seems glad to play a protective role at his son's initiation.

A specific effect that ritual is sometimes believed to have is that of "casting out anger," as Harris (1978) says in writing about the Taita of Kenya. Ethnographers often allude to efforts of a group to rid itself of the burden it suffers from the anger of individuals. Ceremonial expression of anger, letting it out or "spitting" it out, is frequently used. Wilson (1971, 28) reports that ritualized confession, "speaking out," with use of fairly uniform symbols occurs almost the length of Africa, from the Sudan to the Cape.

Concern with directing and controlling aggression is so persistently involved in religion that some writers have given aggression a prime position in attempts to explain the origins of religion. This is true of the French literary scholar René Girard (1977). Speculating about the motives that give rise everywhere to diverse forms of religion, Girard seems to argue that aggression is the universal source. (His terminology and whole mode of thought are so different from ours that we cannot be certain he would agree with our inference.) We cannot agree that religion has any one exclusive source of support, but Girard's evidence makes a strong case for aggression control as one source of major importance.

SELF-ASSERTION VERSUS DEPENDENCE
(NORMS OF HUMILITY AND COMPETENCE)

Every candidate in an initiation ceremony goes through a humbling experience, in which the danger of excessive self-assertion is countered by a stern reminder of basic dependence on others. Perhaps the most exaggerated form of this humbling experience occurs among some African peoples in what Turner (1969, 166-203) calls "rituals of status elevation," such as the installation of a chief or king. Here the common people have the rare privilege of demeaning the very person who is about to be placed in a high, often sacred, position above them.

The taboos and seclusion many societies impose on warriors who have killed an enemy or taken a head are also humbling experiences. Do these rituals serve as training experiences, increasing the probability that the newly powerful or prestigious person will not assert his power or prestige too disruptively in the future? That is the assumption of the Wilsons, who in writing about the Nyakyusa have treated the subject of humility and competence as aspects of morality (Godfrey Wilson, 1936; Monica Wilson, 1951a, 1971). In the moral code of the Nyakyusa, humility is the value emphasized; competence seems also to be valued, but only in moderation. It is all right to work hard on one's garden and to carry heavy loads of wood, but not to make a show of it or boast about it. To be stingy, particularly with milk and meat, is reprehensible; one who is able should be feasting his neighbors. If your garden is too productive, it is taken to indicate that you may be sorcerizing your neighbor, drawing away the fertility from his garden. Belief that sorcery is effective thus serves, even in the absence of any actual practice of sorcery, to enforce norms of humility. As we have seen in Chapter 6, this economic leveling effect of belief in wizardry appears in many places and may indeed be a major reason for the persistence of the belief. Where, as in many African groups (Marwick, 1970; LeVine 1973, 140), Westernization has disrupted the traditional interdependence of neighbors and kinsmen and has stirred up individual competition, the motivation for belief in wizardry and for its practice has been heightened. As we saw in Chapter 11, the result under conditions of rapid social change is sometimes that where other aspects of the aboriginal religion are diminished, the importance of wizardry may actually increase.

Encouragement of the positive side of humility, appropriate dependence on kinsmen, neighbors, and community, is an obvious theme of many rituals. This is particularly clear in the Navaho of Arizona and New Mexico, whose rituals center around healing. In Navaho healing rituals, participation of others besides the patient is emphasized. The "sing" is directed at putting at least one distressed individual back into harmony with the group, and indeed with the whole universe. While one person is the designated patient for whom the ritual is conducted, similar benefits may be gained by other participants. Restoring or maintaining appropriate interdependence seems to be a theme also of healing rituals among the Apache, the "rituals of affliction" of the Ndembu (Turner, 1968), and the community healing of the Kung (Katz, 1982). In all these cases, the rituals are characteristically performed in the presence and with the active participation of the relatives, friends, and neighbors important to the patient.

Experiences of ethnographers nicely illustrate how, on this dimension of humility and competence, many traditional peoples occupy a position very different from our own. Somewhere in our reading on pastoralists we came across an ethnographer who had been surprised to be taken to task for mentioning in conversation that it was *he* who had provided an animal to be sacrificed—a violation of local norms of humility.

Yet we do find rare instances where a traditional society provides rituals to facilitate reduction of interdependence. Both instances occur in New Guinea. Whiting (1941, 145) reports for the Kwoma a ritual for the "unmaking of kinship ties." Koch (1974, 98) reports a similar ritual for the Jalemo. Inasmuch as the desire to use these rituals and formally dissolve obligations and expectations presumably arises out of severe antagonism, we would, of course, view these rituals as a control pertinent to aggression as well as to dependence and self-assertion.

We began this section with mention of rituals that, by enforcing temporary humility, may tend to prevent the extremes of competence that are so strongly rewarded in our society. But if the extreme of high competence may be a threat in a traditional society, a sufficient degree of competence is obviously a necessity. And many rituals seem to play some role in encouraging and rewarding competence. Ceremonies of initiation out of childhood, whether the transition be to adulthood or to some intermediate status, mark a change in expected behavior—away from childhood dependence on mother, for instance. Female initiation ceremonies, indeed, are generally placed in time precisely to announce and adjust to the fact that the girl is now competent to produce a baby. First-kill rites seem calculated to strengthen and publicize a boy's pride in attaining adult competence in the food quest. And it may be that planting and harvest rituals serve as constant reminders and regulators of the general skill and effort that all in the community must exert.

NORMS OF CONFIDENCE

By norms of confidence, we refer to customs in the management of anxiety, which we may equally well call insecurity. What particular anxieties are central in the concerns of a particular people varies, but for any one focus of anxiety, or for anxieties in general, societies differ in how reassurance is obtained so that confidence may be maintained.

Reassurance in the face of insecurity is what Freud, in *The Future of an Illusion* (1961), says religion gives to people. Human beings can never master the universal privations intrinsic to their being mortal and social, nor can they ever totally master the more variable frustrations and uncertainties that unpredictably beset them. Rational thought is the realistic tool for getting as close as possible to the goal of complete mastery, but it can never take one all the way. Religion is the substitute, offering a fantasy of mastery for which each person's infantile view of all-powerful parents offers a model.

Freud's theory was hardly novel with him, we would suppose, remembering for instance the old American labor song warning about the false comforts of religion: "You'll eat pie in the sky bye and bye." That religion often provides a comforting but unrealistic fantasy of security is clearly enough suggested by many of the details of religious behavior all over the world, but nowhere is it so convincingly shown as in religion in societies undergoing rapid change. Religion as an attempt to manage insecurity is evident in many of the instances we reviewed in Chapter 11 of religious movements in societies threatened by alien forces. Its importance is clear, however, only as a temporary response to insecurity; reality often puts a brutal end to fantasy.

A major source of insecurity underlying two of the great sets of religious movements we have surveyed is economic. In some instances, the insecurity resides in comparison with more affluent intruders; in others, the basic command of essential resources may be threatened.

Cargo cults, as we have said, are especially characteristic of Melanesia, but similar movements have arisen elsewhere. They are built around attempts to obtain, with the help of mystical beings, the advanced technology displayed by the aliens or the products of that technology, such as canned food or better weapons.

It seems significant that cargo cults apparently did not develop among the Maya or Aztecs. In both regions direct destruction of the native economy was not a main feature of the impact of aliens. In Central Africa cargo cults were rare; yet Middleton reports on a persistent one in northwestern Uganda and nearby regions, the Allah water or Yakan cult, beginning in the 1880s. The ritual centered on the drinking of magical water, and it was expected that the water

> would preserve them from death; that their ancestors would come to life; that their dead cattle would come to life; that they could flout government orders with impunity and need not pay tax; that they would be immune against rifles which would fire only water, and that they would obtain rifles to drive the Europeans from the country. The rifles were to be brought in boats along the Kaia and Nile rivers, and. . .they were believed to be brought by a spirit. (1963b, 92-93)

In tracing the probable origins of this Yakan cult, Middleton (1963b, 86, 100) stresses the impact of severe epidemics (affecting both people and cattle), famines, and military threats from outside; the effect of these events on their society was phrased by the Lugbara as having "destroyed the world as they had known it" (ibid., 100).

Economic need is apparent in the various revivalistic movements of North American Indians. Many tribes had experienced complete extinction of their former way of making a living, as well as dispossession even from their homelands. The fantasies of return to precontact life, with the disappearance of the destroyers and the return of buffalo herds to the Plains, were surely among much else an outcome of economic frustration. We conjecture that extremity of disruption of the economy and lack of a model of replacement that can actually be seen at hand will be conditions that jointly favor the development of movements seeking to restore the old economy.

Economic sources of insecurity seem to be important in the rise of millenarian movements in more complex societies, too. But both there and in simpler societies, it is not economic needs alone for which religion may provide a partial substitute for the satisfaction that is not found in reality. Other sources of anxiety are clearly, though less pervasively, illustrated by what is known about religion under alien pressure. Threats that disease or injury pose to individual life or comfort are present everywhere, and syncretic religions are likely to include some provision for unrealistic coping with this source of anxiety. Healing is, for instance, a conspicuous part of many ceremonies of the Native American Church (which blends the use of peyote with elements of Christian worship) and of the Shaker religion developed by Native American churches of the northwestern United States. Conversion to one or another of the competing Christian sects in Nigeria seems to have been greatly influenced by expectation of successful treatment of individual illness or other misfortune.

The insecurity that gives rise to new religions may not, of course, have any one specific source. Anthony Wallace (1956), reviewing religious movements among the Delaware Indians through 300 years, argues that the relevant deprivation is not of "food, shelter, and other economic wants" but something more general and diffuse, "loss of confidence in a familiar and expectedly reliable pattern of social relations" (p. 19).

A common source of insecurity in societies threatened by outside forces is uncertainty about their continued existence and about their social identity. The role of religion in expressing the ethnic unity of the group seems important, for example, in Fortes's (1987) analysis of religion among the Tallensi of Ghana. Here, as we have seen in Chapter 11, the syncretic religions he studied derived from two related societies that had merged during the preceding century. Their religious beliefs and practices have shown a mixture of modification, maintenance, and interaction. Some of the rituals of each require crucial participation by members of the other group. Thus the newly developing religion promotes the partial unity of the entire merged society while at the same time maintaining the integrity of each of the merged components. Fernandez, from his detailed analysis of the Bwiti cult in Gabon and the Congo Democratic Republic, is led to a generalization about African religious protest movements: that they "have long been acting to restore to their participants autonomy and integrity in their social and cultural life" (1964, 531).

This function of ritual during social change is well illustrated by facts cited in Chapter 11 about Javanese immigrants to New Caledonia. Their Javanese ceremonial shifted from the expression of neighborliness it had had in Java to an expression of Javanese identity among migrants to multiethnic communities in New Caledonia. A similar role of ritual in affirming social identity is cited by Nadel (1954, 230-231) in his study of Nupe religion. Nupe who live in the multicultural city of Lagos hold on to traditional Nupe religion more purely than do those who live in Nupe villages and towns. For the latter, their identity as Nupe is so repeatedly confirmed by the practical circumstances of their life, that the hints of a broader identity as Muslims poses no threat. The former, in immediate proximity to non-Nupe, find comfort in religious practices and beliefs that proclaim their distinctiveness, and they are more likely to keep the Muslim aspects of their religion separate from the Nupe aspects.

The sense of ethnic unity provided by religion may extend beyond previous boundaries. This is one of the effects Middleton ascribes to the Yakan or Allah water cult:

> The cult was able temporarily to ally groups from the many small tribes threatened by the Azande and Arabs, and this aspect of it, that of enabling members of different groups to merge their identity as adherents of a single new cult, was also apparent in the later phase. (1963b, 86)

Political power is another aspect of life in which insecurity may be felt, where the insecurity may be reduced in reality as well as in fantasy by such developments as an increased sense of ethnic unity. Religious movements directed, with some degree of realism, at establishing a greater measure of autonomy, and thus political power, include the Paliau movement among the Manus (Schwartz, 1962), the messianic outbreak expressed in the Sun Dance of the Comanche (Hoebel, 1941), and many millenarian movements in various parts of the world. All had their fantasy components, and many ultimately led to a real increase in political power.

Whatever the sources of anxiety, the contribution of religion to its management need not be entirely unrealistic; ritual and the accompanying beliefs may be so deeply embedded in the realistic routines of making a living that they may become a necessary part of it. For health needs and for many other needs, the realistic gains from religion seem to us a clear addition to the unrealistic gains that Freud recognized so well.

COGNITION: CONTINUITY VERSUS CHANGE

The psychological effects we have been tracing for religion all have their cognitive side. Rituals that help restrain sexuality, or that offer temporary freedom, do so in part by clearly indicating to everyone what is expected or permitted. The same is true for rituals pertinent to control of aggression, self-assertion versus dependence, and anxiety. The rituals may not merely provide cues about what is to be done. They may also provide lessons or exercises in how to do it, as when a male initiate learns the ceremonies by which he may establish contact with the ancestors, or the menarcheal girl learns how to put her new mystical power to use in healing. The cognitive content of ritual, in short, is an essential component of its effects on diverse motives and their satisfaction.

Yet there is something more general in the cognitive effects of ritual, an effect on a person's view of the world and of self and on the strength and character of cognitive motivation. Rituals serve to place the individual in the society, to help form and strengthen the individual's identity. In

Erikson's portrayal of the development of personal identity in our society (1950), rituals are not very conspicuous, but in many other societies, they are of prime importance in the formation of personal identity. They contribute to the person's cognitive map of the world and his or her place in it. James Hillman (1975) provides, from his Jungian background, a useful way of thinking about this. Each person develops a unique set of meanings, and from these continuously constructs a unique human life, placing each experience into a framework or context of comparison. Rituals with their accompanying myths and practices are a prime source, then, that the individual draws on in building his or her inner world of meaning and an influence on the desire to form this inner world of meaning.

The importance of religion in providing a view of the world comes out repeatedly in studies of societies undergoing rapid change. European administrators of colonies often found natives strangely resistant to proposed changes whose practical importance seemed extremely obvious to the administrators. For the Madang district of New Guinea, for example, Lawrence (1963) describes the terrible frustration of apparently benevolent administrators in attempting to persuade people to adopt alien techniques of food production of obviously high efficiency. The background lay, in Lawrence's view, in the persistence of a view of the world that made ritual an essential component of any economic activity, and in the failure of the Westerners to teach the secrets of the ritual that in the natives' belief must normally accompany Western techniques of production. The beliefs and rituals accompanying the indigenous economy had been well integrated into a view of the world that had a staying power of its own. Aspects of religion originally supporting the indigenous way of life and contributing to the reduction of insecurity continued even when they had become a source of insecurity. It seems a reasonable inference—though Lawrence is not concerned with making it—that the world view provided by a religion is part of what religion provides to human life.

Studies of syncretism in Africa by Peel (1968a, 1968b) and by Horton (1971) argue strongly for an influence of the intellectual function of religion. Peel presents his argument as somewhat distinctive of the Yoruba; Horton argues that it is of much more general validity for Africa (without considering its bearing on the rest of the world). In the precontact religion, mystical beings were at once objects of communion in religious practice and agents of central importance in the explanation and control of events in daily life. The Christianity brought by missionaries was one in which this latter use, the intellectual appeal to divinity for explanation of natural events and human action, had almost totally disappeared in recent centuries; so Christianity offered a satisfactory replacement and extension only for the communion aspect of native religion. The blending with this of the intellectual aspect is seen as a major reason for the success of the syncretistic cults, the separatist or Africanist churches, in attracting members away from the missionary churches and in making their own fresh converts. In the terms used by the psychologist David Bakan in his book *The Duality of Human Existence* (1966), the syncretistic cults add to the communion appeal of the modern Christian churches the agency appeal that has remained strong in the indigenous religions.

The intellectual function of religion is a central feature of Horton's explanation of selective conversion to the proselytizing religions, Islam and Christianity, active in Africa now and in past centuries. The background of his theory is relevant to the explanation of religious variation among various stable societies as well. The theory views religious beliefs as cosmology, expressing an interpretation of the world that provides a basis for explaining, predicting, and (through ritual) controlling events in the real world. If a people are completely absorbed in social relationships within their community, they will form a cosmology that is local; the supernatural figures in it will be interpretations of the individuals and their ancestors and of the places and things of the local community. If a people are greatly involved also in relationships beyond their community and society, then their cosmology will include a supreme being who is concerned with the larger world. A society that, on contact with alien administrators or missionaries, already has this broader cosmology will be more receptive to a world religion. Horton supports this thesis with cross-cultural comparisons among a restricted number of African societies for which there are excellent data available on the original culture, the conditions of contact, and the course of religious change. He strengthens his argument by demonstrating parallels in the response to Christianity and to Islam and by reference to within-society variations in religious change (1962, 1971, 1975). Horton is, in effect, arguing that the study of religion under acculturation in Africa supports a general interpretation of religion as responsive to cognitive needs and, through satisfaction of cognitive needs, contributing to a variety of realistic interactions with the social and even physical environment. (Ifeka-Moller [1974] argues against Horton's intellectualist interpretation. She does not seem to us to invalidate it, but we agree with her argument that more directly practical motives and the search for secure identity also provide important support for religion.)

A part of the worldview religion presents to people is a sense of continuity, a feeling of union with their own and their society's past and future. So far as successful, this makes for development of a norm of stability, of routine. New cults that form under acculturative stress often give great importance to the ancestors, even greater importance than in the earlier religion of the society, and a sense of continuity is one apparent gain. The consistency of cosmology from precontact to postcontact time on which Horton builds his theory is another instance of continuity. So are the parallels between precontact religion of the Maya and Aztecs and the aspects of Catholicism emphasized in the syncretic religion that developed in their regions. Cargo cults, with their emphasis on acquiring the material advantages of the aliens, are reported (Lawrence, 1964, 29) to have been favored by the aboriginal individualism and materialism of many Melanesian societies. The many modern African religious movements centered around a living prophet as leader could more easily develop in cultures that already had a strong prophetic tradition in their earlier religion.

These examples may suggest a general conservatism of religion. Yet a tradition of religious change may itself be one of the features of continuity, so that the balance arrived at in some societies may be more toward novelty than toward routine. Herskovits (1962, 419) argues that the dynamism characteristic of precontact African religions prepared for a great flexibility of new religious movements growing out of them.

The importance of cognitive motives seems to vary enormously from person to person, and doubtless from one society to another. For the philosophers whom Paul Radin (1927) leads us to expect to find occasionally even in the simplest societies, they may be dominant motives in life. For everyone they are of some consequence. Religion may serve to stabilize and unify the way people view the world, and yet may encourage a questioning attitude. For fewer people than for the other norms we have considered, perhaps, but in similar ways, religion thus may help establish a balance—in this case a balance between tendencies to draw on the familiar and to create the new, a balance between norms of routine and of novelty.

SUMMARY

Religion is found in traditional societies to offer, beyond its own intrinsic benefits, satisfaction of numerous specific needs. Some are best seen as typical needs of individuals, some as needs of the society. In either case, the gains are likely to be accompanied by losses as well. The various gains and losses may be seen as a contribution of religion to establishing, for each society or community, norms in the satisfaction and control of basic motives or interests:

1. Norms in the satisfaction and control of sexual interests
2. Norms in the control yet appropriate encouragement of aggression
3. Norms of humility and competence, aimed at suitable balance between self-assertive quest for competence and dependence on others
4. Norms of confidence, balancing need for reassurance in the face of anxiety, with a useful degree of anxiety
5. Norms of routine and novelty in the pursuit of cognitive interests.

For each of these motives or interests, traditional religions help guide people toward achieving a balance between opposed tendencies. The balance may differ from person to person, but retain enough consistency to distinguish the culture of one group from the culture of other groups.

References

Where authors are mentioned in the text but their names do not appear in this list of references, or a society is mentioned without an author being named, it is because the information was obtained from the Human Relations Area Files, available in a number of university libraries, and demand did not seem likely to justify extended citation here. For information about the HRAF, see Levinson (1988) and Ember and Ember (1988), or write to Human Relations Area Files, Inc., P.O. Box 2054 Yale Station, New Haven, CT 06520 (203-777-2334).

Albers, Patricia, & Parker, Seymour. (1971). The Plains vision experience: A study of power. *Southwestern Journal of Anthropology, 27*, 203-233.

Allen, M. R. (1967). *Male cults and secret initiations in Melanesia*. Melbourne: Melbourne University Press.

Anisimov, A. F. (1963). The shaman's tent of the Evenks and the origin of the shamanistic rite. In Henry N. Michael (Ed.), *Studies in Siberian shamanism*, 84-123. Toronto: University of Toronto Press. (*Arctic Institute of North America, Anthropology of the North: Translations from Russian Sources / No. 4*). (Original work published 1952).

Ansbacher, Heinz L., & Ansbacher, Rowena R. (Eds.). (1956). *The individual psychology of Alfred Adler: A systematic presentation in selections from his writings*. New York: Basic Books.

Ardener, Edwin. (1956). *Coastal Bantu of the Cameroons*. London: International African Institute.

———. (1970). Witchcraft, economics, and the continuity of belief. In Douglas, 1970, 141-160.

Armstrong, W. E. (1928). *Rossell Island: An ethnological study*. Cambridge: Cambridge University Press.

Ayres, Barbara. (1967). Pregnancy magic: A study of food taboos and sex avoidances. In Clellan S. Ford (Ed.), *Cross-cultural approaches: Readings in comparative research*, 111-125. New Haven, CT: HRAF Press.

Baal, J. van. (1966). *Dema: Description and analysis of Marind-Anim culture (South New Guinea)*. The Hague: Martinus Nijhoff.

Bahr, Donald M., Gregorio, Juan, Lopez, David I., & Alvarez, A. (1974). *Piman shamanism and staying sickness*. Tucson: University of Arizona Press.

Bakan, David. (1966). *The duality of human existence: An essay on psychology and religion*. Chicago: Rand McNally.

Balandier, Georges. (1970). *The sociology of black Africa: Social dynamics in Central Africa*. (D. Garman, Trans.). New York: Praeger. (Original work published 1955).

Balikci, Asen. (1963). Shamanistic behavior among the Netsilik Eskimos. *Southwestern Journal of Anthropology, 19*, 380-396.

Balzer, Marjorie M. (1980). The route to eternity: Cultural persistence and change in Siberian Khanty burial ritual. *Arctic Anthropology, 17*(1), 77-85.

Barber, Theodore Xenophon. (1969). *Hypnosis: A scientific approach*. New York: Van Nostrand Reinhold.

Barnard, Alan. (1979). Nharo Bushman medicine and medicine men. *Africa, 49*, 68-79.

Barry, Herbert, III, Child, Irvin L., & Bacon, Margaret K. (1959). Relation of child training to subsistence economy. *American Anthropologist, 61*, 51-63.

Barth, Fredrik. (1961). *Nomads of South Persia: The Basseri tribe of the Khamseh confederacy*. Oslo: University Press, and London: Allen & Unwin.

Bartolomé, Miguel Alberto. (1979). Shamanism among the Avá-Chiripá. In David L. Browman & Ronald A. Schwarz (Eds.), *Spirits, shamans, and stars: Perspectives from South America*, 95-148. The Hague: Mouton.

Barton, Roy Franklin. (1946). The religion of the Ifugaos. *American Anthropologist, 48* (4) pt. 2, 1-219. (*Memoir Series of the American Anthropologist*, no. 65).

Basso, Keith H. (1969). *Western Apache witchcraft*. Tucson: University of Arizona Press. (*Anthropological Papers of the University of Arizona*, no. 15).

———. (1970). *The Cibecue Apache*. New York: Holt, Rinehart & Winston.

Bateson, Gregory. (1958). *Naven* (2nd ed.). Stanford, CA: Stanford University Press. (Original edition 1936, Cambridge University Press).

Beals, Ralph Leon, & Hoijer, Harry. (1965). *An introduction to anthropology* (2nd ed.) New York: Macmillan.

Beattie, John H. M. (1964). *Other cultures*. London: Cohen & West.

Beidelman, Thomas O. (1963). Witchcraft in Ukaguru. In Middleton & Winter, 1963, 57-98.

———. (1964). Three tales of the living and the dead: The ideology of Kaguru ancestral propitiation. *Journal of the Royal Anthropological Institute, 94*, 109-137.

———. (1966). *Utani*: Some Kaguru notions of death, sexuality and affinity. *Southwestern Journal of Anthropology, 22*, 354-380.

Benedict, Ruth Fulton. (1938). Religion. In Franz Boas (Ed.), *General anthropology*, 627-665. New York: D. C. Heath.

Bercovitch, Eytan. (1989). Mortal insights: Victim and witch in the Nalumin imagination. In Gilbert Herdt & Michele Stephen (Eds.), *The religious imagination in New Guinea*, 122-159. New Brunswick, NJ: Rutgers University Press.

Bergman, Robert. (1973). A school for medicine men. *American Journal of Psychiatry, 130*, 664-666.

Berndt, Ronald M., & Berndt, Catherine H. (1951). Sexual behavior in West Arnhem Land. *Viking Fund Publications in Anthropology*, no. 16.

Berndt, Ronald M., & Lawrence, Peter (Eds.). (1971). *Politics in New Guinea*. Nedlands: University of Western Australia Press.

Best, Eledon. (1924). *The Maori*. Wellington, New Zealand: Tombs.

Bettelheim, Bruno. (1954). *Symbolic wounds: Puberty rites and the envious male*. Glencoe, IL: Free Press.

Bierhorst, John. (Ed.). (1985). *Cantares Mexicanos: Songs of the Aztecs*, translated from the Nahuatl, with an introduction and commentary, by John Bierhorst. Stanford, CA: Stanford University Press.

Biernoff, David. (1978). Safe and dangerous places. In Lester Richard Hiatt (Ed.), *Australian aboriginal concepts*, 93-105. Canberra: Australian Institute of Aboriginal Studies.

Binford, Lewis R. (1971). Mortuary practices: Their study and their potential. *American Antiquity, 36*(3), pt. 2, 6-29.

Bleek, D. F. (1928). *The Naron: A Bushman tribe of the central Kalahari*. Cambridge: Cambridge University Press.

Bloch, Maurice, & Parry, Jonathan (Eds). (1982a). *Death and the regeneration of life*. Cambridge: Cambridge University Press.

———. (1982b). Introduction. In Bloch & Parry, 1982a, 1-44.

Boas, Franz. (1910). Religion. In F. W. Hodge (Ed.), *Handbook of American Indians north of Mexico*, pt. 2, 365-371. Washington, DC: Smithsonian Institution. (*Bureau of American Ethnology Bulletin 30*, pt. 2).

Boddy, Janice. (1982). Womb as oasis: The symbolic context of pharaonic circumcision in rural Northern Sudan. *American Ethnologist, 9*, 682-698.

Bogoras, Waldemar. (1907). The Chukchee: Religion. *Memoirs of the American Museum of Natural History, 11*, pt. II.

Bohannon, Paul. (1958). Extra-processual events in Tiv political institutions. *American Anthropologist, 60*, 1-12.

Booth, Newell S., Jr. (1977). Islam in Africa. In Newell S. Booth, Jr. (Ed.), *African religions: A symposium*, 297-343. New York: NOK Publishers.

Boston, John. (1971). Medicines and fetishes in Igala. *Africa, 41*, 200-207.

Bourguignon, Erika. (1973a). Introduction: A framework for the comparative study of altered states of consciousness. In Bourguignon, 1973b, 3-35.

———, (Ed.). (1973b). *Religion, altered states of consciousness, and social change*. Columbus: Ohio State University Press.

———. (1989). Multiple personality, possession trance, and the psychic unity of mankind. *Ethos, 17*, 371-384.

Brain, James L. (1977). Sex, incest, and death: Initiation rites reconsidered. *Current Anthropology, 18*, 191-208.

———. (1978). Symbolic rebirth: The Mwali rite among the Luguru of eastern Tanzania. *Africa, 48*, 176-188.

Broude, Gwen J., & Greene, Sarah J. (1976). Cross-cultural codes on twenty sexual attitudes and practices. *Ethnology, 15*, 409-429.

Brown, Judith K. (1981). Cross-cultural perspectives on the female life cycle. In Munroe, Munroe, & Whiting, 1981, 581-610.

Brown, Julia S. (1952). A comparative study of deviations from sexual mores. *American Sociological Review, 17*, 135-146.

Buber, Martin. (1958). *I and Thou* (2nd ed.). (Ronald George Smith, Trans.). New York: Scribner. (Original work published 1923).

Buck, Peter Henry. (1939). *Anthropology and religion.* New Haven, CT: Yale University Press.

Burton, Roger V., & Whiting, John W. M. (1961). The absent father and cross-sex identity. *Merrill-Palmer Quarterly of Behavior and Development, 7,* 85-95.

Butt, Audrey J. (1954). The burning fountain from whence it came: A study of the system of beliefs of the Carib-speaking Akawaio of British Guiana. *Timehri: The Journal of the Royal Agricultural and Commercial Society of British Guiana,* no. 33, 48-60.

———. (1956). Ritual blowing: *Taling*—A causation and cure of illness among the Akawaio. *Man, 56,* 48-55.

———. (1961). Symbolism and ritual among the Akawaio of British Guiana. *Nieuwe West-Indische Gids, 41,* 141-161.

Carroll, Michael P. (1979). The sex of our gods. *Ethos, 7,* 37-50.

———. (1986). *The cult of the Virgin Mary: Psychological origins.* Princeton, NJ: Princeton University Press.

Chagnon, Napoleon A. (1968). *Yanomamö: The fierce people.* New York: Holt, Rinehart & Winston.

Chapple, Eliot D., & Coon, Carleton S. (1942). *Principles of anthropology.* New York: Holt.

Child, Alice B., & Child, Irvin L. (1985). Biology, ethnocentrism, and sex differences. *American Anthropologist, 87,* 125-128.

Chinnery, E. W. Pearson, & Beaver, Wilfred N. (1915). Notes on the initiation ceremonies of the Koko, Papua. *Journal of the Royal Anthropological Institute, 45,* 69-78.

Clements, Forrest E. (1932). Primitive concepts of disease. *University of California Publications in American Archaeology and Ethnology, 32,* 185-252.

Cochrane, Glynn. (1970). *Big men and cargo cults.* Oxford: Clarendon.

Codrington, Robert Henry. (1891). *The Melanesians: Studies in their anthropology and folklore.* Oxford: Clarendon.

Coelho, Ruy. (1949). The significance of the couvade among the black Caribs. *Man, 49,* 51-53.

Cohen, Yehudi A. (1964a). The establishment of identity in a social nexus: The special case of initiation ceremonies and their relation to value and legal systems. *American Anthropologist, 66,* 529-551.

———. (1964b). *The transition from childhood to adolescence.* Chicago: Aldine.

Collins, John James. (1967). Peyotism and religious membership at Taos Pueblo, New Mexico. *Southwestern Social Science Quarterly, 48,* 183-191.

Collins, June McCormick. (1950). The Indian Shaker church: A study of continuity and change in religion. *Southwestern Journal of Anthropology, 6,* 399-411.

Collocott, E. E. V. (1921). The supernatural in Tonga. *American Anthropologist, 23,* 415-444.

Colson, Audrey Butt. (1976). Binary oppositions and the treatment of sickness among the Akawaio. In J. B. Loudon (Ed.), *Social anthropology and medicine,* 422-499. London: Academic Press.

———. (1977). The Akawaio shaman. *University of Arizona Anthropological Papers,* no. 28, 43-65.

Coon, Carleton S. (1931). *Tribes of the Rif.* Cambridge, MA: Peabody Museum. (*Harvard African Studies*, 9).

———. (1971). *The hunting peoples.* Boston: Little, Brown.

Coppet, Daniel de. (1981). The life-giving death. In Humphreys & King, 1981, 175-204.

Cox, Harvey. (1977). *Turning East: The promise and peril of the new orientalism.* New York: Simon & Schuster.

Craemer, Willy de, Vansina, Jan, & Fox, Renée C. (1976). Religious movements in Central Africa: A theoretical study. *Comparative Studies in Society and History, 18*, 458-475.

Crawford, J. R. (1967). *Witchcraft and sorcery in Rhodesia.* London: Oxford University Press.

Crocker, Jon Christopher. (1985). *Vital souls: Bororo cosmology, natural symbolism, and shamanism.* Tucson: University of Arizona Press.

Cunha, Manuela Carneiro da. (1981). Eschatalogy among the Kraho: Reflection upon society, free field of fabulation. In Humphreys & King, 1981, 161-174.

Curley, Richard T. (1983). Dreams of power: Social process in a West African religious movement. *Africa, 53*, 20-37.

Davidson, Basil. (1969). *The African genius: An introduction to African cultural and social history.* Boston: Little, Brown.

Deng, Francis Mading. (1972). *The Dinka of the Sudan.* New York: Holt, Rinehart & Winston.

———. (1978). *Africans of two worlds: The Dinka in Afro-Arab Sudan.* New Haven, CT: Yale University Press.

Dewey, Alice G. (1970). Ritual as a mechanism for urban adaptation. *Man, 5*, 438-448.

Dieterlen, Germaine. (1941). *Les âmes des Dogons.* Paris: Institut d'Ethnologie. (*Travaux et mémoires de l'Institut d'Ethnologie, 40*).

———. (1951). *Essai sur la religion Bambara.* Paris: Presses Universitaires de France. [Quotation is from translation by K. Wolf for Human Relations Area Files.]

Dobkin de Rios, Marlene. (1984). *Hallucinogens: Cross-cultural perspectives.* Albuquerque: University of New Mexico Press.

Douglas, Mary. (1963). The Tele of Kasai. In D. Forde (Ed.), *African worlds: Studies in the cosmological ideas and social values of African peoples*, 1-26. London: Oxford University Press.

———, (Ed.). (1970). *Witchcraft: Confessions and accusations.* London: Tavistock Publications.

Downes, Rupert Major. (1971). *Tiv religion.* [Ibadan], Nigeria: Ibadan University Press.

Downs, Richard Erskine. (1956). *The religion of the Bare'e-speaking Toradja of central Celebes.* 's-Gravenhage: Uitgeverij Excelsior.

Driver, Harold E. (1972). *Indians of North America* (2nd ed.). Chicago: University of Chicago Press.

Durkheim, Emile. (1965). *The elementary forms of the religious life.* (Joseph Ward Swain, Trans.). New York: Free Press. (Original work published 1912).

Duru, Mary Steimel. (1983). Underlying themes in Igbo culture. *Anthropological Quarterly, 56*, 1-9.

Dyk, Walter. (1938). *Son of Old Man Hat: A Navaho autobiography*. New York: Harcourt, Brace.

———, & Dyk, Ruth. (1980). *Left Handed: A Navajo autobiography*. New York: Columbia University Press.

Eliade, Mircea. (1964). *Shamanism: Archaic techniques of ecstasy*. (W. R. Trask, Trans.). New York: Bollingen Foundation.

Elmendorf, William W. (1952). Soul loss illness in western North America. In Tax, 1952, 104-114.

Ember, Carol R., & Ember, Melvin. (1973). *Anthropology*. New York: Appleton Century Crofts.

———. (1988). *Guide to cross-cultural research using the HRAF archive*. New Haven, CT: Human Relations Area Files, Inc.

Erikson, E. H. (1950). *Childhood and society*. New York: Norton.

Evans-Pritchard, E. E. (1937). *Witchcraft, oracles and magic among the Azande*. Oxford: Clarendon.

———. (1953). The sacrificial role of cattle among the Nuer. *Africa, 23*, 181-197.

———. (1956). *Nuer religion*. Oxford: Clarendon.

Faithorn, Elizabeth. (1975). The concept of pollution among the Káfe of the Papua New Guinea highlands. In Rayna R. Reiter (Ed.), *Toward an anthropology of women*, 127-140. New York: Monthly Review Press.

Favret-Saada, Jeanne. (1989). Unbewitching as therapy. *American Ethnologist, 16*, 40-56.

Fernandez, James W. (1961). Christian acculturation and Fang witchcraft. *Cahiers d'Etudes Africaines, 2*, 244-255.

———. (1964). African religious movements: Types and dynamics. *Journal of Modern African Studies, 2*, 531-549.

———. (1965). Symbolic consensus in a Fang reformative cult. *American Anthropologist, 67*, 902-929.

———. (1972). Tabernanthe Iboga: Narcotic ecstasis and the work of the ancestors. In Furst, 1972, 237-260.

———. (1982). *Bwiti: An ethnography of the religious imagination in Africa*. Princeton, NJ: Princeton University Press.

Firth, Raymond. (1934). The meaning of dreams in Tikopia. In E. E. Evans-Pritchard et al. (Eds.), *Essays presented to C. G. Seligman*, 63-74. London: Kegan Paul, Trench.

———. (1951). *Elements of social organization*. New York: Philosophical Library.

———. (1956). *Human types: An introduction to social anthropology* (rev. ed.). London: Nelson.

———. (1964). *Essays on social organization and values*. London: Athlone.

———. (1967a). *Tikopia ritual and belief*. Boston: Beacon Press.

———. (1967b). *The work of the gods in Tikopia* (2nd ed.). London: Athlone.

———. (1970). *Rank and religion in Tikopia: A study in Polynesian paganism and conversion to Christianity*. London: Allen & Unwin.

Fitz-Patrick, David G., & Kimbuna, John. (1983). *Bundi: The culture of a Papua New Guinea people*. Nerang, Queensland: Ryebuck Publications.

Flannery, Regina. (1952). Two concepts of power. In Tax, 1952, 185-189.

Fletcher, Alice C., & LaFlesche, Francis. (1911). The Omaha tribe. *27th Annual Report of the Bureau of American Ethnology*. Washington, DC: Government Printing Office.

Fock, Niels. (1960). South American birth customs in theory and in practice. *Folk [Copenhagen], 2*, 51-69.

Ford, Clellan S. (1945). A comparative study of human reproduction. *Yale University Publications in Anthropology*, no. 32.

Ford, Richard I. (1972). An ecological perspective on the eastern Pueblos. In Ortiz, 1972a, 1-17.

Forde, Daryll. (1964). *Yakö studies*. London: Oxford University Press.

Fortes, Meyer. (1936). Ritual festivals and social cohesion in the hinterland of the Gold Coast. *American Anthropologist, 38*, 590-604. (Reprinted in Fortes, 1970, 147-163.)

————. (1945). *The dynamics of clanship among the Tallensi*. London: Oxford University Press.

————. (1961). Pietas in ancestor worship: The Henry Myers lecture 1960. *Journal of the Royal Anthropological Institute, 91*, 166-191.

————. (1965a). Ancestor worship. In Fortes & Dieterlen, 1965, 16-20.

————. (1965b). Some reflections on ancestor worship in Africa. In Fortes & Dieterlen, 1965, 122-144.

————. (1970). *Time and social structure, and other essays*. London: Athlone.

————. (1987). *Religion, morality and the person: Essays on Tallensi religion*. Cambridge: Cambridge University Press.

————, & Dieterlen, Germaine (Eds.). (1965). *African systems of thought*. London: Oxford University Press.

Fortune, Reo F. (1932). *Sorcerers of Dobu*. New York: Dutton.

————. (1935). Manus religion. *Memoirs of the American Philosophical Society, no. 3*.

Fox, J. Robin. (1964). Witchcraft and clanship in Cochiti therapy. In Ari Kiev (Ed.), *Magic, faith, and healing: Studies in primitive psychiatry today*, 174-200. Glencoe, IL: Free Press.

Frazer, James George. (1922). *The golden bough: A study in magic and religion* (1 volume abridged ed.). New York: Macmillan. (Original work published 1890).

Freud, Sigmund. (1961). *The future of an illusion* (James Strachey, Trans.). New York: Norton. (Original work published 1927).

Furst, Peter T. (Ed.). (1972). *Flesh of the gods: The ritual use of hallucinogens*. London: Allen & Unwin.

Gallup, Gordon G. (1977). Self recognition in primates: A comparative approach to the bidirectional properties of consciousness. *American Psychologist, 32*, 329-338.

Gayton, A. H. (1946). Culture-environment integration: External references in Yokuts life. *Southwestern Journal of Anthropology, 2*, 252-268.

Geertz, Clifford. (1973). *The interpretation of cultures: Selected essays*. New York: Basic Books.

Gell, Alfred. (1975). *Metamorphosis of the cassowaries: Umeda society, language & ritual*. Atlantic Highlands, NJ: Humanities Press.

Gennep, Arnold Van. (1960). *The rites of passage*. (M. B. Vizedom & G. L. Caffee, Trans.). Chicago: University of Chicago Press. (Original work published 1909).

Girard, René. (1977). *Violence and the sacred*. (Patrick Gregory, Trans.). Baltimore, MD: Johns Hopkins University Press. (Original work published 1972).

Gluckman, Max. (1937). Mortuary customs and the belief in survival after death among the south-eastern Bantu. *Bantu Studies, 11*, 117-136.

———. (1944). The logic of African science and witchcraft: An appreciation of Evans-Pritchard's "Witchcraft Oracles and Magic among the Azande" of the Sudan. *Rhodes-Livingstone Institute Journal, 1*(1), 61-71. (Reprinted in part in Marwick, 1970, 321-331).

———. (1949). The role of the sexes in Wiko circumcision ceremonies. In M. Fortes (Ed.), *Social structure: Papers presented to A. R. Radcliffe-Brown*. Oxford: Clarendon.

———. (1972). Moral crises: Magical and secular solutions. In M. Gluckman (Ed.), *The allocation of responsibility*, 1-50. Manchester: University of Manchester Press.

Goddard, Pliny Earle. (1931). *Indians of the Southwest*. New York: American Museum of Natural History.

———. (1934). *Indians of the Northwest Coast* (2nd ed.). New York: American Museum of Natural History.

Godelier, Maurice. (1986). *The making of great men: Male domination and power among the New Guinea Baruya*. (Rupert Swyer, Trans.). Cambridge: Cambridge University Press. (Original work published 1982).

Goldman, Irving. (1963). *The Cubeo: Indians of the northwest Amazon*. Urbana: University of Illinois Press.

———. (1975). *The mouth of heaven: An introduction to Kwakiutl religious thought*. New York: Wiley.

———. (1976). Perceptions of nature and the structure of society: The question of Cubeo descent. *Dialectical Anthropology, 1*, 287-292.

Goldschmidt, Walter. (1971). Arete—Motivation and models for behavior. In Iago Galdston (Ed.), *The interface between psychiatry and anthropology*, 55-87. New York: Brunner/Mazel.

———. (1973). Guilt and pollution in Sebei mortuary rituals. *Ethos, 1*, 75-105.

Goodman, Felicitas D. (1988). *Ecstasy, ritual, and alternate reality: Religion in a pluralistic world*. Bloomington: Indiana University Press.

Goody, Esther. (1970). Legitimate and illegitimate aggression in a West African state. In Douglas, 1970, 207-244.

Goody, Jack. (1959). Death and social control among the LoDagaa. *Man, 59*, 134-138.

———. (1962). *Death, property and the ancestors: A study of the mortuary customs of the LoDagaa of West Africa*. Stanford, CA: Stanford University Press.

Gorer, Geoffrey. (1938). *Himalayan village: An account of the Lepchas of Sikkim*. London: Michael Joseph.

Gough, E. Kathleen. (1958). Cults of the dead among the Nayars. *Journal of American Folklore, 71*, 446-478.

Gould, Richard A. (1969). *Yiwara: Foragers of the Australian desert*. New York: Scribner.

Gourlay, K. A. (1975). Sound-producing instruments in traditional society: A study of esoteric instruments and their role in male-female relations. *New Guinea Research Bulletin*, no. 60.

Gray, Robert F. (1963). Some structural aspects of Mbugwe witchcraft. In Middleton & Winter, 1963, 143-173.

Greenbaum, Lenora S. (1973a). Possession trance in sub-Saharan Africa: A descriptive analysis of fourteen societies. In Bourguignon, 1973b, 58-87.

———. (1973b). Societal correlates of possession trance in sub-Saharan Africa. In Bourguignon, 1973b, 39-57.

Gregor, Thomas. (1977). *Mehinaku: The drama of daily life in a Brazilian Indian village*. Chicago: University of Chicago Press.

Griffin, Donald R. (1976). *The question of animal awareness: Evolutionary continuity of mental experience*. New York: Rockefeller University Press.

———. (1984). *Animal thinking*. Cambridge, MA: Harvard University Press.

Grigson, Wilfrid. (1949). *The Maria Gonds of Bastar* (reissue, with a supplement). London: Oxford University Press.

Grollig, F. X., & Haley, H. B. (Eds.). (1976). *Medical anthropology*. The Hague: Mouton.

Grottanelli, Vinigi L. (1976). Witchcraft: An allegory? In Grollig & Haley, (1976) 321-329.

Guiart, Jean. (1952). John Frum movement in Tanna. *Oceania, 22,* 165-177.

———. (1956). Culture contact and the "John Frum" movement on Tanna, New Hebrides. *Southwestern Journal of Anthropology, 12,* 105-116.

———. (1970). The millenarian aspect of conversion to Christianity in the South Pacific. In Thrupp, 1970, 122-138.

Gunther, Erna. (1949). The Shaker religion of the Pacific Northwest. In Marian W. Smith (Ed.), *Indians of the urban Northwest*, 37-76. New York: Columbia University Press.

Gusinde, Martin. (1917). The Yahgan. *Bulletin of the Bureau of American Ethnology, 63,* 1-247.

Hallowell, A. Irving. (1934). Some empirical aspects of northern Saulteaux religion. *American Anthropologist, 36,* 389-404.

———. (1938). Fear and anxiety as cultural and individual variables in a primitive society. *Journal of Social Psychology, 9,* 25-47. (Reprinted in Hallowell, 1955, 250-265).

———. (1942). *The role of conjuring in Saulteaux society*. Philadelphia: University of Pennsylvania Press. (*Publications of the Philadelphia Anthropological Society, 2*).

———. (1955). *Culture and experience*. Philadelphia: University of Pennsylvania Press.

———. (1963). Ojibwa world view and disease. In Iago Galdston (Ed.), *Man's image in medicine and anthropology*, 258-315. New York: International Universities Press. (Reprinted in Hallowell, 1976, 391-448).

———. (1976). *Contributions to anthropology*. Chicago: University of Chicago Press.

Harding, Thomas G. (1967). *Voyagers of the Vitiaz Strait: A study of a New Guinea trade system*. Seattle: University of Washington Press.

Harner, Michael J. (1973). *The Jívaro: People of the sacred waterfalls*. Garden City, NY: Anchor Press/Doubleday.

———. (1977). The ecological basis for Aztec sacrifice. *American Ethnologist, 4*, 117-135.

———. (1980). *The way of the shaman: A guide to power and healing*. San Francisco: Harper & Row.

Harris, Grace. (1978). *Casting out anger*. Cambridge: Cambridge University Press.

Harris, Marvin. (1974). *Cows, pigs, wars & witches: The riddles of culture*. New York: Random House.

Harvey, Byron. (1972). An overview of Pueblo religion. In Ortiz, 1972a, 197-217.

Hawes, Charles H. (1903). *To the uttermost East*. London: Harper.

Hayano, David M. (1974). Misfortune and traditional political leadership among the Tauna Awa of New Guinea. *Oceania, 45*, 18-26.

Herdt, Gilbert H. (1981). *Guardians of the flutes: Idioms of masculinity*. New York: McGraw-Hill.

Herskovits, Melville J. (1941). *The myth of the Negro past*. Boston: Beacon Press.

———. (1948). *Man and his works*. New York: Knopf.

———. (1962). *The human factor in changing Africa*. New York: Knopf.

———. (1967). *Dahomey: An ancient West African kingdom*. 2 vols. Evanston, IL: Northwestern University Press. (Originally published 1938).

Hertz, Robert. (1960). *Death & the right hand* (Rodney Needham & Claudia Needham, Trans.). Glencoe, IL: Free Press. (Original work published 1907-1909).

Hiatt, Lester Richard. (1971). Secret pseudo-procreation rites among the Australian aborigines. In Hiatt & Jayawardena, 1971, 77-88.

———, & Jayawardena, Chandra. (Eds.). (1971). *Anthropology in Oceania: Essays presented to Ian Hogbin*. San Francisco: Chandler.

Hilgard, Ernest R. (1977). *Divided consciousness: Multiple controls in human thought and action*. New York: Wiley.

Hillman, James. (1975). *Re-visioning psychology*. New York: Harper & Row.

Hoebel, Edward Adamson. (1941). The Comanche Sun Dance and messianic outbreak of 1873. *American Anthropologist, 43*, 301-303.

Hoebel, Edward Adamson. (1954). *The law of primitive man*. Cambridge, MA: Harvard University Press.

Hoernlé, A. W. (1918). Certain rites of transition and the conception of !Nau among the Hottentots. *Harvard African Studies*, no. 2, 65-82.

Hogbin, H. Ian. (1931). Tribal ceremonies of Ontong Java (Solomon Islands). *Journal of the Royal Anthropological Institute, 61*, 24-55.

———. (1936). Mana. *Oceania, 6*, 241-274.

———. (1951). *Transformation scene: The changing culture of a New Guinea village*. London: Routledge & Kegan Paul.

———. (1964). *A Guadalcanal society: The Kaoka speakers*. New York: Holt, Rinehart & Winston.

Hollan, Douglas. (1989). The personal use of dream beliefs in the Toraja highlands. *Ethos, 17*, 166-186.

Holmberg, Allan R. (1950). *Nomads of the long bow: The Siriono of eastern Bolivia*. Washington, DC: Government Printing Office.

Honko, Lauri. (1979). Theories concerning the ritual process. In Lauri Honko (Ed.), *Science of religion: Studies in methodology*, 369-390. The Hague: Mouton.

Horton, Robin. (1960). A definition of religion and its uses. *Journal of the Royal Anthropological Institute, 90*, 201-226.

———. (1962). The high god: A comment on Father O'Connell's paper. *Man, 62*, 137-140.

———. (1971). African conversion. *Africa, 41*, 85-108.

———. (1975). On the rationality of conversion. *Africa, 45*, 219-235, 373-399.

Hsu, Francis L. K. (1965). The effect of dominant kinship relationships on kin and non-kin behavior: A hypothesis. *American Anthropologist, 67*, 638-661.

———, (Ed.). (1971). *Kinship and culture*. Chicago: Aldine.

Hugh-Jones, Christine. (1979). *From the Milk River: Spatial and temporal processes in northwest Amazonia*. Cambridge: Cambridge University Press.

Hugh-Jones, Stephen. (1979). *The palm and the Pleiades: Initiation and cosmology in northwest Amazonia*. Cambridge: Cambridge University Press.

Hultkrantz, Åke. (1953). Conceptions of the soul among North American Indians. Stockholm: Caslon Press. *(Monograph Series, Ethnographical Museum of Sweden*, no. 1).

———. (1967). *The religions of the American Indians*. Berkeley: University of California Press.

Humphreys, Sarah C., & King, Helen (Eds.). (1981). *Mortality and immortality: The anthropology and archaeology of death*. London: Academic Press.

Huntington, Richard, & Metcalf, Peter. (1979). *Celebrations of death: The anthropology of mortuary ritual*. Cambridge: Cambridge University Press.

Ifeka-Moller, Caroline. (1974). White power: Social-structural factors in conversion to Christianity, eastern Nigeria, 1921-1966. *Canadian Journal of African Studies, 8*, 55-72.

Im Thurn, Everard F. (1882). On the animism of the Indians of British Guiana. *Journal of the Anthropological Institute, 11*, 360-382.

Ivanoff, Pierre. (1958). *Headhunters of Borneo*. (Edward Fitzgerald, Trans.). London: Jarrolds.

Jacobson-Widding, Anita. (1986). Beer for the ancestors, sun-hat for the white lady. *Working Papers in African Studies, African Studies Programme, Department of Cultural Anthropology, University of Uppsala*, no. 23.

Jenness, Diamond. (1922). *The life of the Copper Eskimos*. Ottawa: F. A. Acland. *(Report of the Canadian Arctic Expedition, 1913-18, 12*, pt. A).

Jochelson, Waldemar. (1905-1908). The Koryak: pt. 1. Religion and myths of the Koryak. *Memoirs of the American Museum of Natural History*, no. 10.

Jones, G. I. (1970). A boundary to accusations. In Douglas, 1970, 321-332.

Junod, H. A. (1962). *The life of a South African tribe*. New Hyde Park, NY: University Books. (Originally published 1912).

Kaberry, Phyllis M. (1941). The Abelam tribe, Sepik District, New Guinea: A preliminary report. *Oceania, 11*, 345-367.

Kalweit, Holger. (1988). *Dreamtime & inner space: The world of the shaman*. (Werner Wuensche, Trans.). Boston: Shambhala. (Original work published 1984).

Kan, Sergei. (1986). The 19th-century Tlingit potlatch: A new perspective. *American Ethnologist, 13*, 191-212.

Katz, Richard. (1973). Education for transcendence: Lessons from the !Kung Zhu/Twasi. *Journal of Transpersonal Psychology, 2*, 136-155.

———. (1982). *Boiling energy: Community healing among the Kalahari !Kung.* Cambridge, MA: Harvard University Press.

Keesing, Roger M. (1982). *Kwaio religion: The living and the dead in a Solomon Island society.* New York: Columbia University Press.

———. (1984). Rethinking *Mana. Journal of Anthropological Research, 40*, 137-156.

Kelly, Edward F., & Locke, Ralph G. (1981). Altered states of consciousness and PSI: An historical survey and research prospectus. *Parapsychological Monographs*, no. 18.

Kelly, William H. (1949). Cocopa attitudes and practices with respect to death and mourning. *Southwestern Journal of Anthropology, 5*, 151-164.

Kendall, Ann. (1973). *Everyday life of the Incas.* New York: Putnam.

Kennedy, John G. (1967). Nubian Zar ceremonies as psychotherapy. *Human Organization, 26*, 185-194.

Kindaichi, Kyosuke. (1949). The concepts behind the Ainu bear festival (Kumamatsuri). *Southwestern Journal of Anthropology, 5*, 345-350.

Kleinman, Arthur M. (1973). Medicine's symbolic reality: On a central problem in the philosophy of medicine. *Inquiry, 16*, 206-213.

Kluckhohn, Clyde. (1962). *Navaho witchcraft.* Boston: Beacon. (Originally published in 1944 as Vol. 22, no. 2, of *Papers of the Peabody Museum of Archaeology and Ethnology, Harvard University*).

———, & Leighton, Dorothea. (1947). *The Navaho.* Cambridge, MA: Harvard University Press.

Knauft, Bruce M. (1985). *Good company and violence: Sorcery and social action in a lowland New Guinea society.* Berkeley: University of California Press.

Koch, Klaus-Friedrich. (1974). *War and peace in Jalemo: The management of conflict in highland New Guinea.* Cambridge, MA: Harvard University Press.

Kopytoff, Igor. (1971). Ancestors as elders in Africa. *Africa, 41*, 129-142.

Kracke, Waud. (1987). Myths in dreams, thought in images: An Amazonian contribution to the psychoanalytic theory of primary process. In Tedlock, 1987, 31-54.

Krader, Lawrence. (1954). Buryat religion and society. *Southwestern Journal of Anthropology, 10*, 322-351.

Krige, Eileen Jensen. (1968). Girls' puberty songs and their relation to fertility, health, morality and religion among the Zulu. *Africa, 38*, 173-198.

———. (1974). A Lovedu prayer: The light it throws on the ancestor cult. *African Studies, 33*, 91-97.

———, & Krige, Jacob Daniel. (1943). *The realm of a rain-queen: A study of the pattern of Lovedu society.* London: Oxford University Press.

Krippner, Stanley (Ed.). (1977). *Advances in parapsychological research. 1. Psychokinesis.* New York: Plenum.

Kroeber, Alfred L., & Gifford, Edward W. (1949). World renewal: A cult system of native Northwest California. *Anthropological Records, 13*, 1-156.

Kuper, Hilda. (1947). *An African aristocracy: Rank among the Swazi.* London: Oxford University Press.

La Barre, Weston. (1972). Hallucinogens and the shamanic origins of religion. In Furst, 1972, 261-278.

———. (1975). *The Peyote cult* (4th ed. enl.). [Hamden, CT]: Archon Books. (Originally published 1938 as *Yale University Publications in Anthropology*, no. 19).

———. (1980). *Culture in context: Selected writings of Weston La Barre*. Durham, NC: Duke University Press.

La Fontaine, Jean S. (1963). Witchcraft in Bugisu. In Middleton & Winter, 1963, 187-220.

Lambert, William W., Triandis, Leigh Minturn, & Wolf, Margery. (1959). Some correlates of beliefs in the malevolence and benevolence of supernatural beings: A cross-societal study. *Journal of Abnormal and Social Psychology, 58*, 162-169.

Landes, Ruth. (1968). *Ojibwa religion and the midewiwin*. Madison: University of Wisconsin Press.

Lane, Robert B. (1965), The Melanesians of south Pentecost, New Hebrides. In Lawrence & Meggitt, 1965a. 250-279.

———. (1977). Power concepts in Melanesia and northwestern North America. In Raymond D. Fogelson & Richard N. Adams (Eds.), *The anthropology of power*, 365-374. New York: Academic Press.

Langness, Lewis L. (1974). Ritual, power, and male dominance in the New Guinea highlands. *Ethos, 2*, 189-212.

Lantis, Margaret. (1947). Alaskan Eskimo ceremonialism. *Monographs of the American Ethnological Society, 11*.

Larner, Christina L. (1984). *Witchcraft and religion: The politics of popular belief*. Oxford: Basil Blackwell.

Lawrence, Peter. (1963). Religion: Help or hindrance to economic development in Papua and New Guinea? *Mankind, 6*, 3-11.

———. (1964). *Road belong cargo: A study of the cargo movement in the Southern Madang District, New Guinea*. Manchester: Manchester University Press.

———. (1971). Statements about religion: The problem of reliability. In Hiatt & Jayawardena, 1971, 139-154.

———, & Meggitt, Mervyn J. (Eds.). (1965a). *Gods, ghosts and men in Melanesia*. Melbourne: Oxford University Press.

———, & Meggitt, Mervyn J. (1965b). Introduction. In Lawrence & Meggitt, 1965a, 1-26.

Leach, Edmund R. (1969). *Genesis as myth, and other essays*. London: Jonathan Cape.

Leach, Jerry W. (1983). Introduction. In Jerry W.Leach & Edmund R. Leach (Eds.), *The Kula: New perspectives on Massim exchange*. Cambridge: Cambridge University Press.

Lee, Nelson. (1957). *Three years among the Comanches (1855-58): The narrative of Nelson Lee, the Texas ranger*. Norman: University of Oklahoma Press.

Leighton, Alexander H., & Leighton, Dorothea C. (1949). Gregorio, the hand-trembler: A psychological personality study of a Navaho Indian. *Papers of the Peabody Museum of American Archaeology and Ethnology, Harvard University, 40*(1).

Lesser, Alexander. (1933). Cultural significance of the Ghost Dance. *American Anthropologist, 35*, 108-115.

———. (1978). *The Pawnee Ghost Dance hand game*. Madison, WI: University of Wisconsin Press. (Originally published in 1933 as vol. 16 in *Columbia University Contributions to Anthropology*).

LeVine, Robert A. (1962). Witchcraft and co-wife proximity in southwestern Kenya. *Ethnology, 1*, 39-45.

———. (1973). Patterns of personality in Africa. *Ethos, 1*, 123-151.

———. (1982a). *Culture, behavior and personality* (2nd ed.). Chicago: Aldine.

———. (1982b). Gusii funerals: Meanings of life and death in an African community. *Ethos, 10*, 25-65.

Levinson, David. (1988). *Instructor's and librarian's guide to the HRAF archive*. New Haven, CT: Human Relations Area Files, Inc.

Lewis, Gilbert. (1975). *Knowledge of illness in a Sepik society: A study of the Gnau, New Guinea*. London: Athlone.

Lewis, Ian M. (1965). Shaikhs and warriors in Somaliland. In Fortes & Dieterlen, 1965, 204-220.

———. (1966). Spirit possession and deprivation cults. *Man, 1*, 307-329.

———. (1989). *Ecstatic religion: A study of shamanism and spirit possession* (2nd ed.). London: Routledge.

Lewis-Williams, J. David, & Biesele, Megan. (1978). Eland hunting rituals among northern and southern San groups: Striking similarities. *Africa, 48*, 117-134.

Lienhardt, R. Godfrey. (1961). *Divinity and experience: The religion of the Dinka*. Oxford: Clarendon Press.

Lindenbaum, Shirley. (1972). Sorcerers, ghosts, and polluting women: An analysis of religious belief and population control. *Ethnology, 11*, 241-253.

———. (1976). A wife is the hand of man. In Paula Brown & Georgeda Buchbinder (Eds.), *Man and woman in the New Guinea highlands*, 54-62. Washington, DC: American Anthropological Association. (*American Anthropological Association Special Publication*, no. 8).

———. (1979). *Kuru sorcery: Disease and danger in the New Guinea Highlands*. Palo Alto, CA: Mayfield.

Linton, Ralph. (1922a). The sacrifice to the Morning Star by the Skidi Pawnee. *Field Museum of Natural History, Department of Anthropology, Leaflet No. 6*.

———. (1922b). The thunder ceremony of the Pawnee. *Field Museum of Natural History, Department of Anthropology, Leaflet No. 5*.

———. (1923). Annual ceremony of the Pawnee medicine man. *Field Museum of Natural History, Department of Anthropology, Leaflet No. 8*.

Lipkin, Mack, & Lamb, Gerri S. (1982). The couvade syndrome: An epidemiologic study. *Annals of Internal Medicine, 96*, 509-511.

Llewellyn-Davies, Melissa. (1979). Two contexts of solidarity among pastoral Maasai women. In Patricia Caplan & Janet M. Bujra (Eds.), *Women united, women divided: Comparative studies of ten contemporary cultures*, 206-237. London: Tavistock.

Lowie, Robert H. (1909). The northern Shoshone. *Anthropological Papers of the American Museum of Natural History, 2*, 165-306.

———. (1935). *The Crow Indians*. New York: Farrar & Rinehart.

MacClancy, Jeremy. (1986). Mana: An anthropological metaphor for island Melanesia. *Oceania, 57,* 142-152.

MacDonald, W. Scott, & Oden, Chester W., Jr. (1977). *Aumakua;* Behavioral direction visions in Hawaiians. *Journal of Abnormal Psychology, 86,* 189-194.

McKnight, John David. (1975). Men, women, and other animals: Taboo and purification among the Wik-mungkan. In Roy Willis (Ed.), *The interpretation of symbolism,* 77-97. New York: Wiley.

――――. (1967). Extra-descent group ancestor cults in African societies. *Africa, 37,* 1-21.

Mair, Lucy P. (1958). Independent religious movements in three continents. *Comparative Studies in Society and History, 1,* 113-136.

Malinowski, Bronislaw. (1916). Baloma: The spirits of the dead in the Trobriand Islands. *Journal of the Royal Anthropological Institute, 46,* 353-430. (Reprinted in Bronislaw Malinowski, 1954, *Magic, science, and religion.* Garden City, NY: Doubleday Anchor).

――――. (1922). *Argonauts of the western Pacific.* London: Routledge.

――――. (1926). *Crime and custom in savage society.* New York: Harcourt, Brace.

――――. (1929). *The sexual life of savages in north-western Melanesia.* New York: Harcourt, Brace & World.

――――. (1935). *Coral gardens and their magic.* vol. I. New York: American Book Co.

Mandelbaum, David G. (1940). The Plains Cree. *Anthropological Papers of the American Museum of Natural History, 37,* 155-316.

――――. (1965) Social uses of funeral rites. In Herman Feifel (Ed.), *The meaning of death,* 189-217. New York: McGraw-Hill.

Marshall, Harry Ignatius. (1922). The Karen people of Burma: A study in anthropology and ethnology. *Ohio State University Bulletin, 26,* no. 13.

Marshall, Lorna. (1957). N!ow. *Africa, 27,* 232-240.

――――. (1961). Sharing, talking, and giving: Relief of social tensions. *Africa, 31,* 231-249.

――――. (1962). !Kung Bushman religious beliefs. *Africa, 32,* 221-262.

Marwick, Max G. (1952). The social context of Cewa witch-beliefs. *Africa, 22,* 120-135, 215-233.

――――. (1958). The continuance of witchcraft beliefs. In P. Smith (Ed.), *Africa in transition: Some BBC talks on changing conditions in the Union and the Rhodesias,* 106-114. London: Max Reinhardt.

――――. (1965). *Sorcery in its social setting: A study of the northern Rhodesian Cewa.* Manchester: Manchester University Press.

――――, (Ed.) (1970). *Witchcraft and sorcery: Selected readings.* Middlesex: Penguin.

Mayer, Philip. (1970). Witches. In Marwick, 1970, 45-64.

Mead, Margaret. (1935). *Sex and temperament.* New York: Morrow.

――――. (1940). The Mountain Arapesh: II. Supernaturalism. *Anthropological Papers of the American Museum of Natural History, 37,* 317-451.

――――. (1949). *Male and female: A study of the sexes in a changing world.* New York: Morrow.

――――. (1956). *New lives for old: Cultural transformation—Manus, 1928-1953.* New York: Morrow.

Meigs, Anna S. (1976). Male pregnancy and the reduction of sexual opposition in a New Guinea highlands society. *Ethnology, 15,* 393-407.

Merrill, William. (1987). The Rarámuri stereotype of dreams. In Tedlock, 1987, 194-219.

Messenger, John C., Jr. (1959). Religious acculturation among the Anang Ibibio. In William R. Bascom & Melville J. Herskovits (Eds.), *Continuity and change in African cultures,* 279-299. Chicago: University of Chicago Press.

Metcalf, Peter. (1982). *A Borneo journey into death: Berawan eschatology from its rituals.* Philadelphia: University of Pennsylvania Press.

Métraux, Alfred. (1941). Messiahs of South America. *Interamerican Quarterly, 3,* no. 2, 53-60.

———. (1963). The couvade. In J. H. Steward (Ed.), *Handbook of South American Indians,* vol. 5, 369-374. New York: Cooper Square Publishers. (Originally published as *Bulletin 143 of the Bureau of American Ethnology*).

Middleton, John. (1955). The concept of "bewitching" in Lugbara. *Africa, 25,* 252-260.

———. (1960). *Lugbara religion: Ritual and authority among an East African people.* London: Oxford University Press.

———. (1963a). Witchcraft and sorcery in Lugbara. In Middleton & Winter, 1963, 257-275.

———. (1963b). The Yakan or Allah water cult among the Lugbara. *Journal of the Royal Anthropological Institute, 93,* 80-108.

———. (1982). Lugbara death. In Bloch & Parry, 1982a, 134-154.

———, & Winter, Edward Henry. (Eds.). (1963). *Witchcraft and sorcery in East Africa.* London: Routledge & Kegan Paul.

Mischel, Walter, & Mischel, Frances. (1958). Psychological aspects of spirit possession. *American Anthropologist, 60,* 249-260.

Monberg, Torben. (1966). *The religion of Bellona Island: A study of the place of beliefs and rites in the social life of pre-Christian Bellona. pt. 1. The concepts of supernaturals.* Copenhagen: National Museum of Denmark.

Montagu, Ashley. (1974). *Coming into being among the Australian aborigines: A study of the procreative beliefs of the native tribes of Australia* (rev. and exp.). (Original edition 1937). London: Routledge & Kegan Paul.

Montgomery, Rita E. (1974). A cross-cultural study of menstruation, menstrual taboos, and related social variables. *Ethos, 2,* 137-170.

Moore, Omar K. (1957). Divination: A new perspective. *American Anthropologist, 59,* 69-74.

Morgan, Lewis H. (1851). *League of the Ho-de'-no-sau-nee, or Iroquois.* Rochester, NY: Sage & Brother.

Morren, George E. B., Jr. (1986). *The Miyanmin: Human ecology of a Papua New Guinea society.* Ann Arbor: University of Michigan Research Press.

Morton-Williams, Peter. (1960). Yoruba responses to the fear of death. *Africa, 30,* 34-40.

Munroe, Robert L., Munroe, Ruth H., & Whiting, John W. M. (1973). The couvade: A psychological analysis. *Ethos, 1,* 30-72.

———. (1981). Male sex-role resolutions. In Ruth H. Munroe, Robert L. Munroe, & Beatrice B. Whiting (Eds.), *Handbook of cross-cultural human development,* 611-632. New York: Garland.

Murdock, George P. (1949). *Social structure*. New York: Macmillan.

———. (1971). Anthropology's mythology: The Huxley Memorial Lecture 1971. *Proceedings of the Royal Anthropological Institute for 1971*, 17-24.

———. (1980). *Theories of illness: A world survey*. Pittsburgh: University of Pittsburgh Press.

Murphy, Robert F. (1958). Mundurucú religion. *University of California Publications in American Archaeology and Ethnology*, no. 49.

Myerhoff, Barbara G. (1974). *Peyote hunt: The sacred journey of the Huichol Indians*. Ithaca, NY: Cornell University Press.

Myers, Frederic W. H. (1903). *Human personality and its survival of bodily death*. New York: Longmans Green.

Nadel, Siegfried Frederick. (1935). Witchcraft and anti-witchcraft in Nupe society. *Africa, 8*, 423-447.

———. (1954). *Nupe religion*. Chicago: Free Press.

Nash, June. (1968). The passion play in Maya Indian communities. *Comparative Studies in Society and History, 10*, 318-327.

Nash, Manning. (1961). Witchcraft as social process in a Tzeltal community. *América Indígena, 20*, 121-126.

Needham, I. Rodney. (1976). Skulls and causality. *Man, 11*, 71-88.

Newman, Philip L. (1965). *Knowing the Gururumba*. New York: Holt, Rinehart & Winston.

Oosterwal, Gottfried. (1976). The role of women in the male cults of the Soromaja in New Guinea. In A. Bharati (Ed.), *The realm of the extra-human: Agents and audiences*, 323-334. The Hague: Mouton.

Opler, Morris E. (1936a). The influence of aboriginal pattern and white contact on a recently introduced ceremony, the Mescalero peyote rite. *Journal of American Folk-Lore, 49*, 143-166.

———. (1936b). An interpretation of ambivalence of two American Indian tribes. *Journal of Social Psychology, 7*, 82-115.

Ortiz, Alfonso (Ed.). (1972a). *New perspectives on the pueblos*. Albuquerque: University of New Mexico Press.

———. (1972b). Ritual drama and the Pueblo world view. In Ortiz, 1972a, 135-161.

Paige, Karen Ericksen, & Paige, Jeffery M. (1981). *The politics of reproductive ritual*. Berkeley: University of California Press.

Paine, Robert. (1971). Animals as capital: Comparisons among northern nomadic herders and hunters. *Anthropological Quarterly, 44*, 157-172.

Parker, Arthur. (1913). The code of Handsome Lake, the Seneca prophet. *New York State Museum Bulletin 163*.

Parrinder, Edward Geoffrey. (1950). Theistic beliefs of the Yoruba and Ewe peoples of West Africa. In Edwin W. Smith (Ed.), *African ideas of God: A symposium*, 224-240. London: Edinburgh House Press.

Parsons, Elsie Clews. (1939). *Pueblo Indian religion*. vols. I and II. Chicago: University of Chicago Press.

Peel, J. D. Y. (1968a). *Aladura: A religious movement among the Yoruba*. London: Oxford University Press.

———. (1968b). Syncretism and religious change. *Comparative Studies in Society and History, 10*, 121-141.

Pereira de Queiroz, Maria Iseura. (1958). L'influence du milieu social interne sur les mouvements messianiques brésiliens. *Archives de Sociologie des Religions,* no. 5, 3-30.

Peters, Larry. (1981). *Ecstasy and healing in Nepal: An ethnopsychiatric study of Tamang shamanism.* Malibu, CA: Undena Publications.

Piddocke, Stuart. (1965). The potlatch system of the southern Kwakiutl: A new perspective. *Southwestern Journal of Anthropology, 21,* 244-264.

Pineda Giraldo, Roberto. (1961). *Aspects of magic in La Guajira* (Sydney Muirden, Trans.) New Haven, CT: Human Relations Area Files, Inc. (Original work published 1947).

Poole, Fitz John Porter. (1983). Cannibals, tricksters, and witches: Anthropophagic images among Bimin-Kuskusmin. In Paula Brown & Donald Tuzin (Eds.), *The ethnography of cannibalism,* 6-22. Washington, DC: Society for Psychological Anthropology.

Pospisil, Leopold. (1958). Kapauku Papuans and their law. *Yale University Publications in Anthropology,* no. 54.

Postal, Susan Koessler. (1965). Hoax nativism at Caughnawaga: A control case for the theory of revitalization. *Ethnology, 4,* 266-281.

Radcliffe-Brown, Alfred Reginald. (1922). *The Andaman Islanders.* Cambridge: Cambridge University Press.

Radin, Paul. (1914). Religion of the North American Indians. *Journal of American Folk-Lore, 27,* 335-373.

———. (1927). *Primitive man as philosopher.* New York: Appleton. (Dover, 1957.)

Rappaport, Roy A. (1984). *Pigs for the ancestors: Ritual in the ecology of a New Guinea people* (new, enl. ed.). New Haven, CT: Yale University Press.

Raum, Otto Friedrich. (1940). *Chaga childhood: A description of indigenous education in an East African tribe.* London: Oxford University Press.

Ray, Verne F. (1933). *The Sanpoil and Nespelem: Salishan peoples of northeastern Washington.* Seattle: University of Washington Press. (*University of Washington Publications in Anthropology,* vol. 5).

Read, Kenneth E. (1965). *The high valley.* New York: Scribner.

———. (1986). *Return to the high valley.* Berkeley: University of California Press.

Rehfisch, Farnham. (1969). Death, dreams, and the ancestors in Mambila culture. In Mary Douglas & Phyllis Kaberry (Eds.), *Man in Africa: Essays dedicated to Daryll Forde,* 306-314. Garden City, NY: Anchor Books.

Reichard, Gladys A. (1970). *Navaho religion: A study of symbolism,* one-volume ed. Princeton, NJ: Princeton University Press. (Original publication 1950).

Reid, Janice. (1983). *Sorcerers and healing spirits: Continuity and change in an aboriginal medical system.* Canberra: Australian National University Press.

Reinhard, Johan. (1992). Sacred peaks of the Andes. *National Geographic, 181*(3), 84-111.

Ribeiro, René. (1970). Brazilian messianic movements. In Thrupp, 1970, 55-69.

Richards, Audrey I. (1956). *Chisungu: A girls' initiation ceremony among the Bemba of northern Rhodesia.* London: Faber and Faber.

Ridington, Robin. (1971). Beaver dreaming and singing. *Anthropologica, 13,* 115-128.

———. (1976). Wechuge and Windigo: A comparison of cannibal belief among boreal forest Athapaskans and Algonkians. *Anthropologica, 18,* 107-129.

———. (1988). *Trail to heaven: Knowledge and narrative in a northern native community.* Iowa City: University of Iowa Press.

———. (1990). *Little bit know something: Stories in a language of anthropology.* Iowa City: University of Iowa Press.

Rigby, Peter. (1981). Pastors and pastoralists: The differential penetration of Christianity among East African cattle herders. *Comparative Studies in Society and History, 23,* 96-129.

Riley, E. Baxter. (1925). *Among Papuan headhunters.* London: Seeley, Service and Co.

Ring, Kenneth. (1980). *Life at death: A scientific investigation of the near-death experience.* New York: Coward, McCann & Geoghegan.

Rivière, Peter G. (1970). Factions and exclusions in two South American village systems. In Douglas, 1970, 245-255.

———. (1974). The couvade: A problem reborn. *Man, 9,* 423-435.

Roberts, John M., Arth, Malcolm J., & Bush, Robert R. (1959). Games in culture. *American Anthropologist, 61,* 597-605.

———, & Nutini, Hugo G. (1988). Witchcraft event staging in rural Tlaxcala: A study in inferred deception. *Ethnology, 27,* 407-431.

Romanucci-Ross, Lola. (1979). Melanesian medicine: Beyond culture to method. In Peter Morley & Roy Wallis (Eds.), *Culture and curing: Anthropological perspectives on traditional medical beliefs and practices,* 115-138. Pittsburgh: University of Pittsburgh Press.

Rosenblatt, Paul C., Walsh, R. Patricia, & Jackson, Douglas A. (1976). *Grief and mourning in cross-cultural perspective.* New Haven, CT: HRAF Press.

Rowe, John Howland. (1960). The origins of creator worship among the Incas. In Stanley Diamond (Ed.), *Culture in history: Essays in honor of Paul Radin,* 408-429. New York: Columbia University Press.

Ruel, Malcolm. (1970). Were-animals and the introverted witch. In Douglas, 1970, 333-349.

Sagan, Eli. (1974). *Cannibalism: Human aggression and cultural form.* New York: Harper & Row.

Saler, Benson. (1964). Nagual, witch, and sorcerer in a Quiché village. *Ethnology, 3,* 305-328.

———. (1977). Supernatural as a Western category. *Ethos, 5,* 31-53.

Sandner, Donald. (1979). *Navaho symbols of healing.* New York: Harcourt Brace Jovanovitch.

Schapera, Isaac. (1952). Sorcery and witchcraft in Bechuanaland. *African Affairs, 51,* 41-52.

Schele, Linda, & Miller, Mary Ellen. (1986). *The blood of kings.* Fort Worth, TX: Kimball Art Museum.

Schieffelin, Edward L. (1976). *The sorrow of the lonely and the burning of the dancers.* New York: St. Martin's Press.

Schlegel, Alice, & Barry, Herbert, III. (1979). Adolescent initiation ceremonies: A cross-cultural code. *Ethnology, 18,* 199-210.

———. (1980). The evolutionary significance of adolescent initiation ceremonies. *American Ethnologist, 7,* 696-715.

Schwartz, Theodore. (1962). The Paliau movement in the Admiralty Islands 1946-1954. *Anthropological Papers of the American Museum of Natural History, 29,* 211-421.

Seligmann, C. G., & Seligmann, Brenda Z. (1911). *The Veddas*. Cambridge: Cambridge University Press.

Serpenti, Laurentius Maria. (1965). *Cultivators in the swamps: Social structure and horticulture in a New Guinea society*. Assen: Von Gorcum.

Sharp, Henry S. (1986). Shared experience and magical death: Chipewyan explanations of a prophet's decline. *Ethnology, 25*, 257-270.

Shirokogoroff, S. M. (1935). *Psychomental complex of the Tungus*. London: Kegan Paul, Trench, Trubner & Co.

Shternberg, L. I. (1933). *The Gilyak, Orochi, Goldi, Negidal, Ainu: Articles and materials*. Unpublished translation by L. Bromwich and N. Ward from the Russian, available in the Human Relations Area Files.

Slotkin, James Sydney. (1956). *The peyote religion*. Glencoe, IL: Free Press.

Smith, Edwin William, & Dale, Andrew Murray. (1920). *The Ila-speaking peoples of northern Rhodesia*, vol. 2. London: Macmillan.

Smith, Marian W. (1954). Shamanism in the Shaker religion of northwest America. *Man, 54*, 119-122.

Smith, W. Robertson. (1889). *Lectures on the religion of the Semites: First series, The fundamental institutions*. Edinburgh: Adam and Charles Black.

Spier, Leslie. (1927). The Ghost Dance of 1870 among the Klamath of Oregon. *University of Washington Publications in Anthropology, 2*, 39-56.

———. (1930). *Klamath ethnography*. Berkeley: University of California Press.

———. (1935). *The Prophet Dance of the Northwest and its derivatives: The source of the Ghost Dance*. Menasha, WI: Banta. (*General Series in Anthropology*, no. 1).

———, Suttles, Wayne, & Herskovits, Melville J. (1959). Comment on Aberle's thesis of deprivation. *Southwestern Journal of Anthropology, 15*, 84-88.

Spiro, Melford E. (1952). Ghosts, Ifaluk, and teleological functionalism. *American Anthropologist, 54*, 497-503.

———. (1953). Ghosts: An anthropological inquiry into learning and perception. *Journal of Abnormal and Social Psychology, 48*, 376-382.

———. (1966). Religion: Problems of definition and explanation. In Michael Banton (Ed.), *Anthropological approaches to the study of religion*, 85-126. London: Tavistock.

———. (1968). Virgin birth, parthenogenesis and physiological paternity: An essay in cultural interpretation. *Man, 3*, 242-261.

———, & D'Andrade, Roy G. (1958). A cross-cultural study of some supernatural beliefs. *American Anthropologist, 60*, 456-466.

Stephen, Michele. (1987a). Contrasting images of power. In Stephen, 1987b, 249-304.

———, (Ed.). (1987b). *Sorcerer and witch in Melanesia*. New Brunswick, NJ: Rutgers University Press.

Stewart, Kenneth M. (1946). Spirit possession in native America. *Southwestern Journal of Anthropology, 2*, 323-339.

Strathern, Andrew J. (1981). Death as exchange: Two Melanesian cases. In Humphreys & King, 1981, 205-223.

Strehlow, Theodor George Heinrich. (1947). *Aranda traditions*. Melbourne: Melbourne University Press.

————. (1964). Personal monototemism in a polytotemic community. In Eike Haberland, Meinhard Schuster, & Helmut Straube (Eds.), *Festschrift für Ad. E. Jensen*, vol. 2, 723-754. Munich: Klaus Renner Verlag.

Suttles, Wayne. (1960). Affinal ties, subsistence, and prestige among the coast Salish. *American Anthropologist, 60*, 296-305.

Swanson, Guy E. (1960). *The birth of the gods: The origin of primitive beliefs*. Ann Arbor: University of Michigan Press.

Tatje, Terrence, & Hsu, Francis L. K. (1969). Variations in ancestor worship beliefs and their relation to kinship. *Southwestern Journal of Anthropology, 25*, 153-172.

Tax, Sol (Ed.). (1952). *Indian tribes of aboriginal America. (Proceedings of the 29th International Congress of Americanists*, vol. 3). Glencoe, IL: Free Press.

Taylor, Kenneth I. (1976). Body and spirit among the Sanuma (Yanoama) of North Brazil. In Grollig & Haley, 1976, 27-48.

Tedlock, Barbara (Ed.). (1987). *Dreaming: Anthropological and psychological interpretations*. Cambridge: Cambridge University Press.

Tedlock, Dennis. (1975). An American Indian view of death. In Dennis Tedlock & Barbara Tedlock (Eds.), *Teachings from the American earth: Indian religion and philosophy*, 248-271. New York: Liveright.

Thomas, Elizabeth Marshall. (1959). *The harmless people*. New York: Knopf.

Thompson, Laura. (1949). The relations of men, animals, and plants in an island community (Fiji). *American Anthropologist, 51*, 253-267.

Thompson, Donald E. (1954). Maya paganism and Christianity: A history of the fusion of two religions. *Tulane University, Middle American Research Institute*, Publication 10 (Reprinted in Munro, Edmonson, et al., *Nativism and syncretism*, Publication 19 in the same series, 1960).

Thrupp, Sylvia L. (Ed.). (1970). *Millenial dreams in action: Studies in revolutionary religious movements*. New York: Schocken.

Titiev, Mischa A. (1960). A first approach to the problems of magic and religion. *Southwestern Journal of Anthropology, 16*, 292-298.

Tonkinson, Robert. (1981). Church and *kastom* in southeast Ambrym. In Michael Allen (Ed.), *Vanuatu: Politics, economics and ritual in island Melanesia*, 237-267. Sydney: Academic Press.

Traube, Elizabeth G. (1986). *Cosmology and social life: Ritual exchange among the Mambai of East Timor*. Chicago: University of Chicago Press.

Trilles, le R. P. (1932). *Les pygmées de la forêt équatoriale*. Paris: Bloud & Gay. (*Bibliothèque Ethnologique Anthropos, Internationale de Monographies Ethnologiques, 3*, no. 4).

Turnbull, Colin M. (1965). *Wayward servants: The two worlds of the African pygmies*. Garden City, NY: Natural History Press.

Turner, James W. (1986). The water of life: Kava ritual and the logic of sacrifice. *Ethnology, 25*, 203-214.

————. (1987). Blessed to give and receive: Ceremonial exchange in Fiji. *Ethnology, 26*, 209-219.

Turner, Victor W. (1952). *The Lozi peoples of northwest Rhodesia*. London: International African Institute.

————. (1962). Three symbols of *passage* in Ndembu circumcision ritual: An interpretation. In M. Gluckman (Ed.), *Essays on the ritual of social relations*, 124-173. Manchester: University of Manchester Press.

————. (1967). *The forest of symbols: Aspects of Ndembu ritual*. Ithaca, NY: Cornell University Press.

————. (1968). *The drums of affliction*. Oxford: Clarendon.

————. (1969). *The ritual process: Structure and anti-structure*. Chicago: Aldine.

————. (1971). Themes and symbols in an Ndembu hunter's burial. In Mario D. Zamora, J. Michael Mahar, & Henry Orenstein (Eds.), *Themes in culture: Essays in honor of Morris E. Opler*, 270-284. Quezon City, Philippines: Kayumanggi Publishers.

Tuzin, Donald F. (1974). Social control and the Tambaran in the Sepik. In A. Epstein (Ed.), *Contention and dispute: Aspects of law and social control in Melanesia*, 317-351. Canberra: Australian National University Press.

————. (1978). Politics, power, and divine artistry in Ilahita. *Anthropological Quarterly, 51*, 61-67.

————. (1980). *The voice of the Tambaran*. Berkeley: University of California Press.

Tylor, Edward B. (1891). *Anthropology: An introduction to the study of man and civilization*. New York: Appleton.

Urban, Greg. (1988). Ritual wailing in Amerindian Brazil. *American Anthropologist, 90*, 385-400.

Vayda, Andrew P. (1961). A re-examination of Northwest Coast economic systems. *Transactions of the New York Academy of Sciences, ser. 2, 23*, 618-624.

Villa Rojas, Alfonso. (1969). The Tzeltal. In Robert Wauchope & Evon Z. Vogt (Eds.), *Handbook of Middle American Indians*, vol. 7, 195-225. Austin: University of Texas Press.

Vinci, Alfonso. (1959). *Red cloth and green forest*. (James Cadell, Trans.). London: Hutchinson.

Voget, Fred W. (1951). Acculturation at Caughnawaga: A note on the native-modified group. *American Anthropologist, 53*, 220-231.

————. (1959). Towards a classification of cult movements: Some further contributions, *Man, 59*, 26-27.

Wallace, Anthony F. C. (1956). New religions among the Delaware Indians, 1600-1900. *Southwestern Journal of Anthropology, 12*, 1-21.

Warner, W. Lloyd. (1958). *A black civilization: A social study of an Australian tribe* (rev. ed.). Chicago: University of Chicago Press. (Original edition 1937).

Weiner, James F. (1986). Men, ghosts and dreams among the Foi: Literal and figurative modes of interpretation. *Oceania, 57*, 114-127.

Weltfish, Gene. (1965). *The lost universe*. New York: Basic Books.

Weyer, Edward Moffat. (1932). *The Eskimos: Their environment and folkways*. New Haven, CT: Yale University Press.

Whiting, Beatrice B. (1950). Paiute sorcery. *Viking Fund Publications in Anthropology*, no. 15.

Whiting, John W. M. (1941). *Becoming a Kwoma: Teaching and learning in a New Guinea tribe*. New Haven, CT: Yale University Press.

————, & Child, Irvin L. (1953). *Child training and personality: A cross-cultural study*. New Haven, CT: Yale University Press.

Whyte, Martin King. (1978). Cross-cultural codes dealing with the relative status of women. *Ethnology, 17,* 211-237.

Wierzbicka, Anna. (1989). Soul and mind: Linguistic evidence for ethnopsychology and cultural history. *American Anthropologist, 91,* 41-58.

Williams, F. E. (1932). Trading voyages from the Gulf of Papua. *Oceania, 3,* 139-166.

———. (1936). *Papuans of the Trans-Fly.* Oxford: Clarendon.

Willis, Roy G. (1968). Changes in mystical concepts and practices among the Fipa. *Ethnology, 7,* 139-157.

———. (1970). Instant millenium: The sociology of African witch-cleansing cults. In Douglas, 1970, 129-139.

———. (1972). Pollution and paradigms. *Man, 7,* 369-378.

Wilson, Godfrey. (1936). An African morality. *Africa, 9,* 75-98.

———. (1939). Nyakyusa conventions of burial. *Bantu Studies, 13,* 1-31.

Wilson, Monica Hunter. (1951a). *Good company: A study of Nyakyusa age villages.* Boston: Beacon.

———. (1951b). Witch beliefs and social structure. *American Journal of Sociology, 56,* 307-313.

———. (1957). *Rituals of kinship among the Nyakyusa.* London: Oxford University Press.

———. (1959). *Communal rituals of the Nyakyusa.* London: Oxford University Press.

———. (1971). *Religion and the transformation of society: A study in social change in Africa.* Cambridge: Cambridge University Press.

Winter, Edward Henry. (1963). The enemy within: Amba witchcraft and sociological theory. In Middleton & Winter, 1963, 277-299.

———. (1964). The slaughter of the bull: A study of cosmology and ritual. In Robert Alan Manners (Ed.), *Process and pattern in culture: Essays in honor of Julian H. Steward,* 101-110. Chicago: Aldine.

Witherspoon, Gary. (1977). *Language and art in the Navajo universe.* Ann Arbor: University of Michigan Press.

Wolf, Eric R. (1955). Types of Latin American peasantry: A preliminary discussion. *American Anthropologist, 57,* 452-471.

Woodburn, James. (1982). Social dimensions of death in four African hunting and gathering societies. In Bloch & Parry, 1982a, 187-210.

Worsley, Peter M. (1957). *The trumpet shall sound.* London: Macgibbon & Kee.

Young, Frank Wilbur. (1965). *Initiation ceremonies: A cross-cultural study of status dramatization.* Indianapolis, IN: Bobbs-Merrill.

Index of Names

Names of societies reported on, and names of authors, are indexed for their appearances in the text, but not for appearances in the list of references. Societies are sometimes named by the political entity within which they are located; in any event, the name is intended to apply here only to the local group studied, except where a broader application is implied. Authors are indexed even when they are mentioned on a page only by implication (through the use of *et al*).

Abelam, 16
Aboagye, P.A.K., 109
Acoma, 190
Adler, Alfred, 22
Afkhaz, 35
Ainu, 29, 34, 72, 80, 82
Akawaio, 87, 129-31, 135
Akoa Pygmies, 82
Albers, Patricia, 22
Algonquians, 24, 48, 94
Allen, M.R., 151, 163
Alvarez, A., 137
Amba, 101, 118
Anang Ibibio, 214, 216
Andamanese, 48, 60, 71, 182, 183
Anisimov, A. F., 80, 87, 88, 94
Ansbacher, Heinz L., 22
Ansbacher, Rowena R., 22
Apache, 181, 229 *See also* Cibecue Apache; Mescalero Apache; Western Apache
Aranda, 146, 185
Arapaho, 225
Arapesh, 156, 157, 159, 160
Ardener, Edwin, 101, 102
'Aré'Aré, 178
Armstrong, W. E., 158
Arth, Malcolm J., 63, 64
Arunta, 158
Ashanti, 40, 51
Athabascans, 48, 83, 93
Avá-Chiripá, 84, 90
Aymara, 146
Ayres, Barbara, 143
Azande, 83, 97, 98, 99, 113, 225
Aztecs, 18, 58, 80, 210-11, 231

Baal, J. van, 159
Bacon, Margaret K., 21, 38
Bahr, Donald M., 137
Baka, 168
Bakan, David, 234
Bakweri, 102
Balandier, Georges, 215
Balikci, Asen, 90

Balinese, 20, 44, 167
Balzer, Marjorie M., 219
Bambara, 35, 155
Banyang, 101
Bara, 183
Barasana, 29, 32, 157, 159, 160, 162
Barber, Theodore Xenophon, 87
Barnard, Alan, 121
Baroya, 160
Barry, Herbert, III, 21, 38, 150, 151, 153
Barth, Fredrik, 60
Bartolomé, Miguel Alberto, 84, 85, 87
Barton, Roy Franklin, 56
Basseri, 60
Basso, Keith H., 16, 104, 114, 117, 119
Bateson, Gregory, 152
Beals, Ralph Leon, 3
Beattie, John H. M., 109
Beaver, 16, 21, 84, 93 *See also* Dunne-za
Beaver, Wilfred N., 151
Beidelman, Thomas O., 111, 114, 176, 185
Bella Coola, 188
Bellona Islanders, 171
Bemba, 35, 148, 149, 225
Benedict, Ruth Fulton, 24, 26, 48
Benin, 51
Berawan, 184
Berbers, 25, 26
Bercovitch, Eytan, 86, 119
Bergman, Robert, 129
Berndt, Catherine H., 158, 159
Berndt, Ronald M., 108, 158, 159
Best, Eledon, 17
Bettelheim, Bruno, 156
Bierhorst, John, 211
Biernoff, David, 26
Biesele, Megan, 41
Bimin-Kuskusmin, 19
Binford, Lewis R., 180

Bleek, D. F., 58
Bloch, Maurice, 181
Boas, Franz, 24
Boddy, Janice, 149
Bogoras, Waldemar, 58
Bohannon, Paul, 100
Booth, Newell S., Jr., 213
Borneo, 183
Bororo, 38, 67
Boston, John, 16
Bourguignon, Erika, 86, 91
Brain, James L., 153, 162
Broude, Gwen J., 157
Brown, Judith K., 153
Brown, Julia S., 81
Buber, Martin, 68
Buck, Peter Henry, 17
Bundi, 59
Burton, Roger V., 155
Buryat, 32
Busana, 157
Bush, Robert R., 63, 64
Bushmen, 48
Butt, Audrey J., 129, 130

Carroll, Michael P., 62, 66
Cewa, 115, 116
Chaga, 39, 40, 161, 225
Chagnon, Napoleon A., 15, 24
Chapple, Eliot D., 142
Child, Alice B., 151
Child, Irvin L., 21, 38, 110, 133, 151
Chinnery, E. W. Pearson, 151
Chinook, 24, 188
Chipewyan, 15
Chukchee, 41, 43, 57, 58
Cibecue Apache, 16 *See also* Apache
Clements, Forrest E., 132
Cochiti, 105
Cochrane, Glynn, 206, 207
Cocopa, 176
Codrington, Robert Henry, 10, 11, 13
Coelho, Ruy, 144

Cohen, Yehudi A., 148, 152
Collins, John James, 210
Collins, June McCormick, 207
Collocott, E. E. V., 17, 20
Colson, Audrey Butt, 87, 129, 131
Comanche, 226, 233
Conibo, 87, 88
Coon, Carleton S., 19, 48, 49, 82, 142
Copper Eskimo *See* Copper Inuit
Copper Inuit, 36
Coppet, Daniel de, 178
Cox, Harvey, 44
Craemer, Willy de, 213
Crawford, J. R., 96
Cree, 16
Creek, 189
Crocker, Jon Christopher, 67
Crow, 16, 22, 58, 73, 82
Cubeo, 154, 158, 159, 226
Cunha, Manuela Carneiro da, 174, 176
Curley, Richard T., 216

Dahomeans, 78
Dale, Andrew Murray, 39
D'Andrade, Roy G., 63
Davidson, Basil, 213
Delaware, 232
Deng, Francis Mading, 168, 169
Dewey, Alice G., 219
Dieterlen, Germaine, 155, 169, 178
Dinka, 19, 39, 42, 59, 60, 74, 75, 76, 168-69
Dobkin de Rios, Marlene, 88
Dobuans, 107, 108, 116
Dodd, Robert, 168
Dogon, 155, 169, 178
Douglas, Mary, 115, 119
Downes, Rupert Major, 76
Downs, Richard Erskine, 176
Driver, Harold E., 58, 152
Dunne-za, 15, 37, 83
Durkheim, Emile, 49, 62
Duru, Mary Steimel, 213
Dyaks, 44
Dyk, Ruth, 125
Dyk, Walter, 125, 126, 127

Eliade, Mircea, 70
Elmendorf, William W., 134, 135
Ember, Carol R., 3, 4
Ember, Melvin, 3, 4
Enga, 134
Erikson, E. H., 234
Eskimo, 48
Evans-Pritchard, E. E., 19, 39, 41, 59, 76, 83, 97, 98, 99, 100, 103, 104, 113
Evenk, 80, 87, 88

Faithorn, Elizabeth, 158
Fang, 85, 89, 141, 213, 215
Favret-Saada, Jeanne, 116, 117
Fernandez, James W., 85, 89, 141, 213, 215, 216, 232
Fijians, 193 *See also* Lau Fijians
Fipa, 139
Firth, Raymond, 4, 8, 11, 12, 20, 26, 29, 30, 68, 85, 160, 174, 177, 191, 192, 199

Fitz-Patrick, David G., 59
Flannery, Regina, 14
Fletcher, Alice C., 25
Fock, Niels, 146
Foi, 86
Ford, Clellan S., 157
Ford, Richard I., 189
Forde, Daryll, 100, 198
Fore, 19, 108, 134
Fortes, Meyer, 52, 53, 55, 64, 169, 198, 199, 215, 232
Fortune, Reo F., 107, 116, 174
Fox, J. Robin, 105
Fox, Renée C., 213
France, 117
Frazer, James George, 2, 3, 138
Freud, Sigmund, 138, 224, 230

Gahuku, 4, 157
Gallup, Gordon G., 31
Garia, 40
Gayton, A. H., 36, 189
Gebusi, 176
Geertz, Clifford, 3
Gell, Alfred, 158, 196
Gennep, Arnold Van, 142, 161
Gifford, Edward. W., 188
Gilyak, 29, 34, 44, 71, 72
Girard, René, 228
Gisu, 100, 101, 117, 118, 228
Gluckmann, Max, 113, 116, 162, 175
Gnau, 123-24, 137, 138
Goajiro, 40, 41, 42
Goddard, Pliny Earle, 58, 69, 188
Godelier, Maurice, 160
Goldman, Irving, 29, 154, 159, 226
Goldschmidt, Walter, 21, 183, 227
Gond, 159
Goodman, Felicitas D., 86
Goody, Esther, 102
Goody, Jack, 166, 173, 175, 176, 177, 179, 182
Gorer, Geoffrey, 159, 225
Gough, E. Kathleen, 53
Gould, Richard A., 6
Gourlay, K. A., 160
Gray, Robert F., 100, 101, 115
Greenbaum, Lenora S., 92
Greene, Sarah J., 157
Cregor, Thomas, 100, 157
Gregorio, Juan, 137
Griffin, Donald R., 31
Grigson, Wilfrid, 159
Grottanelli, Vinigi L., 109
Guadalcanal, 13
Guiart, Jean, 206, 207
Gunther, Erna, 207
Gururumba, 157
Gusii, 110, 115, 118, 180
Gusinde, Martin, 71, 151

Hadza, 168
Haida, 58
Haiti, 91
Hallowell, A. Irving, 4, 15, 35, 57, 82, 84, 94, 122, 137
Harding, Thomas G., 195
Harner, Michael J., 5, 15, 18, 24, 80, 87, 88, 106
Harris, Grace, 77, 228
Harris, Marvin, 115
Harvey, Byron, 189

Hausa, 158
Hawaiians, 89
Hawes, Charles H., 72
Hayano, David M., 160
Herdt, Gilbert H., 159
Herskovits, Melville J., 78, 90, 214, 215, 236
Hertz, Robert, 179
Hiatt, Lester Richard, 161
Hilgard, Ernest R., 87
Hillman, James, 234
Hoebel, Edward Adamson, 227, 233
Hoernlé, A. W., 24
Hogbin, H. Ian, 12, 13, 107, 157, 192
Hoijer, Harry, 3
Hollan, Douglas, 85
Holmberg, Allan R., 58, 167
Honko, Lauri, 142
Hopi, 58, 69, 154, 177, 190
Horton, Robin, 3, 50, 51, 113, 234, 235
Hsu, Francis L. K., 55
Hua, 160
Hugh-Jones, Christine, 29
Hugh-Jones, Stephen, 29, 32, 157, 159, 160, 162
Huichol, 44, 45, 209
Hultkrantz, Åke, 48, 170
Huntington, Richard, 179, 183

Iatmul, 152
Iban, 18
Ibo *See* Igbo
Ifaluk, 108, 119, 171
Ifeka-Moller, Caroline, 235
Ifugao, 18, 44, 56, 225, 226
Igbo, 100, 213
Im Thurn, Everard F., 174
Inca, 42, 49, 58, 74, 210
Inuit, 57, 58, 167, 227
Iraqw, 79
Iroquois, 24, 204, 209
Ivanoff, Pierre, 44, 45

Jackson, Douglas A., 51, 167, 170, 179
Jacobson-Widding, Anita, 184
Jalemo, 230
Javanese, 219, 232
Jenness, Diamond, 167
Jívaro, 5, 15, 17, 18, 24, 87, 88, 106, 158
Jochelson, Waldemar, 42, 58
Jones, G. I., 100
Jung, Carl Gustav, 126
Junod, H. A., 79, 101

Kaberry, Phyllis M., 16
Kaguru, 111, 114, 176, 185
Kagwahiv, 84
Kaluli, 175
Kalweit, Holger, 70
Kan, Sergei, 69, 190
Kapauku, 144, 146
Karen, 147
Katz, Richard, 19, 21, 121, 122, 229
Keesing, Roger M., 13, 107
Kelly, Edward F., 86
Kelly, William H., 176
Kendall, Ann, 106
Kennedy, John G., 137
Keraki Papuans, 159

Khanty, 219
Khoikhoi, 24, 58
Kimam, 15, 20, 158
Kimbuna, John, 59
Kindaichi, Kyosuke, 72
Kipsigis, 110
Kiwai Papuans, 154
Klamath, 14, 15
Kleinman, Arthur M., 140
Kluckhohn, Clyde, 71, 103, 104, 110, 111, 113, 114, 115, 126
Knauft, Bruce M., 176
Koch, Klaus-Friedrich, 230
Kopytoff, Igor, 53
Koryak, 42, 43, 58
Kota, 183
Kpe, 102
Kracke, Waud, 84
Krader, Lawrence, 32
Krahó, 174, 176
Krige, Eileen Jensen, 20, 54, 69, 102, 136
Krige, Jacob Daniel, 54, 102, 136
Krippner, Stanley, 108
Kroeber, Alfred L., 188
Kung San, 19, 20, 21, 23, 37, 38, 41, 82, 121-22, 137, 227, 229
Kuper, Hilda, 177
Kwaio, 107
Kwakiutl, 24, 48
Kwoma, 45, 156, 157, 170, 171, 230

La Barre, Weston, 88, 207
LaFlesche, Francis, 25
La Fontaine, Jean S., 100, 101, 110, 117, 118
Lamb, Gerri S., 144
Lambert, William W., 63, 64
Landes, Ruth, 123
Lane, Robert B., 14, 38
Langness, Lewis L., 161
Lantis, Margaret, 190
Lapps, 34, 40, 73
Larner, Christina L., 115
Lau Fijians, 29
Lawrence, Peter, 1, 5, 6, 40, 108, 163, 207, 234, 235
Leach, Edmund R., 158
Leach, Jerry W., 194
Lee, Nelson, 227
Leighton, Alexander H., 125
Leighton, Dorothea C., 71, 125
Lele, 115
Lepcha, 35, 36, 159, 225
Lesser, Alexander, 204, 205
LeVine, Robert A., 110, 180, 223, 224, 229
Lewis, Gilbert, 123
Lewis, Ian M., 4, 5, 93
Lewis-Williams, J. David, 41, 152
Lienhardt, R. Godfrey, 19, 39, 42, 59, 74, 75, 76, 169
Lindenbaum, Shirley, 19, 108, 133, 134, 161
Linton, Ralph, 16, 18, 58, 80
Lipkin, Mack, 144
Llewellyn-Davies, Melissa, 162
Locke, Ralph G., 86
LoDagaa, 165-66, 168, 176, 177, 182, 183
Lopez, David I., 137
Lovedu, 54, 69, 102, 136

Lowie, Robert H., 16, 22, 49, 58, 73
Lozi, 54
Lugbara, 53, 55, 60, 78, 100, 110, 169, 176, 231
Luguru, 153, 162
Lunda, 137, 139
Luo, 110

MacClancy, Jeremy, 13
MacDonald, W. Scott, 89
McKnight, John David, 53, 161
Mair, Lucy P., 205
Malaita, 13
Malinowski, Bronislaw, 12, 20, 107, 114, 141, 158, 185, 191, 193, 194
Mambai, 161, 196-97
Mambila, 176
Mandelbaum, David G., 16, 183
Manus, 59, 138, 174, 205, 233
Maori, 11, 17, 191
Marind-anim, 159
Marshall, Harry Ignatius, 147
Marshall, Lorna, 23, 82, 121, 227
Marwick, Max G., 114, 115, 213, 229
Masai, 162
Maya, 58, 80, 210-11, 231
Mayer, Philip, 115, 118
Mbundu, 158
Mbuti, 36, 37
Mead, Margaret, 151, 156, 160, 201, 202, 206
Meggitt, Mervyn J., 163
Mehinaku, 106, 157
Meigs, Anna S., 160
Merrill, William, 84, 169
Mescalero Apache, 209
Messenger, John C., Jr., 214, 215, 216
Metcalf, Peter, 179, 183, 184
Métraux, Alfred, 143, 146, 212
Middleton, John, 53, 60, 78, 96, 100, 102, 110, 169, 176, 213, 231, 233
Miller, Mary Ellen, 80
Mischel, Frances, 91, 92
Mischel, Walter, 91, 92
Miyanmin, 107, 108
Mohawk, 209
Monberg, Torben, 171
Montagu, Ashley, 158
Montgomery, Rita E., 143, 144
Moore, Omar K., 34
Morgan, Lewis H., 72
Morren, George E. B., Jr., 107
Morton-Williams, Peter, 173
Motu, 195
Mundugumor, 151
Mundurucú, 18, 24, 35, 158, 178
Munroe, Robert L., 143, 144, 145, 146, 147, 153
Munroe, Ruth H., 143, 144, 145, 146, 147, 153
Murdock, George P., 132, 137, 146, 147, 224, 225, 228
Murngin, 108, 127-29, 137
Murphy, Robert F., 18, 24, 35, 178
Myerhoff, Barbara G., 44, 45, 209
Myers, Frederic W. H., 172

Nadel, Siegfried Frederick, 8, 9, 118, 218, 226, 232
Nalumin, 86, 119
Nambicuara, 158
Nash, June, 211
Nash, Manning, 105
Navaho, 42, 63, 71, 103, 104, 105, 110, 111, 113, 115, 124-27, 129, 137, 229
Nayars, 53
Ndembu, 139, 149, 154, 158, 227, 228, 229
Needham, I. Rodney, 18
Netsilik Inuit, 37, 71, 90
Newman, Philip L., 157
Nharo See San
Nubians, 137
Nuer, 19, 39, 41, 59, 76
Nupe, 8, 118, 218-19, 226, 232-33
Nutini, Hugo G., 111
Nyakyusa, 17, 100, 112, 114, 141, 176, 199-200, 217, 227, 229
Nzema, 109

Oden, Chester W., Jr., 89
Ojibwa, 26, 35, 38, 122-23, 137
See also Saulteaux
Omaha, 25
Ona, 48, 71
Ontong-Javanese, 13, 192, 193
Oosterwal, Gottfried, 160
Opler, Morris E., 181, 182, 209
Orok, 29
Orokaiva, 44, 151
Ortiz, Alfonso, 189, 190
Ovimbundu, 40

Paige, Jeffery M., 144, 145, 152
Paige, Karen Ericksen, 144, 145, 152
Paine, Robert, 34
Paiute, 23, 71, 104, 105, 113
Papago, 137
Parker, Arthur, 204
Parker, Seymour, 22
Parrinder, Edward Geoffrey, 56
Parry, Jonathan, 181
Parsons, Elsie Clews, 177, 189
Pawnee, 16, 18, 58, 80, 205, 225
Peel, J. D. Y., 214, 216, 234
Pende, 213
Pentecost Islanders, 38
Pereira de Queiroz, Maria Iseura, 212
Peters, Larry, 87
Piddocke, Stuart, 190
Pineda Giraldo, Roberto, 40
Pondo, 112, 113, 116, 217
Poole, Fitz John Porter, 19
Pospisil, Leopold, 144
Postal, Susan Koessler, 209
Pygmy, 23, 48, 100 See also Kung San

Quiché, 40

Radcliffe-Brown, Alfred Reginald, 60, 71, 182
Radin, Paul, 25, 26, 57, 173, 236
Rappaport, Roy A., 57, 113, 178, 195, 196

Rarámuri, 84, 169
Raum, Otto Friedrich, 161
Ray, Verne F., 22
Read, Kenneth E., 4, 157
Rehfisch, Farnham, 176
Reichard, Gladys A., 125
Reid, Janice, 127, 128, 129
Reinhard, Johan, 58
Ribeiro, René, 212
Richards, Audrey I., 148
Ridington, Robin, 14, 15, 17, 21, 37, 83, 84, 93
Riffians, 19
Rigby, Peter, 214
Riley, E. Baxter, 154
Ring, Kenneth, 173
Rivière, Peter G., 106, 146, 147
Roberts, John M., 63, 111
Romanucci-Ross, Lola, 138
Rosenblatt, Paul C., 51, 167, 170, 179
Rossel Islanders, 158
Rowe, John Howland, 49
Ruel, Malcolm, 101

Sagan, Eli, 19
Saler, Benson, 4, 105
Salish, 24
Sambia, 159
Samoyeds, 37
San, 58, 121-22, 152 *See also* Kung San
Sandner, Donald, 63, 126
Sanpoil, 22
Santo Domingo, 190
Saulteaux, 4, 15, 57, 64, 82, 84, 94, 122-23
Schapera, Isaac, 101
Schele, Linda, 80
Schieffelin, Edward L., 176
Schlegel, Alice, 150, 151, 153
Schwartz, Theodore, 202, 206, 233
Sebei, 183, 227
Seligmann, Brenda Z., 51, 71, 167
Seligmann, C. G., 51, 71, 167
Semang, 48
Seneca, 72, 209
Serpenti, Laurentius Maria, 12, 16, 20, 158
Sharp, Henry S., 15
Shavante, 106, 158
Shilluk, 17
Shirokogoroff, S. M., 87
Shona, 184
Shoshone, 49
Shternberg, L. I., 71
Siouans, 24
Siriono, 58, 167
Slotkin, James Sydney, 207
Smith, Edwin William, 39
Smith, Marian W., 207
Smith, W. Robertson, 141
Somali, 5, 40, 93

Soromaja, 160
Spier, Leslie, 14, 15, 204, 214
Spiro, Melford E., 3, 63, 108, 119, 158, 171
Stefansson, Vilhjalmur, 71
Stephen, Michele, 108, 114
Stewart, Kenneth M., 91
Strathern, Andrew J., 181
Strehlow, Theodor George Heinrich, 52, 185, 186
Suttles, Wayne, 190, 214
Swanson, Guy E., 48, 49, 50, 54, 55, 62
Swazi, 177

Taita, 77, 228
Tallensi, 51, 52, 53, 55, 198-99, 215, 232
Tamang, 87
Taos, 210
Tarahumara *See* Rarámuri
Tasmanians, 48
Tatje, Terrence, 55
Taylor, Kenneth I., 136
Tedlock, Dennis, 52, 174
Tewa, 190
Thomas, Elizabeth Marshall, 37
Thompson, Donald E., 211
Thompson, Laura, 29, 44
Thonga, 40, 79, 100
Tikopia, 11, 12, 20, 30, 44, 68, 85, 158, 159, 160, 191, 192, 193
Titiev, Mischa A., 142
Tiv, 76, 100
Tlingit, 69
Tonga, 17, 20
Tonkinson, Robert, 13
Toraja, 85, 176
Traube, Elizabeth G., 161, 196, 197
Triandis, Leigh Minturn, 63, 64
Trilles, le R. P., 82
Trinidad, 91
Trio, 106
Trobriand Islanders, 12, 20, 114, 141, 185, 193-95
Truk, 158
Tsembaga, 56, 113, 178, 195-96
Tsimshian, 188
Tswana, 101
Tuareg, 19
Tungus *See* Evenk
Tupi-Guarani, 212
Tupinamba, 158
Turnbull, Colin M., 37
Turner, James W., 192, 193
Turner, Victor W., 54, 137, 139, 149, 227, 228, 229
Tuzin, Donald F., 157, 160, 228
Tylor, Edward B., 170
Tzeltal, 146

Umeda, 158, 196

Urban, Greg, 180

Vansina, Jan, 213
Vanuatu, 13, 14
Vayda, Andrew P., 190
Vedda, 51, 71, 167
Villa Rojas, Alfonso, 146
Vinci, Alfonso, 143, 146
Voget, Fred W., 209

Waiwai, 146
Walbiri, 158
Wallace, Anthony F. C., 232
Walsh, R. Patricia, 51, 167, 170, 179
Wambugwe, 100, 101, 115
Warner, W. Lloyd, 108, 127, 128, 129
Weiner, James F., 84
Weltfish, Gene, 16
Western Apache, 104, 105, 114, 119 *See also* Apache
Western Mono, 189
Weyer, Edward Moffat, 37, 71
Whiting, Beatrice B., 23, 71, 104, 113
Whiting, John W. M., 45, 110, 133, 143, 144, 145, 146, 147, 153, 155, 157, 170, 230
Whyte, Martin King, 61, 62
Wierzbicka, Anna, 169
Wikmungkan, 161
Wiko, 162
Williams, F. E., 159, 195
Willis, Roy G., 103, 139
Wilson, Godfrey, 229
Wilson, Monica Hunter, 100, 112, 113, 114, 141, 176, 199, 217, 218, 227, 228, 229
Winter, Edward Henry, 79, 96, 101, 118
Witherspoon, Gary, 126
Wogeo, 13, 156
Wolf, Eric R., 113
Wolf, Margery, 63, 64
Woodburn, James, 168
Worsley, Peter M., 206

Xhosa, 213

Yahgan, 48, 71, 151
Yakö, 100, 198
Yanoama, 40, 136, 143, 146
Yanomamo, 15, 24
Yao, 116
Yokuts, 36, 189
Yoruba, 56, 173, 214, 216, 234
Young, Frank Wilbur, 152

Zulu, 20
Zuni, 23, 52, 174, 190

Index of Topics

Afterlife
  character, 174-79
  duration, 174-76
  reward and punishment in,
    176-79
  and wish to avoid extinction,
    173, 176
Aggression
  as motive underlying religion,
    228
  projection of, 171
  regulation of, 226-28
  satisfaction in wizardry,
    110-11
  by spirits, 137-38
Altered states of consciousness
    See also Trance experiences
  in cargo cults, 202
  in syncretistic religions, 207
Ancestors
  role in cargo cults, 202-3
Ancestor worship
  examples, 52-55
  frequent inappropriatness of
    term, 52
Ancestral spirits
  how their status is achieved,
    184-85
  importance related to
    economy, 54
  presence at sacrifice, 77, 79
  relation to kinship system,
    54-55
  under religious change in
    Africa, 217-18
  role in enforcement of
    morality, 176
Anger *See* Aggression
Animal parts
  religious use of, 33
Anxiety
  as motive underlying religion,
    230
  relation to wizardry, 111-12
  sources in economy, 231-32
  about survival of the group,
    225-26, 232
Awareness
  assumed in animals, 30-31

Baraka
  defined, 19
  and mystical power, 19, 25
"Big man"
  as background of revival
    movements, 206
  definition, 12

Bodily functions in male
  distorted beliefs, 160-61

Cannibalism
  a danger from excess of
    mystical power, 21
  and human sacrifice, 80
  a source of mystical power,
    18-19
Cargo cults, 201-3
  compared with African
    syncretism, 213-14
  compared with Native Ameri-
    can movements, 203, 205-7
Ceremonies. *See* Initiation
    ceremonies; Rites; Ritual
  first-salmon, 188
Childbirth, normal
  myths about male invention,
    159-60
Christianity
  incorporation of elements in
    Ghost Dance, 205
  influence on cargo cults, 202
  influence on peyote religion,
    209
  influence on Shaker religion,
    208
  and syncretistic religions of
    Middle and South America,
    210-12
  and syncretistic religions in
    Africa, 212-19
Cognitive effects of religion,
    233-36
Communication
  as communion vs. reciproca-
    tion, 68-69
  in festivals, 191
  religious acts as, 66-67, 191
  skepticism about messages,
    67-68
  versus expression, 66
Complexity of society
  and locus of mystical power, 26
  and syncretistic religions, 210
Conception, beliefs about male
  role, 157-58
Conjuring *See also* Spirit
    possession
  as communication with
    animal spirits, 38
Consciousness. *See* Awareness
Couvade
  definitions, 143-44
  frequency, 144
  theories of function, 144-47

Culture hero
  defined, 19
  examples, 60-61

Death
  problems posed by, 166-68
  disposition of body, 167,
    179-80, 183-84
  explanation of, 167, 182-83
  loss of person, 167, 180-81
  relation to surviving spirit,
    168, 181-82
Dependence, regulated by
  religion, 229-30
Destiny animals, 40
Divination
  as communication, 81-83
  cultural guidance, 81-82
  as guide to therapy, 125-26
  role of animals, 33-34
  and wizardry, 99
Dramatization, 114
Dreams
  acquiring mystical power, 15,
    16
  and belief in afterlife, 171
  as messages, 83-86

Envy
  of each sex, by the other, 163
  of men, by women, 163
  of women, by men, 155-63
Evil, problem of, 118, 125
Exchange, ritual, 192-97
Explanations, psychological
  versus sociological, 109, 116-
    17, 144-45, 152-53
Expressive function, 109

Festivals
  definition, 187
  examples, 187-200
  realistic effects of, 189-90
Foragers. *See* Hunting-
    gathering societies

Gains from religion, 221-36
  to group, 222-23
  to individual, 221-22
Ghost Dance, 204-5
Group identity
  assisted by peyote religion,
    209
  and confidence, 232-33

Group identity (cont.)
  and syncretistic religion, 215-16, 218-19
Guardian spirits
  animals as, 38-39
  source of mystical power, 14-16

Hallucinogenic drugs See Psychotropic drugs
Healer, training to be a, 106
Herding societies
  bloody sacrifice characteristic, 41-43
  comparison with hunting societies, 34, 38-39
  ensuring equitable distribution, 43
  identification with domestic animals, 38-41
  self-reliance and mystical power, 21
High god See Major god
Humility vs. competence, norms of, 228-30
Hunting-gathering societies
  animal reincarnation, 32
  ensuring equitable distribution, 37-38
  ensuring future supply, 34-35
  ensuring gain in mystical power, 38-39
  ensuring success in hunt, 35-37
  as locus of revival movements, 206-7
  sacrifice of bears and dogs, 72
  and self-reliance, 21
  types of mystical being, 57

Identity See Group identity
Illness
  beliefs about causes
    diversity, 129-30
    examples, 121-31
    related to motivational themes, 133-34
  mystical explanations and therapies
    disturbed social relations, 139-40
    intrusion, 136-37
    magic, 138-39
    soul loss, 134-35
    spirit attack, 137-38
    spirit possession, 135-36
    variation by region, 132
    violation of taboos, 137
    widespread similarities, 132
  occasion for sacrifice, 75
  therapeutic practices examples, 121-31
Inheritance
  of mystical power, 17, 18
  of witchcraft, 98
Initiation ceremonies
  and encouragement of competence, 230
  of female
    comparison with those of male, 150-55
    examples, 148-49
    first-fruit rites, 152
    mutilations in, 159
    and mystical power, 16
    and sexual frankness, 20
  of male

example, 149-50
first-kill rites, 41, 152
  mutilations in, 155, 156
  and mystical power, 16
  and regulation of sexuality, 226
  relation to economy and complexity, 151
  theories of function, 152-53, 155
Insecurity See Anxiety
Intellectual functions of religion, 234-36
Intrinsic values of religion, 221
Islam
  and religious change in Africa, 212-14, 218-19

Kaiko ceremony, 195
Kava ceremony, 191
Killing
  as source of mystical power, 17-19
Kiva, in Pueblo religions, 210
Kule expeditions, 194

Life events
  as messages from mystical beings, 81-82
Losses from religion, 221-36
  to individual, 222
  to society, 222-23

Magic
  definition, 3
  in festivals, 193-95
  good magic, 99
  included in definition of religion, 3-4
  relation to practical procedures, 193
  in response to illness, 138-39
  in rituals of childbirth, 147
Major god
  and ascribed versus achieved status, 50-51
  and contact with outside world, 50-51
  definition, 48
  relation to complexity, 48-49
  relation to economy, 48-49
Mana
  Melanesian concepts, 10-13
  Polynesian concepts, 11-13
  "Masters" of animal species in hunting societies, 35-37, 57
  source of mystical power, 15
Mastery, need for See Understanding
Medical practices, realistic, 120
  adopted from scientific medicine, 128-29
Medicine bundles
  and mystical power, 16, 21
Mediumship, spiritual
  definition, 12
  and support for belief in afterlife, 172
Menstruation
  beliefs about male role in causing, 159
  and health, 157
  myths about male menstruation, 159

Missionary message
  and political power, 215
  response influenced by economy, 214
Morality
  role of ancestral spirits, 176
  and traditional religions, 6, 25
Mortuary rites See Rites, funeral
Musical instruments
  and myths about men and women, 160
Mystical beings
  animal versus human form, 64
  attributes of, 56
  benevolence-malevolence, 63-64
  relation to type of games, 63
  definition, 47
  four broad categories, 47
  gender of, 61-63
  human beings as, 61
  number of in one society, 56
  subcategories, 56-60
  relation to economy, 57-60

Nature spirits, 57-58
Near-death experiences, 173
Norms to which religion contributes
  Aggression control, 226-28
  Anxiety vs. confidence, 230-33
  Continuity vs. change, 233-36
  Self-assertion vs. dependence, 228-30
  Sexuality, 224-26

Offerings, 71-72 See also Sacrifice
Orphanhood and religious leadership, 202

Pastoral economies See Herding
Plants in religion, 43-45
Possession See Spirit possession
Potlatch, 190
Power, mystical
  associated with place, 25
  changes in African syncretism, 218
  dangers of, 17
  definition, 4
  divine sources, 19
  evil use, 21
  gaining through Ghost Dance, 205
  inborn, 23-24
  indigenous terms for, 24-25
  and knowledge, 14
  and mana, 10
  personal versus impersonal, 25-26
  positive versus protective use, 24
  and realistic power, 4-5
  in sacrifice, 75
  and self-reliance, 20-21
  of words, 19-20
Prayer, 70-71, 216
Pregnancy, beliefs and practices, 143
Priest
  distinguished from shaman, 70

Projection
and belief in afterlife, 171
Prophet Dance, 204
Prophets
role in revival movements,
206, 214
Pseudomenstruation, male, 156-
57
Psychokinesis, 108-9
Psychotropic drugs
acquiring mystical power, 15
dual role in kava ceremony,
191-92
role in shamanistic experience, 88, 106
role in synerotistic religions,
207, 209
Purification rites, male, 157

Realistic effects of religion
ensuring food distribution,
196
food and pregnancy, 143
gain in political power, 233
increasing group solidarity,
197-99
in rituals surrounding birth,
147
Rebirth imagery in male
rituals, 161-62
Reincarnation
of animals, 32, 34, 188
and kula expeditions, 194
of people in animals, 32
of recently or remotely
deceased, 51-52
source of mystical power, 15,
20
varied conceptions of, 185-86
Religion, definition, 2, 4-5
Renewal
rituals of, 199-200
world, 188
Residence, patrilocal, 145
Rites See also Ceremonies;
Festivals; Initiation
ceremonies; Ritual
of advancement toward
adulthood, 148-55
calendrical, 142, 187
crisis, 142
funeral
aggression at, 227-28
duality of, 179-84
example, 165-68
and pollution, 183
of intensification, 142
of marriage, 142
of status elevation, 228-29
Ritual See also Ceremonies;
Initiation ceremonies;
Rites
importance in traditional
religions, 141
"Rubbish men", 207

Sacrifice
of bears, 42, 72
bloody versus bloodless, 41
as communication, 72-80
of dogs, 42-43, 72
among foragers, 72-73
geographical distribution, 42, 80

among herders and
cultivators, 73-80
human, 73, 80, 211
of pigs, 195-96
providing for spirits, 77-79
and scapegoating, 76
Security, sought in religious
movements, 203
Self-assertion, regulated by
religion, 229
Semen, beliefs about role in
growth, 158-59
Sexual abstention, 106
Sexual fantasy and wizardry,
112
Sexual identity
and couvade, 144-45
Sexuality, regulation of, and
religion, 224-26
Sexual license, 225-26
Shaker religion, 207-8
Shaman
distinguished from priest, 70
respect for, 17
training of, 87-88
Shamanistic travel, 90
Socialization, and wizardry,
110, 114
Sorcery See also Wizardry
definition, 97-98
killing as prerequisite, 18, 103
techniques, 100, 107, 127
Soul
attributed to animals, 32
multiple, 32
survival of, belief in, 168-74
experiences supporting
belief, 170-74
as explanation of puzzling
facts, 172
varied conception of, 169-70
Soul loss explanation of illness,
134-35
relation to couvade, 146-47
Spirit mediumship, 94-95
Spirit possession
description of experience, 91
gains from, 91-92
social correlates of, 92-93
a source of illness, 90, 135-36
a source of trance, 90-94
transformation as extreme,
93-94
Spirits of the dead
danger to the living, 51, 121,
123-24
universality of belief in, 51,
168
Spiritual continuity and growth
male role in, 147, 153-55, 156
Status
and mystical power, 17, 20-21
"Supernatural"
criticism of the term, 47, 60,
61, 122
Supernatural beings See
Mystical beings
Survival See Soul, survival of

Taboos
associated with "masters",
36-37
as negative magic, 138-39
violation of, and illness, 137

Theology, Western
compared with Nuer concepts,
59
Totemism, 28-30
Traditional religions
compared with world
religions, 1, 2, 5-7
defined, 1, 28
economy, relation to, 9
sex roles, relation to, 9
Trance experiences
frequency, 86
as messages, 86-90

Understanding
religion as a quest for, 33, 207
wizardry and quest for, 112-
13, 118
Usefulness
as an influence on religion, 33
in religion of hunting peoples,
34-39

Vision quest
adapted in memory to adult
role, 22-23
as background of revival
movements, 206
favored by egalitarian values,
23
route to mystical power,
14-15, 22
and self-mutilation, 73
Visions See also Vision quest
messages from mystical
beings, 89-90

Witchcraft See also Wizardry
beliefs about witches, 100-101
definition, 97-98
inheritance, 98
as physical substance, 98, 100
Wizardry See also Sorcery;
Witchcraft
in African syncretism, 213, 218
aggression, relation to,
110-11, 115
anxiety, relation to, 111-12
beliefs about wizards, 104
cleansing movements, 103
and conformity, 113-14
costs of, 119
definition, 96
effect on social relations,
101-2, 106-8, 113-17
effect on social structure,
115-17
frequency of accusations, 104,
105
"obstetric" function, 115
present in nearly all societies
in North America, 105
in sub-Saharan Africa, 100
punishment for, 99, 102, 105-6
and quest for understanding,
112-13
sexual fantasy in, 112
and social control, 113-14
worldview, effects on, 11
Work of the Gods, 191-92
Worldview
provided by a religion, 234-36